EPISTEMOLOGICAL INTEGRATION:
ESSENTIALS OF AN ISLAMIC METHODOLOGY

EPISTEMOLOGICAL INTEGRATION

ESSENTIALS OF AN ISLAMIC METHODOLOGY

Fathi Hasan Malkawi

Translated from the Arabic by Nancy Roberts

THE INTERNATIONAL INSTITUTE OF ISLAMIC THOUGHT
LONDON • WASHINGTON

THE INTERNATIONAL INSTITUTE OF ISLAMIC THOUGHT
P.O. BOX 669, HERNDON, VA 20172, USA
www.iiit.org

LONDON OFFICE
P.O. BOX 126, RICHMOND, SURREY TW9 2UD, UK
www.iiituk.com

ISBN 978-1-56564-557-8 *limp*
ISBN 978-1-56564-569-1 *cased*

Typesetting and cover design by Sideek Ali

In the Name of God, Most Gracious, Most Compassionate

بسم الله الرحمن الرحيم

And unto thee [O Prophet] have We vouchsafed this divine writ, setting forth the truth, confirming the truth of whatever there still remains of earlier revelations and determining what is true therein. Judge, then, between the followers of earlier revelation in accordance with what God has bestowed from on high, and do not follow their errant views, forsaking the truth that has come unto thee. Unto every one of you have We appointed a [different] law and way of life. And if God had so willed, He could surely have made you all one single community: but [He willed it otherwise] in order to test you by means of what He has vouchsafed unto you. Vie, then, with one another in doing good works! Unto God you all must return; and then He will make you truly understand all that on which you were wont to differ.

(*Sūrah al-Mā'idah* 5:48)

Contents

Evolution of the Concept of Method in Islamic and Western Thought

5

Schools of Islamic Methodology

6

Sources and Tools of Methodology

7

Methodological Principles and Values

Foreword

NOW IS THE WINTER OF OUR DISCONTENT – Shakespeare's famous opening line to Richard III seems an entirely appropriate way to describe the current state of affairs afflicting the Muslim world and its own sense of despair. Although Islamic civilization is by no means at the point of collapse and has never quite entered the dark ages of its medieval European counterpart, nevertheless its clear demise is a profound reminder of what it has lost, and more importantly, what it has the potential to regain. For where there is winter there is summer.

This work makes the case that fundamental to any Muslim recovery is laying the foundations of sound thinking and values (rooted in the Qur'an and the Sunnah) and developing practical means by which to bring the fruits of that knowledge, whether goals or ideas, into a working arena. In other words for significant change to emerge there needs to be an interchange of an effective epistemology with a clear defined action-rooted methodology to help, according to the author, bring to an end the current state of decline. The aims are clearly laid out from the start. Not that valiant effort has not been made in this regard but, according to Malkawi, the approach has been somewhat skewed in the direction of ideas rather than the ways and means to realise and implement them.

Epistemology and Methodology lie at the heart of this theory. Although the terms sound heavy going and grandiose, readers should not be put off. Malkawi simply employs them to convey ideas precisely and as stepping stones to develop more large-scale thought. Lay readers will not be confused as both terms are carefully demystified, that is, defined in detail with explanation of their relationship to each other clearly shown. Whatever the case, the point is that these are solution-based words used to develop a strong line of reasoning few would dispute.

It is necessary to make clear that Malkawi does not set out to replicate the past (that is craft empire) but rather to renew the intellectual vitality, energy and spiritual understanding of Muslim thought and achievement, to renew that is the motivating force of a once vigorous Islamic civilization in a modern context.

The framework of Malkawi's argument is straightforward. The world that we know and live in is governed by *tawḥīd*. What is eluding Muslims is to bring two elements into fruition and then into harmony with each other within a framework of this concept (*tawḥīd)*. One of these is thought (both in content and process) governed by values, and the other is developing the best means to implement the aims, objectives, and goals of this thought process in the most realistic and viable fashion.

Where does thought come from? How is it constructed? These are important facets of the study. The problem is that much of it does not evolve in a free flowing independent way, as we would imagine, but is itself a product of culture and the dominance of surrounding modes of thinking, which in themselves are simply modes of understanding or perceiving the world and our place within it. Today thought is largely governed by secular systems of perception, whether in science, philosophy, the social sciences or the humanities. Precluding reference to the Divine the influence of this system is felt intensely across the Muslim world and its weight bears down on almost all forms of study. Let us be clear, this is not to imply a value judgement on this knowledge by any means, but rather to pose the question, is it rational to borrow wholeheartedly, without careful distinction, from a model (or a worldview) which is a product of its own cultural-specific, historical environment, employing its own culture-specific terminology, to obtain knowledge and understanding of the human condition and the Muslim predicament? To appreciate this is to understand something of what Malkawi is trying to convey.

This takes us to Malkawi's insistence on being clear about our aims and our worldview. For instance, what are the goals and objectives of mankind, surely not infinite progress and technical advancement as ends in themselves, without a higher objective, or even maximization of welfare according to a utilitarian outlook? An important element of Malkawi's argument is examination of humanity's position in this world both in terms of an outlook of welfare (*khilāfah*) and awareness of Man's existence as not merely a single unit but as part of a larger collective, a social unit or Ummah. And of course there is an almost rhythmic relationship between the two. Ummah overcomes ideas of race or class and even culture to place *tawḥīd* as the central defining force of the relationship of man as single unit to man as social unit and what all this entails both epistemologically and methodologically. This work analyses in detail many of these and other issues to chart a way forward for Muslims.

In sum, Islam is not best expressed in art or magnificent buildings, (although art has its place), this is not its supreme achievement, but in spirituality and thought (based on the Qur'an and Sunnah) and creative realization of that thought in the pure present. If we are to carry over anything from the past it is this.

This study is being published to widen discourse, invite scholars to respond, and hopefully pave the way for further research. Since it deals with some critical and difficult issues, doubtless readers may agree with some of the issues raised, and disagree with others, but it is hoped that for the most part both general and specialist readers will benefit from the perspective offered and the overall issues examined in the book.

Where dates are cited according to the Islamic calendar (hijrah) they are labelled AH. Otherwise they follow the Gregorian calendar and labelled CE where necessary. Arabic words are italicized except for those which have entered common usage. Diacritical marks have been added only to those Arabic names not considered modern. English translations taken from Arabic references are those of the translator.

The IIIT, established in 1981, has served as a major center to facilitate serious scholarly efforts based on Islamic vision, values and principles. The Institute's programs of research, seminars and conferences during the last thirty years have resulted in the publication of more than four hundred titles in English and Arabic, many of which have been translated into other major languages.

Foreword

We express our thanks and gratitude to the author for his cooperation throughout the various stages of production. We would also like to thank the translator, Nancy Roberts, as well as the editorial and production team at the IIIT London Office and all those directly or indirectly involved in the completion of this work including, Shiraz Khan, Dr. Maryam Mahmood, and Sara Mirza. May God reward them for all their efforts.

IIIT LONDON OFFICE
January 2014

Preface

THE literature produced by the Islamization of knowledge project has consistently stressed the importance of both the epistemological and the methodological dimensions of efforts to reform and revive Islamic civilization. The epistemological dimension, which has to do with the theoretical content of human thought, concerns itself with drawing the proper distinctions among the various levels of thought, namely, facts, concepts, principles and theories, viewed from a comprehensive Islamic perspective. As for the methodological dimension, it has to do with the practical side of human thought: ways of thinking, research procedures, and incentives for action. Yet despite the importance of the epistemological dimension with its various topics and issues, it is the methodology for dealing with these topics and issues that has received the greatest attention in the Islamization of knowledge project. This project can be summed up in terms of the following four focal points, each of which is associated with two specific concerns:

1) The Islamic worldview, which includes the Islamic epistemological system and Islamic methodology.
2) Methods for dealing with the sources of Islamic knowledge, which include the Holy Qur'an and the Prophetic Sunnah.
3) Methods for dealing with our written heritage, including both the Islamic heritage and the human heritage as a whole.
4) Methods for dealing with reality, including both reality as it is (through field studies of facts on the ground and nature of things, events and phenomena), and reality as it ought to be (through futuristic studies).

These four focal points and their associated concerns make clear that the subject of methodology forms the warp and woof of the Islamization of knowledge project. Everyone would agree that systematic, orderly thinking is necessary for the success of any action, since it is through this type of thinking that we are able to map out how we will reach the goal we hope to achieve. Awareness of the need for orderly thinking is not merely a product of our own times. On the contrary, throughout recorded history human beings have demonstrated an awareness of the need for systematic thinking. This awareness has not been restricted to a single culture, nor to a single specialization or area of interest. Nevertheless, many people – whether individuals, groups, or entire nations – fail to achieve their goals, be they short-term or long-term, because they have neglected to determine the best means of reaching these goals.

The terms "method" and "methodology" have a certain mystique about them, as evidenced by their frequent use in the writings of those concerned with literary enjoyment, ideological competition, rousing rhetoric, proselytizing, and putting forth academic or scientific claims. All these individuals make use of methodology and claim to possess methods that are superior to those of their rivals – not to mention those who are accused of having no methods at all – in the areas of thought, word and action alike.

Over the past fifty years a number of academics and other figures have attempted to purge Arab-Islamic thought and its associated methodology of mistaken notions. Others have attempted to make use of inductive *uṣūlī* methods to explain the prosperity and distinctiveness of Islamic culture, while others have sought to explain the regression of Islamic civilization as resulting from the juristic method that prevailed among earlier Arab Muslim thinkers, thereby robbing Arab Islamic thought of its creative momentum. Still others have argued that this same juristic method laid foundations and established criteria for interpreting religious texts, thereby depicting the principles of jurisprudence as a theory of hermeneutics, in which case they become a closed system!

However, this type of evaluation lends more attention to the historical application of Islamic ways of thinking and the heritage they produced than it does to the principles that inhere in the original sources of these ways of thinking, that is, in the Qur'an and the

Prophetic Sunnah. Nor does it give sufficient attention to the purposes these sources were intended to fulfill and the broad horizons such principles can open up to us in numerous fields of knowledge and spheres of life.

Epistemological integration – which is a comprehensive, systematic integration of the sources and means of knowledge – constitutes the frame of reference for Islamic methodology. Epistemological integration is a necessity that is fully consistent with human nature. Variety is a natural, authentic phenomenon that should be accepted and put to good use. Hence, there is a genuine need for cooperation and integration, since variety is basic to human nature, with people coming from a variety of ethnic backgrounds, speaking different languages, being descended from different tribes, and so on. Variety is also fundamental to conceptualizations, beliefs, and religious faith and practice. (If God had so desired, He would have made all people everywhere into a single community, but He chose to do otherwise). Similarly, variety is fundamental to the functions people perform and the skills they master, their preferences, their tastes, and so on.

The need for integration takes two different forms, one internal and the other external. What I am terming the internal need for integration is manifested in the need for loving relationships and bonds of compassion and trust among the members of a single society or community, as well as peace treaties and charters that engender trust and confidence among different communities and societies. As for the external necessity of integration, it arises from people's mutual dependence on one another for the provision of life's necessities.

Every methodology is associated with both mental activity and practical procedures for searching out solutions to problems and answers to questions, which lead to the acquisition of knowledge and the construction of thought systems. Next comes concrete action to apply solutions to actual situations. Hence, the integration of thinking, research and practice is a principle of methodology in general. However, Islamic methodology in particular has taken this principle and formulated its significance in clear, eloquent terms. The numerous Qur'anic references to "...those who have attained to faith and do good works..." (Qur'an 2:25, 82; 3:57; 4:57 and elsewhere) affirm the need to integrate thought and practice, knowledge and action, and to integrate efforts to both create prosperity on earth and earn reward in the life to come.

Methodology of Epistemological Integration: Essentials of Islamic Methodology is an attempt to construct a program which helps to spread awareness of methodology and, at the same time, to offer practical training in the thoughtful investigation of issues relating to science and knowledge in a variety of fields. The book's title affirms the distinctive types of integration that characterize Islamic methodology, including the integration of sources, tools, and schools of thought; the integration of existing realities with desired ideals; and the integration of quantitative descriptions that take place through the evaluation and precise measurement of the subject or problem under study with qualitative descriptions which clarify the underlying meanings of phenomena.

My interest in the subject of this book began early in my work as a teacher trainer, and later as a university professor. A number of the chapters in this book were presented in training courses in the 1990's in Jordan, then in other countries. I have organized numerous sessions with scholars and researchers on issues relating to methodology, as well as with individuals who specialize in training in methodological thinking. I took part in all the discussion sessions that were held by the International Institute of Islamic Thought (IIIT) in Cairo between 2005 and 2008 in order to plan the writing of the book *Islamic Methodology*,[1] Chapter One of which contains material from the present work. In the course of writing this book, particularly the chapters dealing with the sources and tools of methodology and methodological schools respectively, I benefited greatly from the contributions of the scholars and thinkers who took part in these sessions. I have benefited similarly from comments I have received from participants in the aforementioned training courses. Hence, I offer my sincere thanks and appreciation to everyone who took part in those sessions, programs and activities.

The ideas presented in this book make up the basic topics of many training courses I have organized over the years. Courses that aimed to encourage systematic action in a particular area of field bore titles such as, "The Problems of Academic Research in Islamic Studies" and

"Educational Research and Its Applications to the Islamic Sciences in Universities." As for courses whose purpose was to encourage systematic thought and action in general, they bore titles such as, "Academic Research Methods from an Islamic Perspective," "Reforming Islamic Ways of Thinking and the Islamization of Knowledge," "Islamic Methodology" and "Epistemological Integration Methodology." Not surprisingly, then, those who participated in these courses own copies of the earliest versions of some chapters of this book! It is also worth noting that all these courses address themselves to university faculty members and graduate students. Regular readers of *Islāmīyat al-Ma'rifah* will also notice that paragraphs from some chapters have appeared previously in my editorials for the journal.

The experience of organizing training courses on Islamic methodology and its applications to various fields of knowledge, including education, psychology, economics, international relations and others, has repeatedly confirmed the need for a book that presents methodological concepts, principles, sources, tools and schools of thought in a clear, concise and accessible manner. Trainers can then simply reproduce each chapter in the form of activities, examples and real-life situations. This need was uppermost in my mind as I drafted the material for this book. Consequently, the book contains models for activities, examples and situations, yet without digression or excessive detail in the body of the text. Therefore, the trainer is free to exercise his or her own discretion by choosing whatever best suits his or her own experience and areas of expertise, the needs of his or her trainees, and the nature of their specializations. Nevertheless, the appendix to this book contains comments and observations on training requirements and additional models for training session plans.

It should be stressed from the outset that this book is not intended as a substitute for the book *Islamic Methodology*,[2] which resulted from a collective effort to provide a reference book for IIIT's courses on Islamic methodology. A sizable two volumes of more than 1,200 pages in length that reflects the rich experience and expertise of numerous scholars and thinkers, *Islamic Methodology* consists of a detailed presentation of issues and topics in systematic thought and methodological philosophy. This kind of detailed treatment is necessary for those readers who wish to go deeply into the philosophical foundations of methodological thought and research, whereas the present work was written specifically as a textbook for the purposes of teaching and training.

IIIT has organized numerous conferences to heighten awareness of the need to construct an Islamic methodology of thought and research, and to spread what might be termed the "methodological culture," particularly among university professors and graduate students. In so doing, IIIT has been implementing the action plan that was laid by the IIIT in a book which sums up the IIIT's thought, vision, mission and plan of action.[3] These include a conference organized by the IIIT in cooperation with the University of Khartoum in 1987, the proceedings of which were published in three volumes,[4] and another organized by the IIIT in cooperation with the Emir Abdelkader University in Algeria in 1989, the proceedings of which were published in a single volume.[5] In addition, the IIIT assigned Dr. Muhammad Amarah the task of writing a reference work which summarizes the essential features of Islamic method. This work was written and published by the IIIT in cooperation with al-Azhar University in 1990.[6]

Nor is the present work intended as a replacement for the various reference works used by university students on the subject of academic research methods. Books of this nature tend to deal with the steps and procedural operations which address themselves directly to the research problem, as well as relevant questions that need to be answered or hypotheses that need to be tested, whereas the present work deals with aspects of methodological thought. In this way it helps in the critical analysis of other technical works and provides a guide to their use, because many of these books, particular university textbooks translated from other languages, may be based on premises which themselves call for critical analysis in order to determine how consistent, or inconsistent, they are with the Islamic intellectual frame of reference.

Given the fact that this book attempts to toe a practical line, with training as its focus, readers may look in it for particular "skills," which are, quite naturally, the center of attention in any training program. However, it should be remembered that skills are not limited to manipulative or practical skills. Rather, the basic topic of this book is "thinking skills," that is, skills that revolve around "intellectual action," which are no less important than the manipulative and practical skills associated with vocational and technical work.

This book is composed of seven chapters. Chapter One presents the concept of epistemological integration and its relationship to the unity of knowledge, the principle of divine unity, and the Islamic worldview. It also draws attention to certain obstacles to the achievement of epistemological integration. Chapter Two presents the twin concepts of method and methodology and explicates the importance of methodological awareness, while presenting some concepts of direct relevance to methodology. Chapter Three discusses the topic of methodological awareness, and describes signs of methodological inadequacy which call for remedial action. Chapter Four treats the evolution of the concepts of method and methodology in both Islamic thought and Western thought. Chapter Five discusses the sources and tools of knowledge and the concept of epistemological integration. Chapter Six presents a specific vision of the principles and values of Islamic methodology, while Chapter Seven provides an introduction to methodological schools of thought within the Islamic worldview. The book then concludes with a summary of the principles explicated in its various chapters.

Attention should be drawn to the fact that the semi-final draft of this book was examined by a number of notable scholars whose friendship I cherish, and with whom I have engaged in fruitful dialogue over the years. Of these associates I mention, in particular, those who offered me valuable observations and important corrections, many of which made their way into this book in its current form. These individuals include Dr. Ahmed Fouad Pasha, Professor of Physics and the Philosophy of Science and former Vice-President of Cairo University, Dr. Yomna al-Khouli, Head of the Philosophy Department at Cairo University, Dr. Sayyid Umar, Professor of Political Science at Helwan University, and Dr. Muhammad Amarah, noted Islamic thinker and author. To all these individuals I extend heartfelt thanks and sincere appreciation, and prayers for God to reward them richly for their efforts.

I expect the publication of this book to yield a growing interest in the topic of epistemological integration from an Islamic perspective and its associated methodology. I also hope the value of the book's contents will be put to the test. To that end, I welcome feedback on the suggestions offered in the book's various chapters, and I encourage readers to send me their comments, observations and any suggested improvements to the book, all of which might well find their way into future editions.

O God, teach us what we do not know, enable us to benefit
from what we learn, and increase us in knowledge!
Praise be to God, Lord of the worlds.

AIMS OF THE BOOK

A. Theoretical and Cognitive Aims

1. To clarify the concept of epistemological integration and its relationship to the unity of knowledge, *Tawḥīd*, and Islamic worldview as the governing frame of reference.
2. To explain the concepts of "method", "methodology" and subsidiary concepts derived from these, as well as epistemologically related concepts such as: methodological awareness, methodological inadequacy, methodology of thought, research methodology, methodology of conduct, sources of methodology, tools of methodology, principles of methodology, methodological principles, epistemological integration, and the epistemological integration model.
3. To trace the development of the concepts of "method" and "methodology" in both Islamic thought and Western thought, and to identify the critical junctures in this development and the ways in which such development has been manifested in scientific and epistemological production and cultural advancement.
4. To draw attention to the importance of research into methodological issues, and the central place occupied by methodology in academic research in the various fields of human knowledge, including the Islamic legal sciences (*ʿulūm al-sharīʿah*), the humanities, the social sciences, and the natural and applied sciences.
5. To identify the sources and tools of Islamic methodology and their unique characteristics, and to demonstrate the integrative and complementary relationship between methodological sources, methodological tools, and between the sources and the tools of methodology.
6. To identify the principles of Islamic methodology and their relationship to the governing value system, the ways in which these principles and values manifest themselves in the nature and defining features of knowledge, and the ways in which epistemological integration is reflected in the methodology of thought, research methodology, and the methodology of conduct.
7. To derive an equation for epistemological integration as a frame of reference for Islamic methodology.

B. Practical and Operational Aims

1. To foster awareness of the science of methodology and its implications for thought and research, as well as the application of Islamic methodology to questions relating to science, knowledge, and life.
2. To enable readers to organize training courses on the topic of epistemological integration methodology.
3. To think of issues of life, work and relations with others based on methodology of epistemological integration.
4. To do research within an Islamic framework and acquire sound knowledge base in dealing with issues of life, elevating the level of performing duties effectively, and build sound relations with others.
5. To conduct personal and public life according to the principle of integration of revealed knowledge and knowledge of practical facts and realities of life.

1

Concepts of Relevance to Epistemological Integration

GOALS OF THIS CHAPTER

1. To define the term "epistemological integration" and to clarify related concepts and ideas.
2. To clarify the relationship between epistemological integration and the unity of knowledge.
3. To explain how epistemological integration is based on the principle of divine unity.
4. To locate epistemological integration within the Islamic worldview.
5. To draw attention to the obstacles and constraints that hinder achieving epistemological integration.
6. To justify having epistemological integration as a frame of reference for Islamic methodology in relation to thought, research, and sound ways of dealing with questions relating to knowledge and behavior.
7. To build a model for epistemological integration in the following three areas: integration of sources, integration of tools, and integration of sources and tools together.

INTRODUCTION

Certain terms tend to come to the fore in writings pertaining to this field or that, where their use becomes widespread without sufficient attempts to define their meanings clearly. Consequently, one may find a given term being used in different and even contradictory senses in different contexts. This may also have happened in connection with the term "epistemological integration."

The term "epistemological integration" (*al-takāmul al-maʿrifī*) has frequently been used in reference to individuals who have an encyclopedic knowledge of things. Such persons may be acquainted with numerous fields of knowledge, if only in a general sort of way. In this connection, reference is sometimes made to Muslim scholars who achieved epistemological integration in the sense of possessing an encyclopedic knowledge, since they were well-versed in language, literature, Islamic jurisprudence, the Qur'anic sciences, the Hadith sciences, history, and possibly even astronomy, medicine or mathematics. Imam al-Ṭabarī, for example, was a Qur'anic exegete, a historian, a jurist, a linguist, and a poet. Ibn Khaldūn was primarily a political adventurer; however, he came to be known as a historian and the Chief Justice of the Mālikī school of jurisprudence in Egypt, while many consider him to have been a pioneer in sociology, economics, education and other fields. Ibn Sīnā (Avicenna) was a philosopher and physician, while Ibn Rushd (Averroes) was a jurist, a scholar of the principles of jurisprudence (*uṣūlī*), a physician, and a philosopher. Similarly, Ibn Taymiyyah wrote in the fields of jurisprudence, the principles of jurisprudence, the Prophetic Sunnah, Islamic mysticism (Sufism), and logic.

The phenomenon of creative production in more than one field of knowledge was clearly a distinguishing feature of the age in which many well-known Muslim scholars lived. However, this phenomenon had also been widely known among ancient scholars, thinkers and philosophers in Greek civilization and elsewhere. The practice of devoting oneself entirely to a single specialization is thus a recent phenomenon in human history; it has emerged in response to the unprecedented expansion that has taken place in human knowledge over the past century, with the result that it has become virtually impossible for a single scholar to specialize in more than one field. Indeed, a single field may well be divided into numerous sub-specializations, each of which is so vast that a single individual can hardly master it.

Around the middle of the twentieth century, the British Lord S. P. Snow remarked on the communication gap that had come to exist between those specializing in social sciences and the humanities and those specializing in the natural and applied sciences. The situation had grown so dire that Lord Snow described each of the two groups as possessing a culture of its own that had nothing to do with the other. In his well-known work entitled, *The Two Cultures*, he called for the integration of these two estranged "cultures."[1]

In ancient times sages and scholars spoke of integration between knowledge and action.[2] Ibn Rushd affirmed the possibility of linking wisdom and the divinely given law, while Ibn Taymiyyah affirmed the concept of integration in his insistence that there can be no contradiction between a correct understanding of divinely revealed texts and what is clear to human reason. Similarly, al-Qushayrī and other Sufis combined "the path" (*al-Ṭarīqah*), that is, the Sufi way of life, and "the truth" (*al-ḥaqīqah*), that is, the truths revealed in the Qur'anic revelation. This was followed by attempts to integrate principles, theories and scientific research on one hand, and their practical applications on the other as "pure" science and technology joined hands. In the early twentieth century it became clear that Physics stood in need of Mathematics, and Biology in need of Chemistry, which led in turn to the development of interdisciplinary research, publications and instruction, since it was now recognized that evolution and development in one of the sciences are dependent upon other sciences as well. A number of ideas have since been put forward in connection with the integration of science and religion. Similarly in the field of education, increasing efforts have been made to construct integrated curricula. There is now a greater awareness of the need for ideas related to the integration of tradition with modernity, and so on.

This chapter aims to clarify concepts relating to epistemological integration in its historical and modern contexts and how they relate to other concepts such as the unity of knowledge, worldview, classification of schemes of knowledge, and Islamization of knowledge. In addition, an attempt will be made to explain the nature of the issues with which epistemological integration concerns itself, and the obstacles in the way of achieving epistemological integration. This chapter will provide an introduction to the discussions in later chapters of the forms integration has taken within the Islamic framework, particularly in relation to the links between the various sources of knowledge, between the various means of acquiring knowledge, and between such sources and means.

First: EPISTEMOLOGICAL INTEGRATION VS. THE UNITY OF KNOWLEDGE

The issue of epistemological integration is both ideational-intellectual and methodological in nature in that it is linked with mental activity, research practices, and ways of dealing with ideas. However, the purpose for dealing with the issue of epistemological integration and the method by means of which it is dealt with will determine the epistemological category into which this issue is placed. Epistemological integration might be classified, for example, as a branch of philosophy – ontology, epistemology, or ethics – in which case it takes on an abstract, theoretical dimension. It might also be classified as a type of cultural, social activity when the purpose for which it is undertaken is to provide necessary resources and to transform them into political, economic or social activity in order to facilitate life for people on the practical level, in which case it takes on a social, applied dimension. Investigation of the topic of epistemological integration might also be limited to the task of dealing with the various epistemological fields and evaluating the need for each of these fields in designing programs and curricula for educational institutions, in which case the issue takes on a didactic-pedagogical dimension.

> Epistemological integration: Either a theoretical, abstract, philosophical issue, or a practical, applied, social issue.

There are two dimensions to the process of epistemological integration: a productive dimension and a consumptive dimension. In its productive dimension, integration is a form of intellectual creativity which requires special skills. Thus, for example, the process of integrating the Qur'anic sciences, the humanities and the social sciences in their contemporary Western formulations calls for a scholar and researcher, who draws inspiration from God's guidance in understanding the aims and intents of religious texts and rulings and how to apply them to real-life situations and events within a contemporary cultural framework. This understanding involves an important analytical and deconstructive effort. At the same time, however, the researcher will need to be familiar with the reality that relates to a particular epistemological field or specific issue, be it economic, social, or educational, on both the quantitative and qualitative levels. And this necessarily means the ability to deconstruct the issue at hand, identify its elements, and understand the mechanism by which it operates and its underlying theoretical assumptions or premises. This process of deconstruction is a necessary precondition which, if fulfilled, will be the foundation for the achievement of epistemological integration between the two fields of concern in a critical, creative construction process. This constructive process is generally accompanied by an evaluation of the elements that will go into the new amalgam, and the matrix of relationships that bring them together for a new purpose or aim.

> The process of epistemological integration has two dimensions: a productive, scientific, creative dimension, and a consumptive, pedagogical, applied dimension.

As for the consumptive dimension of epistemological integration, it has to do with the use of the intellectual structures upon which integration rests in order to understand the phenomena or issues under investigation, identify the distinguishing elements of knowledge in its integrative framework, and facilitate the communication of this knowledge to others. The difference between the productive and the consumptive dimensions of epistemological integration might be likened to the difference between the physicist who discovers a given natural law or the technologist who develops an instrument or machine based on this law, and the technician who works in a factory in which this instrument or machine is used.

In order to clarify the role and importance of integration within the various fields of scientific activity, noted educator Ernest Boyer divided scientific activity into four phases. The first phase is that of *discovery*, which consists in the epistemological efforts involved in research procedures in specific fields of knowledge. The second phase is that of *application*, namely, reflection on how to put the knowledge discovered to practical use. The third phase is that of *instruction*, or the communication of knowledge in such a way that it is bequeathed from one generation to the next. And the fourth phase is that of *integration*, where structure is integrated or combined with meaning. It is this final phase that gives the three earlier phases of scientific activity their true meaning and significance. Stressing the nature and importance of integration, Boyer held that it is only through integration that research becomes truly trustworthy.[3]

The Unity of Knowledge: A Practical Foundation for its Integration

The concept of epistemological integration is linked to the concept of the unity of knowledge, which constitutes the logical foundation for such integration. I will be devoting the present discussion to the concept of epistemological integration in particular, postponing the discussion of the various concepts connected with the unity of knowledge to another occasion. Nevertheless, the Islamic principle of divine oneness; i.e., *tawḥīd*, will be present in discussions of both the unity of knowledge and epistemological integration.

The modern age has been highly successful in keeping its promise of expanding knowledge and progress in providing for life's external, material requirements. However, the price has been exorbitant. For modernity has left us with a frightening legacy of unprecedented problems on a global scale, problems which threaten the very future of humanity and of the planet we live on. Exponential growth in information and data has resulted in a mass of knowledge so vast that, in order for us to be able to cope with it, it has had to be divided up into separate fields and specializations, and the more our knowledge increases, the more it has to be divided and fragmented. As chemist Allen Utke points out, this phenomenon has given rise to educational systems and societies which are engrossed in a process of dividing and subdividing knowledge into a growing number of specializations and sub-specializations. Out of this process have emerged individuals with a reductionist view of the world who focus excessively on parts of the truth that are immediate and direct, while losing touch increasingly both with history and with the larger, more comprehensive picture of the cosmos. Hence, as we come to know more and more about fewer and fewer things, we know less and less about more and more things.[4]

We are, without a doubt, living through an extraordinary, perilous phase of history the end of which is difficult to predict. Some researchers are of the opinion that humanity is slipping into a new dark age, and that human society and civilization are in great danger. Indeed, we are living in an era in which, for the first time in history, the specter of the end of Planet Earth itself appears to be looming on the horizon. However, despite the dark picture some have painted of the state of humanity and the planet on which we live, Utke is optimistic about the possibility of entering a new phase of history, or post-modern era. Utke attempts to draw up a plan which, though admittedly imperfect, he believes will help pave the way for such an age. According to Utke, the new age of lights (which is how he refers to the post-modern age) will be accompanied by revolutions in which the forces of matter and mind intermingle to bring about radical changes in human behavior toward nature as well as, by necessity, changes in people's view of the world and psychological inclinations, which will differ significantly from those exhibited during the age of modernity. There will be a shift away from a shallow focus on present reality characterized by narrowness, irresponsibility, dogmatism and violence, and toward a more comprehensive, inclusive way of thinking about the Absolute Truth. The new age of lights, in Utke's view, will also be accompanied by a methodological revolution that moves away from the emphasis on the individual, be it the personal "I," the national "I," or the religious "I," and toward a re-emphasis on the human "we" as we move into the future.

Utke justifies his optimism based on the observation that in the early twentieth century, the old world and its reductionist methods began taking in larger and larger doses of what might be termed "cosmic unity consciousness." Unity consciousness has been spread, for example, through the Theory of Relativity and its applications, new understandings of the relationship between energy and matter,

Quantum theory, and Grand Unified Field Theory. Those who promote such consciousness stress the study of the various parts of reality together with the realization that in the final analysis, these parts are actually nothing but an illusion, since everything, ultimately, permeates everything else. The knowledge and information in our possession draw our attention away from the whole and toward the parts (from the one to the many). However, there is an ongoing recognition that the whole is greater than the sum of its parts.

This new science recognizes that definitive knowledge, complete understanding, and total certainty of the truth are ideals that will never be realized. In their place it offers a new truth, namely, that the universe is not in a simple, static, disconnected state that has no meaning, like some mindless machine, and that human beings did not appear in this universe by accident or mere chance. Rather, the universe appears to be cohesive, its parts connected to one another. It also appears to be growing in a conscious fashion, its structure and features integrated, while human beings appear to be a means of achieving the purpose for which the universe was created, in that the human mind appears to be the most complex entity known to us. One might venture the claim that the new science, through the powerful message it presents about the new reality, is heralding the dawn of the long-awaited new age, the post-modern age, in which the unity of knowledge can be realized.[5]

Some scholars' belief that sciences will ultimately be unified finds support in the conclusions reached by Muslim physicist Muhammad Abdus Salam, known for his work in the area of electroweak theory. This theory, on the basis of which Abdus Salam was awarded the Nobel Prize in Physics in 1979 together with two of his colleagues, is a unified mathematical and rational description of electromagnetism and the weak interaction, which was the most advanced theory that had been formulated up to that time on ways of unifying the fundamental forces of nature. The validity of this theory was confirmed in later years through experiments conducted in the laboratories of the European Organization for Nuclear Research (CERN) in Geneva, Switzerland in the particle accelerator known as the Super Proto Synchrotron, which led to the discovery of the W and Z gauge bosons. The electroweak theory continues to form an important part of the standard model of particle physics.[6]

Models of Islamic Discourse on the Unity and Integration of Knowledge

Within the context of Islamic discourse relating to the unity of knowledge, many Muslim scholars in the past spoke of the need to preserve the unity of the sciences and of knowledge in general by virtue of the fact that they were all connected to a single source, that is, God Almighty. This connection was acknowledged regardless of whether knowledge took the form of revealed texts, or information that God had enabled human beings to acquire through research and investigation. Suffice it in this regard to note the efforts of al-Ghazālī, Ibn Rushd, and Ibn Taymiyyah.

In the modern era, by contrast, faced with the West's unprecedented scientific and industrial superiority, numerous Muslim intellectuals began falling under the influence of Western ideologies that raise a barrier between science and religion. In consequence, a large number of contemporary Muslims have taken it upon themselves to address the dangers involved in separating Islam from science and the need to reestablish the vital link between them based on the principle of divine unity.

The issue is related fundamentally to the integrative nature of the natural and biological sciences themselves. Ongoing progress in the realm of scientific knowledge and research in the philosophy of science have revealed the interdependence, complementarity and systematic nature of contemporary scientific knowledge. This, in turn, has revealed the need to activate what Ahmed Fouad Pasha has referred to as,

> a universal, comprehensive view of the various phenomena of the universe and life. Such a view causes the apparent barriers among the various branches of knowledge to vanish in such a way that intermeshing, integrated sciences take the place of discrete, separate ones. In fact, all of them can be included within a single orderly structure.... One of the most telling examples of the complementarity and interdependence of modern sciences is the emergence of Cybernetics, which is based on numerous fields of learning, including Mathematics, Logic, Mechanics, Physiology, and others... The twin features of complementarity and systematicity are significant because they confirm the fact that human knowledge progresses and evolves in a marvelous harmony toward more and more abstraction and generalization. Abstraction and generalization are features that characterize human

thought which is imbued with belief in the divine unity, and which one finds within the framework of Islamic life and doctrine.[7]

Similarly, Muzaffar Iqbal affirms the need to join the words "Islam" and "science" in such a way that we are speaking not only of a link between them, but about complete unification. The reason for this, in Iqbal's view, is that it would make no sense for Islamic discourse to speak of two separate or independent paths to the truth. Even when there are varied ways of expressing the one truth or differing means of arriving at this truth, they will remain connected to one another via a central node with a unifying function.[8]

The late Isma^cīl al Fārūqī, together with the Islamization of knowledge school that developed at the International Institute of Islamic Thought and a number of universities and research centers, held that the crisis being faced by the contemporary Muslim community results from the division that has been set up between the religious and secular educational systems. In al Fārūqī's view, the Muslim community has difficulty benefiting from the contemporary sciences in their present form, whether the humanities, the social sciences, or even the natural sciences. The reason for this is that although these sciences all represent aspects of an integrated view of the truth, the world, and history, they are treated as though they were foreign to Islam. Hence, the solution to this crisis lies in unifying the traditional Islamic educational system and the contemporary secular educational system into a single system that combines the best of both. Such a combined system would develop the knowledge offered by the various educational systems by formulating it from an Islamic perspective, that is, by Islamizing it.[9]

Seeking to achieve the same cultural aim for the Muslim community but in terms that differ from those used by the Islamization of knowledge school, Ziauddin Sardar – together with a number of his associates in what has come to be known as the Ijmāliyyīn School[10] – has added his voice to the discussion of the unity and integration of knowledge. According to the Ijmāliyyīn School, all sciences, including the natural sciences, are socially constructed and functional in nature; that is to say, they are tools and means of action, their value being determined by their practical usefulness. According to this school, the sciences arise out of specific assumptions about truth and humanity and the relationship between human beings and nature. Moreover, given the fact that every civilization constructs its own sciences, all modern sciences are, therefore, Western sciences. Consequently, it will be difficult to construct Islamic sciences anywhere but in an Islamic cultural environment by means of a radical construction process that establishes integrative ties among its various components.[11]

There is, in addition, an Islamic discourse on the unity of knowledge based in spiritual experience. This discourse views knowledge from a traditional perspective, which was expressed by the civilizations of the East within a metaphysical framework based on principles derived from the timeless teachings of the divine revelation in its various forms. This being the case, the traditional sciences enjoy a sacredness derived from the sacredness of nature itself, which in turn derives its sacredness from the revelation due to its recognition of Nature as a composite of the signs of God. Hence, the knowledge human beings acquire about the world and the knowledge they receive from the Creator constitute a single unit. Even the methodologies of these sciences can trace their roots to a single source. Thus, the knowledge available to human thought through mystic (Sufi) philosophy opens up numerous possibilities because, being linked ultimately with God in His transcendence, it establishes a link among all the knowledge-related activities in which thought engages.[12]

This philosophical, Sufi discourse has been adopted by a group of contemporary scholars, foremost among whom are Seyyed Hossein Nasr, Syed Muhammad Naquib al-Attas, Mehdi Golshani, and their disciples in Malaysia, Iran, Turkey, and the United States of America. It is clear that this vision is based on meditative philosophy and, as such, goes beyond the ethical determinants of action in the universe to a metaphysic which sees nature as an entity with spiritual significance. Consequently, this philosophy holds that contemporary science, which lacks a sense of the sacred, is leading humanity to the brink of an abyss. In this respect it finds itself in agreement with many scholars who, though their thought arises out of an entirely different analytical philosophy, have similar expectations of the fate that awaits the human race on Planet Earth in light of problems foreseen, unforeseen, and unacknowledged.

The Relationship Between the Classification of the Sciences and the Unity and Integration of Knowledge

Efforts to classify the sciences are relevant to the issue of the unity and integration of knowledge. Muslim scholars representing a variety of intellectual trends – among them philosophers, theologians, leading Sufi thinkers, jurists, historians, and others – have sought to discover the order that underlies the various fields of knowledge and the relationships among them.

The classification of the sciences is one of the essential keys to understanding the Islamic intellectual heritage. Muslim scholars' efforts in this field over the centuries may be viewed as attempts to elucidate various links among these sciences, since it is these links which form the criterion for classification. Classification tends naturally to focus either on elements of similarity and unity, or on elements of contrast and diversity, though in some cases there is a need to focus on both.

The notion of the classification of the sciences is rooted in ancient history. One ancient method of classification involves categorizing the sciences according to the criterion of abstraction in keeping with Aristotelian thought. This method of classification places the most abstract sciences at the top of the pyramid, considering them to be more significant than the practical sciences. The most important thing to be noted here is the attempt to separate the sciences by affirming their autonomy and their graded order of importance.

Although most Muslim scholars have been influenced by this method of classification, particularly those who adhere to the Aristotelian philosophical school, some of them have striven to ensure that their classification reflects the Islamic worldview and its requirements. We find, for example, al-Fārābī, Ibn Ḥazm, Ibn Khaldūn, Ibn al-Qayyim, and Tash Kubra Zadeh organized the sciences into a classificational structure that served educational purposes, and which thus reflected the realistic view of the sciences that had arisen within the Islamic environment. Given the number and variety of the sciences,

Muslim scholars' efforts to classify them focused on features that were proper to the Islamic worldview. These features include, for example, logically based order, internal consistency, graded levels of importance, continuity on the level of content, complementary, interdependence, and a unified orientation toward the service of Islamic religious truth.[13]

There are important differences among the bases of classification employed by Muslim scholars and their respective epistemological schools. Al-Fārābī, for example, belonged to the Peripatetic (Aristotelian) School, al-Ghazālī represented the Scholastic and Sufi school of thought, while Quṭb al-Dīn al-Shīrāzī hailed from the Illuminist School. Nevertheless, they all agreed that the highest level of knowledge is the knowledge of God Almighty, and that human beings ought to strive to achieve other types of knowledge in the service of knowing God.[14] Therefore, all other forms of knowledge should be interconnected, complementary, and organically linked to the knowledge of God. In the view of these scholars, the fact that all sciences originate from a single divine source is the foundation for the ultimate integration and unity of knowledge.

Second: THE PRINCIPLE OF GOD'S ONENESS AS THE FOUNDATION FOR EPISTEMOLOGICAL INTEGRATION

Muslim scholars agree unanimously that the oneness of God (*al-tawḥīd*) is the foundation of Islam and that which gives Islamic civilization its identity. Many non-Muslim scholars also acknowledge that the concept of the oneness of God in Islam is to be distinguished from its counterpart in the other monotheistic religions,[15] both in its conceptualization of the one God, and in the implications of this conceptualization for the Creator's relationship to His creatures.

Ismaᶜīl al Fārūqī's Vision of the Unity and Integration of Knowledge

Ismaᶜīl al Fārūqī devoted an entire book to the subject of *al-tawḥīd*, or the oneness of God,[16] in which he expounded the integrated nature of the monotheistic perspective and the way in which it brings together the theoretical-philosophical and the practical-applied dimensions of culture and civilization. Al Fārūqī's treatment of the issues of the unity and complementarity of the various branches of knowledge is free of many of the complexities with which the Islamic heritage has been burdened in the name of Islamic philosophy and scholastic theology, and he made a powerful case for reforming Islamic thought and the contemporary Islamic approach to vital issues.

Together with other Muslim scholars, al Fārūqī viewed *al-tawḥīd* as an all-encompassing perspective on reality, the cosmos, time, place, human history, and human destiny. The concept of *al-tawḥīd* applies to the entire Islamic way of life. Islam does not divide the world into sacred and profane, nor does it classify values as "religious" vs. "secular." Similarly, it makes no distinction between "men of religion" and "men of the world." Seen from the Islamic perspective, these are artificial distinctions and classifications that belong historically to non-Islamic traditions.[17]

The concept of *al-tawḥīd* leaves its mark on all aspects of Islamic culture and civilization by establishing clearly defined links between them. In its grand inclusiveness, Islam brings about a reformulation of every element of its civilization in varying degrees of depth, from minor modifications in outward forms to radical changes in functions, since it is function which shapes essential relationships. When Muslims developed the science of *al-tawḥīd*, they combined within it the areas of logic, the theory of knowledge, metaphysics, and ethics.[18]

Islamic monotheism (*tawḥīd*) draws a crucial distinction between the transcendent Creator and the created universe. It is the will of the Creator which defines creatures' existence, their behavior, and their organic structure. The reality of God's oneness is manifested in the fact that the universe is founded upon orderly behavior. Such orderliness points to the unity of the authority that brought such order into being, namely, the one God, glory be to Him. If there were numerous deities in the universe, it would be thrown into disorder, because it would be incapable of answering to two masters at one and the same time. For this reason, affirmation of God's oneness is of vital importance in religion, since it plays a distinctive role in shaping human beings' beliefs in this life, and determining what recompense will be theirs in the life to come.

Acknowledgment of God's unity – *al-tawḥīd* – presupposes by necessity an acknowledgement of the unity of truth as well. Al Fārūqī explains how *al-tawḥīd*, as a methodological principle requiring the unity of truth, is based on three subsidiary principles having to do with the nature of the sources from which human beings acquire knowledge. The first of these principles is the rejection of all that is inconsistent with the truth. The second is the disavowal of contradiction. And the third is openness to new evidence.[19]

The first of these three principles excludes falsehood, illusion, and conjecture from the realm of Islamic belief, while still allowing room for criticism and scrutiny. Anything that deviates from the truth or fails to conform to it in some degree is unacceptable in Islam, be it legislation, a personal or social ethical principle, or a way of understanding the world. This protects the Muslim from being swayed by mere opinion or whim. Any claim that is not accompanied by supporting evidence is mere conjecture, which can never replace the truth. Muslims are individuals who speak nothing but clear truth, and who accept nothing but the truth even if it goes against their desires and aspirations, or conflicts with their personal interests or the interests of those near and dear to them.

The second principle, which has to do with the absence of contradiction, represents the essence of rationalism, and without it there is no escape from doubt and uncertainty. If a contradiction cannot ultimately be resolved, this means there is no way of arriving at the truth. Contradictions may, of course, appear in a person's thinking and statements. There may also be contradictions in our superficial understanding of the relationship between revelation and reason. Islam denies the logical possibility of such contradictions when there is a true, complete understanding of revelation; it also presents an explanation of the way in which apparent contradictions can be eliminated.

In al Fārūqī's view, neither reason nor revelation holds sway over the other. If revelation were allowed to hold sway over reason, there would be no basis for distinguishing one text of the revelation from another, or between two different ideas presented by the revelation on a particular topic. Without allowing for the role of reason, it would be impossible to resolve the contradictions or inconsistencies that arise in our understanding of the texts of the revelation. The various texts of the revelation are themselves characterized by internal consistency, and the correct understanding of them prevents the appearance of contradiction. However, this or that text of the revelation may appear to be inconsistent with reason; that is, it may appear to conflict with certain outcomes of rational investigation and understanding. When this happens, Islam teaches us that the contradiction that has appeared is not the end, and that we should rethink either our understanding of the revelation, the outcomes of our rational investigation, or both.

Although Islam rejects the possibility of an irresolvable contradiction between reason and revelation, the concept of *al-tawḥīd* – as an expression of the oneness of truth – encourages us to reexamine whatever appears to be a contradiction. The reason for this is that some dimension of reality may have eluded us so that, if we were to take this dimension into consideration, the apparent contradiction would be resolved. *Al-tawḥīd* requires seekers of truth to engage in another reading of the divine revelation when they sense that there is some logical contradiction in it, since this additional reading may remove the ambiguity and clarify meanings they have not been able to understand, thereby resolving the contradiction. Hence, rethinking one's reasoning or understanding may bring about harmony, not among the texts of the revelation themselves – since these texts are above being subjected to human judgment – but, rather, between the texts and human beings' understanding of them. This harmonization process brings our understanding of revelation into conformity with the data we have gathered and discovered through reason. Hence, the notion that there might be contradictions between revelation and reason is attractive only to those with weak minds. Muslims are behaving rationally when they insist on the unity of the two sources of knowledge, namely, revelation and reason.[20]

On this point al Fārūqī appears to be in agreement with Ibn Taymiyyah. Al Fārūqī rejected the views of al-Rāzī, Ibn Rushd, and other like- minded Muslim philosophers and theologians who assumed the possibility of contradictions between revelation and reason, while viewing reason as the final authority and the means by which revelation is understood. Similarly, he parted ways with al-Ghazālī, who agreed with the philosophers and theologians on the possibility of contradictions between revelation and reason while viewing revelation, not reason, as the final authority.

The third principle of *al-tawḥīd* as an expression of the oneness of truth is that of openness to new or conflicting evidence or data. This principle protects the Muslim from the need to join liberal, unbelieving schools of thought; at the same time, it protects him or her from extremism, or a conservatism so strict that it leads to rigidity and stagnation. Adoption of this third principle of *al-tawḥīd* gives rise to intellectual humility. Such humility leads us to say, "God knows best" when confronted with conflicting evidence or apparent contradictions between revelation and reason, since we know that the truth is too great to be fully comprehended or fathomed by human beings.

Moreover, just as *al-tawḥīd* serves to confirm the absolute oneness of God Almighty, it likewise confirms the unity of sources of truth. God is the Creator of the natural world from which human beings derive knowledge:

> He it is who has made the sun a [source of] radiant light and the moon a light [reflected], and has determined for it phases so that you might know how to compute the years and to measure [time]. None of this has God created without [an inner] truth. Clearly does He spell out these messages unto people of [innate] knowledge: for, verily, in the alternating of night and day, and in all that God has created in the heavens and on earth there are messages indeed for people who are conscious of Him! (*Sūrah Yūnus*, 10: 5-6)

The object of knowledge consists of the things and events of Nature, which are creations of God. It is a certainty that God Almighty knows these things and events, and it is equally certain that God is the source of revelation. Moreover, God gives human beings something of His vast, all-encompassing, perfect knowledge.

Al-tawḥīd invites human beings to draw connections between God as Creator and the pursuit of knowledge in its various spheres. The reason for this is that when human beings perceive the work of God in all events and things, they are observing the work of divine creation. When they observe the action of God in Nature, they are engaging in the natural sciences, since the divine creation in Nature is none other than the patterns and laws that God has deposited in the natural realm. Similarly, when human beings perceive the work of divine creation in themselves or their societies, they are engaging in the human and social sciences. If, as a result of human striving and searching, the cosmos reveals the operation of orderly patterns and laws as manifestations of God's will, then, from the Muslim's perspective, the cosmos is a living theatre which God created by His action and command.[21]

Seyyed Hossein Nasr's Vision of the Unity and Integration of Knowledge

Seyyed Hossein Nasr and a number of his disciples offer another way of thinking about the implications of *al-tawḥīd* for the unity and integration of knowledge. Nasr agrees with other Muslim scholars on the importance of the principle of *al-tawḥīd*, the hierarchical ordering of the sciences, and the view of *al-tawḥīd* as the highest form of knowledge and the final goal of all the Muslim's intellectual strivings. By contrast, however, Nasr focuses primarily on the natural sciences; he also placed great importance on philosophy and traditional Islamic metaphysics, which he and other like-minded scholars view as the entry point for understanding the relationship between scientific and religious knowledge. Consequently, they use the same metaphysical terminology that was current among Muslim thinkers such as al-Rāzī, Ibn Sīnā, al-Shīrāzī, Ikhwān al-Ṣafā, and others.

One of these terms is cosmology, or cosmological knowledge, which is employed as a point of entry to the study of nature. Cosmology is a branch of metaphysics in which the macrocosm, or the greater cosmos, is compared to the microcosm, or the lesser, human "cosmos." Within the context of cosmology, to observe Nature is to observe the action of the Creator, and the legitimacy of the ongoing pursuit of the natural sciences depends on the degree to which these sciences reveal the overall unity, connection, interdependence, and complementarity that characterize the divine creation. Hence, scientific knowledge that conforms to the spirit of Islam is knowledge which derives its legitimacy from the fundamental doctrine of Islam, that is, *al-tawḥīd* in all its varying senses, and which strives ultimately to integrate particulars within a single comprehensive whole. There may be many different explanations, interpretations, and levels of thinking. However, what remains is the principle according to which the created world consists of the unity of unified entities, whereas God the Creator alone enjoys what Nasr terms "the unity of the Unique."[22]

The organic link between scientific knowledge and the knowledge of God's oneness means that scientific knowledge is encompassed and integrated within the knowledge of God's oneness, because the divine revelation is the source of metaphysical knowledge of the diverse world with which the sciences deal. However, the conceptual tools for integration need to be derived from cosmological knowledge. This cosmological knowledge is capable of providing tools for conceptual integration, because the aim of integration is to provide the kind of scientific knowledge that sets forth the complementarity of all things and the way in which the levels of the hierarchy or order in the universe are linked to each other and to the spiritual realm. Consequently, it provides knowledge that allows for the integration of multiple and varied entities into a single unit.[23]

Osman Bakar's Vision of the Unity and Integration of Knowledge

In an approach similar to Seyyed Hossein Nasr's, Osman Bakar uses the term "cosmological knowledge." This cosmological knowledge is spiritual in nature. The laws that govern the various systems within creation are not all equally general and comprehensive. Rather, there is a hierarchical order to this generality and comprehensiveness. Biological laws, for example, are higher than chemical and physical laws, because biological laws have to do with living beings, which possess an existential reality that is higher than that possessed by other entities. However, these same biological laws are subject to a higher set of universal laws of a spiritual nature. When attempts are made to bring about an objective unification of known laws in the realms of physics and biology, we may reach a point beyond which we have no choice but to take into account laws that govern supernatural orders. In other words, we must recognize that natural laws are of limited comprehensiveness and generality.

The natural and mathematical sciences are limited sciences having to do with specific spheres of truth, whereas the higher truth of *al-tawḥīd* is a metaphysical science having to do with realities that lie beyond human perception.

The science of metaphysics is the most general of all the sciences, because it concerns itself with the higher truth that encompasses all other truths. Cosmological knowledge, which concerns itself with the structure and qualitative content of the cosmos, lies somewhere between the higher knowledge of *al-tawḥīd* and the particular sciences. In the traditional Islamic sciences, cosmology was classified as part of metaphysics; this is what we find, for example, in the enumeration provided by al-Fārābī, and it was from cosmology that the other particular sciences were derived. Cosmological knowledge thus constitutes the conceptual framework for the unity of the material and spiritual sciences.[24]

In keeping with the same approach, Osman Bakar employs the terms "spiritual knowledge" and "universal soul." The term "spiritual knowledge" refers to the knowledge of God and His oneness or unity. This knowledge does not necessarily have to do with the divine essence, which we are forbidden to think about. Rather, it has to do with the effects and actions of the Creator throughout the created universe. According to Bakar, the Muslim's knowledge of the Creator is the knowledge of the universe in its capacity as one effect of the Creator's action. Awareness of the relationship between God the Creator and the created cosmos, or between the principle of divinity and its manifestations in the cosmos, is the primary foundation for the unity of scientific and spiritual knowledge.

An understanding of this relationship requires us to go back to the fundamental source of knowledge in Islam, that is, revelation, which consists of the Qur'an and the Prophetic Sunnah. The Muslim looks upon the Qur'an as the springhead of both intellectual and spiritual energy. As such, the Qur'an is viewed as the springhead of all knowledge and all sciences, not because it contains the knowledge itself but, rather, because it inspires the Muslim to develop a distinctive vision of the unity among the various spheres of knowledge. The notion of this unity arises out of an awareness of the unity of the Divine and its applications to the various spheres of human knowledge. For, although human beings acquire knowledge from various sources and in a variety of ways, all types of knowledge derive ultimately from God the All-Knowing. The Qur'anic vision affirms that our knowledge of material and spiritual realities is possible because God has given us the necessary capabilities to possess such knowledge.[25]

Among Muslim scholars, cosmology requires that one relate to the natural world in a manner that is connected to the higher orders of truth. When studying the natural world, including the biological sciences, Muslim scholars affirm the relationship between this world and spiritual entities that lie beyond human perception. Hence, they recognize that the question of the origin of life on earth cannot be solved based on the evidence of natural entities alone, because life is not simply a material, natural form of existence. Rather, it is a vital capacity or force that has penetrated the world of material things. The molecular physiological activities associated with life's various forms are not themselves the source of life. Rather, they are simply manifestations of life on the natural level. The Islamic cosmological principle which is considered the basis for deciphering the mystery of life is the notion of "the universal soul." This universal soul is the soul or spirit of the natural order. As such, the universal soul is to the natural order what your soul or spirit is to your body.

It is this universal spirit which gives the entire cosmos its vital energy, an energy that we observe in the life of plants and animals. This universal spirit which exists in God's creatures, its relationship to human beings' knowledge of the universe's functions, capacities and distinguishing features, and the ways in which these relate to the natural order are essential for the integration of the biological sciences. Moreover, as will be clear from the foregoing, we perceive the existence of this spirit based on our belief in *al-tawḥīd*, or the oneness of God.

Despite the importance of developing cosmology and its link to the unity of knowledge, it is not necessary to abandon the empirical method and the modern tools of scientific research and investigation that have proved so successful in the quantitative study of nature. However, we do need to make radical changes in our orientations toward reality and knowledge. Acceptance of the notion of cosmology has a significant impact on research methodology, since those committed to the scientific method have to give up the claim that it is the only way to know things and acknowledge the existence of other paths to knowledge which are equally valid.[26]

Third: EPISTEMOLOGICAL INTEGRATION IN THE ISLAMIC WORLDVIEW

Our discussion of epistemological integration begins with the Islamic worldview, which has enabled the Muslim mind to develop a sound understanding of the universe, life, and human beings.

"Worldview" is:

- a modern philosophical term referring to an all-inclusive view of the world that takes all parts, elements, components and systems into account.
- a vision of the true nature of things within the broadest possible framework. Such a vision consists of authoritative rules and frameworks for thought and action within the society's overall value system.
- the lense through which the human mind perceives the realities of the universe, life, and human beings.
- a set of answers to the existential, epistemological, and value-related questions that arise in relation to these realities and the relationships among them.

The human mind acts instinctively to distinguish varied, multiple and separate entities from each other based on the features and traits that are proper to each of them. It also perceives these entities as belonging to a category or set which represents a larger unit. Such entities are located at specific time-place coordinates and there are definable relationships between them. Features and traits are also perceived by the human mind in relation to patterns of human behavior, social issues, religious values, and the like.

Any behavior or activity in which an individual engages or which prevails in this or that community within a society will be understood in light of an overall worldview. In other words, the image of existence reflected in our minds has a direct impact on our actions, our social conduct, and our individual and communal lives. In short, every one of us lives in accordance with his view of the cosmos – his worldview.[27]

An Islamic worldview is an expression of the overall belief-based conceptualization embodied in Islamic doctrine. This conceptualization offers a comprehensive explanation of existence. It also gives rise to individuals' concrete way of life and the rules that govern their behavior in light of their understanding of their place in the universe and the purpose of their existence.[28]

Abu Bakr Muhammad Ahmad's Study on Epistemological Integration and its Applications to University Curricula

One of the most comprehensive treatments of the subject of epistemological integration is a detailed study entitled, "Epistemological Integration and Its Applications to University Curricula." The study was written by Abu Bakr Muhammad Ahmad Ibrahim at International Islamic University of Malaysia (IIUM).[29] The researcher relied on a critical analysis of numerous writings of direct or indirect relevance to the concept of epistemological integration and related concepts, particularly the concept of the Islamization of knowledge. The study includes interviews conducted by the author with a number of researchers and thinkers. These are followed by an overview of the academic programs and pedagogical practices at IIUM's Faculty of Islamic Revealed Knowledge and Human Sciences, which has adopted and applied the concept of epistemological integration. On the basis of his research, the author concludes that epistemological integration is closely linked with the Islamization of knowledge. If the Islamization of knowledge can be properly described as a vision, then epistemological integration can be described as a feature that marks the educational process at academic institutions that have adopted this vision.[30]

As for the vision itself, it is, in actuality, a worldview that calls for an intellectual and cultural reform enterprise from an Islamic perspective. This enterprise involves three steps. The first step is to reexamine the sources of Islam in light of their governing values and overall aims, and to critique the legacy handed down through these sources and founded upon these values and aims. The second step is to engage positively with contemporary human knowledge as it relates to innate human tendencies, patterns, and dispositions, while subjecting this input to a critical analysis that will free it from philosophical accretions that are inconsistent with the facts at hand. These two initial steps are analytical and deconstructive in nature. As for the third step, which is constructive and creative in nature, it is to reformulate current knowledge within the Islamic worldview based on the integration of the guidance provided by divine revelation, the patterns and laws of nature, and human beings' attempts to understand the universe in its natural, social and psychological dimensions. Taken together, these three steps can help bring individual Muslims and the Muslim community as a whole out of the state of backwardness in which they find themselves. In fact, they promise to bring them to a place where they can make distinctive contributions to the direction being taken by human culture and civilization.

In this sense, epistemological integration is not merely an epistemological process but, in addition, a psychological and educational process whose aim is to liberate the Muslim mind, nurture the Muslim psyche, and motivate Muslims to be accomplish, create and reform.[31]

> The Islamic worldview calls for an integrated, three-step intellectual enterprise for the purpose of reform and cultural advancement.

Worldview in the Thought of AbdulHamid AbuSulayman

AbdulHamid AbuSulayman has published a set of works whose aim is to analyze the crisis in the Muslim mind, will and psyche, and to propose needed measures for dealing with these crises. AbuSulayman has also published a book on the Qur'anic cultural worldview, a worldview which he formulated in the process of completing his earlier writings. The book clarifies the monotheistic, integrational dimension of the Islamic worldview, which AbuSulayman describes as being a systematic, scientific, and comprehensive vision of love and goodness that puts resources to the best, most constructive possible use. As such, this vision provides the foundation for releasing Muslims' potentials and molding their characters, psyches and instincts in keeping with the

Qur'anic message via the forces of love, goodwill, conscience, reason and knowledge. When guided by sound doctrine and sincere faith and armed with the Qur'anic vision, Muslims can begin to flesh out these realities in society and build a constructive, spiritually-minded, well-intentioned human civilization.[32]

The Muslim mind has been able to develop a clear, sound understanding of the universe, life, and human beings via a comprehensive Islamic worldview based on a careful, reflective reading of two 'books.' The first of these 'books', which is perceived through the physical senses, is the universe with the things, events, phenomena and interrelationships that human beings have put to use in their capacity as God's *khalīfah*[33] (vicegerents) on earth. The second 'book', which exists in the form of a written revelation, is the Qur'an with its guidance, knowledge, wisdom, and decrees. In Islam's early days Muslims 'read' the universe in its natural, social and psychological dimensions with both their minds and their physical senses, introducing into this reading both the world of human experience and the world beyond human perception. They thus employed their knowledge of the universe to construct the foundations of a rightly guided human civilization that towered above both those civilizations which had preceded it and those that came after it. In addition, they engaged in an insightful, careful reading of the divine revelation in the form of both the Qur'an and the Prophetic Sunnah.

Based on these "two inseparable, thoughtful readings,"[34] epistemological integration has been achieved by combining the various aspects of the material universe (things, events, and phenomena), the social universe (laws and patterns of change, equilibrium through struggle and alternation), and the psychological universe (right guidance, depravity, faith, culture, and unbelief). This process has likewise involved combining the Qur'anic revelation, the Prophetic Sunnah, thoughtful consideration, the tools of concrete observation, and interpretation. In other words, it has involved integrating human, sense-based reception of both the physical universe and the written revelation with what we receive from the world beyond the senses relating to the origin and evolution of the universe through our study of divine revelation with its various reports and narratives.

As a result of this combination of the two 'readings' referred to above, the Muslim community was able to play the roles of pioneer, witness, benefactor, and leader for a period of time. Eventually, however, hearts were hardened, and the Muslim community imported the battle between reason and revelation from other nations and communities which only knew how to read the superficial phenomena of the life of this world. As a consequence, Muslims' reading of the world around them changed: their vision was blurred, their minds were dulled, their perception deteriorated, and thus began their regression.[35]

It was the Qur'anic worldview that gave birth to the mindset of the Prophet's Companions, may God be pleased with them, and the Qur'anic foundations of their cultural achievement contributed immeasurably to the renewal of human civilization by expanding and elevating human beings' rule-governed reason and moral awareness. The result was the beginning of a new era in which the laws of the universe were put to practical, creative uses, and efforts were made to guide the course of human civilization in keeping with human beings' obligation to adhere to moral and spiritual principles.[36] This achievement was possible by clarity of vision, integration of the Islamic sources of knowledge (revelation, human nature, and the laws, patterns and facts of the universe), and adherence to the criterion of objective, orderly scientific reasoning. There is no benefit to be gained from atomistic, haphazard efforts which fail to perceive the system underlying Islamic civilization and the laws that govern its interaction with its surroundings. Yet it is precisely this kind of intellectual and scientific lack of awareness that has thwarted reformers' efforts, numerous and protracted though they have been, to revive the Muslim community.

The Islamic vision for human civilization arises out of the notion of God's absolute unity. Similarly, it is the principle of *al-tawḥīd* that gives rise to the Qur'anic vision of the unified, integrated nature of the universe, whose structure and components constitute unity within integrated diversity, and integrated diversity in unity.[37] The Islamic worldview employs a uniquely Qur'anic, monotheistic approach to epistemological integration. It begins with the oneness of God the Creator, the oneness of the created universe, the oneness of the human being who has been appointed God's steward on earth, and the oneness of the divine gift given to human beings through God's teaching Adam the names of all things (see *sūrah al-Baqarah* 2:31), then continuing to provide human beings with divine revelation to guide them by means of the written word:

> O children of Adam! Indeed, We have bestowed upon you from on high [the knowledge of making] garments to cover your nakedness, and as a thing of beauty: but the garment of God-consciousness is the best of all. Herein lies a message from God, so that man might take it to heart. O children of Adam! Do not allow Satan to seduce you in the same way as he caused your ancestors to be driven out of the garden: he deprived them of their garment of [God-consciousness] in order to make them aware of their nakedness. Verily, he and his tribe are lying in wait for you where you cannot perceive them! Verily, We have placed [all manner of] satanic forces near unto those who do not [truly] believe. (*Sūrah al-Aʿrāf* 7:26-27)

The revelation goes on to remind us of the lesson to be learned from Cain's slaying of his brother Abel, saying, "Thereupon God sent forth a raven which scratched the earth, to show him how he might conceal the nakedness of his brother's body. [And Cain] cried out, 'Oh, woe is me! Am I then too weak to do what this raven did, and to conceal the nakedness of my brother's body?' – and was thereupon smitten with remorse" (*sūrah al-Mā'idah* 5:31).

The monotheistic approach involves acknowledging the integration and interdependence that exist between the divine revelation embodied in Nature, and that embodied in the written word. In this way it does away with the problems associated with the correspondence between reason and revelation. Furthermore, the monotheistic approach involves integrating the sciences of revelation and the acquired sciences having to do with the universe in its natural, social and psychological dimensions. These latter sciences are necessary for human (*khilāfah*) vicegerency on earth, the proper exercise of authority over the natural world, and human development and progress. The use of this approach in efforts to achieve epistemological integration tends to foster moderation in all things, since there is no sense of opposition between the various aspects of existence: individual and community, matter and spirit, this world and the world to come, self and other, rights and duties, responsibility and reward or punishment.

The various members of the human body are integrated in performing their respective functions; however, the limbs are not as important as the heart or the brain.[38] Similarly, the various sciences can be integrated without all of them being on the same plane in their relationship to the truth and, therefore, of the same importance or priority.

Although God Almighty is the ultimate source of knowledge, He has made knowledge available to human beings through two sources: the written revelation and the created universe, and has provided human beings with two means for acquiring knowledge: reason and sensory perception. Reason operates when we seek to understand these two sources and put them to use in the service of human vicegerency (*khilāfah*) on earth. Similarly, sensory perception comes into play when we use our senses to observe and experiment on the things, events, and phenomena of the universe, or to arrive at the meanings of the texts of revelation as they apply to human experience.[39]

The monotheistic worldview continuously links the various spheres of knowledge about which the Qur'an speaks. This link is so consistent, in fact, that the boundaries between these spheres nearly disappear, as do the boundaries between the Muslim's various practical concerns. The Qur'anic texts connect this earthly life with the life to come, the world beyond sense perception with the world of sense perception, and so on. Even more important, however, is the way in which they affirm the unity and complementarity of the sources and aims of knowledge.

Perhaps the most significant indication of this unity and complementarity is the Qur'an's use the word "sign" (*āyah*) to refer not only to the written words in the Qur'anic text, but, in addition, to the concrete phenomena we observe in the physical, social, and psychological realms. We read: "And on earth there are signs (*āyāt*) [of God's existence, visible] to all who are endowed with inner certainty, just as [there are signs thereof] within your own selves: can you not, then, see?" (*sūrah al-Dhāriyāt* 51:20-21). When the Qur'an invites us to go about the Earth and investigate the beginnings of creation, it is as though God Almighty were linking the story of the creation of humankind as it is narrated in the verses of the Holy Book with what we find in fossils, for example, where we see the traces of life engraved in stone or buried beneath the soil. When it invites us to reflect on the fates of the peoples, nations and civilizations that went before us so as to learn from the past, we realize that although the guidance the Qur'an wants us to obtain is a gift of grace and mercy from God, we can also acquire it, in part, through the effort we expend in our study of history, archeology, anthropology, comparative religion, sociology, and so on. Similarly, when the Qur'an urges us to examine God's signs on the horizons and within ourselves – through the cosmological and psychological sciences – it is affirming the complementarity that exists between these sciences and the study of divine revelation.

> The concept of integration is found in the writings of al-Rāzī, Ibn Rushd, al-Ghazālī, and Ibn Taymiyyah.

Ibn Rushd repeatedly affirmed this complementarity. He stated, "Existent entities point to the Maker through our knowledge of their workmanship, and the more complete our knowledge of their workmanship, the more complete will be our knowledge of the Maker." He went on to say:

> The divinely revealed law commends the act of reflecting on existing entities and urges us to engage in such reflection. Hence, it is clear that according to the divinely revealed law, this pursuit is, if not obligatory, then at least commendable. The fact that the law urges us to give reasoned consideration to existing entities and requires us to gain knowledge of them in this way is made clear by numerous verses in the Book of God, may He be blessed and exalted. We read, for example, '...Learn a lesson, then, O you who are endowed with insight!' (*sūrah al-Ḥashr* 59:2), and 'Have they, then, never considered [God's] mighty dominion over the heavens and the earth, and all the things that God has created...?' (*sūrah al-Aʿrāf* 7:185). Such passages urge us explicitly to give thought to the created universe...Therefore, when those who believe in and seek to obey the divinely revealed law consider existing entities, they should first become familiar with the specific objects [before them], because these objects are the means by which such consideration can take place, just as instruments are the means by which work can be accomplished...."[40]

The Arabic word *āyah* is used in the Qur'an to refer to both a verse of the Qur'anic text, and to a manifestation or sign of God's presence and power in the realms of nature, society and the life of the psyche.

Abū Ḥāmid al-Ghazālī also treated the question of the structural unity of knowledge. According to al-Ghazālī, the Qur'anic verses which speak about the stars can only be understood with help from astronomy, the verses that have to do with health can only be understood based on the study of medicine, and so on. Al-Ghazālī wrote:

> ...These sciences, both those we have enumerated and those we have not enumerated, are encompassed by the Qur'an. Rather, all of them have been dipped, as it were, out of a single sea – one of the many seas belonging to God Almighty – namely, the sea of actions. One of God's actions, for example, is that of [bringing about] healing and illness.... This action can only be recognized by those who have a perfect knowledge of medicine...Another of His actions is the determination of ways in which one can achieve knowledge about the sun, the moon, and their stations as God has numbered them...no one but those who know the make-up of the heavens and the earth can perceive the true nature of the sun and the moon in keeping with their divine reckoning, nor their eclipses, nor how the night gives way to the day, nor how one of these two celestial bodies rotates around the other. [And the knowledge of these things] is a science unto itself.[41]

Hence, although al-Ghazālī and Ibn Rushd differed on the subject of epistemology, they agreed on the need for the integration of knowledge, with al-Ghazālī seeing such integration in the structure of knowledge itself (integrality), and Ibn Rushd seeing it in the various sciences' need for one another (complementarity).

In a specialized work spanning eleven volumes, Ibn Taymiyyah presented an exhaustive discussion of the sciences human reason has generated, be they philosophical or natural, in comparison with the texts of divine revelation. Ibn Taymiyyah was of the view that there cannot be any contradiction between the two types of sciences. Rather, that which is truly rational will never conflict with the proper understanding of divine revelation. Ibn Taymiyyah stated:

> I have reflected on this in the context of what people generally disagree about, and I have found that the things that conflict with explicit texts properly understood are nothing but sophisms whose invalidity can be easily recognized through reason. In fact, reason confirms the validity of the opposing claims which are in agreement with the divinely revealed law.[42]

Fourth: DANGERS AND OBSTACLES ALONG THE PATH TO EPISTEMOLOGICAL INTEGRATION

Human beings were created with an urgent, ongoing need to classify things, organize them into groups, analyze them into their component parts, recombine the parts, etc. Perhaps it is this need that has led to the emergence of the various epistemological fields and their branches.

Notwithstanding the efforts of scholars who are working along and across the boundaries of existing specializations and affirming the commonalities among the sciences, most of the scientific and technological discoveries made over the past several decades have come about thanks to the efforts of specialized scientists working in their respective fields. Scholars with narrow specializations will continue to make significant scientific accomplishments, and the vast majority of scholars – young ones among them in particular – will strive to prove themselves through specialized work. Such scholars may feel that working in the areas of integration and unification would come at the expense of opportunities for competition and academic excellence, which would threaten their futures.

This kind of fear is reinforced when efforts to address problems relating to over-specialization and the resultant atomization of knowledge result in the emergence of personalities with a distressingly superficial understanding of things. In such situations, the results of epistemological integration are not encouraging; in fact, nothing is a greater hindrance to progress than the "jack of all trades, master of none" who chatters constantly about generalities in this field or that, but lacks the ability to delve deeply into any of them.[43]

There is a danger that, under pressure to find evidence supporting claims of unity and complementarity, those who support epistemological integration may search for links among the sciences or relationships among the data that have no real existence. Such efforts may backfire or produce futile or laughable results. At the same time, some studies may have the appearance of methodological rigor, when in fact they are filled with specialized jargon that conceals their superficiality and incoherence. However, an even greater danger lies in the natural human tendency to find what one is looking for, or what one is expecting to find. This tendency can lead a researcher unknowingly into error, thereby undermining the external validity of his research design.

It is difficult to find scholars whose academic research models reflect a vision of the unity and complementarity of the sciences, a fact which hinders efforts to promote work based on such a vision and to expand the range of its applications. This difficulty emerges especially in the search for instructors who are skilled at teaching their particular specializations using interdisciplinary or cross-disciplinary methodologies.

One of the most serious obstacles facing new ideas and their applicability is the tendency to misunderstand those who advocate these ideas, or to misrepresent or misapply the ideas themselves. The sincere desire to adopt and promote an idea is not enough to persuade others of it, or to create the circumstances conducive to its acceptance and application. Rather, the idea also needs to be correctly understood and represented. One common misunderstanding of epistemological integration is the belief that it can be achieved simply by establishing a university degree program in which students are able to take subjects from a variety of areas – subjects relating to Islamic law, for example, alongside sociology and other courses relating to social issues – in the hope that integration will take place on the level of the student's intellectual orientation. A textbook might contain contemporary formulations of its subject matter based on assumptions that are inconsistent with religious thought. Alternatively, it might present religious texts thought to be relevant to the specialized material, or the contributions of Muslim scholars and thinkers through history on the subject being taught. However, such a mishmash of information may not involve any sort of epistemological integration. Rather, it may be nothing but a forced combination that distorts the subject under study, and which may produce outcomes that are at odds with the aims of epistemological integration.

Once universities have made the decision to teach the natural sciences, the social sciences and the humanities with a view to highlighting their unity and complementarity, they will need to redesign their curricula in such a way that it serves the aims of epistemological integration. The curriculum adopted should, for example, train specialists in scientific fields to make wise decisions when researching issues relating to the social sciences and designing their applications in industry, business and services. Similarly, it should equip specialists in the humanities and the social sciences to make wise choices and relate in a discerning fashion to issues of relevance to the natural sciences.

At the same time, specializations and epistemological fields related to the nature of human thought, the history of science, cultural assumptions, the nature of values, ethics, esthetics, patterns of environmental and human development, comparative religion, and other fields that raise vital existential questions (about our origin as human beings, our evolution, and our destiny) also call for receive greater interest and attention in curriculum design.

Those responsible for university education need to help students understand that graduates who will be working in various professions in the coming generations of the twenty-first century will need more than just copious amounts of information. Information has become readily accessible, and will become still more accessible with the increasing globalization of higher education. When this occurs, there will be a need for new types of skill, competence, and wisdom. Specifically, what will be needed is the ability to combine and integrate the right information at the right time, to think critically about the information at one's disposal, to weigh the available options and alternatives, and to make prudent choices. After all, in the words of one modern thinker, "We are drowning in information, while starving for wisdom."[44]

The task of unifying the human, social and natural sciences is a decidedly difficult one. But how many such difficult tasks have already been accomplished? Open-heart surgery, spaceship design, and human gene mapping have all become routine procedures despite the fact that they are extremely demanding in terms of the nature of the knowledge and skill they involve, the enormity of the concerted efforts required to execute them, and the exorbitant sums of money they consume. All of these things have been made possible because they were backed by a resolute will and competent scientists devoted wholeheartedly to their achievement.

CONCLUSION

Many of those who have discussed the unity of knowledge (or the unity of the sciences), be they natural scientists or specialists in philosophy, the history of science, or the history of religion, view this unity in a reductionist fashion such that all types of knowledge and science are subsumed ultimately under a single broad discipline: the natural sciences, for example, or the religious sciences. This reduction takes place by interpreting the facts and theories of the sciences, or by identifying the final authority for this interpretation, or by arguing for the unity of the source from which these sciences spring.

The belief in this type of unity generally rests upon an all-inclusive worldview. The worldviews adopted by these scholars and scientists have some elements in common, while differing with respect to other elements depending on the nature of the metaphysical authority or point of reference to which the writers ascribe. However, the implications of affirming the unity or complementarity of the sciences are not clearly evident in applied scientific writings. Rather, they are latent and concealed within key phrases that point to them indirectly, and can only be derived through a profound and detailed analysis of the philosophical assumptions underlying the text.

In view of the variety of concepts relating to the unity and complementarity of the sciences and their association with specific metaphysical points of reference, these concepts are frequently accompanied by a certain degree of confusion or ambiguity, as a result of which they fail to achieve significant practical outcomes. The term "complementarity" may convey a clearer meaning than that of "unity," especially if by "complementarity" we mean that a specific science needs to be completed or complemented by one or more other sciences in order to progress and develop, or that in order to understand a particular science, we need to be familiar with other sciences as well.

The concept also remains an open one to which new dimensions can be added whenever the need arises. So, for example, it is easy to see that the efforts of scientists in a particular specialization need to be complemented by the efforts of other scientists within the same specialization in order for them to resolve a particular scientific problem or achieve some specific concrete goal. In this situation, integration consists in bringing together individual scholars' efforts to construct a shared vision that is deeper, broader, and more objective. Such a process can help to achieve concrete results and facilitate the scientific and academic community's acceptance and recognition of the notion of epistemological integration. This phenomenon is illustrated in the case of Nobel Laureate Muhammad Abdus Salam, who was awarded the 1979 Nobel prize in Physics. In his acceptance speech, Abdus Salam mentioned the names of more than fifty other scientists who had been involved in the specialized research on the basis of which he had received the prize, noting that these scientists had built on each other's work and engaged in ongoing, frank dialogue. Some of them had tested out others' hypotheses experimentally before Abdus Salam and his colleagues arrived at their theory on the unification of fundamental forces.[45]

Epistemological integration may mean combining the efforts of scholars from various specializations in order to deal with specific problems, particularly those relating to major strategic issues and contemporary scientific and technological development in areas such as medicine and space exploration. A fundamental aspect of this type of integration is managing the scientific enterprise and organizing the roles of those taking part in it so as to provide the information needed during each phase of the project, cope with emergencies, and deal with new developments. The history of modern science provides numerous examples of the importance of integrating the efforts of scholars with a variety of scientific, technical, and administrative specializations toward carrying out specific and highly complex projects. One such example is the Manhattan Project,[46] which led to the manufacture of the first atom bomb in the United States in 1946. Another is the goal of sending a man to the moon, which President John F. Kennedy committed himself to achieving before the end of the 1960's, and which was in fact achieved in 1969.[47]

Still other forms of integration entail combining the efforts of scholars from different generations such that each generation builds on the experience of the generation that went before it. In fact, it is difficult to imagine how any given generation could have achieved what it achieved had it not been for the achievements of the preceding generation. The same goes for integration of the efforts of different peoples and nations, as history tells us that virtually every nation's civilization has been the outcome of interaction with, absorption of, and cultural borrowing from, other nations, both its contemporaries and its predecessors. In this connection Ibn Rushd holds that although the Greeks were pagans, this should not prevent us from making use of the scientific facts they discovered or the conclusions they reached, since otherwise we would end up reinventing the wheel, so to speak. Rather, we should begin where others have left off. It would not be easy for a single individual, generation or nation to obtain singlehandedly everything necessary to construct a human civilization. In the words of Ibn Rushd, "It would be difficult, in fact, impossible, for a single person to obtain on his own everything he needs in this respect."[48]

Lastly, it should be noted that distinguishing between the unity and complementarity of the sciences does not require us to affirm one feature in order to negate another. Affirming the unity of the sciences is not to deny their complementarity, just as affirming the complementarity of the sciences is not to deny their unity. Rather, the use of one or the other of these two terms is a matter of approach. When we affirm the unity of the sciences we are describing the relationship among them on the ontological level; this is the metaphysical, theoretical approach. When, by contrast, we affirm the complementarity of the sciences, we are describing the relationship among them on the epistemological level; this is the practical, educational approach.

The purpose of this chapter has been to highlight the value of epistemological integration from a monotheistic (*tawḥīdi*), Islamic perspective and the place of such integration in the Islamic approach to thought, research, and behavior. It is this approach, or methodology, which will occupy us in detail in the chapters that follow.

2

Method and Methodology: The Nature of Concepts and the Importance of Investigating Them

GOALS OF THIS CHAPTER

1. To clarify the meanings of the Qur'anic concept of "method" (*minhāj/manhaj*) and its relationship to other relevant Qur'anic terms, such as *ṣirāṭ*, *sabīl*, *hudā*, and *nūr*.
2. To distinguish between *minhāj/manhaj* (road, way, method) in the sense of a manner of arriving at a place or a goal, and *manhajiyyah* (methodology) as a way of going about a task.
3. To highlight different aspects of the need for a discussion of the terms *manhaj/minhāj* and *manhajiyyah*.
4. To provide examples of contemporary Islamic awareness of the importance of *manhaj* and *manhajiyyah*.
5. To clarify the meanings of the concepts of worldview, epistemological system, guide model and hermeneutical model, and how *manhajiyyah* relates to them.

INTRODUCTION

It is generally agreed that the issue of methodology in Islamic thought is a matter of major importance. Methodology is equally important in relation to thought, research for the purpose of acquiring, testing, and applying knowledge, investigating the sources and foundational principles of Islam, studying the Islamic heritage and the overall human heritage, and dealing with the conditions currently facing the Muslim community and the world as a whole.

Numerous Muslim thinkers and researchers, both ancient and modern, have written about the importance of methodology, the need for systematic, orderly thought, and the signs of imbalance and dysfunction in the Muslim mind. The signs of backwardness in the Muslim community that are so widespread at the present time point to a serious methodological imbalance in thought, research, and ways of relating to reality. Consequently, all members of the Muslim community, and its intellectual leaders in particular, should be encouraged to master the art of systematic thought and action in life's various spheres and on its various planes.

Like the methodologies proper to other frameworks, Islamic methodology is based on unchanging principles and rules. At the same time, Islamic methodology consists of a number of elements that change and develop in keeping with scholars' accumulated experience, expertise and evolving interpretations, as well as the norms adhered to by the scholarly community in this or that field of knowledge or in this or that generation. Some of these elements are shaped by the issues and problems under investigation, the norms that prevail among scholars and researchers during a particular era, the inspired, innovative, and creative interpretations of certain individual scholars, and/or the manner in which society deals with crises, misfortunes, and newly emerging issues and events.

What has been written about methodological rules and principles consists of human interpretations which may be either right or wrong, not divinely revealed legal rulings relating to specific concrete situations. As a consequence, there is an ongoing need to research and discuss methodology and systematic thinking, the aim being to validate those aspects of existing methodology that are correct and effective, and to correct those aspects that are flawed. Every generation has the obligation to reinterpret, renew its understanding and its vision, and push the limits of knowledge to new horizons. In so doing, it must derive inspiration from the divine purposes for humanity while leaving the way open for future generations to make their own innovative contributions. What is referred to in Islamic circles as reinterpretation of the Islamic heritage may be the equivalent of what is referred to in other circles as academic research. And, like the innovative interpretation of the Islamic heritage in days of old and Islamic thought from one age to the next, modern academic research is associated with methods that change and evolve.

Reinterpretation remains both an adventure and a risk due to the influence of demagogues in the Muslim community who work to keep people tied to obsolete ways of thinking, and who bestow academic titles on individuals who do not deserve them. For this reason, the only people who dare to engage in reinterpretation are the most stouthearted scholars, and even they undertake it with a degree of trepidation. This is worrisome. Still more worrisome, however, are the practices of those who, enthralled with this or that method, promote it indiscriminately among others, and in the midst of turmoil and methodological anarchy, circulate slogans the effects of which may well be unwholesome despite the fact that the slogans themselves contain words of truth.

Given that research into methodology has been marked by various types of rhetorical eloquence and theoretical description, it is to be hoped that scholars' and researchers' efforts will make the transition to the phase of what we might term methodological eloquence and systematic practice. This is a serious responsibility. However, it does not relieve individuals of their own responsibility to investigate things for themselves and to give things careful thought in order to gain insight into their private and public affairs, and to fulfill the obligations entailed by their religion. Those who seek knowledge will be rewarded more richly, both in this life and in the life to come, than those who do not. Hence, each of us needs to make an effort to acquire knowledge, and just as we should condemn demagoguery in relation to research methods driven by ignorance and capriciousness, we must likewise condemn the elitism and classism that isolate those that possess knowledge and sound methods, treating their understanding as something no one else could possibly attain.

First: MINHĀJ/MANHAJ AND MANHAJIYYAH: THE CONCEPT AND THE TERM

(1) *Denotations of the Qur'anic Term*

The Arabic terms *nahj*, *manhaj*, and *minhāj* (or *manhajiyyah/ minhājiyyah*) appear frequently in modern writings, particularly in critical, philosophical and historical studies. The terms *nahj*, *manhaj* and *minhāj* are synonymous, referring to a clear, straight road or path that leads one easily to one's destination. These words also convey the sense of traveling quickly down a road because of its straightness and freedom from obstacles, or accomplishing a task quickly due to the clarity of the manner in which it is to be done.[1]

All three words are derived from the root *n-h-j*, which bears the sense of becoming clear, or being or becoming a clear road or path. In the Qur'an God declares, "Unto every one of you have We appointed a [different] law (*shir*ʿ*ah*) and way of life (*minhāj*)" (*sūrah al-Mā'idah* 5:48). The terms *nahj* and *minhāj* are sometimes differentiated slightly, with the former being defined as "a straight path," and the latter as "a continuous, clear path." In a hadith passed down on the authority of Ibn ʿAbbās, may God be pleased with him, we read, "The Messenger of God (ṢAAS)* did not pass away until he had left you all on a clear path." The verbs *nahaja/anhaja* also convey the sense of panting, gasping, or being out of breath. As ʿĀ'ishah is related as saying, "He led me along, and I was gasping for breath (*wa innī la anhaju*)." In another hadith we read, "He saw a man panting, that is, gasping for breath as though he were having an asthma attack, because he was obese."[2]

Al-Qurṭubī writes, "*Al-minhāj* is a continuous path; it is also *al-nahj* and *al-manhaj*, that is, a clear path. Al-Rājiz speaks, for example, of "...water, the quenching of thirst, and an open road (*ṭarīqun nahj*)."[3] The term *minhāj* occurs once in the Qur'an, where God Almighty states:

---

*(ṢAAS) – *Ṣallā Allāhu* ʿ*alayhi wa sallam*: May the peace and blessings of God be upon him. Said whenever the name of the Prophet Muhammed is mentioned.

> And unto thee [O Prophet] have We vouchsafed this divine writ, setting forth the truth, confirming the truth of whatever there still remains of earlier revelations and determining what is true therein. Judge, then, between the followers of earlier revelation in accordance with what God has bestowed from on high, and do not follow their errant views, forsaking the truth that has come unto thee. Unto every one of you have We appointed a [different] law (*shirʿah*) and way of life (*minhāj*). And if God had so willed, He could surely have made you all one single community: but [He willed it otherwise] in order to test you by means of what He has vouchsafed unto you. Vie, then, with one another in doing good works! Unto God you all must return; and then He will make you truly understand all that on which you were wont to differ. (*Sūrah al-Mā'idah* 5:48)

Commentators have suggested numerous explanations of the words *shirʿah* and *minhāj*. Some of them have suggested that the word *shirʿah* refers to the contents of the Qur'an, while the word *minhāj* refers to the contents of the Sunnah. "And *shirʿah* is also *sharīʿah*, or that with which one begins to approach something. One might say, for example, *sharaʿa fī kadhā*, that is, he began to do such-and-such. The term *sharīʿah* can also refer to the path to a watering-place. As for the term *minhāj*, it refers to a clear, easy path, while the plural *sunan* refers to paths or ways."[4]

As such, these two terms refer to the practical rulings God has laid down for each of the peoples and communities of the world, although there is only a single religion before God. The differences between one *sharīʿah* and another are the differences between one set of rulings and precepts and another based on differences in the various communities' circumstances, living conditions, temperaments and predispositions, potentials, life experiences, and so on. As God revealed His will to the messenger He had sent to each people or community, it became apparent that the new set of precepts would abrogate all or some of those that had been sent down to previous prophets and messengers. In the words of al-Qurṭubī, "A particular thing might be forbidden in one *sharīʿah* while being permitted in another, and vice-versa. Similarly, a particular ruling might be lenient in one *sharīʿah* and more severe in another. Such differences are due to God Almighty's unfathomable wisdom and irrefutable arguments which, were we cognizant of this divine wisdom, would be clearly apparent to us."[5]

Just as each community or nation has a *sharīᶜah*, each of them also has a *minhāj*, that is, a way of life which it pursues in keeping with its *sharīᶜah*, whose guidance helps to purify people's souls. Thus if it is correct to say "the Islamic *sharīᶜah*," it is also correct to say, "the Islamic methodology."

(2) *Qur'anic Terms of Relevance to Minhāj/Manhaj*

The essential meaning of the term *manhaj/minhāj*, namely, 'way' or 'path', occurs scores of times in the Qur'an in the form of words such as *sabīl, ṣirāṭ, ṭarīq and ṭarīqah*. The contexts in which these terms appear are associated consistently with right guidance and error. We are told, for example, that God Almighty leads people to *sawā' al-sabīl*, that is, "...the right path" (*sūrah al-Baqarah* 2:108; cf. 28:22). Believers ask God to lead them along the straight path (*al-ṣirāṭ al-mustaqīm*), the path of those upon whom God has bestowed His grace, thereby guiding them to the right way – not those who have earned God's wrath and lost their way, but, rather, those who recognize the right path and commit themselves to it. They pray, saying, "...Guide us the straight way (*al-ṣirāṭ al-mustaqīm*) – the way of those upon whom Thou hast bestowed Thy blessings, not of those who have been condemned [by Thee], nor of those who go astray!" (*sūrah al-Fātiḥah* 1:6-7). "...God speaks the [absolute] truth: and it is He alone who can show [you] the right path (*al-sabīl*)" (*sūrah al-Aḥzāb* 33:4). The revelation sent by God Almighty leads to the truth and to a straight way: "They said, 'O our people! Behold, we have been listening to a revelation bestowed from on high after [that of] Moses, confirming the truth of whatever there still remains [of the Torah]: it guides towards the truth, and onto a straight way (*ṭarīq mustaqīm*)" (*sūrah al-Aḥqāf* 46:30). God declares that steadfast adherence to the path will cause abundant rain and blessing to flow down. God says, "[Know,] then, that if they [who have heard Our call] keep firmly to the [right] path (*al-ṭarīqah*), We shall certainly shower them with blessings abundant," (*sūrah al-Jinn* 72:16).

Another Qur'anic term with a related meaning is *sunnah* (plural, *sunan*). One of the ways in which God blesses people is to lead them along the paths trodden by their righteous forebears, since they are clear paths that will lead them to their intended destinations. These paths are a source of wisdom and experience that will benefit those who travel them: "God wants to make [all this] clear unto you, and to guide you onto the [righteous] ways of life (*sunan*) of those who preceded you, and to turn unto you in His mercy: for God is All-Knowing, Wise" (*sūrah al-Nisā'* 4:26).

It will be clear from the foregoing that the terms *minhāj*, *ṭarīq*, *ṣirāṭ*, *sunnah*, *hidāyah* (guidance), and *nūr* (light) share a number of significations in common, as they all have to do with human striving to tread the straight, clear path that leads to their intended destination and goal. If human beings' purpose in this earthly existence is to worship God in the broadest sense, to be God's stewards (*khalīfah*) on earth, and to achieve human development, then the *minhāj* is the means of achieving this end, or the path leading to this goal. This means or path will take the form of various intermediate goals. One might strive, for example, to go from one physical location to another along a path in a specific direction, or to move from one epistemological state to another along paths of research, study and the acquisition of knowledge. Alternatively, the goal may be to move along God's straight path from this earthly life, the realm of testing and affliction, to the life to come, the realm of reward and recompense.

Guidance along God's path is contrasted with going astray from it, and God knows best who will be guided aright and who will lose his or her way: "Call thou [all mankind] unto thy Sustainer's path (*sabīl*) with wisdom and goodly exhortation, and argue with them in the most kindly manner: for, behold, thy Sustainer knows best as to who strays from His path, and best knows He as to who are the right-guided" (*sūrah al-Naḥl* 16:125). And just as the path is associated with guidance, this guidance is associated with light:

> And thus, too, [O Muhammad,] have We revealed unto thee a life-giving message, [coming] at Our behest. [Ere this message came unto thee,] thou didst not know what revelation is, nor what faith [implies]: but [now] We have caused this [message] to be a light (*nūr*), whereby We guide whom We will of Our servants:... (*Sūrah al-Shūrā* 42:52)

Faith is the light we need in order to walk along the path to which God's revelation points. Similarly, faith confirms that it is indeed the path that leads to our intended destination, that is, to God Himself, the final authority and the source from which everything originates and to which it must return. By faith we can be assured that we are on "...the straight way (*ṣirāṭ mustaqīm*) – the way that leads to God, to whom all that is in the heavens and all that is on earth belongs. Oh, verily, with God is the beginning and the end of all things!" (*sūrah al-Shūrā* 42:52-53). "O you who have attained to faith! Remain conscious of God, and believe in His Apostle, [and] He will grant you doubly of His grace, and will light for you a light wherein you shall wa alk, and will forgive you [your past sins]: for God is much-forgiving, a dispenser of grace" (*sūrah al-Ḥadīd* 57:28).

God Almighty has committed Himself to guiding people to the right path. To this end He makes the path plain while warning us that there are paths that lead to error rather than to truth. "And [because He is your Creator,] it rests with God alone to show you the right path: yet there is [many a one] who swerves from it. However, had He so willed, He would have guided you all aright" (*sūrah al-Naḥl* 16:9).[6] The terms *manhaj*, *sabīl*, and *ṣirāṭ* all refer to a path or way that leads to the fulfillment of a specific purpose for which human beings strive to obtain knowledge or benefit of some kind. However, they can also refer to the path one follows in this life in order to attain to the life to come. In other words, they include the idea of a path that leads to a life of perfection, and it is in this sense that the term *manhaj* is used most frequently in the Qur'anic revelation.

(3) *Variant Uses of the Term Manhaj*

There is an intimate link between the terms *minhāj* and *maqṣid* (intention, aim). In his commentary on Imam al-Bayḍāwī's *Minhāj al-Wuṣūl ilā ʿIlm al-Uṣūl*, al-Subkī states:

> *Minhāj* – the title of this book – means 'road' or 'path.' One arrives at something at the end of a road or path. Hence, when al-Bayḍāwī speaks of *minhāj al-wuṣūl ilā ʿilm al-uṣūl* (the '*minhāj* of arrival at the knowledge of principles'), he means the

> path by means of which one arrives at the knowledge of principles. We might speak, for example, of *ṭarīq Mekkah*, 'the Mecca road', by which we mean the road by means of which one arrives in Mekkah. Arrival is not part of the road; rather, arrival takes place at the end of the road. Or, one might say, arrival is the road's purpose or goal.[7]

The value of a *minhāj* is that one takes it as a path to reach one's intended destination, or *maqṣid*. One thus moves in the direction of the intended destination. It is in the nature of movement to be directional, and in this movement, through which people commence their journey along a straight path toward their goal or destination, they have a history which they write by means of their movement and purposeful striving. Movement is meaningless without a path that has a beginning, a direction, and an end.

The aforementioned terms are often synonymous, and are used interchangeably. However, they can also be used with varied meanings. Thus, one might speak of *al-manhaj al-islāmī* (the Islamic path, method or approach) or *al-manhaj al-mārkisī* (the Marxist path, method or approach) in reference to an epistemological system or a worldview, philosophy, or an overall idea about the cosmos, life, and human beings. When we speak of *al-manhaj al-tarbawī* (educational method or approach) in Islam, we are speaking of a specialized science. Similarly, we speak of Shāfiʿī's *manhaj fī al-uṣūl* – Shāfiʿī's method or approach to Islamic principles – or *manhaj al-Muʿtazilah fī al-Kalām*, that is, the Muʿtazilites' approach to, or method of, studying theology. In such situations, the term *manhaj* or *minhāj* refers to the philosophy or school of thought to which a particular researcher, thinker, scholar, or group of thinkers or scholars belongs. We might say that a certain study employed the historical method (*al-manhaj al-tārīkhī*) or the empirical method (*al-manhaj al-tajrībī*), in which case we are referring to a style of research that involves specific procedures and ways of doing things.

(4) *Methodology (Manhajiyyah) vs. Minhāj/Manhaj (Method)*

Some situations call for a study plan (*manhaj dirāsī*), that is, a set of materials and skills that have been specified for the purpose of achieving certain educational aims. Other situations call for a scientific method (*manhaj ʿilmī*), that is, a scientific manner of going about research based on observation, the formulation and testing of hypotheses, and drawing and generalizing conclusions. As for the Arabic term *manhajiyyah*, it can sometimes be translated as "Methodism," which refers to the philosophy of religious renewal that emerged in eighteenth century Europe. Methodism witnessed its early beginnings at Oxford University, where the study of religion and evangelism was undertaken on systematic, orderly bases. Adherents of this philosophy are still known as Methodists.[8]

The term *manhajiyyah* can also be rendered in English as "methodology," which is defined as "the science of method," or "a branch of logic which analyzes the principles and procedures that govern research and investigation in a given field of knowledge." The term "methodology" can also be used to refer to the theoretical foundations of a given philosophical school, that is, its fundamental assumptions, premises and concepts.[9]

Method (manhaj): Research procedures
Methodology (manhajiyyah): The science that concerns itself with these procedures

"Methodology" thus refers to a modern discipline that concerns itself with methods and ways of engaging in research and investigation, and which is of relevance to all sciences. However, it is most closely related to the history of science, the philosophy of science, and, most particularly, the theory of knowledge. The term can form part of any science; it can also form a branch of any epistemological field (physics, history, etc.) that studies this field's logic and structure, and means of acquiring knowledge and research methods proper to this field. One might refer, for example, to the methodology of the science of history.

Given the foregoing, "method" can be defined as the procedures proper to a given epistemological field, while "methodology" can be defined as the science that concerns itself with these procedures and which identifies their distinguishing features such as purpose, clarity, and integrity.[10]

Modern Arabic dictionaries define the term *manhajiyyah* in a variety of ways. These range from the definitions cited above from *Webster's New World College Dictionary* to those given for the term *manhaj*. Most of these dictionaries trace the word's meaning to one or more of the foreign dictionaries from which they were translated. The dictionary of philosophical terms published by the Arabic Language Academy in Cairo defines the term *manāhij al-baḥth* (research methods) as a branch of logic that studies method in general, as well as the specific methods proper to the various sciences.[11] By contrast, the philosophical encyclopedia edited by Abd al-Rahman Badawi unites the science of method with the science of logic, that is, the rules of thought in the partial sciences.[12]

Authors have used these three terms with various but similar senses, although they may add dimensions derived from a particular field of knowledge or from a general intellectual framework. Without attempting to trace these various usages, suffice it to note that the Arab writers who have used these terms most frequently have attempted in their usage to combine the meanings the terms bear in the Arab Islamic heritage with the translations of their uses in English and French, particularly in specialized dictionaries in these two languages. The various senses associated with the term *manhaj/minhāj* continue to range from specific, limited meanings to senses derived from a general intellectual framework. It has been used, for example, to refer to an aspect of the philosophy of sciences having to do with ways of thinking and general rules applied to the search for truth in the sciences, which influence the course of the mind and define its processes until it arrives at a known outcome.[13] As for the term methodology, it largely parallels what was known in the history of science and philosophy, in both ancient Greek civilization and Arab-Islamic civilization, as the "science of logic." Parallel terms from the Islamic heritage include Shāfiʿī's "principles of jurisprudence" (*uṣūl al-fiqh*) and al-Ghazālī's "scientific standard" (*miʿyār al-ʿilm*) or "investigative criterion" (*miʿyār al-naẓar*). Al-Ghazālī states:

> Their assertion that logical arguments need to be made airtight is correct. However, logic is not their sole province. Rather, it is the source to which we

refer in the art of argumentation as reasoned reflection. However, they have given it the name "Logic" to make themselves look impressive. We might also refer to it simply as "debate" or "mental perceptions" (*madārik al-ʿaql*).[14]

Methodology also has a parallel in what al-Tahānawī refers to as "how work is to be done" when he states, "That which is, in and of itself, an instrument for obtaining something else must be related to the manner in which this something is to be obtained. As such, it is related to the manner in which a task is to be accomplished."[15]

It is clear, then, that the terms *manhajiyyah* and *manhaj/minhāj* intersect with human ways of thinking, as well as with logic as a branch of philosophy; with the theory of knowledge and epistemology as a branch and science of philosophy; and with methods of searching for knowledge in this or that field. All three of these terms are used in relation to knowledge, which in turn touches on all realms of existence, both the seen and the unseen, and on both the individual and communal levels. In the last analysis, however, such knowledge is limited by the limitations on human beings' capacity for perception and understanding.

Knowledge-related Methodological Assumptions

- Assumptions relating to the knower or researcher
- Assumptions relating to the object of research and knowledge
- Assumptions relating to the tools of knowledge

Given the fact that knowledge in its various fields is the sphere in which methodology operates, we would expect a methodology to be associated with a set of knowledge-related assumptions. Moreover, we would expect these assumptions to cover three areas,[16] namely, (1) the knower or researcher (a positive attitude, openness to new data, integrity, an inclusive perspective), (2) the object of research and knowledge (for example, the testability and knowability of the object, and the possibility of replicating such knowledge in others), and (3) the tools of knowledge (reliance on data, reliance on the rules of reason in relating to the data, putting data on trial, evaluating data in light of its realistic validity, etc.).

It will also be clear from the foregoing that the sphere of operation for methodology encompasses all fields of knowledge in their various categorizations, whether they pertain to revelation, reason, Islamic law, nature, society or other topics. Methodology may have to do with the manner in which we think about these fields, the research conducted to acquire, test and apply knowledge, or day-to-day conduct and scientific practices engaged in based on the guidance provided by such knowledge. However, the terms *manhaj/minhāj*, *nahj* and *manhajiyyah* are more closely linked to scientific research and its associated procedures than they are to issues relating to thought and individual conduct and practice. The various meanings associated with these terms have been linked with specific research topics, as well as the groups into which such topics can be classified based on the relevant criteria.[17] Consequently, the methodological issues that arise most frequently have to do with the tools and procedures used to gather research data such as tests, experiments, questionnaires, surveys, interviews and the like.

Our purpose in this chapter is not to detail such matters. Rather, our aim is to confirm and emphasize the importance of engaging in thought and research in an orderly manner that will enable us to achieve our aims in the clearest, most direct way possible. These thought processes have more to do with what we might term the philosophy of research, the philosophy of science generally speaking, or the philosophy of method. In this chapter our aim has been to consider the topic of method – *manhaj* – and related issues, leaving to future chapters the matter of how method is to be put into practice.[18]

If methodology (*manhajiyyah*) is the science that concerns itself with ways of thinking about, relating to and investigating a particular subject, then it will also include a preconceptualization and overall vision of this subject's component elements. It will also yield detailed plans and approaches that define the way to achieve relevant aims by means of practical procedures and operational methods. After all, there can be no action or execution of a plan or procedure without some sort of forethought and prior conceptualization.

Second: THE IMPORTANCE OF RESEARCH INTO ISLAMIC METHODOLOGY AND SYSTEMATIC THINKING

(1) *The Need to Research Islamic Methodology*

Islamic methodology has to do with the process of thinking Islamically and the nature of the ideas that arise from this process. Hence, it is associated with Islam's overall aims and intents. The issue of methodology in its intellectual dimension is thus inseparable from the way of life that Islam seeks to promote and nurture in Muslim society. The aim of Islamic thought is to establish an Islamic way of life in this earthly realm so that it becomes a passageway to felicity in the life to come. If Islamic thought diverges from an Islamic way of life or is isolated from people's daily concerns, it will lose its effectiveness and life will pass it by. Similarly, if Muslims' way of life diverges from Islamic thought, it will lose its way and cease to be truly Islamic, falling into the labyrinths of non-Islamic values and conceptions. However, even when Islamic life and thought are in harmony, Islamic methodology will yield a variety of distinct approaches and methods in keeping with the distinctive features of the different sciences and epistemological fields.

The issue of methodology is one of a number of questions relating to the philosophy of science, which is divided by modern classifications into numerous areas of scientific knowledge and their sub-specializations. An examination of the contemporary literature dealing with the Islamic perspective on the various areas of the philosophy of science yields little apart from scattered individual efforts having to do with the history of the Islamic scientific heritage. As for other topics that fall under the rubric of the philosophy of science – having to do with an analysis of the language, history, method and theory of science and everything of relevance to its evolution and progress – they have yet to be subjected to a careful academic treatment from an Islamic perspective.[19]

The need to study Islamic methodology is multifaceted. The epistemological practices that prevail in today's world, particularly in powerful, influential societies, are not haphazard or impulsive. Rather, they are based on methodological foundations with clearly defined principles, values and premises. In order for us to understand these societies and their impact on our countries, then discern the ways in which we need to confront and relate to them, we will need to familiarize ourselves with their methods, that is, how they operate. We must then adopt an appropriate methodology of our own in light of our Islamic view of the world. Any discussion or comparison of these contrasting methodologies will necessarily involve a discussion of their respective principles and theoretical foundations.[20]

Those engaged in the Islamization of knowledge view the issue of Islamic methodology as a major factor in the intellectual crisis being faced by the Muslim community. Consequently, they recognize the need to join efforts to construct and clarify such a methodology as a basic foundation of the Islamic culture and civilization that the Muslim community seeks to establish. Unfortunately, however, there is a dearth of Islamic literature and research on the topic of method and methodology in their capacity as epistemological fields. We also find that few Muslim writers have forged a path toward constructing methodological foundations, that is, an Islamically grounded theoretical perspective on method (*manhaj*). The few writings available on this topic are, for the most part, attempts to draw attention to the problem of method, the importance of applying a systematic perspective, engaging in systematic reading and interpretation, etc. Rarely, however, do we find systematic *practice* on the part of Muslim specialists in the various epistemological fields.

In what follows I summarize what a number of contemporary Muslim thinkers and scholars have to say about the importance of research into Islamic methodology. Within the space of a single chapter it would be difficult, if not possible, to analyze all scholars' contributions to the discussion and treatment of any given topic. Hence, my aim here will simply be to confirm the existence of a methodological awareness that constitutes a foundation for the contemporary Islamic intellectual reform movement. The present choice of authors and writings is thus not intended to understate the importance of other contemporary reformist Muslim thinkers whose contributions do not appear here. Nor is it intended to understate the seriousness of the destructive methodological orientations adopted by numerous contemporary thinkers who – in the name of deconstruction, interpretation, secularism, modernism, post-modernism, and the like – have attempted to drive a wedge between modern Muslims and their religious principles and heritage.[21]

Issues for Investigation

- Search on the Internet for five studies (either academic or professional) that aim to construct the desired Islamic methodology, or which trace the methodological efforts of Muslim writers and scholars.
- Search on the Internet for five studies (academic or professional) that undertake a critical analysis of destructive methodological orientations.

(2) *Examples of Modern Islamic Awareness of the Issue of Methodology*

Isma^cīl al Fārūqī

Isma^cīl al Fārūqī viewed methodology as central to the Islamization of knowledge enterprise. In his explanation of the question of methodology, al Fārūqī[22] began by defining the nature of the effort required to rebuild the Muslim community and empower it to carry out its God-given responsibilities. He based this approach on the notion that the Muslim community is suffering from a serious loss of direction which threatens its ability to shoulder its responsibility to lead the world. Al Fārūqī was convinced that the source of the malady afflicting the Muslim community is the prevailing educational system, which was established under Western colonialism and perpetuated by national governments after winning their independence. This system is based on a split between two parallel educational systems. One of these is a secular public educational system, which is little more than a distorted version of the system found in the West. Although it is responsible for graduating society's leaders, this secular system fails to provide learners with an Islamic way of thinking because its content is devoid of an Islamic perspective on the world. The other is a traditional Islamic educational system that is out of touch with reality, and whose graduates have such a circumscribed role that they are unable to compete with the graduates of the secular public educational system.[23]

In al Fārūqī's view, the way to begin addressing the crisis facing the Muslim community is to unify the two educational systems described above into a single system that aims to instill an Islamic worldview in students' minds and familiarize them with the nature of Islamic civilization and its defining features. Such a system would aim to reformulate all branches of modern knowledge from an Islamic perspective in the context of a well-rounded curriculum. This would enable members of the Muslim community to construct a contemporary Islamic knowledge that combines revelation and reason, thought and action and, in so doing, leads to earthly prosperity and felicity in the world to come. In short, it would be a monotheistically based system in every sense of the word.

Topic for Discussion

There has been a great deal of talk about the need to unify the modern secular educational system and traditional Islamic education. However, the more important question is: How can this be accomplished?

It follows, then, that the methodology required for this purpose can be derived neither from the prevailing Western methodology, nor from traditional Islamic methodology. Al Fārūqī observes in this connection that the Muslim community has lost the monotheistically inspired methodology on the basis of which Muslim society and civilization were originally built. After the Muslim community was afflicted with successive catastrophes, its academic leaders lost confidence in their ability to nurture and preserve Islamic character, and were content to cling to the apparent meanings of the texts of Islamic law without consideration for its higher intents and aims. In so doing they closed the door to innovative interpretation, viewing any reform of the tradition inherited from their pious forebears as a blameworthy innovation.

These developments took place at a time when the West was in the ascendency in the areas of political power, industrialization, and colonial discovery and expansion. As a consequence, the West took over most of the Islamic world. It even confronted the Ottoman caliphate and did away with it, then partitioned what remained of the Muslims' states. Under the sway of ignorance, backwardness and colonialist pressure, high-ranking Muslim leaders in Turkey, Egypt, and India attempted to launch a renaissance on Western foundations in the hope that life might course anew through the Muslim community. However, Westernization did nothing but alienate certain sectors of the Muslim community from their Islamic faith in some countries, and open a divide in others between the secular Western system and the traditional Islamic system.[24]

Consequently, al Fārūqī saw the modern Muslim community as being divided between two methodologies: a secular Western methodology, and a traditional Islamic methodology, both of which are equally powerless to revive and reform the Muslim community. In al Fārūqī's view, the ineffectiveness of traditional Islamic methodology has two primary causes. The first cause has to do with the fact that traditional Islamic methodology confines the concept of ijtihad, or reasoned interpretation, to the area of jurisprudence, which is in turn confined to the legal rulings and laws set down by early schools of jurisprudence. In so doing, this methodology disregards the broad, inclusive Qur'anic understanding of the term "jurisprudence" (Arabic, *al-fiqh*, which means literally "understanding"), and which was appreciated rightly by the great jurists of Islam. The Qur'anic concept of jurisprudence, or fiqh, includes the notion of understanding, realization, perception, the acquisition of knowledge, and specification of the fundamental principles of life and reality. By contrast, however, today's jurists have so confined themselves to the practice of issuing legal rulings (fatwas) concerning what is permissible and what is not that they have lost the ability to take on the responsibilities that were shouldered by earlier scholars of Islamic jurisprudence.

The second reason for the ineffectiveness of traditional Islamic methodology is its propensity for distancing itself from earthly concerns. Engrossed in the pursuit of mystical ideals, proponents of this methodology have tended to neglect practical issues, leaving them instead to the world's tyrants, megalomaniacs and workers of corruption. At the same time, of course, Sufism remained the sole source of openness and spiritual vitality during the period of stagnation in Islamic thought. Through the spiritual discipline and purity it fostered in its adherents, Sufism helped to protect and preserve Muslim identity and provide a degree of spiritual satisfaction. It was Sufis who, by providing a good example to others on the level of personal conduct and relations with others, drew many people to Islam. It was also Sufis who, during certain critical periods of history, stirred up others to engage in armed resistance against tyrannical foes. However, this source of vitality has also dried up to a significant extent, advocating an isolationist, quietist approach based on sheer intuition and subjective experience which has perpetuated the alienation between reason and revelation.

In response to this state of affairs al Fārūqī called for the formulation of a new methodology the likes of which traditional jurists could never have anticipated. The methodology al Fārūqī envisioned is derived from a new understanding of the nature of principles or sources (*uṣūl*) in Islam. According to this new understanding, the principles or sources of Islam are viewed not as principles of Islamic jurisprudence in its traditional sense, but, rather, as sources of Islamic knowledge.[25] Al Fārūqī called for the Islamization of knowledge as a necessary starting point for overcoming the dichotomy in the educational system, the dichotomy in the life of the Muslim community as a whole, and the ineffectiveness of traditional Islamic methodology. Al Fārūqī defined numerous features of the desired methodology, which revolves overall around the principles of Islamic monotheism (*tawḥīd*). As such, it is a monotheistic methodology based on the oneness of the Creator, the oneness of the creation, the oneness of knowledge, the oneness of life, and the oneness of humanity.[26]

AbdulHamid AbuSulayman

AbuSulayman has drawn attention to the methodological issues in contemporary Islamic thought and the importance of methodological, systematic thinking. In addition to writing and publishing on the subject of methodology, AbuSulayman has founded institutions whose activities and programs have promoted awareness of its importance. Indeed, the terms "method" and "methodology" occur in nearly every paragraph of what he has written.[27]

There are those who claim that there is no such thing as an "Islamic methodology." Such people argue that methodology is an objective tool that is independent of the culture of the researcher and the topics he or she is researching. By contrast, AbuSulayman holds that there exists an Islamic methodology which can be clearly distinguished from the methodologies of other cultures and peoples. However, he does not view this methodology as a revealed text in relation to which human beings are mere recipients. Rather, it represents a human effort to understand the interaction that needs to take place between the instructions contained in the revealed text and the issues people face on the ground in order to fulfill the religion's purposes and aims. This methodology is in a constant state of evolution and development, in an ongoing response to newly arising circumstances and challenges.

The concept of method, the course of its development, its initial successes and its subsequent failures are matters that call for study and investigation. AbuSulayman has found, for example, that the Islamic method that was developed and applied in the early phases of Islamic history, and which involved integrating the two God-given sources of knowledge – the written revelation and the created universe – liberated human reason and released its powers. Consequently, this method helped lay the foundations of Islamic civilization and contributed to the progress of the world's nations in virtually all areas. However, this same method proved unable to resolve a number of difficulties relating to the understanding of revealed texts, such as the issue of abrogation in the Qur'an, or certain financial and economic practices of relevance to the question of usury. In AbuSulayman's view, the traditional method ceased to be effective because of problems that soon began to emerge in the social and political life of Muslim society. As rulers began taking arbitrary control of public administration and policy, Muslim scholars retreated, or were forced to retreat, from society's public issues and concerns to occupy themselves solely with theoretical juristic and intellectual issues. As a consequence, Muslim scholars from that time on contented themselves with subordination and imitation rather than the creative use of their reason.

AbuSulayman may not have written prolifically on the topic of Islamic methodology. However, in everything he wrote, he emphasized the need to develop such a methodology and to put it to use for the purpose of recovering the Qur'anic view of the world and culture. He also emphasized that the Islamic intellectual reform which he advocated was essentially a methodological issue, and that the efforts expended in this area should not be haphazard, but founded on a disciplined, scientific plan. Like al Fārūqī, AbuSulayman has frequently taken issue with what both thinkers have referred to as "the traditional methodology" that was developed by jurists and scholastic theologians in the early centuries of Islam, but whose development was later aborted, thereby hindering the progress of Muslim society and civilization over the centuries.

AbuSulayman has posited a number of processes that are essential to Islamic methodology. The most important of these are: understanding Islamic texts based on the higher aims and intents of the religion, viewing all texts relevant to the topic under investigation in light of one another, and interpreting these texts within the temporal and geographical context in which they were written as a way of discerning the most prudent way to apply them to current realities. It bears noting that AbuSulayman practices the methodology he preaches, particularly in the way he relates to texts, in the realms of economic thought, international relations, psychology and education alike. And this practice has often led him to unexpected conclusions.

Taha Jabir Alalwani

The central place occupied by the issue of "method and methodology" in Alalwani's thought is easily discernible, although space does not permit us to trace this theme throughout al-Alwani's works. In the present context it will be sufficient to examine the working paper he presented in 1989 at the First Seminar for Advisors of the International Institute of Islamic Thought. In this paper Alalwani presented the five focal points of the Islamic intellectual reform project: thought, method, science and knowledge, culture and civilization, and the Islamic and human heritage.[28] Alalwani later expanded these four themes into the following six: (1) formulation of the Islamic worldview, (2) construction of the Islamic methodology, (3) the Qur'an, (4) the Prophetic

Sunnah, (5) the Islamic heritage, and (6) the contemporary humanist heritage, which Alalwani identified as the field of operation for this desired methodology.[29]

Issues for Discussion

- How was the notion of integrating the two sources of knowledge (written revelation and the created world) manifested in the early phases of Islamic history?
- How did this integration contribute to the construction of an Islamic methodology capable of resolving issues that were newly arising at that time?

In his subsequent writings Alalwani stressed the need to build Qur'anically inspired foundations for what he termed a "cosmic Qur'anic methodology." Alalwani holds that,

> ...apart from *al-tawḥīd*, the notion of Qur'anic method is the most important of all Qur'anic concepts. Consequently, a single verse such as *sūrah al-Mā'idah* (5:48) must not be the sole basis for formulating the concept Qur'anically. Rather, one must read all the verses that, together, form a network of subthemes and Qur'anic terms revolving around the notion of method (*minhāj*)...Such terms include *al-ṣirāṭ al-mustaqīm* (the straight path), *al-sabīl* (the way), *al-hudā* (right guidance), *al-nūr* (light), *al-ittibā*ʿ (following, emulation), *al-iqtidā'* (emulation, following an example), *al-shifā'* (healing), *al-uswah al-ḥasanah*) (good example), and *al-ṭarīq* (road or way)...[30]

When connected to other, related terms, the Qur'anic term *minhāj* can be seen to refer to a clear, straight path with easily discernible landmarks and an unmistakable beginning and end. Alalwani states that,

> the person who travels this path can rest assured of reaching his intended destination. This is why God Almighty has drawn a link between *minhāj* (way of life) and *shir*ʿ*ah* (law). There is a law – a *shir*ʿ*ah* – that people want and need in their search for uprightness, integrity and truth as they strive to organize their lives, carry out their duties as God's stewards [*khalīfah*] on earth, and achieve true justice among themselves. However, these aims can only be achieved by means of a clear, easily discernible path...Hence, the *minhāj* needs to provide exacting criteria on the basis of which we can discern higher aims and intents, regulate our behavior, obey God's law, and tread the path of right guidance...[31]

In Alalwani's view, contemporary scientific methodology and reasoning are "an advanced stage along the path leading toward a cosmic methodology, the sole source of which is the Qur'an, because the Qur'an is the only book capable of accommodating, purifying, and elevating scientific methodology to the level of a cosmic methodology. It is the only book capable of bringing scientific methodology out of its crisis, releasing its potentials, and protecting it from the perils and threats of relativism, probability, and the tendency to make final pronouncements without clear foundations."[32]

For this reason, Alalwani stresses the need to bring to light the "logic" of the Qur'an and what he terms "the cosmic Qur'anic methodology." This methodology is distinguished by a set of Qur'anic methodological determinants of which he details three: (1) *al-tawḥīd* as the pivotal element of the Qur'anic worldview, (2) combining the "two readings," that is, our reading of the Qur'an and of the created universe, and (3) the structural unity of the Quran and the cosmic truths it encapsulates. Alalwani then links these three Qur'anic methodological determinants with construction of the epistemological integration methodology we are advocating. He explains:

> The Majestic Qur'an is a single book in its structure and in its organic unity, and every single word it contains is preserved by means of these structural unity. The act of bringing together the 'two readings' is the most important methodological step, and the most significant methodological factor in revealing the remaining Qur'anic methodological determinants.[33]

It was his ongoing reflection on *sūrah al-Mā'idah* 5:48, "Unto every one of you have We appointed a [different] law (*shirᶜah*) and way of life (*minhāj*)" that led Alalwani to develop his understanding of the word *minhāj* in its Qur'anic sense. In the beginning he followed Ibn ᶜAbbās, al-Shāfiᶜī, and other commentators, who understood the term *minhāj* to refer to the Prophetic Sunnah, which helps us to see how to apply the teachings of the Qur'an. He later leaned toward the view that the term refers to the science known as the fundamentals or principles of jurisprudence (*ᶜilm uṣūl al-fiqh*). By the year 2010, however, he had concluded, that just as the Holy Qur'an contains the divinely revealed law (al-Shariʿah) in all of its details, it also contains the way or path we are to follow (*al-manhaj*) with all of its determinants, and that just as God Almighty has completed the religion for us, bestowing grace upon us in all perfection and detailing the divinely revealed law for us, so also has He deposited within His written revelation a path or method (*minhāj*) which is capable of ratifying and directing all of the various methods (*manāhij*) human beings have formulated....In order for human understanding to reach a level where it can properly apprehend the Qur'an, it needs an introduction that begins from the individual researcher's epistemological ceiling, that is, from the level people have attained thus far in their ways of thinking and reasoning, and the reason-related phase through which humanity is passing, because only in this way will we know what questions to pose about the crisis we face and its attendant difficulties. As for the answers to these questions, they are revealed by the contents of the Qur'an on the same level where we find ourselves. In other words, the answers provided by the Qur'an are always in keeping with the epistemological ceiling that obtains at any given time in human history.[34]

Alalwani goes on to say:

It is to be hoped, after methodological awareness has spread, that those who have dealings with the various sciences, particularly those relating to divine revelation, will be able to rethink both these sciences and the divine revelation, and to look critically at relevant issues and questions that call for further examination in light of the guidance provided by the Qur'an's own methodological determinants. We are fully confident that this methodological orientation will restore the vitality and effectiveness of these sciences, rendering them susceptible to being confirmed and directed by the Qur'an and achieving "the revival of the religious sciences" to which so many religious authorities of early times and godly scholars have aspired.[35]

Nevertheless, Alalwani reminds his readers that, ultimately,

the issues of relevance to method will not be fully clarified, nor will its tools be complete until it has become the topic of discussion – that is, until scholars' dialogues and exchanges have brought them to maturity and its premises have been empirically tested.

Alalwani calls upon scholars with specializations in the various branches of science,

> to unearth 'the Qur'an's epistemological methodology,' thereby enabling the Muslim community to clarify the rules governing this approach and, with its help, to resolve the problems that face the wider human family. For the Qur'an, like its Source, is generous and ever-giving, and its wonders never cease.[36]

Taha Abd al-Rahman

From early in his academic career, Moroccan philosopher Taha Abd al-Rahman noted that the Muslim community was suffering from "a serious methodological shortage." The reason for this is that many of those who are undertaking a reexamination of Islamic methods have less mastery of rational methods than did the scholastic theologians of Islamic history, and are less skilled than their intellectual forebears were at gleaning and using sound rational evidence. According to Abd al-Rahman, we are indebted to scholastic theologians for the ways in which they confronted non-Islamic faith currents and rationalistic, atheistic philosophical orientations by going beyond a focus on the principles and foundations of Islamic doctrines to the introduction and use of theoretical and dialectical methods and approaches. Consequently, he calls upon the Muslim community to recover its creative energy in the realm of intellectual and theological production in order to confront the materialist and historistic tendencies that dominate the modern world, and to prepare itself for this confrontation with the necessary methodological equipment.[37]

Taha Abd al-Rahman takes issue with the manner in which many researchers study and evaluate the Islamic heritage, because they employ a methodology that has been adopted unthinkingly from a cultural context other than their own. In Abd al-Rahman's view, it would be better for such researchers to derive their own methodology through adherence to a set of theoretical and practical principles, the most important of which is to acquire a comprehensive knowledge of the methods and approaches used by early Muslim scholars and thinkers from various scientific fields, as well as a good knowledge of modern methods and approaches. In so doing, researchers can go beyond the practice of imitation and the borrowing of theories to that of innovative interpretation and the formulation of original methods, approaches, and theories.[38]

Abd al-Rahman describes the methodology he employs in his dialogue and debate with modern researchers as an "infra-methodology." According to Abd al-Rahman, this "infra-methodology",

> involves debate, which was the dialectical practice in which the early Muslims specialized and which we have adopted as our topic of study, analysis and evaluation. [We also employ] an 'ultra-methodology', which we have made use of in this investigation, analysis, and evaluation.[39]

Abd al-Rahman derives his methodological techniques and theoretical concepts from two precise sciences that have only recently gained wider circulation – viz., Linguistics and Logic – by "inverting" their tools, principles, and content. At the same time, he affirms the importance of the methods and approaches employed by Muslim scholastic theologians and of giving thought to "the things they were right about, so that we can benefit from them in assessing the degree of 'creative energy' in their production."[40] Applying his methodology in the context of theological debate, he undertakes a sober, critical analysis of Muhammad Abid al-Jabiri's notion of "the critique of the Arab mentality," which tends toward rhetoric and metaphor, and Muhammad Arkun's idea of "the critique of the Islamic mentality," which emphasizes the derivation of legal rulings.[41]

Taha Abd al-Rahman has dealt in many of his writings with the thought of his contemporary and colleague, Muhammad Abid al-Jabiri (1936-2010), and the latter's approach to evaluating the Islamic heritage. Abd al-Rahman distinguishes between the "differential evaluation" in which al-Jabiri engages, and which he seeks to refute, and the "integrative evaluation" which he himself has adopted. At the same time, Abd al-Rahman sets out to familiarize readers with traditional Islamic methodology, and begins by specifying several aspects of a contemporary application of the traditional method. These include the clarification of concepts, definitions and principles, formulation of claims, compilation of evidence, and the critique of various points of view. Hence, Abd al-Rahman's work is not "merely theoretical discourse on the traditional method."[42] Rather, in evaluating the Islamic tradition, he adheres to, a methodology which derives its essential characteristics from principles that lay at the heart of traditional Arab Islamic practice. In intent, this practice was a function-based methodology, not a content-based one, a practical methodology rather than a theoretical one. It was a methodology based on firm foundations, and which did not simply present facts without analysis or discussion....This functional methodology...led to ten outcomes that were supported by clear evidence. Some of these outcomes were oppositional, and some of them served to build foundations. The oppositional results revealed the weaknesses in the empirical view of tradition, while the foundational results, which revealed the benefits of the integrational view of tradition, were divided into two groups: (1) those having to do with overlapping integration, and (2) those having to do with approximative integration."[43]

Though a contemporary philosopher himself, Taha Abd al-Rahman views most Arab researchers associated with philosophy as little more than disciples who imitate the philosophers of the West on the pretext of being engaged with global modernism. He writes, "Look at the modern Arab philosophizers, who 'interpret' if others interpret, who 'dig' if others dig, and who 'deconstruct' if others deconstruct...." Considering "where bad philosophizing has led this [Muslim] community," Abd al-Rahman undertook an in-depth study of statements made by philosophy's innovative interpreters. He began investigating philosophy the way a scientist investigates natural phenomena, that is, "through observation, description and explanation." In so doing, he left the beaten path by challenging the commonly held notion that philosophy is mere words, asserting that in fact, philosophy is "double-speak in action." He refers to his work as "the jurisprudence of philosophy," concerning which he has published the first of two volumes. The purpose of this project is to "liberate philosophical discourse." In other words, it aims,

to replace the practice of recording philosophical statements that have been passed down from others and which bequeath you nothing but dependency with the practice of recording philosophical statements that have a solid grounding, and which bequeath you the ability to form your own opinions. In other words, they give you the ability to make the transition from conformity and imitation to innovative interpretation and renewal.

After all, he states, "the [true] philosopher is free even if they put a yoke around his neck and a lock on his mouth."[44]

Taha Abd al-Rahman's approach to liberating philosophical discourse and the practice of "the jurisprudence of philosophy" have served to rehabilitate Qur'anic terms that had been abandoned by the would-be philosophers who do nothing but imitate thinkers in the West. Using the meanings of these Qur'anic terms as his foundation, Abd al-Rahman has constructed concepts and terms which, taken together, constitute the machinery of what he terms his "conceptual factory," which has its own distinctive pillars, mechanisms and models. His simple but detailed explanations enable readers to familiarize themselves with "the technical operations which the philosopher undertakes in manufacturing and using terms and concepts, thereby producing a distinctive, autonomous intellectual discourse that splits statements up as much as it generates points of view." Abd al-Rahman urges readers to throw off the shackles of imitation and tradition and to plunge into the sea of renewal, not preoccupying themselves with imitators' grumbling and complaints over,

> the difficulty or impossibility of being creative in our philosophical production, bemoaning our circumstances and heaping blame on our lack of understanding, yet without doing anything to show us practical ways of recovering our ability to be creative...In fact, when we found ... what we thought would lead us to this practical solution, and when we spoke as precisely and as accurately as we could about the means by which we could develop our philosophical creativity, these imitators urged us to give up our striving to achieve creativity, to be content with what we could learn from Western philosophers, and to pass on their sayings unthinkingly to our progeny. So, they have gone from shedding crocodile tears over the loss of creativity to waging war on those who go in search of it.[45]

Not content simply to talk about methodology, Taha Abd al-Rahman puts it into practice. After providing a detailed description of his methodology's intellectual premises, practical steps and procedures, he encourages his readers to adopt these for themselves.

Ahmad al-Raysuni

Ahmad al-Raysuni occupies a place of respect in numerous fields, in all of which he is known for his systematic approach. As a scholar of the principles of jurisprudence, al-Raysuni is interested in the topic of renewal, particularly as it pertains to the higher aims and intents of Islamic law (*al-maqāṣid*). Al-Raysuni notes that Islamic methodological thought has been intimately associated with scholastic theology. This association has not been entirely successful, since one of the difficulties into which ancient Islamic thought fell was precisely on account of this association, and its failure to take proper account of the higher intents of Islamic law on the level of either content or method. Consequently, Muslim thinkers need to be cognizant of both the higher intents of Islamic law and aims-based method.[46]

Al-Raysuni mentions a number of reasons for being concerned with *al-maqāṣid*, or the higher aims of Islamic law, one of which is that *maqāṣid*-based (aims-based) thought is, first and foremost, systematic thought. He states, "With respect to their foundations and their purposes, their universals and their particulars, their divisions and their ranks, their paths and their procedures, *al-maqāṣid* constitute a distinctive manner of thinking and seeing, analyzing and evaluating, drawing conclusions and putting things together."[47] If our manner of thought is based on *al-maqāṣid*, our thought will be purposeful and able to define its objective. This will in turn determine the priority and legitimacy of a given line of thought and, hence, the feasibility of pursuing it. The need to concern ourselves with *maqāṣid*–based thought becomes even clearer when we realize that many thinkers and theorists lack the ability to see how interests and sources of harm should be prioritized in the various areas of life. They also lack the kind of synthetic mentality that would enable them to examine life's particulars in such a way that they can draw the necessary connections between them and perceive the larger, more universal issues and questions to which they point. A *maqāṣid*-based method or approach enables us to synthesize things and to place them in their proper order. For in light of the higher intents of Islamic law we are able to draw inferences, put pieces together, see how things compare, and how they are to be ordered. As al-Raysuni observes, "Induction is the most advanced of all approaches, while universal, inductive knowledge is the most advanced and powerful knowledge there is."[48]

It is only natural that innovative interpretation (ijtihad), whether in the realm of the principles of jurisprudence, or in the realm of *al-maqāṣid*, should require a degree of academic competence. However, in al-Raysuni's view, mere academic competence is not enough to qualify an individual to engage in innovative interpretation. In addition, one must have what he terms "methodological commitment." When we are engaged in making academic judgments on ideas and points of view, there must be generally accepted "methodological rules."[49] When there are a range of interpretations – some sectarian, others denominational, geographical, individual, theological, or political – the result is a descent into a kind of chaos and laxity. In such a situation, al-Raysuni asserts, the solution has to be "balanced and scientific. It must involve a methodical approach based on rules and principles. This was the type of approach that was developed and perfected by Imam Muḥammad ibn Idrīs al-Shāfiʿī."[50] This methodical formulation of rules and principles applicable to the practice of innovative interpretation and juristic reasoning was marked by a kind of inflexibility and exactitude, both of which were needed in order to deal with chaos and laxity. Al-Raysuni observes:

> It appears, in hindsight, that it would have been more helpful for the trend al-Shāfiʿī established toward restraint and control to stop, or at least become more moderate, once it had introduced a suitable degree of balance and thoughtfulness into the interpretative and investigative process. Instead, however, this trend continued in the direction of even greater severity and control until it began to shift from rules-creation to complication. So eventually it came to place shackles on innovative interpretation and investigation.[51]

Even though al-Shāfiʿī's juristic school took the lead in the realm of *uṣūlī* thought,[52] other schools – the Ḥanafī, the Mālikī, and the Ẓāhirī – made significant contributions to the dialogue with Shāfiʿī scholars. In addition, al-Raysuni states, "we find that a number of juristic scholars were known for their open-minded approaches and styles of writing on the subject of the principles of jurisprudence or juristic application."[53]

Al-Raysuni has demonstrated the kind of methodological commitment to which he calls others. He has applied methodological rules to his discussion of a number of issues of relevance to the relationship between texts and human interests, illustrating his points with examples relating to the fast of Ramadan, women's manner of dress, and cutting off the hands of thieves. He has demonstrated this same methodological commitment in his outstanding work on "the theory of persuasion and preference" (*naẓariyyat al-taqrīb wa al-taghlīb*), whose features he has clarified and whose importance he has brought to light. Al-Raysuni has shown this theory, which encompasses and gives rise to a large number of rules that have served to guide Islamic thought down the centuries, to be one of the major underpinnings of Islamic juristic principles. It is, in al-Raysuni's words, "a methodological device which is complete and ready for use, and which can be used safely and with confidence." The effectiveness of this theory and its methodological value in relation to the principles of jurisprudence have been demonstrated through its use in treating numerous current issues relating to jurisprudence, Qur'anic interpretation and Hadith. This theory is foundational to Islamic legislation, thought, and evaluation.[54]

In his book entitled, *Al-Kulliyyāt al-Asāsiyyah li al-Sharīʿah al-Islāmiyyah* (Basic Universals of Islamic Law), al-Raysuni applies a comprehensive methodology to the process of demonstrating the perfection of the Islamic law, defining priorities relating to intellectual pursuits and outreach, and strengthening the monotheistic foundations that unite the Muslim community with its various currents and schools of thought. According to al-Raysuni there are four types of Islamic universals, each of which relates to a specific realm. The first relates to doctrine, the second to the higher aims and intents of Islamic law, the third to morality, and the fourth to legislation. These universals help both Muslim scholars and the Muslim community as a whole to draw up methodological rules that can guide them both to the beginning of the road and to its end. The source of these universals is the Holy Qur'an, which is the beginning. In fact, it is "the beginning of the beginning." Al-Raysuni states:

> Its clear, unambiguous verses – which form the essence of its message – are the source of Islamic universals. Consequently, we must focus our sight and our understanding on these clear, unambiguous verses: calling them to mind, seeking insight through them, steeping ourselves in them. It is on the basis of these verses that we must relate to all other verses of the Qur'an, as well as to the Prophetic Sunnah and the events of the Prophet's life. Given this order of priority, we have a basis for relating to the Prophet's Companions fiqh – their understanding of things (I use the word fiqh here in this more general sense, not in the derived sense of jurisprudence), the fiqh (understanding) of the imams and the jurists, and our academic heritage overall. When we find ourselves perplexed and disquieted by the complexities of our lives, let us appeal once again to the beginning, and to the beginning of the beginning, knowing that there we will find refuge, safety and peace of mind.55

Those who read al-Raysuni's books will find that there is a clear method to his writing that sets him apart from other scholars. With the exception of this Masters and PhD dissertations, all of his books are small and deal with very limited, specific themes. Their ideas are masterfully organized, they reveal a constructive, reformist, practical bent, and they are so free of digressions and verbosity that all the ideas in a given book could be summed up in just a few words. Yet every sentence and every paragraph in the book has its place.

Take, for example, his book *Al-Shūrā fī Maʿrakat al-Binā'* (*Al-Shūrā*: The Qur'anic Principle of Consultation, A Tool for Reconstruction and Reform), which treats both general issues and particular questions of direct relevance to modern-day life. Relying heavily on the principles-based (*uṣūlī*) method and both principles-based and legislative rules, al-Raysuni examines verses from the Qur'an, passages from the Prophet's biography and the Prophetic Sunnah, and the jurisprudence of the Prophet's Companions and of later juristic scholars in the space of a mere one hundred and eighty pages. This piece of writing embodies a distinctive approach marked by both originality and a commitment to grounding statements in their documentary and historical sources. Taking care not to rehash things that have been said before, al-Raysuni inquires into what is new and beneficial. To this end, he limits himself to a treatment of contemporary issues, new angles, and questions or aspects of questions that have received little attention in the past.[56]

Al-Raysuni concludes that consultation is not only a theme of relevance to political science and a set of mechanisms for decision-making in the public sphere. In addition, it is intended to be a way of life for the individual Muslim, Muslim society, and the Muslim state in relation to all issues, both private and public. This study by al-Raysuni also shows that consultation is an approach to thought and investigation in search of the truth in science and the right course of action in the social sphere, and a way of building relationships and regulating transactions on the level of society and state and in the realm of international relations.

Nevertheless, this study makes clear that it is not sufficient simply to declare consultation to be a principle for ordering private and public life, or to say that commitment to this principle may lead to the desired reform. Rather, in order for the aims of freedom and justice to be realized, the members of society must establish the detailed laws, mechanisms and practical procedures necessary to make consultation a concrete reality.

Third: BASIC CONCEPTS OF RELEVANCE TO METHODOLOGY

Scholars and thinkers use specific terms to convey their ideas, beliefs, and ways of thinking. These terms are methodological tools which help us to understand the factors that determine many cultural and social phenomena. Modern academic literature is replete with terms expressive of concepts that are closely related and, to a great extent, overlapping. There is a range of attitudes and schools of thought on how acceptable it is to use these terms. Some of these terms are used to convey a meaning that is conveyed by other terms as well, and some researchers have no qualms about using a number of terms synonymously, not because they make no distinction between the words, but because they see them as all belonging to a single thought group. In the course of his discussion, the researcher will be concerned primarily not with terms, but with an idea, and as long as the idea comes across clearly, it makes no difference (or so he assumes) which term the reader or hearer associates it with!

We find, for example, that some of the researchers to whom reference will be made shortly are not concerned to distinguish between science (*ʿilm*) and knowledge (*maʿrifah*), religion and philosophy, worldview and epistemological model, worldview and ideology, epistemological system and epistemological model, the philosophy of science and the theory of knowledge, theory and paradigm, methods and methodology, or the object of scientific research and scientific method. Those who do concern themselves with such distinctions may find themselves in a forest dense with trees of varying sizes, shapes and colors, any one of which may take on a new size, shape or color before their very eyes!

It is undoubtedly helpful and important to know the roots of terms, their semantic evolution, and the relationship these bear to intellectual clarity (or chaos), particularly during periods of cultural interaction between peoples and nations. Such interaction is taking place in our own day with the globalization of ideas and practices and mutual borrowing of concepts and terms. During such periods of exchange, weaker nations may fear the loss of their historical, linguistic and cultural identities. Hence, a writer may wish to avoid the use of a this term or that for fear that its meaning may be laden with foreign cultural associations. However, the alternative term chosen might itself be laden with associations from the writer's own cultural background. Be that as it may, human civilizations have often witnessed the migration of terms from one culture to another and from one epistemological field to another. When a term migrates, efforts are made to settle it in its new environment so that in its new habitat it will bear specific meanings that are not necessarily bound to its country or culture of origin.

Jungle of shapes, colors and directions

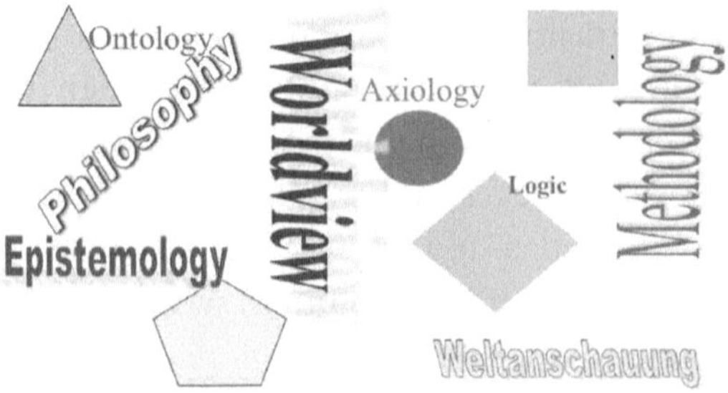

Worldview

The concept of "worldview" is one that has moved out of its original habitat in philosophy and taken up residence in numerous other epistemological fields, particularly the natural and social sciences. The importance of the concept of worldview will be clear when we realize the degree to which worldview impacts the ways in which we perceive the world we live in, our place in that world, and the way we understand the natural and social sciences.

The concept of worldview is found in fields of knowledge as varied as religion, philosophy, the social and natural sciences, the arts, applied sciences such as medicine and engineering, and so on. Religious terms such as faith, doctrine and macro-conceptualization express the ideas, concepts and beliefs that address the major existential questions which the term "worldview" attempts to answer. These are the same questions with which philosophy has concerned itself from the dawn of human history. They also make up the essential content of the philosophy of any of the modern sciences, the theories that underlie these sciences, and their methods of research. Virtually every film we see in the cinema or on television, from comedy to tragedy, is presenting us with specific values and views of the world. There is no such thing as a film that presents a "neutral" story that is not colored by the author's, actor's, producer's or director's beliefs and cultural values.[57]

Although many new terms have come into use among scholars in various fields over the centuries, there are some individuals who prefer not to use any term which is not found in the Qur'an or the Prophetic Sunnah on the pretext that some of these terms may have roots and associations that obscure their intended meaning and distance them from the concepts the writer wants to convey. Beginning in the 1950s, the late Sayyid Qutb worked on linking the ways of thinking and acting required by Islamic doctrine, and the overall idea one has about the universe, life, and human beings. In his book, *Khaṣā'iṣ al-Taṣawwur al-Islāmī wa Muqawwimātuhu* (The Distinguishing Features and Components of Islamic Conceptualization), Sayyid Qutb discussed the importance of using a particular term that would express Islam's "overall idea about the universe, life, and human beings." Qutb was not satisfied with the terms "doctrine," "overall idea," or "Islamic philosophy." Instead he chose the term "conceptualization" (*taṣawwur*). According to Qutb, worldview in its Islamic framework is an expression of the overall belief-related conceptualization presented by Islamic doctrine. This conceptualization, which contains a comprehensive explanation of existence, provides realistic guidelines for human activity in light of human beings' understanding of their place in the cosmos and the ultimate purpose of their existence.[58]

An overarching vision is the basic starting point for epistemological work on all aspects of a given project, and one's methodological approach is of relevance to both the project's ends and its means. In fact, it would seem that all aspects of human behavior can be attributed ultimately to worldview. Hence, there is ample reason to look further into the significance of worldview in the realms of individual and social life and academic activity. Such an investigation is certain to confirm the central role played by worldview in everything we do. This is not to deny the importance of other factors, such as state of mind, and one's physical and social surroundings. However, worldview – from the epistemological point of view, at least – is more important by far than any other factors of relevance to human behavior because it is the only framework in which human reason can operate to acquire knowledge. Consequently, worldview constitutes the foundation for any epistemological theory.

People form an overall picture of themselves and of the world around them within the limits imposed by the location from which they are viewing things, the angle they take, their natural, psychological and social environment, and the prevailing system of thought with its linguistic components and authoritative frameworks. It is this overall picture – variously referred to as cosmic vision, overall idea, cosmic conceptualization, general philosophy, comprehensive explanation, explanatory paradigm, or ideology – that has come to be known widely as worldview.

Exercise

How can worldview be put to use as the foundation for a theory of knowledge? Cite examples of this use.

Seen from the Islamic perspective, worldview is not merely a theoretical, theological issue. Rather, it operates on three interconnected, integrated levels. First, worldview is a mental perception of the natural, social and psychological realms. As such, it is like a set of stationary and moving pictures which draw people's attention and call them to reflect and contemplate with the aim of acquiring understanding and insight. Second, worldview is an attitude toward the world, a state of mind that requires one to relate actively and constructively to the world, in peace and harmony, reverence and respect, desire and wonderment. Third, worldview is a plan to change the world, that is, a set of goals through the achievement of which people hope to make the world more harmonious and balanced, and to put resources to use towards creating a better life for themselves and others in the realization that our earthly life is a place of preparation for life in the world to come.

It would be a mistake to deny the political and economic aspects of the crisis in which the Muslim community finds itself, or the corruption of our ruling regimes and the hostility of our adversaries. However, it would be an even greater mistake to disregard the intellectual and cultural dimension of our crisis, which manifests itself in our view of ourselves and of the world around us.

Worldview in Islamic Thought

- A mental perception of the natural, social and psychological realms.
- An attitude that requires one to establish a relationship with these realms.
- A plan to change the world.

Worldview is related to our overall perception of the Creator, the universe, life, and the human race, and how we answer the ultimate (or initial) questions about human life in this universe: When? Why? Whither? The answers we provide to such questions will impact our mental perceptions and our actions. Similarly, they will impact the way in which a community or nation sees itself and its place among other communities and nations.

Exercise

How can an individual's view of himself be part of his worldview?

Worldview in this sense undoubtedly formed part of Muslims' geographical jurisprudence, that is, the juristic rulings of relevance to land and home and the legal rulings pertinent to residing in a country, migrating there, or migrating elsewhere. This juristic perspective was part of the political jurisprudence that governed Muslims' relationships with others both within "the abode of Islam" (*dār al-islām*) and elsewhere. Many studies indicate that this political jurisprudence did not develop and mature to the degree that the jurisprudence pertaining to acts of worship and individual religious rites did. At the same time, Islamic jurisprudence witnessed a development whereby people were classified in terms of their attitude to the Islamic message. A group of people might, for example, be termed "a nation of response" (*ummah istijābah*), that is, a nation that had accepted the Islamic message and begun carrying it to others, while another would be termed "a nation of invitation" (*ummah daʿwah*), that is, a nation to whom the message of Islam was still being directed. However, this categorization simply perpetuated a divisive view of the world. Consequently, there is a need for thorough methodological studies that investigate what elements have led to the formation of this juristic vision within the contemporary Muslim mentality, and the respective places of Qur'anic authority, events in the life of the Prophet, and the Prophetic Sunnah, in determining these elements. In short, we need to explain the persistence of the divisive juristic perspective that has been passed down by Islamic tradition. Similarly, we need to ask how relations between Muslims and others have been understood both in historically Muslim countries and elsewhere, and how they ought to be understand in the present and the future.[59]

If contemporary individual Muslims' worldview were determined by their place in this world, they would no longer see themselves as distant from others either historically or geographically. On the contrary, they would find themselves vitally linked to other parts of the world, and responsive to what happens to others just as others are responsive to what happens to them. Worldview has thus become an explanatory paradigm for understanding the nature of the problems that arise between different groups of people, while the act of clarifying how people's worldviews compare in terms of both differences and similarities has become a way of dealing with and overcoming these problems.

> *An Issue for Discussion*
> How can Islamists use their worldview in formulating a methodology for contemporary Islamic discourse?

If Islamists were to use worldview as a unit of analysis for ideas, attitudes, individuals and institutions, they might be better able to understand the perspectives of others. Even more helpful, perhaps, would be for them to explain their own worldview to others in terms that others can truly understand.

A worldview is, essentially, the view one holds of oneself, and on the basis of which one's view of others is formed. This view will permeate a person's way of looking at other individuals, both those who share many of the same convictions and commitments and those who do not. Similarly, it will permeate the way a person views the adherents of various religions, juristic currents, schools of thought, partisan organizations and social institutions, each of which he views as something "other," and different from himself.

The various aspects of an individual's worldview interact with elements of religious doctrine, which instills a particular understanding of the universe, life, and human existence, as well as with the human knowledge he or she has acquired in the natural, social, and behavioral sciences. Worldview is affected by a wide of factors, including concepts such as the roundness of the Earth and its movement, space exploration, issues relating to geographical and astronomical jurisprudence, human interaction with natural elements and phenomena, the concept of the self and its various ways of behaving, human personality types, and the plurality of human societies and their varying values and norms.

It is clear, then, that an individual does not necessarily construct his or her own worldview. Rather, it comes into being in every individual's mind in a more or less spontaneous manner. As such, worldview is a component of human beings' innate makeup given their tendency to be influenced by the intellectual environment in which they live and to assimilate prevailing social customs and traditions. An individual is shaped by family upbringing during the early phases of his or her development. However, this does not mean that the educational system and the media are incapable of influencing the formation of an individual's worldview, or of modifying worldview after it has been formed through the design of suitable interventions.

AbuSulayman believes that the thought and culture of the Muslim community has undergone palpable distortions that have prevented its cultural enterprise from fully achieving its aims. He states:

> The first and most serious of these distortions was the distortion of the Islamic worldview that provided the framework for the Muslim community's thought and culture. As a consequence, it ceased to be a positive, comprehensive, monotheistic worldview capable of providing well-founded, universal guidance for Muslims' thought, ethics, relationships and systems.[60]

AbuSulayman sees this distortion as one of the reasons the social sciences failed to develop in the Arab world from an early date.[61] Distortion in the Islamic worldview led in turn to methodological distortion which resulted in a one-dimensional, unbalanced view of the sciences and knowledge. The various epistemological fields were divided into religious sciences (which were classed as "central") and worldly sciences (which were viewed as "marginal"). As a consequence, thought began to atrophy and the worldview that discerns the order and unity of the universe died out. The effect of this development, according to AbuSulayman, was to "deprive the Muslim community of the growth of the social sciences which complement the universals of the divine revelation and its guidance by providing the proper direction for Islamic social life and renewing it and developing its concepts, its institutions, and its resources alongside growing knowledge, potentials, and escalating challenges."[62]

Paradigm

The concept of paradigm has been attributed to the American scholar Thomas Kuhn (1922-1996), who began his career as a researcher in theoretical Physics. When he began reflecting on historical events that represented important way stations in the growth and advancement of scientific knowledge, his interest shifted to the history and philosophy of science, in which connection Kuhn was influenced by the works of James Conant.[63] However, Kuhn acknowledged that it was the works of Michael Polanyi on personal and tacit knowledge that led him to the "strange" conclusions he reached.[64]

Kuhn's ideas are based on the concept of "paradigm" and scientific revolutions. According to Kuhn, it is in the nature of the scientific mind always to engage in research within the parameters of a particular paradigm, or standard model, which embodies a view of the world that is comprehensive, scientific, methodical, and metaphysical. In Kuhn's view, worldview lies at the heart of academic and scientific activity. Hence, it plays a critical role in scientific practice, since it defines the link between the data, the content of observations, the importance of problems, and the acceptance of solutions. Worldview supplies us with our values, criteria and research methods. In short, every model or paradigm that defines the way in which science progresses is an all-inclusive view of the world.

Scientific revolutions take place in response to ordinary scientific practice in keeping with the prevailing paradigm, since ordinary practice is what generally leads to the appearance of anomalies which later form springboards for change and revolution. These anomalies lead to the discovery of new, unexpected phenomena, or things that were not known before. This may lead ultimately not to the development of existing theories but, rather, to their total abandonment and subsequent replacement with other, newer, theories. In other words, there are times when an existing paradigm is no longer capable of explaining observed phenomena, in which case it becomes a harbinger of an approaching shift, and the existing paradigm is overthrown in a scientific revolution. The scientific revolutions that have taken place in the West have been associated with names such as Copernicus, Newton, Lavoisier, Darwin, and Einstein.

Progress in science, according to Kuhn, is not a result of a linear accumulation of knowledge. Rather, it takes place as a result of radical changes in which new theories replace previous theories that have lost their explanatory power. When a scientific revolution takes place, the scientific community rejects a scientific theory that has heretofore been accepted by all in favor of a different theory. Every scientific revolution produces a subsequent shift in the problems that are posed for scientific research and the way in which the scientific community determines which problems merit researchers' attention. Every revolution alters the scientific imagination in ways that we need in order to understand the world more clearly. These shifts and the debate that accompanies them are the distinguishing features of scientific revolutions.[65]

The publication of Kuhn's book, *The Structure of Scientific Revolutions*, in 1970 fell like a bombshell into the fields of science and the philosophy of science, and for better or for worse, its reverberations are still being felt to this day. The notion of a paradigm in the sense of a standard model was based on the intimate link that exists between history and the philosophy of science. This link was established in a way that Edwin Hung has described as a worldview revolution, a revolution in the way we view life.[66] Scientific research and the nature of scientific reasoning really did undergo a revolution after we realized that such research always takes place within the parameters of a particular view of the world.

Basically, Kuhn took the concept of "paradigm" to mean scientific achievements that had been recognized worldwide because they supplied the research community with both problems and solutions. In fact, Kuhn meant two things by the word "paradigm": (1) Scientific content embodied in laws, methods, and theoretical, metaphysical explanations, which in turn represent a highly general worldview, and (2) the significance and nature of the scientific community's achievements embodied in the rules and regulations that researchers generally agree on using in the ordinary practice of science.

> Kuhn's "paradigm" relies on
> (1) scientific theories and (2) research methods that are prevalent in the society.

Kuhn asserts that paradigm shifts and scientific revolutions result in a change in worldview because, when they take place, scientists are obliged to deal with a seemingly new world. After the Copernican revolution, for example, astronomers came to live in what appeared to be a different world. Similarly, after Lavoisier discovered oxygen, he found himself operating in a world that seemed different from the one in which he had been operating previously. Of course, the world as it really was had not changed. Rather, it only appeared to scientists that they were operating in a different world. The world as it appears to the observer results from realms of perception and modes of understanding. It is the world constructed by the human mind. Hence, the change had taken place in the subject, not in the object.

The Explanatory Model

The concept of worldview overlaps with a number of epistemological methodological tools which are used by thinkers when analyzing phenomena, events and ideas with the aim of achieving a comprehensive view of disparate topics. Such a view helps the thinker or researcher to link the whole with the parts, the universal with the particular, the general with the specific, so that he or she gains a fuller, more comprehensive grasp of the phenomenon under study. One of these tools is what Abdelwahab Elmessiri refers to as "the explanatory model," which might be defined as "a set of characteristics that have been transformed into a coherent picture that has so permeated our minds and consciousness that we see all of reality through it, since it is an integrated vision of existence."[67]

This explanatory model is an epistemological map which is constructed by the human mind. One arrives at such a model by abstracting a great number of relationships, details and facts, then linking them to construct an overall pattern that takes the form of a comprehensive perceptual map. This "perceptual model" is the tool human beings employ in perceiving reality. However, the act of perception takes place for the most part in an unconscious manner that becomes part of an individual's psyche, inborn disposition, and immediate perceptions based on his culture, the details of his life, and the objects, symbols, signs, images, dreams and various cultural products that go to make up his world.

Perceptual models are paired with conscious, creative "analytical models" which a researcher formulates based on his reading of various texts and his observation of phenomena. By means of such analytical models, the researcher deconstructs reality, then reconstructs it in such a way that the reality or text before him comes to be understood and absorbed on a profounder level. Analytical models serve to broaden the range of the explanatory model through the phenomena and data that the model attempts to explain. Since these data challenge the model and expose its areas of weakness, it will sometimes be necessary to modify the model so that its explanatory capacity is increased. Hence, the relationship between the explanatory model and reality consists of an interchangeable spiral.[68]

Those who read Elmessiri's writings may draw a correlation between his "explanatory model" and Thomas Kuhn's "paradigm" given the closely related senses in which Elmessiri uses the two terms. However, Elmessiri also uses the terms differently in certain respects. He frequently uses the term "explanatory model" almost synonymously with the term "worldview." Hence, one should be cautious when reading Elmessiri's works to distinguish in what precise sense he employs this term. Elmessiri's language is not easily conformable to the traditional terms one finds in the dictionary. Nor can it be brought easily into conformity with the terms employed by other researchers in similar or identical senses. Elmessiri employs a terminology which he is at pains to make uniquely his own. Moreover, he strives constantly to ensure that he uses each term consistently, that is, with the same meaning, in all of his writings. Consequently, it might be difficult to understand fully what he means by this or that term based on a cursory reading of one of his works. Rather, one needs to have some familiarity with his various writings in order to gain a good grasp of his terminology. One reason for this is that Elmessiri uses his terms in a variety of epistemological fields: the history of science, literature, philosophy, politics, etc. Thus, for example, the term *maʿrifī* (literally, "of or pertaining to knowledge," and generally rendered in English as "epistemological") as used by Elmessiri does not bear the same significance it does in other writers' works, where it is sometimes associated with the theory of knowledge (as it is in English language dictionaries), or the philosophy of science (as in French language dictionaries). As used by Elmessiri, the word *maʿrifī* has to do with what is universal and ultimate. Hence, Elmessiri's explanatory model does not correspond entirely to Kuhn's paradigm, however great the resemblance between them. Rather, Elmessiri's "explanatory model" is closest in meaning to the term "comprehensive worldview."

Nasr Arif has used the term "epistemological model" (*numūdhaj maʿrifī*) in a manner that corresponds to Kuhn's "paradigm."[69] Nevertheless, he has attempted to establish the meanings of relevant terms such as science/knowledge (*ʿilm*), epistemological model (*numūdhaj maʿrifī*), theory (*naẓariyyah*), method (*manhaj*), explanatory model (*numūdhaj tafsīrī*), etc. by tracing each of them back to its Latin origin and tracing the term's semantic development in its European context from the days of ancient Greece to the days of post-Modernism. Hence, the authoritative point of reference for this analysis was a Western European one. This may have been done in compliance with the requirements of the Ph.D. thesis in which the aforementioned analysis appears, and which was written for Cairo University's Political Science Department. However, Nasr Arif went on to produce pioneering academic works in which he applied a different methodology in his treatment of issues relating to Arab Islamic tradition in the political sciences.

The Epistemological System

The elements that go to make up the theory of knowledge, or epistemology, are sometimes referred to as "the epistemological system." We had occasion to mention earlier that the first focal point of the Islamization of knowledge project is construction of a worldview, and that the two fundamental issues of relevance to this focal point are epistemological system and methodology. An epistemological system concerns itself with issues of relevance to the history and evolution of human knowledge, the sources and tools of this knowledge, methods of classifying knowledge, and a clarification of its functions.

Sources of knowledge are most closely linked to worldview, while tools of knowledge are most closely linked to methodology. Divine revelation and the universe are two complementary sources of knowledge within the Islamic worldview, while reason and the sensory faculties are two complementary tools for relating to divine revelation and the universe for the sake of acquiring knowledge and putting it to use. Hence, it is worldview (the greater range of vision) that determines both the sources and tools of knowledge, while the nature of these sources and tools (the epistemological system, which is a subsphere within worldview) defines the methods of dealing with the knowledge acquired. Methodology can thus be seen to be a subsphere within an epistemological system or theory of knowledge. Given this overlap and mutual interdependence, we find that many thinkers and writers use the terms "worldview," "epistemological system" and "methodology" interchangeably.[70]

A Suggested Model of the Relationship Between Worldview, Epistemological System and Methodology

This suggested explanatory model begins with Islamic doctrine, which represents the belief system. One's belief system has to do with the greater existential issues and ultimate questions relating to the Creator, the universe, human beings and life. This system bears close resemblance to what we are terming cosmic vision, or worldview. The primary fact within this system is the existence of God as Creator, which human beings have an inborn ability to perceive. God Almighty created human reason with the built-in capacity to understand the world, and He created the world in a way that makes it understandable. This is a universal, natural knowledge that exists within human reason all over the world and which constitutes what we are terming "natural life structures." Such structures are an element shared by all worldviews.

The structures formed by the Muslim mind having to do with God the Creator, prophethood, the Last Day, etc. are comprised of numerous detailed concepts. Some of these are epistemological structures which the individual obtains through the acquisition of knowledge. Taken together, they constitute what we term "the epistemological system," which recognizes certain sources and tools of knowledge, as well as certain ways of acquiring and using such knowledge.

The epistemological system and the belief system are linked by certain key concepts having to do with human beings' place in the universe and the Muslim community's place among other communities.

Hence, terms such as "community," "caliphate," "empowerment" and "resource utilization" are part of the epistemological system and, at the same time, part of the belief system.

Given the centrality of the Islamic belief system and the epistemological structures it forms within the Muslim mind, there is a value-related, ethical framework that will take shape as a result of an overall Islamic understanding of things. This ethical framework or value system, which clarifies issues relating to truth, justice and goodness, complements and intermingles with the epistemological system.

> The Islamic system = the system of doctrine + the system of knowledge + the value system.[71]

These three systems are interlocking and interdependent. Hence, our understanding of the elements of one of these systems will reflect on our understanding and way of relating to the other two. The elements that make up the epistemological system will necessarily be defined in light of the doctrines pertaining to the seen and unseen worlds, the nature and purpose of the universe, the nature of human beings and their place in the universe, and the nature of life, from the way it began to the way it will come to an end. Similarly, the conduct people engage in and their attitudes toward the values of truth, justice and goodness will be determined by their understanding of the outcomes of such conduct, outcomes which are defined based on the source of their beliefs.

The Islamic worldview, which takes all parts, elements, components and systems into consideration, is marked by an integrative view of knowledge that has enabled the Muslim mind to develop a distinctive perspective. As a vision of the true nature of things within their more inclusive framework, the Islamic worldview includes authoritative rules and frameworks for thought and behavior as parts of the society's overall value system. It defines the way in which the human mind perceives the realities of the universe, life, and human beings, as well as the answers to the major existential, epistemological and ethical questions that pertain to these realities and the relationships among them.

It is in the nature of human reason to distinguish between entities that are varied and separate based on the features that set them apart from one another. At the same time, it recognizes them as belonging to categories or groups that make up larger units. Such entities are located at particular coordinates within time and space and are related to each other in defined ways. Distinguishing features are also perceived by human reason as they pertain to types of behavior and conduct, social issues, religious values, and so forth.

As noted earlier, our mental images of existence have a direct impact on our actions, our social conduct, and our individual and communal lives. Hence, all individual and collective behavior arises out of an overall worldview.[72]

CONCLUSION

This chapter has concerned itself with the concept of method (*manhaj*) from a Qur'anic point of view, and clarified the distinction between method (*manhaj*) and methodology (*manhajiyyah*) in their modern technological usage. We have discussed the need for research and writing on issues pertaining to method and methodology, and the importance of promoting a methodological culture among members of the Muslim community at large. We have examined some of the forms methodological awareness has taken, and the ways in which contemporary scholars and thinkers have understood method and methodology. This chapter has also touched on a number of key concepts of direct relevance to method and methodology, particularly those of worldview, epistemological system, paradigm, and explanatory model. The following chapter will discuss the ways in which the concept of method has been treated by scholars in the Islamic tradition.

It has been noted that modern scholars hold differing views on the importance of method and methodology and the extent to which they are needed in the context of modern Islamic reform. Some scholars point to the ways in which method manifests itself in specific Islamic sciences such as the principles of jurisprudence, scholastic theology and logic. Some hold that method consists of general rules governing thought and research in all academic disciplines, while others see it as consisting of rules that pertain specifically to this discipline or that. Seen from such a viewpoint, there is one method that pertains to scholars of Hadith, another that pertains to interpreters of the Qur'an, another to scholars of jurisprudence, another to philosophers, another to natural scientists, and so on.

Some contemporary Muslim scholars are content simply to apply a given method to whatever they say or write, while others speak explicitly about their method and the ways in which they reach their conclusions. There are some whose understanding of method has remained static, while others' understanding of method and its implications within the Islamic context has evolved, and may still be developing and changing.

The approach we have followed in this book is to adopt the Qur'anic point of reference as a guide to the definitions of concepts. The concept of method – *manhaj/minhāj* – as seen from the Qur'anic perspective is characterized by both generality and comprehensiveness, in which respect it is like all other Qur'anic concepts. Nevertheless, there is no denying the fact that any meaning we associate with the term *manhaj/minhāj* will inevitably be a particular meaning which is tied to a specific time, place, and set of circumstances and experiences. We find, for example, that the method of the Prophet's Companions, may God be pleased with them, was that of receiving things on the authority of the Messenger of God. In other words, it was what we have come to know as the Sunnah as passed down on the authority of Ibn ʿAbbās and other narrators, which clarifies the meanings of the Holy Qur'an, thereby providing us with a way (*manhaj*) in which to emulate the Prophet. The term *manhaj/minhāj* also refers to a set of rules that regulate the process of deriving precise legal rulings from their original sources. Given this sense of the word *manhaj/minhāj*, the principles of jurisprudence constitute a methodological science par excellence. Similarly, the Hadith sciences are methodological sciences which employ a set of processes involving precise definition, scrutiny, documentation, and criticism of both the account's chain of transmission and its text. All of these are methodological processes. Nevertheless, every hadith scholar has a method of his own which is distinct from those of other hadith scholars. And the same applies to all other sciences pertaining to divine revelation and realms of human discovery and reason.

Method is associated with general rules that regulate the ways in which human thought deals with knowledge-related issues and themes. It is also associated with specific rules that pertain to particular sciences. Some methods and rules are colored by the worldview adopted by scientists and researchers. There is, for example, one positivist method that is based on the adoption of modernist views, and another that is based on post-modernist perspectives. Similarly, there is a Christian religious method, an Islamic religious method, and so on.

Although the examples discussed in this chapter may give the impression that there is a high degree of awareness of the importance of method, the literature on methodology outside the Islamic sphere may be just as plentiful and thorough as what we encounter on the Islamic side. In fact, it may reflect an even greater awareness of the methodological crisis through which some disciplines are passing, particularly the social sciences and the humanities.

There are also a number of matters that deserve note:

- Most of the research and studies on prevailing scientific practice adhere to customs, traditions and procedures that researchers have not traced back to their origins, and the authoritative point of reference for which they have not attempted to identify. Rather, they content themselves with the knowledge that these methods are familiar and widely practiced. Alternatively, they may not adhere to any particular method at all, or a method that one could not easily describe or define.
- The studies that we might view as direct applications of Islamic methodology – that is, studies that explicitly adopt this methodology and consciously adhere to its principles – are quite rare.
- Discussions of method and methodology are generally restricted to academic and professional studies rather than including practical applications of Islamic methodology to thought, research and conduct.
- Although there is some awareness of the need to develop an Islamic methodology, there is still little awareness of the principles and

distinguishing features of such a methodology. Weaker still is the awareness of what we have termed "the methodology of epistemological integration" – which we are advocating in this book and encouraging others to develop.

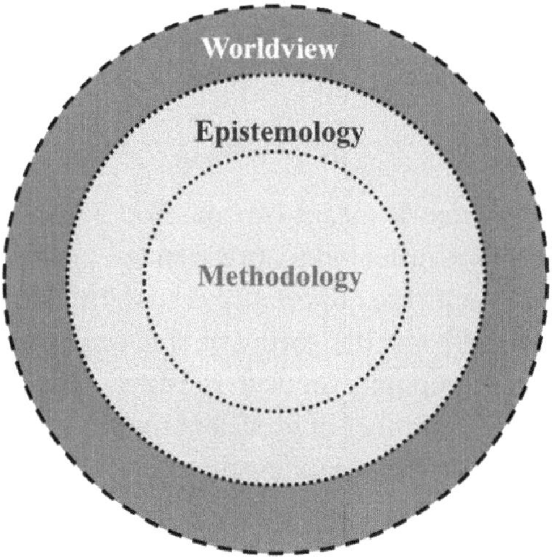

Circles of belonging

3

Methodological Awareness and Methodological Defects

GOALS OF THIS CHAPTER

1. To clarify what is meant by "methodological awareness" and its relationship to other types of awareness.
2. To demonstrate the importance of understanding both method and methodology and the forms of this understanding to be found among contemporary theorists of Islamic thought and action.
3. To identify a number of prevalent methodological defects and the ways in which they manifest themselves in the life of the Muslim community.

INTRODUCTION

When, in our everyday language, we express the need for political awareness, cultural awareness, developmental awareness, awareness of the higher aims and intentions of Islamic law, and so on, we affirm our aspiration for knowledge and understanding of reality in one or more of its various dimensions (its political dimension, its economic dimension, its cultural dimension, etc.), as well as the need to reform this or that aspect of reality. Awareness, then, is a term used to describe human beings' consciousness of themselves and their surroundings.

The term "awareness" includes the acts of bringing things together, understanding, preservation and memory. The "wide-awake ear" of which the Qur'an speaks is not a physical ear that picks up sound waves in the material world. Rather, it is an ear that understands and makes sense of what it has heard, then puts this understanding to good use.[1]

Similarly, the Messenger of God pronounced blessings on those who hear his words and absorb their meaning, then pass them on to others.[2] Methodological awareness is a conscious understanding of existing reality and of the way to change it for the better.

The Muslim intelligentsia exhibits a degree of methodological awareness. However, in many cases such awareness is only partial in that it pertains to a single aspect of reality, being based on involvement in a particular academic or practical specialization. Such an awareness is limited to the description of a phenomenon and an appreciation of its various dimensions; it also tends to be spontaneous and instinctive. However, it is hoped that methodological awareness can be developed into an all-encompassing discernment that is based on purposeful contemplation and governed by a comprehensive view of the world. This type of discernment, which applies value-based standards that entail ethical responsibility, expands continuously into new areas and delves more deeply into its subject matter until it becomes "a living methodological culture" capable of contributing to the reform of the Muslim community.

Hence, what we mean by methodological awareness is a realization of the need for a detailed, comprehensive understanding of the nature of reality, its difficulties, and its requirements. It is an awareness of how to deal with reality based on systematic, law-governed, purposeful planning uninfluenced by personal reactions or the pressure that arises from the need to make immediate decisions. Methodological awareness entails the realization that the reality in which we live needs to be reformed by means of a sound methodology and an appeal to an all-inclusive worldview. Such reform requires that we begin at the beginning, then persevere with integrity and determination, making use of the required means and methods and exerting patient effort until the desired reform has been achieved.

Given the fact that we have yet to achieve this level of methodological awareness, there is a need to help people realize the importance of understanding and applying method, that is, of constructing a system of methodological thought, research and conduct. We continue to observe numerous types of methodological inadequacy, that is, the lack of a comprehensive worldview and resulting defects in our understanding of how to relate to reality, interpret phenomena, and discern the link between causes and effects. Each of these types of methodological inadequacy manifests itself in our lives in a variety of ways. Hence, when we encounter some defect or imbalance in our life and thought, we need to reflect on the methods of relating to objects, ideas and phenomena that have led to this defect or imbalance, for only in this way will we take possession of the "methodological equipment" needed for reform.

First: METHODOLOGICAL AWARENESS

If the Muslim community wants to recover its lost pride and glory, rise to its global responsibilities and serve as a leader of human civilizations, then it will have to cultivate methodological awareness. Given the fact that methodology is the science of reading road signs, as it were, methodological awareness is something we cannot do without. After all, the road ahead may prove to be long and strewn with obstacles, and the journey may involve numerous stages. What with the bends in the road that could cause us to lose our way and the steep grades we will need to ascend in order to broaden our horizons, there will be many a slippery, treacherous slope on which our feet could stumble and slip. In situations such as these, it is methodology that will serve as our source of guidance along the path.[3]

Methodological awareness calls for clarity in the construction of methodology and in the means by which we make the transition from the Islamization of knowledge to the process of program implementation on the ground. This type of clarity calls in turn for the ability to distinguish between the process of constructing concepts and that of building authoritative frameworks on the basis of which to verify these concepts' effectiveness. Author Mona Abu al-Fadl refers to this type of discernment as "the methodological knot."[4] She points out that we cannot untie this methodological knot and make the needed cultural leap without first developing the methodological awareness required to deal with the Islamic sources of theorization.

The first Islamic component of this methodology has to do with the way in which we relate to the Holy Qur'an. Abu al-Fadl notes that there are few models for dealing with the Qur'anic discourse which arise from a comprehensive perspective and which strive to apply this perspective to both social realities and to fields of specialized knowledge. The scattered individual efforts being made in this connection have failed thus far to bring about a qualitative change in the prevailing epistemological climate, which suffers not only from lack of organization, confusion, and superficiality, but, in addition, from on unremitting onslaught of external intellectual influences.[5]

It may be helpful in this connection to note the link between methodological thought and the mechanisms of human thought in their various forms and on their various levels. It has been said that a science is more accurately defined by its method than by its subject matter; it can be granted, at the very least, that a science is defined by its method and its subject matter in tandem. Human beings' acquisition of knowledge and understanding is a process that is at once active and reactive. A given researcher's methodology will be influenced by his or her mentality, state of mind, and all the various factors that go to make up his or her personality. At the same time, methodology contributes to shaping the overall consciousness and cultural patterns of a society or community which serve, in turn, to determine which research topics are given priority and which criteria are employed in evaluating research and its outcomes.

Our way, or methodology, of thinking influences our awareness of reality. When we attempt to convey reality as we perceive it, what we convey is not reality itself. Rather, we approximate reality to a greater or lesser degree depending on the degree to which our way, or methodology, of thinking is, or is not, appropriate.[6] This attempt is linked to the outcome of an interaction between three elements. The first element is the preconceptions in our minds. These preconceptions generally take the form of a set of principles and values which are either innate, or which originate in social structures and conditions. The second element is the tools employed by the mind, cognitive and emotional processes, and the mind's intuitive, imaginative and volitional capacities. As for the third element, it consists in objective facts, including the quantitative and qualitative features of the reality being experienced and its connection to other realities around it. The human mind organizes these elements within what is termed human experience, which makes up the content used by human consciousness in its attempt to understand and interpret natural and social phenomena and to put them to use in the quest for greater understanding and sounder behavior.

Human Awareness of Reality Results From the Interaction of Three Elements

1. Preconceptions in the human mind
2. The tools employed by the mind, cognitive and emotional processes, and intuitive capacities
3. Objective facts linked to reality

An individual's awareness of reality may be a bogus one, because social conditions may impose restrictions and conditions that require a person to identify with the prevailing culture and the collective consciousness (or lack thereof). This phenomenon is one of the causes underlying cultural and intellectual stagnation in a society. Nevertheless, in every society there are a few individuals who have the will to excel and be creative. Such people, who exercise their freedom with autonomy and distinction, transcend the prevailing consciousness in their society because they understand reality in a new way and interpret their experiences in a pioneering spirit. As a consequence, they may succeed in spreading a new awareness and way of thinking. If such people gain a major following, their ideas may be put into practice with the result that there is a renaissance, and the hoped-for renewal takes place.

Awareness of the backwardness into which the Muslim community has fallen has manifested itself in the writings of numerous advocates of reform over the past century and a half. However, this awareness has come across as confused and scattered, being based on a number of one-dimensional, deficient methodologies. Some, for example, have advocated a Salafi approach based on reverence for the past, unqualified praise for the early generations of Muslims, a total break with Western approaches, and efforts to undermine Western accomplishments by focusing exclusively on their disadvantages and shortcomings. However, these same individuals, when they think about their worldly interests, have no hesitations about sending their children to be educated based on Western methods or enjoying the fruits of these methods! And they fill their homes, their offices and their streets with Western-made – or, at least, Western-invented – appliances, electronics and the like. Others, by contrast, call for a modernist approach that involves all manner of self-flagellation. By virtue of a selective reading of Islamic history, these so-called modernists highlight those events and examples that justify the demolition of history in its entirety and a total break with the past. As for the West, it is portrayed as being so endowed with bounty and genius that it alone deserves to occupy a position of authority and leadership.[7]

The crisis of Islamic awareness illustrated by these approaches may have deepened in the minds of many people. The first reason for this is that the proponents of these approaches from both extremes have, in most cases, been people in positions of authority in the Muslim community, whether in their capacity as government figures, or as intellectual leaders. This crisis of awareness has deepened as a result of the frustration and despair that have weighed so heavily upon many people as a result of the successive military and political defeats the Muslim community has suffered, and the fall of leaders who were once beacons of hope. However, some clouds have a silver lining, and these defeats, however unwelcome, often served to catalyze a rebirth of consciousness even among those who considered themselves to be the Muslim community's leaders in the realm of thought and culture.[8]

The most serious form of awareness-related deception or confusion has to do with method or approach. The loss of methodological awareness can cause us to go off track in relation to our methods and their functions. We might even be tempted to apply the term "method" or "approach" to some entity that has nothing to do with either of these. For methodology in the true sense is a source of right guidance, something that helps us to develop a sound awareness. If "method" (*manhaj*) is a road or path that leads to the desired destination, then it will, by definition, clarify the way to get where we hope to go. And to the extent that its premises and orientation are sound, it will serve as a faithful guide that will point out the landmarks we need in order to reach our intended goal.[9]

At any rate, there appears to have emerged a growing awareness of the need for method and methodological thinking since the mid-twentieth century in various parts of the Islamic world, with "method" becoming a major preoccupation among scholars and specialists in the various branches of knowledge, in intellectual circles, and among those concerned with the Islamic call. Some scholars have written methodological studies in the science of the propagation of Islam.[10] Others have advocated the emulation of the Prophet's approach to spreading the Islamic message.[11] Still others have selected methodologically-related texts from the writings of specific Muslim thinkers,[12] or collected newspaper articles with relevance to the methodological enterprise.[13]

> Read in entirety the passage in the Holy Qur'an which relates the story of God's prophet Abraham, upon him be peace: "And thus We gave Abraham [his first] insight into [God's] mighty dominion over the heavens and the earth – and [this] to the end that he might become one of those who are inwardly sure....Those who have attained to faith, and who have not obscured their faith by wrongdoing – it is they who shall be secure, since it is they who have found the right path" (*sūrah al-Anʿām* 6:75-). Reflect on the methodological implications of this story. Then discuss whether the "methodology" employed by Abraham in his manner of addressing his people about his search for the true God – based on the evidence God had presented to him – might be viewed as expressive of the meaning of scientific methodology or methods of scientific research. Consider what methodological implications would follow if these events had taken place before Abraham's call to be a prophet, and what methodological implications follow from their having taken place following his call.

In specialized academic circles, the science of origins or principles is discussed as a research method[14] that reveals the need to renew the knowledge we have for the purpose of addressing the contemporary methodological crisis. When Islamic doctrine is discussed, attention turns to relevant research methods as a means of studying contemporary Islamic thought and the methodological elements that make up the study of the principles of the religion. The Islamic religion is a way of life that encompasses the realms of doctrine, worship, ethics, and legislation. Taken together, these elements constitute the approach adopted by the first generation of Muslims. This first generation was then succeeded by individuals who turned this approach into a motley mixture of theological and philosophical questions, emotional-mystical experiences, and dry, isolated acts of piety. It was this situation that led to the emergence of reformers who worked to restore cohesion to the structure of Islamic method and lifestyle.[15]

How can the science of principles help in the formulation of a precise scientific methodology of thought? Give two examples, and explain.

When the conversation turns to the defining features and foundations of Islam's practical method, we find it to be manifested in the Prophetic Sunnah, which is itself the practical interpretation of the Qur'an. In his book entitled, *Kayfa Nataᶜāmalu maᶜa al-Sunnah al-Nabawiyyah: Maᶜālim wa Ḍawābiṭ* (How to Relate to the Prophetic Sunnah: Guideposts and Benchmarks), Sheikh Yusuf al-Qaradawi observes that "the Prophet was himself the Qur'an interpreted, and Islam in bodily form.…It is Muslims' obligation to know this detailed prophetic approach, which is defined by a distinctive comprehensiveness, integration, balance and ease. Muslims thus need to familiarize themselves with ways of improving their understanding and relating to the Prophetic Sunnah." Al-Qaradawi goes on to add that "the Muslims' primary crisis in this age is a crisis of thought." This crisis, he states, manifests itself most clearly in the difficulty people face in understanding and applying the Prophetic Sunnah, particularly in the context of certain Islamic revival currents, "given the fact that adherents of such movements are frequently influenced by their misunderstanding of the sacred Sunnah."[16] Author Abd al-Jabbar Said has also identified a number of faulty approaches to dealing with the Prophetic Sunnah.[17]

However, some researchers are of the view that Muslim hadith scholars developed a highly systematic approach to their field early in the history of the study of the Prophetic Sunnah. One modern critique of the Hadith sciences goes so far as to say that early approaches to the study of the Prophetic Sunnah constituted "a complete scientific theory that had reached a high degree of perfection and exactitude."[18] Another scholar has asserted that this science represents "the Islamic miracle in the realm of the Prophetic Sunnah," and that even the various branches of this science, including, for example, the science of differences among hadiths, have become complete sciences in their own right.[19]

Since the days of Ibn Khaldūn, the issue of methodology in the realm of historical studies has been unclear to many, who have relied on the texts passed down from their forebears as though their contents were unquestionable facts and, as a result, have fallen into methodological errors. The same is true of those who have attempted to adopt the methods of Orientalists who – though they undoubtedly made some valuable contributions – worked in the interests of colonialism. In the thrall of their Western superiority complex, Orientalists began writing history "from behind a glass wall. Consequently, they failed to grasp the threads that were guiding events [in the Near East], and were, in consequence, ignorant of Islam's defining traits in its own world and time."[20]

One of the most important tasks facing Islamic thought today is that of guiding the ongoing dialogue toward the theme of methodology. As one noted Muslim thinker asks rhetorically, "Is the crisis in which Muslims have found themselves for so long anything, in essence, but a crisis of thought and methodology?"[21] In the area of literature, the search for an Islamic methodology of literary criticism has become a major priority given the incommensurability between Western methods of literary criticism and Muslims' present-day experiences with literary creativity. There needs to be an alternative Islamic approach to literary criticism which reflects the Muslim character, psyche, and aspirations. Efforts need to be made to define the horizons of this approach, test out its tools, and clarify its components. This need is growing increasingly urgent as foreign approaches attract a larger and larger following. According to one Muslim thinker:

> The world around us has progressed in the development of research methods and approaches to thought, action and application. However, many of the practices being pursued by the Muslim community suggest that no real attempts are being to made to keep pace [with non-Muslim methodologies] and that, instead, the Muslim community is capitulating to materialist, consumeristic approaches and methods that are at odds with Islamic civilization and values. There is a need to

> study these imported methods and approaches so that we can benefit from whatever aspects thereof are consistent with an Islamic worldview while, at the same time, we strive to establish a distinctive approach of our own that gives and takes within parameters that preserve its own constituent elements and defining features.[22]

In the area of literary criticism and terminological studies, al-Bushaykhi explains that "method is our community's number one problem, and we will never take off either academically or culturally until we have found our way to the most sensible and prudent of methods. We ask God regularly to 'guide us along the straight path.' Hence, we must be keen to ensure that our path is straight in all we do, and that the efforts we expend toward straightening our path are commensurate with the path's own importance. It is knowledge that defines human beings. Similarly, it is knowledge that brings about people's advance as a result of their having adhered to a particular path or method that enables them to know what they had never known before. And although comprehension is part of the path, its most important part is what comes after this, namely, analysis, explanation and putting the pieces together."[23]

In the realm of thought, Taha Abd al-Rahman stresses the need for a contemporary religious vigilance in the Islamic world in connection with what he terms "intellectual backing." In other words, there is a need to support the Muslim faith experience by the use of the most modern, persuasive rational approaches, and by showing how faith experience is grounded in these approaches. According to Abd al-Rahman, negligence in this area has led us in directions that have rendered us vulnerable to attacks by our opponents. He states, "If the vigilant acquired methodological skills by going deeper into the experience of faith, they could establish a new form of Islamic thought that would fortify and sustain this vigilance."[24]

AbdulHamid AbuSulayman holds that reform of the Muslim community can only take place through family upbringing and educational institutions, and that solving the educational conundrums we face requires the development of "a methodological science...and an organized, ongoing scientific study that goes beyond limited, haphazard reflections." Such a study involves an examination of the methodology of reform and change, and of the way to develop the knowledge necessary for reform (which is what education and upbringing are). This process is what he describes as "serious academic study" which he distinguishes from "superficial random observation."[25]

According to AbuSulayman, there are three conditions that need to be met in order for renewal and reform to take place. The first of these is psychological strength and courage. The second is a sound, superior way of thinking. The third is a clear worldview whose aim is to bring benefit to all. When discussing the impacts of the failure to meet these conditions, AbuSulayman places highest priority on a systematic way of thinking. He states, "the historical split that came about in the Muslim community between intellectual leadership and political leadership led to ... an unbalanced approach, which led in turn to the demolition of psychological strength and the loss of [the distinctively Islamic] worldview.[26]

Conditions for Renewal and Reform in the View of AbdulHamid AbuSulayman

1. Psychological strength and courage
2. A sound, superior way of thinking
3. A clear worldview whose aim is to bring benefit to all

Although the issue of method is, first and foremost, a thought-related matter, the task of engaging with it is not restricted to thinkers and researchers in the realm of theoretical philosophy. Rather, those who posit the theories that make up the foundation of the Islamic movement, be they intellectuals or not, hold that the issue of method "is one of the most important intellectual issues ever to face the contemporary Islamic movement, since there is a natural link between method and movement. Someone who wishes to move in a prudent, well-guided manner needs to specify the goal toward which he or she wishes to move, as well as the path he or she intends to follow in order to reach this goal. It is an issue that calls for urgent attention, because a misunderstanding of it may be costly, delaying the achievement of one's goal or causing one to lose one's way altogether. It may also result in stagnation, despair, and numerous other outcomes that could be disastrous for the progress of the movement."[27]

> If we adopt AbdulHamid AbuSulayman's three conditions for Islamic renewal and reform, how can the family in its capacity as an educational institution fulfill these conditions?

Among the dimensions he views as missing from the thought and practices of contemporary Islamic movements, Alalwani identifies the methodological dimension as the most significant and urgent.[28] In Alalwani's view, this situation calls for the development off a comprehensive methodological understanding which can bring together the dual readings of the Qur'an and the created universe. Through a comprehensive reading of both these realities with an emphasis on becoming, interaction, and the historical logic of change, we can enter the world of the Holy Book with a clear methodology. By means of such a methodology we can overcome the difficulty that prompted the writing of the groundbreaking *Faṣl al-Maqāl fī mā bayna al-Ḥikmah wa al-Sharīʿah min Ittiṣāl* (The Definitive Word on the Connection Between Wisdom and the Divinely Revealed Law) by Ibn Rushd, *Tahāfut al-Falāsifah* (The Incoherence of the Philosophers) by al-Ghazālī and Ibn Rushd's response to al-Ghazālī in his book, *Tahāfut al-Tahāfut* (The Incoherence of the Incoherence). It was in response to this same difficulty that Ibn al-Ṣalāḥ (d. 643) declared logic "unlawful," and Ibn Taymiyyah attempted to do without the minor premise of a syllogism and offer an alternative premise from the Qur'an for the sake of preventing contradiction between revelation and reason.[29]

These, then, are examples of theorists in the realms of thought, science and political and religious movements with an awareness of method and its importance. However, awareness of the need for a method is one thing, while possession of an actual method is something else. Similarly, awareness among certain select individuals is one thing, while a general awareness on the part of the scholarly community or those who work to propagate Islam, not to mention the society as a whole, is another.

Methodological awareness is not simply a new slogan to be added to the list of things the Muslim community lacks in order to achieve its own distinctive cultural presence. Rather, it is a rational and practical definition of a set of methodological requirements that need to be circulated, researched, studied and critiqued in order to foster an overall mentality in the Muslim community founded on an awareness of method and the best approaches to be followed. Sayf al-Din Abd al-Fattah has listed four elements that are needed in order to construct a sound methodological awareness: (1) awareness of the sources for Islamic methodological theorization, (2) awareness of the available Western methodological potential and the ability to access it, (3) awareness of methodological applications and the ability to interpret the sources of Islamic theorization, and (4) awareness of the difficulties involved in methodological application and ways of overcoming them.[30]

Once these elements are present, those who do possess methodological awareness will need to translate this awareness into practical action in their respective disciplines and academic specializations.

Second: SIGNS OF METHODOLOGICAL IMBALANCE IN THE LIFE OF THE MUSLIM COMMUNITY

A variety of factors contributed to the Muslim community's descent into the cultural backwaters in which it has found itself for the past several centuries. Still other factors perpetuate this discouraging situation despite reformers' sincere efforts to improve things, while elements that are basic to the desired cultural advances are notably absent.

Contemporary Muslims' psyches, on the individual and collective levels alike, exhibit various types of imbalance or dysfunctionality that have hindered Muslims' ability to engage in effective action. These imbalances are manifested, on one hand, in the mental or ideational dimension of people's psyches, that is, in the worldview that determines Muslims' perceptions of the universe, life, and human beings, and which has become confused and unclear in a variety of ways. Imbalances can also be seen in the psychological, emotional dimension of Muslims' characters in the form of weakness of will, an inability to take initiative, and a lack of boldness and courage.

The Imbalance in Modern-Day Muslims' Psychological Makeup Manifests Itself in Two Aspects of Their Personalities

1. The intellectual or ideational aspect, where one observes a lack of clarity in their worldview and resultant perceptions.
2. The psychological-emotional aspect, where the imbalance manifests itself in the form of a weak will and lack of initiative.

It would be helpful to subject the various types of imbalance in these two dimensions of Muslims' inner lives to a thorough study and analysis. There is, however, still another type of imbalance that afflicts Muslims' efforts on both the individual and collective levels. This imbalance, which affects both of the aforementioned aspects of Muslims' psyches – the ideational and the emotional – manifests itself in Muslims' way of thinking about matters of understanding, feeling, and practice. It is a methodological imbalance that has to do with the manner in which an idea is translated into a concrete reality, or the way in which a mental conviction is turned into an actual life practice. The value of an idea is only realized fully when there is a way for it to be converted into concrete action. The seriousness of this methodological imbalance may be seen in the fact that it prevents individuals with good ideas from presenting these ideas in a sound manner, that is, from bringing them out of the realm of mental abstraction and ideals and into the realm of day-to-day life. People's ideas may be formulated in a distorted manner that prevents others from understanding them and receiving them well. The following are specific expressions of this methodological imbalance:[31]

(1) *Imbalance in One's Worldview*

A sound approach to dealing with an issue requires that one examine it within the larger sphere to which it belongs, that is, in its capacity as one of a number of elements, some of them similar and some of them disparate, that go to make up a more comprehensive set. This approach enables the researcher to see the various parts against the background of a greater whole, and to reveal the defining characteristics of the issue at hand from a variety of vantage points. By so doing he can relate to the issue or phenomenon with a proper appreciation of the potential effects of his actions.

The comprehensive approach called for by the Islamic worldview contributes to the possibility of linking the worlds of the seen and the unseen, beneficial and harmful aspects of this or that phenomenon, present and future considerations, the situation in a particular location and the broader environment that surrounds it, as well as immediate and remote effects of actions and events. Methodological imbalance in this context reveals itself in attempts to restrict a given issue or phenomenon to a single dimension to the exclusion of others, the consideration of a limited number of the available facts, and/or what is immediately and directly apparent in the situation at hand. This type of methodological imbalance sometimes takes the form of searching for the truth in a narrow, limited space within the various realms of knowledge by looking, for example, only at what has come down to us historically to the exclusion of more recent developments. This partial or atomistic approach to the study of written history may limit itself to the juristic aspect of things without attempting to grapple with the foundational sources represented by the Qur'an and the Prophetic Sunnah. Alternatively, it might focus exclusively on the textual aspect of an issue and its ramifications without giving thought to areas of application in relation to questions about the universe, matter, and human progress and civilization. Similarly, one might restrict himself to a single school of thought or jurisprudence without taking account of other schools whose perspectives might provide him with fuller insight into things, or enrich his mind by giving expression to a broader understanding of the religion and its higher purposes or aims.

This imbalance sometimes becomes visible through an incomplete view of time, which results in the practice of limiting one's assessment of things to a limit period of history. The aims and purposes of the Islamic religion can only be realized through a legal ruling if such a ruling takes into consideration the past (to derive lessons from it), the present (to address its problems and issues), and the future (by anticipating the ruling's potential effects and ramifications). The most notable failing in this connection is the tendency to neglect the future, and the inability to assess future requirements as part of the planning process. In reality, ijtihad, or reasoned interpretation, is simply the act of joining one period of time with another. The process of ijtihad involves seeking guidance from revelation, which stands over and above time, in order to arrive at solutions to the issues that arise in the present. In so doing, the practitioner of ijtihad is enlightened by the interpretations of his or her forebears, who were in turn interpreting the religion's foundational texts in light of their own circumstances, while anticipating the effects of today's solutions on the future and its associated developments.

The same type of imbalance results difficulties in assessing the relative importance of issues and what rulings apply to them. Elevating the status of particular ethical principles, actions and rites as though they were the heart of the Islamic message and the ruling criterion of action in isolation from the religion's overarching principles and the requirements of the situation at hand distort these overarching principles and undermine the effectiveness with which the Islamic message can be propagated. When certain individuals or factions cling tenaciously to what they have determined to be of greatest importance, the outcome is disputes and divisions. What they have forgotten is that they are disputing over a simple matter of differing assessments or interpretations of certain peripheral issues. When Muslims allow such differences to divide them, they sacrifice far more vital interests such as their unity and their ability to join their efforts for the sake of promoting their religion and enabling the Muslim community to advance.

These imbalances result from the loss of a comprehensive, overarching vision which enables us to assess things in accordance with their true significance and order them based on their relative degrees of importance. Those who have lost sight of this overarching vision treat what is minor and particular as though it were major and universal. One of the distinguishing features of a comprehensive perspective is the ability to make assessments on the basis of sound comparisons between things and situations: to discern the difference between what important and what is more important, what is harmful and what is more harmful, what is beneficial and what is more beneficial. Without this ability, we lose our capacity to set sound priorities, and thereby to serve the Muslim community's best interests. This type of methodological defect also impairs our ability to understand the principles of realism, causality, and comprehensiveness as they affect Muslims' thoughts and actions. As a result, it constitutes a major hindrance to progress toward the desired Islamic cultural advances.

(2) *Impaired Ability to Understand and Deal With Reality*

The impairment or defect being spoken of here has to do with the way in which we look at the natural world and the world of human beings. This defect may manifest itself in a failure to give proper consideration to reality, relying instead abstract conceptualizations, be they mental abstractions on the order of Greek philosophy and its derivatives, or spiritual abstractions on the order of Gnosticism and its outcomes. The Holy Qur'an has brought human reason out of such abstraction and into a realistic understanding of the universe and the human beings who inhabit it. The signs we observe on the horizons (that is, in the natural world) and in our own souls are a source of knowledge, understanding, and guidance. However, this methodological defect may take the form of a pious otherworldliness that overlooks the realities of life and the requirements of human society. There is also a type of social otherworldliness which neglects broad sectors of society due to the isolation of the educated elite and their unwillingness to involve themselves in the concerns of the masses, or an indifference to reality that grows out of despair of changing the way things are. Such despair may lead individuals to avoid dealing with the issues of the day, accuse others of unbelief, or even engage in violence. And to make matters worse, Muslims sometimes give up trying to understand not only their own situation, but, in addition, the situations of peoples and nations around them.

The eventual outcome of this disregard for facts is an ignorance that robs people of the ability to cope with reality. It will be noted in this connection that Western societies have been able to build advanced civilizations as a result of a thorough study and understanding of reality in its various dimensions and details. Given this tendency to think and act unrealistically in relation to the facts of human life in general and Islamic life in particular, there have even been attempts to abolish realism entirely in the realms of both thought and practice.

Disregard for reality has manifested itself on the part of certain groups of Muslims in a tendency to cling to an abstract, idealized image of Islamic history to which they flee for refuge from their own situations. Their understanding of the methodology of reform is limited to attempts to reproduce partial images of the ideal and impose them on present-day reality, or automatic appeals to the Salafi ideal whenever and wherever they are called upon to do cope with the new and unfamiliar.

Many Muslims are ignorant of the impact of global developments on their understanding or discovery of certain principles of religion and the ways in which these principles are applied to contemporary situations. Many aspects of Muslims' understanding of principles are reflections of what they observe among non-Muslims rather than being grounded in their own texts and traditions. We find, for example, that freedom, equality, justice and consultation have come to be associated in modern times with institutions and laws that many Muslims would like to see established in their own countries. Nevertheless, there is a tendency to deny the impact made by the application of these principles in the non-Muslim world on Muslims' understanding of them.[32] This tendency is indicative of a methodological defect in Muslims' thinking which can be observed even among some well-respected contemporary Muslim scholars.[33]

Disregard for Muslims' real-life circumstances may have been reinforced in some Muslim sectors by still another methodological defect, namely, adoption of the situation in the West as the ideal example of advancement and progress. This defect can be seen on the practical level in the practice of devising reform programs derived from a Western idealism that is not well suited to Muslims' situations, since they fail to reflect the cultural, social and religious particularities of Muslims' lives and circumstances. The danger represented by this view of reform lies in the fact that those who adhere to it are highly placed, influential decision makers even though they enjoy a very limited popular base and are quite isolated from the common people.

> Give three other examples of a methodologically-based failure to understand and deal with reality.

(3) *Failure to Link Causes to Effects*

Failure to acknowledge causality and, as a consequence, to fall back on superstitious explanations for phenomena, is a serious methodological defect. Causality is viewed in Islam as a law that governs nature, society, and the human psyche within the framework of the divine governance of the universe. Human beings' relationship to the natural world is governed by causes which may or may not be within human control. Such causes and natural laws are operative at all times unless God wills to overrule them in specific cases and for particular ends which human beings have no way of predicting ahead of time, and for which they bear no responsibility.

This methodological defect may reveal itself in a failure to take account of natural causes on the pretext of relying entirely on God, or the belief that acknowledging natural causation is inconsistent with Islamic doctrine according to which God Almighty is the Sole Actor in the universe. Those who think and behave in this manner see earthly phenomena, including human beings, as bearing little or no responsibility for outcomes because, in their belief, outcomes are the province of God alone rather than being the results of previous causes in time. At the other extreme, there are individuals who rule out the supernatural element altogether in the realm of causation. Such individuals are of the belief that outcomes are brought about by natural causes alone without any divine interference or intervention.

Methodological errors such as these undermine the kind of scientific mentality that prompts a researcher to engage in the logical steps of analyzing, arranging and classifying the elements of a given problem or phenomenon in order to identify the true causal relationships that exist among these elements, which in turn makes it possible to discover solutions, cures, and the like.

Give three other examples of a failure to link causes with effects.

(4) *Failure to Discern Truth, and Working at Cross-Purposes With Reality*

Consider the following example of a failure to heed truth, and even to work at cross-purposes with it: Smoking has become an epidemic of worldwide proportions, albeit in varying degrees. There is not a state on the face of the earth today whose officials are unaware of the harmful effects of smoking. Nevertheless, states themselves invest in the tobacco industry, or allow the construction of cigarette factories by local or international investors on the pretext of promoting a free market when, in reality, what they want is the taxes that will be levied on the industry,[34] or increased job opportunities. Decision makers in these various states know full well that the sums spent on treatment for smoking-related illnesses are far greater than the income that accrues from tobacco plants and cigarette factories.

According to the World Health Organization (WHO 2008) report on the global tobacco epidemic, the number of smokers worldwide in the year 2008 came to more than one billion, or around one-third of the entire population worldwide. The blight of smoking brings a greater death toll than all the wars being waged around the globe. According to the same report, scientific studies have demonstrated decisively that both smoking and second-hand smoke cause death, illness and disability, while "tobacco use causes 1 in 10 deaths worldwide – more than 5 million people a year. By 2030, unless urgent action is taken, tobacco's annual death toll will rise to more than eight million."[35]

The report indicates that 80 percent of the world's smokers are in low- to medium-income developing countries. Most of the states in the world have responded to calls by the WHO to increase awareness of the harmful effects of smoking, while the number of smokers in high-income countries is declining. However, the percentage of those who smoke in developing countries, particularly in Arab-Islamic countries, is on the rise.[36]

The dangers of smoking are not limited to the health risks that threaten smokers and those around them. They also include the financial burdens caused by the purchase of tobacco, the cost of which sometimes consumes up to one-quarter of a family's entire income.

This type of economic waste is clearly beyond reason. So, given the known facts about smoking, why is no Islamic legal ruling forthcoming on its dangers? And what is to prevent the governments of Arab and Islamic countries from making decisive political and economic decisions to curb or prevent the production, import and use of tobacco?

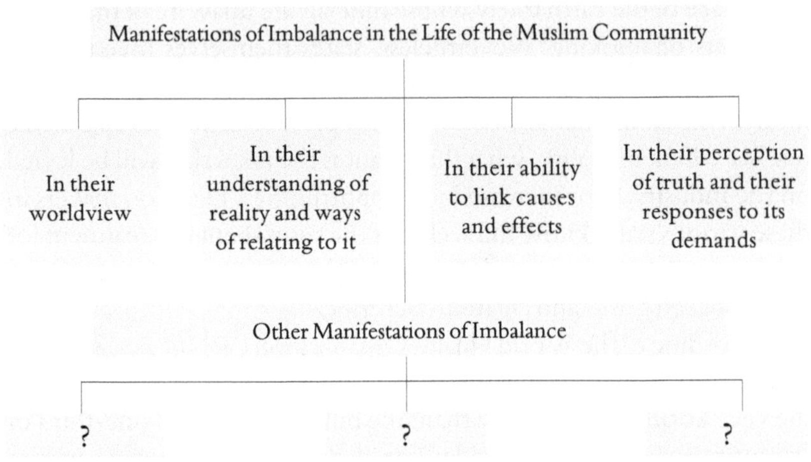

Training Session: Trainees are Divided Into Five Groups

- After discussing the manifestations of methodological imbalance in the understanding of reality and ways of relating to it, the first group gives six examples of these manifestations.
- The second group comes up with six examples of methodological imbalance in relation to the ability to link causes and effects.
- The third group comes up with six examples of methodological imbalance in relation to the Muslim community's worldview.
- The fourth group comes up with six examples of methodological imbalance in relation to perceptions of truth and ways of responding to its demands.
- The fifth group proposes three additional types of methodological imbalance in the life of the Muslim community and gives two examples of each.

4

Evolution of the Concept of Method in Islamic and Western Thought

GOALS OF THIS CHAPTER

1. To trace the evolution of the concept and meanings of method (*manhaj*) in both Islamic thought and Western thought.
2. To clarify the relationship between the concept of method in the Islamic heritage and growth of knowledge in scientific disciplines.
3. To observe the link between the emergence of methodological rules and the sciences dealing with Islamic texts.
4. To show how the meanings of texts, human social conditions and the natural world come together in Islamic methodology.
5. To note defects in the historical evolution of method in Western thought.
6. To discuss the contributions made by Aristotle, Francis Bacon, and René Descartes to the development of the concept of method in Western thought.
7. To affirm the impact of evolving human experience on the evolution of the concept of method.
8. To compare the trajectory of the development of the concept of method and methodological practices in the Islamic and Western heritages.

INTRODUCTION

This chapter will present a brief overview of the history of method. The focus here will be on the term "method" or other terms of direct relevance to it, with attention given to the most significant phases of the term's evolution. Thus far we have presented the historical development of the concept of method in Islamic thought without reference to its evolution in Western thought. In what follows, however, we set out to identify the role played by method in the various phases of interaction between Western and Islamic thought.

The Arabic words *manhaj* and *minhāj* are both found in the Holy Qur'an, the Hadith literature, and other Arabic texts. However, the word *manhaj* has come to be used more frequently in modern parlance. The terms *minhāj*, *nahj* and *manhaj* are associated individually with particular contexts. However, each of them refers to essentially the same reality, namely, the soundest, safest path to assured knowledge and understanding. Muslim thinkers, who became aware of the importance of method early in Islamic history, could see clearly that method (*manhaj*) tended to be colored by whatever school of thought, philosophy or jurisprudence it was associated with. This was the case regardless of whether the school concerned was Islamic in origin and outcome, or combined the general culture of Islamic society with intellectual currents originating in Greek, European, or Oriental Illuminationist thought.

Western thinkers tend to trace the history of method back to the era of Greek philosophy; they then jump to the developments that took place the European Renaissance, and end with a discussion of the methodological crisis revealed in the statements of certain post-Modernists. However, we attempt in our discussion of Western thought on method to identify all the major way stations of its history, including phases involving cultural interaction and borrowing that other historians of thought may have passed over.

First: EVOLUTION OF THE CONCEPT OF METHOD IN ISLAMIC THOUGHT

During the life of the Prophet Muhammad, for example, the revelation would be bestowed on him from on high, whereupon he would communicate it to those around him, asking his scribes to write it down and deliver it to the Muslim community. In the course of communicating verses of the Qur'an to others, the Prophet would sometimes clarify and explain the Qur'anic text. However, he was careful to avoid allowing the Qur'anic revelation to be confused with his own speech. It was for this reason that, according to Muslim scholars, the Prophet wisely refrained from allowing people to write down hadiths in the way they were writing down the words of the Qur'an.

> "Method" during the days of the Prophet Muhammad consisted in the Prophet's communication of the words of the divine revelation, and the Companions' reception of the revelation.

The Holy Qur'an and hadiths – that is, the words and actions of the Prophet as recorded and passed down through chains of trustworthy narrators – were thus the two primary sources of knowledge which ordered life in the early Muslim society, and it was these that formed the basis for the processes of teaching and learning. As one would expect, the Prophet's Companions were not in agreement about everything after the Prophet's death. Consequently, the Companions' consensus (ijmaʿ) on this or that issue or question was viewed as a third source of reliable knowledge. In cases concerning which there was no explicit text in either the Holy Qur'an or the Prophetic Sunnah, Muslim scholars drew analogies between these new cases and previous, similar cases that had received explicit mention in the Holy Qur'an or the Sunnah. For this reason, analogy (*qiyās*) was included as a fourth source of Islamic knowledge. Consensus and analogy may be viewed as types or cases of ijtihad, or reasoned interpretation; therefore, ijtihad has also been classed as a source of knowledge after the Qur'an and the Sunnah.

> "Method" during the lifetimes of the Prophet's Companions consisted in deriving legal rulings from the Qur'an and the Sunnah through the process of ijtihad.

These, then, are the sources that made up the methodology on the basis of which Muslims derived knowledge in the specific sense of legal rulings. For this reason scholars referred to them as sources of legislation. At times scholars would go beyond the conclusions reached through analogical reasoning, basing their rulings instead on the value, spirit and fundamental purpose of the action being ruled on. This process was referred to by scholars as *istiḥsān*, or juristic preference.[1]

First-generation Muslims felt that the Holy Qur'an and the Prophet's explanations and applications thereof were sufficient to order their day-to-day affairs. Consequently, after the Prophet's death, consensus (ijmaʿ), analogical reasoning (*qiyās*), juristic preference (*istiḥsān*) and the processes of defining human interests and the overarching aims of Islamic law were all forms of reasoned interpretation (ijtihad), the goal of which was to increase their understanding of the meanings of the Qur'anic revelation and what they had come to know through the Prophetic Sunnah. The process of recording the Islamic sciences, voweling the relevant texts, and regulating the ways in which these texts were used called for the development of specific new approaches. The various sciences that were developed at that time included the principles of jurisprudence, the principles of exegesis, principles of Hadith study, and scholastic theology. These newly developed disciplines were an outgrowth of Muslim reasoning, they were without precedent in the history of the sciences, and they provided a means of ordering Muslims' concrete affairs on the basis of Islamic law. Consequently, they constituted an Islamic methodology par excellence.

However, when we reflect on the principle source of this Islamic knowledge – the Qur'an itself – it becomes clear that the Qur'an was not only addressing the first generation of Muslims concerning the sciences they needed to establish. Nor was it addressing Muslims alone. Rather, it was addressing the entire human race, providing them with the source of guidance they needed to order all their affairs. The Qur'an continues to address believers and unbelievers alike, engaging them in dialogue and debate, telling them stories of bygone nations, encouraging them and warning them, and offering them evidence to which they are obliged to make some response. The Qur'an deals with life's affairs in their social, political and economic aspects alike while entering the inner recesses of people's hearts and minds. It points to the marvels of the world we live in from the level of the infinitesimal to the vastest expanses of the universe. By means of its various styles of rhetoric – story-telling and parables, dialogue and questioning, enticement and threat – the Qur'an stimulates the mechanisms of perception and awareness in human beings in such a way that they put them to use as sources of knowledge, while holding them responsible ultimately for these uses and their outcomes.

This type of reflection helped Muslim scholars to appreciate the Qur'an's focus on informing people and directing them to what they ought to do, a focus whose aim is to help people both to achieve their interests in this earthly realm and to lead a life that earns them God's pleasure in the world to come. These aspect of knowledge have their origin in the written revelation. Further reflection gave them an appreciation of the way the Qur'an encourages us to contemplate and meditate on the realities both within ourselves and in the outer world. Through these mental processes human beings are able to discover the laws God has established on the psychological, social and cosmic planes, and, having grasped these realities, to legislate the laws needed to order life's affairs, to establish a community devoted to truth and justice, and to construct an enlightened civilization. These aspects of knowledge have their origin in the universe as a whole with its vast array of objects, living beings, events and phenomena. And just as human life is a unified whole in which there is no division between the requirements of this world and the world to come, so also should human beings relate to the two sources of knowledge – revelation and nature – in an integrated, holistic manner.

> The natural and social sciences, when linked to the guidance contained in the Qur'an, lead toward a fuller understanding of phenomena and events.

The process of reflecting on these two dimensions – the inward and the outward – calls for use of the various tools available to us as human beings. It would not be fitting for us to neglect the use of our immediate physical senses. Take, for example, the role played in the reception of auditory stimuli by the sense of hearing, or of visual stimuli by the sense of sight. Nor should we neglect to verify the validity and reliability of the data we receive, ensuring that it provides an accurate description of objects and events both quantitatively and qualitatively. This perceptive and analytic process can only take place through the use of the heart or the mind, which attributes meaning to all the input we receive. The Qur'an combines these two types of tools – sensory perception and the rational faculty – with a sense of responsibility, making clear that hearing and sight in their capacity as sensory faculties, and the mind as the faculty of understanding and awareness, need to be used together. We are not meant to stop at outward forms, passing sensations, or hasty, superficial assessments of things. Rather, the Qur'an calls upon us to use our physical senses and our faculty of discernment in a profound, deliberate manner, examining phenomena from all angles and reaching conclusions with care. Only then can we combine all elements of our observations, experiences and experiments in a manner in which all elements of the judgment process are called into play, and the available evidence, data and proofs are in clear focus.

> The use of sensory perception and reason serve to generate and test knowledge, then put it to use.

With such considerations in mind, we can better understand the Qur'anic insistence on the need for both sensory and mental perception. We read, "...Go over all the earth and behold..." (*sūrah al-ʿAnkabūt* 29:20); "...Consider whatever there is in the heavens and on earth!..." (*sūrah Yūnus* 10:101); "Art thou not aware of thy Sustainer [through His works]? – how He causes the shadow to lengthen [toward the night] when, had He so willed, He could indeed have made it stand still: but then, We have made the sun its guide; and then, [after having caused it to lengthen,] We draw it in towards Ourselves with a gradual drawing-in" (*sūrah al-Furqān* 25:45-46); "...What do you think? If of a sudden all your water were to vanish underground, who [but God] could provide you with water from [new] unsullied springs?" (*sūrah al-Mulk* 67:30); "Behold, then, [O man,] these signs of God's grace – how He gives life to the earth after it had been lifeless!..." (*sūrah al-Rūm* 30:50); "...No fault wilt thou see in the creation of the Most Gracious. And turn thy vision [upon it] once more: canst thou see any flaw? Yea, turn thy vision [upon it] again and yet again: [and every time] thy vision will fall back upon thee, dazzled and truly defeated." (*sūrah al-Mulk* 67:3-4). Examples of such statements abound in the Qur'an. The Qur'an makes mention of specific phenomena that God has placed at human beings' disposal in order that they might put them to use and benefit from them and, in response, realize that they are blessings from God. In fact, such blessings are incalculable:

> [And remember that] it is God who has created the heavens and the earth... and has made the rivers subservient [to His laws, so that they be of use] to you; and has made the sun and the moon, both of them constant upon their courses, subservient [to His laws, so that they be of use] to you; and has made the night and the day subservient [to His laws, so that they be of use] to you. (*sūrah Ibrāhīm* 14:32-33).

> The evidence gleaned from research and observation are linked to elements of the Qur'anic methodology.

A methodology that does not rely on reality with its array of objects, events and phenomena, and which fails to employ deliberate, repeated observation, thorough descriptions and precise calculations followed by experimentation and practical application will never lead to reliable, verifiable knowledge. Similarly, any methodology which does not involve gathering all data of relevance to the topic of study, be they visual, audio, or in the form of Islamic legal texts, will fail to yield the reliable knowledge it is intended to yield.

The Qur'anic revelation sets forth the research methodology that will lead to documented, and documentable, knowledge. Just as the "written signs" contained in the Qur'an affirm definitive rulings on certain questions and issues, they also insist on the necessity of seeking out the "visible signs" to be found within ourselves and in the created world around us. These "visible signs" enable us to discover the patterns and laws that govern existing phenomena and the changes and events associated with them. Why not speak, then, of "a Qur'anic research methodology," or, at the very least, of a research methodology that derives its distinctive features from the Qur'an? Generalizing a bit further, we can speak of "an Islamic research methodology." If, then, a given writer speaks specifically of "*the* Islamic methodology," he is referring to the methodology he himself (or she herself) has observed in the Qur'anic discourse.

Exercise

Give three examples of ways in which one might reconcile the "written signs" found in the Qur'an with the "visible signs" found in the created world for the sake of formulating an Islamic research methodology.

The Qur'an has a miraculous, generous quality about it in that the meanings it conveys accommodate whatever level human knowledge has achieved. In other words, they expand and grow along with our human knowledge and understanding. Consequently, different readers will come away from the Qur'an with different understandings of the verses that refer to the elements of the Qur'anic – or Islamic – research methodology. Scholars' views of this methodology will differ in keeping with the degree of understanding and insight God has granted them, and depending on how much insight they have gained into geographical or temporal contexts.

Unless we appreciate the importance of the sensory and empirical pathways to knowledge, including field studies, experimentation, application and the like, all of which are advocated by Islamic research methodology, our understanding of the Holy Qur'an will remain incomplete. The Prophet's perspective on this Qur'anic principle may be seen in the fact that he would sometimes suspend judgment on this or that issue until more data had become available. In some cases he would wait for a revelation from Heaven, and in others, information based on what he had observed or heard from those around him. We find, for example, that the Prophet had been about to forbid married Muslim men from engaging in sexual relations with their wives during the period between the birth of a newborn and the time the child was weaned. He had intended to issue this prohibition based on his belief that sexual relations would negatively impact the newborn, particularly if they resulted in another pregnancy while the newborn was still nursing. However, he noticed that this practice was having no ill effects on the children of the Byzantines and the Persians. Consequently, he decided not to forbid it after all. Similarly, the Prophet had been of the belief that pollinating date palms was nothing but a misguided practice of the people of Medina, and that God Almighty would permit the date palms to bear fruit just as other trees did without human intervention. However, it then became apparent to him that date palms failed to bear when people stopped pollinating them. Hence, he modified his position on this matter. In so doing, he affirmed the importance of empirical observation and practical experimentation. He freely acknowledged that he himself lacked expertise in such matters, since his tribe in Makkah had never owned date palms, and that those with experience in this area were more knowledgeable than he was.

Exercise

Present other examples illustrating the fact that the Prophet would wait for more facts to emerge between issuing a verdict on a given issue.

With the variety of perspectives and tools relevant to the treatment of this or that topic of research, worldview remains the principle factor determining the approach to be applied as well as the outcomes of such application. For example, when criticizing hadiths, Muslims make use of the historical method just as Orientalists or materialists do. However, there is an essential difference between the Islamic and Orientalist approaches. This difference owes to an unbridgeable differences between their respective foundations and frames of reference. In this connection N. J. Coulson states,

> ...it must, of course, be frankly recognized that the Muslim and Western methods of Ḥadīth criticism are irreconcilable because they rest on totally different premises. Between the dictates of religious faith on one hand and secular historical criticism on the other there can be no middle way of true objectivity.[2]

The significance of method for the Islamic sciences first became apparent as a result of the concern to preserve the sayings of the Prophet and to protect them from corruption and falsification. The systematic use of chains of transmission (*isnād*) was developed into a science, as were the principles of hadith, also known as the science of hadith terminology (*ʿilm muṣṭalaḥ al-ḥadīth*). Strict rules were developed for determining the reliability of every narrator in a given chain of transmission, a process which led to the development of the science of contestation and validation (*ʿilm al-jarḥ wa al-taʿdīl*) and "the science of men" (*ʿilm al-rijāl*), that is, the study of the personal histories and moral characters of men who had transmitted accounts from the life of the Prophet, as well as other sciences relating to the Prophetic Sunnah. Numerous books were written on such topics, including *al-Jarḥ wa al-Taʿdīl* (Contestation and Validation) by Ibn Abī Ḥātim (d. 327 AH /938 CE), *Al-Kifāyah fī ʿIlm al-Riwāyah* (On the Science of Narration) by al-Khaṭīb al-Baghdādī (d. 463 AH/1070 CE), *Mīzān al-Iʿtidāl fī Naqd al-Rijāl* (The Measure of Moderation in the Critique of Men) by al-Dhahabī (d. 748 AH/1348 CE), and *Lisān al-Mīzān* (a reworking of al-Dhahabī's "Measure of Moderation") by Ibn Ḥajar al-ʿAsqalānī (d. 852 AH/1448 CE).

> The elements of method evolved with the emergence of the science of the principles of the Prophetic hadith.

Moreover, although most of these books focused on methods of verifying the validity and reliability of accounts relating to the life of the Prophet, they also contained general methodological rules that were applicable to all sciences, particularly the nascent science of historiography, whose evolution culminated in the appearance of Ibn Khaldūn's renowned *Muqaddimah* (the preface to his book on history entitled *Kitāb al-ʿIbar wa Tārīkh al-ʿArab wa al-ʿAjam al-Barbar wa man Jāwarahum min Dhawī al-Sulṭān al-Akbar*), which contained rules for systematic historical writing.

> *Exercise*
>
> Looking at Ibn Khaldūn's *Muqaddimah*, find the rules he sets forth for systematic historical writing, and list the errors Ibn Khaldūn identifies in the writings of other historians.

Early in the history of Islam there emerged gifted thinkers with the capacity to instruct others in the matters of their religion. Each of these outstanding scholars came to have his own authoritative frame of reference and individual approach. Thus, while Mālik ibn Anas (d. 179 AH/795 CE), who interpreted Islamic law for Muslims living in Madinah, was instructing people in jurisprudence based on his copious knowledge of hadith, Abū Ḥanīfah in Iraq was basing his teaching on a relatively narrower store of hadith knowledge (relative, that is, to Mālik's knowledge). Nevertheless, Abū Ḥanīfah's contribution was to employ reason in the understanding of the various types of situations that called for legal rulings.

> Muslim scholars adopted distinct approaches to the derivation of juristic rulings.

Then came Imam al-Shāfiʿī (d. 205 AH/820 CE), who combined the approaches of Mālik and Abū Ḥanīfah. Al-Shāfiʿī documented and advocated the method he had adopted in his volume entitled *al-Risālah* (The Message). Al-Shāfiʿī's *Risālah* served as the foundation for writing about what later came to be known as the principles of jurisprudence (*ʿilm uṣūl al-fiqh*), a systematic science par excellence.

As Islamic society began occupying itself with philosophical studies and as the natural sciences and scholarly works translated from Greek, Persian and other languages began making their way into Arab Islamic culture, there arose a need for systematic writings that would set down rules for scientific investigation. Use was made initially of reasoning from analogy and logical proofs, after which this approach was expanded and applied on a broader basis. Noting the insufficiency of this approach, scholars added the approach of reasoning or inference from induction. Specialized books were written on the classification of the sciences, their general methods, and their applications to particular sciences. Such books included *Mafātīḥ al-ʿUlūm* (Keys to the Sciences) by al-Khawārizmī (d. 226 AH/840 CE), a treatise entitled *al-Tawfīq ʿalā Tārīkh Ikhtiṣār al-Najāh bi Ikhtiṣār al-Ṭarīq* (A Brief Treatise on the Swiftest Path to Salvation) by Ibn Ḥazm (d. 457 AH/1064 CE), *Miʿyār al-ʿIlm* (The Measure of Knowledge) by al-Ghazālī (d. 505 AH/1111 CE), *Manāhij al-Adillah fī ʿAqā'id al-Millah* (Approaches to Evidence Concerning Religious Doctrines) by Ibn Rushd (d. 595 AH/1198 CE),

Al-Muʿīd fī Adab al-Mufīd wa al-Mustafīd (A Review of Writings on Instruction and Learning) by al-ʿAlmawi (d. 981 AH/1573 CE), *Tadhkirah al-Sāmiʿ wa al-Mutakallim fī Adab al-ʿĀlim wa al-Mutaʿallim* (A Reminder to Listener and Speaker: Rules of Etiquette for Students and Teachers) by Ibn Jamāʿah (d. 672 AH/1273 CE), *Kashshāf Iṣṭilāḥāt al-ʿUlūm* by al-Tahānawī (A Listing of Scientific Terminology), (d. 553 AH/1158 CE), and many others.

Every group of scholars had its own scientific logic and methodological tools. Hadith scholars had their methods of dealing with the sciences of narration and hadith terminology, exegetes had their methods of studying traditions, rhetoric and language, juristic rulings, and mystical interpretations; jurists and specialists in the principles of jurisprudence had methods of reasoning from analogy and induction, theologians had their methods of argumentation, dialogue and debate; the Sufis had their methods of mystical and experiential interpretation, while natural scientists had their methods of induction and hands-on experimentation.

It may go without saying that sensory perception needs to be paired with rational comprehension in order for human beings to construct true knowledge. Nevertheless, some Muslim scholars have gone to great lengths to detail and demonstrate this necessity. Al-Ḥasan ibn al-Haytham (d. 430 AH/1038 CE), for example, stipulated that sensory input and the mind have to work together in order for one to arrive at certainty,[3] and he supported his claim by quoting from Galen. He then proceeded to explain the anatomy of the eye and the way in which human sight takes place in both its material, physiological dimension and its psychological, cognitive dimension. Ibn al-Haytham also discussed the role of memory and the sensory signals the person receives, and how he or she takes in part of the image being seen and uses this to reconstruct the remaining parts.

Methodological literature cites al-Ḥasan ibn al-Haytham's contribution to the evolution of scientific and empirical method in the context of Islamic history. Ibn al-Haytham wrote that he was well-versed in the sciences of the ancients, and that he had found what he was looking for in Aristotle's writings on the science of logic, the natural sciences and theology, which together constitute the heart of philosophy.

According to Ibn al-Haytham, Aristotle began by establishing universals and particulars, generalities and specifics, as well as logical terms. Impressed with the neatness of Aristotle's system, Ibn al-Haytham applied himself to the pursuit to what he termed the three "sciences of philosophy," that is, mathematics, the natural sciences, and theology. He steeped himself in their basic principles and undertook a thorough study of their rulings. In addition, he classified the various branches of these three sciences as a means of clarifying and explaining their more obscure aspects.[4]

However, after mastering the sciences of the ancients, which had yet to arrive at the use of induction and empirical experimentation, Ibn al-Haytham went beyond these sciences. In his research into physical sight, he employed a method which he described with a detailed precision rarely found among either his contemporaries or his predecessors. Ibn al-Haytham described his method as follows:

> We begin our research with a thorough investigation of the facts and the states of visible entities, identifying the distinguishing features of particulars. Then, based on a process of induction, we glean that which is relevant to the sense of sight and the act of seeing, noting phenomena that are stable and unchanging, and which appear to the viewer as they are in reality. Then, gradually and in an orderly manner, we refine our criteria while critiquing the premises [on which our work is based], exercising reserve with respect to the conclusions we reach. In all that we investigate and examine, we make it our aim to exercise prudence and caution rather than surrender to mere impulse. And in all we detect and critique, we seek Truth itself, not merely conjecture or opinion. It is hoped that in this way, we will arrive at the Truth – which brings joy to the heart – and, in so doing, reach the goal wherein lies perfect certainty. By virtue of cautious critique, we will have won the Truth, which does away with doubts and disputes.[5]

Similarly, the physician Abū Bakr al-Rāzī (d. 313 AH/925 CE) spoke of the need for experimentation and analogical reasoning in connection with his treatment of patients. Al-Rāzī discussed patients' hospital records and statistics relating to various cases, describing the conclusions he reached based on them in what are referred to in modern parlance as "retrospective studies." He wrote:

> I have kept these records over a number of years in the hospitals in Baghdad and al-Rayy, as well as in my own home. I have recorded the names of those whose cases correspond to what is written in these books, as well as the names of those whose cases do not correspond to it on a case-by-case basis. The cases that do not correspond to what is written in existing medical writings are as numerous as the cases that do. This lack of correspondence is a serious matter, and, just as in other crafts and professions, the prudent individual should not place full, unthinking confidence in what has been recorded in the past. Nor should he make generalizations or begin a treatment on the basis thereof. The reason for this is the nearly two thousand patients whose cases do not correspondent to existing medical writings. Hence, I have refrained from issuing a definitive judgment based on what I have observed except when the evidence is so clear and incontrovertible as to be beyond doubt. For some time I have continued, through experimentation and analogical reasoning, to work on a treatment for acute diseases, taking care not to make any mistake at a patient's expense, while also taking care not to allow an existing illness to go on longer than necessary.[6]

Hence, method among Islamic thinkers has been in evidence historically in more than one field of study. In fact, its manifestations can be traced in virtually all fields. Systematic or methodological thought is associated with specific rules and principles in both the Holy Qur'an and the Prophetic Sunnah. Similarly, it was evident in the practices of the Companions and Successors of the Prophet, while the writings of hadith scholars and jurists lent it greater definition and established its rules and premises. The concept and practice of method were further defined and classified in the works of scholastic theologians, philosophers, mystics and historians. Nevertheless, the field which is known preeminently for its concern for method is the science of the principles of jurisprudence, which lay the foundations for Islamic legislation. As one writer has remarked, works on the principles of [Islamic] legislation and jurisprudence contain "logical analyses and methodological rules that bear a clear philosophical stamp. Indeed, what we find in this discipline is nearly identical to the rules and foundations of modern research methods."[7]

It will be noted that the Holy Qur'an urges us to employ an overall epistemological approach which links the visible cosmos with the written revelation in their capacity as sources of knowledge. This same approach links the use of reason and sensory input in their capacity as tools for relating to everything in both the created universe and the written revelation. In relation to human efforts and striving, this approach links the benefits of this earthly life with reward in the life to come; similarly, it connects the realms of thought, scientific research, and concrete practice.

Exercise

Design a chart showing the evolution of Islamic methodology in its various phases and fields. The chart should contain the following elements: the methodology of reception, the methodology of chains of transmission and documentation, the methodology of jurisprudence, the methodology of the principles of jurisprudence, the methodology of scholastic theologians, variety and integration in methodology, empirical scientific research methodology, mystical/experiential methodology, methodological defects and the backwardness of the Muslim community, methodological dependency and the disintegration of the Muslim community, methodological awareness, and acquiring the methodological faculty in the realms of thought, research, and behavior.

Second: EVOLUTION OF THE CONCEPT OF METHOD IN WESTERN THOUGHT

The prevailing pattern of historiography in Western thought is based on two primary foundations: (1) recorded human history excluding religious sources, and (2) the history of the European peoples excluding that of other peoples, or, at the very least, undermining their importance.[8] Hence, the history of philosophy, the history of science, and the history of civilization itself begins in Greece and ends in Western Europe and its North American extensions!

When discussing the first foundation above, we should bear in mind that the little that has been recorded of the history of human civilization confirms that people of all nations have used their minds and developed the sciences and the arts. They have formulated legal systems and constructed edifices whose remains stand to this day, and some of which are even classed among the wonders of the world. When the Greeks' turn came along, they built upon the efforts of those who had preceded them. In other words, they did not start from scratch. In his *History of Greek Philosophy*, author Yusuf Karam notes that "the Eastern peoples who predated the Greeks had theories that embodied their perspectives on all the issues that were later classified as being philosophical in nature. In fact, for every idea the Greeks came up with, we find a similar, Eastern, idea which preceded it, or a principle upon which it may have been based."[9]

As for the exclusion of religious sources, this may have resulted from the conflict that raged during Europe's Middle Ages between science and the institutional church. When this conflict ended with the triumph of science, religious authority was isolated from the history of science and human wisdom.

Topic for Discussion

Given the tendency by Western historians of human thought to exclude religious sources from their study of history, first explain the reason for this phenomenon, then discuss its consequences.

However, we cannot rule out the possibility that prophets and messengers appeared in Greece with divine guidance. After all, we know them to have appeared among the Hebrews, the Arabs, and other peoples. The Holy Qur'an states unequivocally that peoples in all ages and all places have been visited by divinely inspired messengers who came bringing both warnings and glad tidings in their own languages. God declares, "[We sent all these] apostles as heralds of glad tidings and as warners, so that men might have no excuse before God after [the coming of] these apostles; and God is indeed almighty, wise" (*sūrah al-Nisā'* 4:165). How, then, can we rule out the possibility that Greece, too, was visited by divinely inspired apostles? If our authoritative basis for this certainty is the Qur'an, it should be borne in mind that even the Qur'an itself has not told us about all the apostles that have been sent to humankind. As God declared to the Prophet Muhammad, "[And indeed, [O Muhammad,] We sent forth apostles before thy time; some of them We have mentioned to thee, and some of them We have not mentioned to thee..." (*sūrah Ghāfir* 40:78).

In his book *ʿUyūn al-Anbā' fī Ṭabaqāt al-Aṭibbā'* (Noteworthy Reports on the Various Classes of Physicians), Ibn Abū 'Uṣaybiʿah tells us that some philosophers, when they were unable to answer questions that had been addressed to them, would refer their questioners to the Prophet. In the first section of his book, Ibn Abū 'Uṣaybiʿah cites sayings about the divine and prophetic principles underlying the science of medicine, drawing examples from Greek history. He quotes Galen as having said that Asclepius, the first of the ancient Greeks to have spoken about medicine, had spoken by divine inspiration. We are told that "the kings descended from his line used to claim that he was a prophet." Galen also tells us that "Asclepius, who lived before the Great Deluge, was a disciple of Agathodaemon the Egyptian, and was recognized as a prophet by the ancient Greeks and Egyptians. It was Asclepius who launched the craft of medicine among the Greeks..." Ibn Abū 'Uṣaybiʿah goes on to add that:

> Asclepius was such an adept physician that he was able to heal patients whose recovery others had despaired of. Some claimed that God Almighty had honored him by exalting him to the status of the angels. It has been said that Asclepius was the prophet Idris, upon him be peace.[10]

Al-Masʿūdī states that in ancient times, particularly in the days of the great Brahman king, India was the land of knowledge and wisdom where the iron and gold industries developed along with astronomy, and numerology. The first of the cosmic principles developed in ancient India is described by al-Masʿūdī as "the First Principle, which gives all existent entities their existence while generously bestowing Its goodness upon them." Moreover, although al-Masʿūdī believed Brahman to have been a king, he makes mention of those who believe him to have been God Almighty's messenger to India, as well as those who claim that he was Adam himself, peace be upon him.[11] In the same work, al-Masʿūdī describes Zoroaster as ruler of the Mazdaists, who brought them the book known as the Zend Avesta (Arabic, *al-Zamzamah*).[12]

Scholar Nadim al-Jisr proposes that many aspects of the wisdom found among the ancients originated in the form of prophetic messages. He states, "For God's guidance on the lips of the Apostles is more ancient than the Greeks and their philosophy. In fact, I think it probable that much of the philosophy of the ancients in Egypt, China and India represents the remnants of prophetic teachings that history has forgotten, and whose bearers have come to be classified as mere philosophers whereas, in fact, they may have been prophets or their followers."[13]

In all fairness, it should also be noted that some Western thinkers do recognize the efforts of peoples and nations that preceded the Greeks in relation to certain aspects of wisdom and philosophy. Hans-Georg Gadamer, for example, sees no possible beginning for philosophy anywhere but in the works of Plato and Aristotle. At the same time, however, he holds that these two philosophers were the portals through which the floodwaters of the period that preceded them came rushing. This being the case, they were historians of the pre-Socratic era. Pre-Socratic philosophy originated in Central Asia, and what is termed epic literature and philosophy both predate Socrates; in fact, they predate most of the written heritage that has come down to us. Moreover, the language in which they were written was the language that was spoken by the Greeks, a fact which Gadamer describes as "one of the great puzzles of human history." He notes that the Greeks did not invent writing by means of an alphabet. Rather, they took it and completed it by drawing on the Semitic alphabet in a process that took two hundred years at most.[14]

Pre-Socratic Greek Methods

In his *History of Greek Philosophy*, Yusuf Karam notes that the most ancient Greeks known to us were the Ionians. A prominent scholar by the name of Thales (624-546 BC) traveled widely through the East and delved deeply into the Babylonian and Egyptian sciences. Thales adopted the empirical method and attempted to engage in induction and proof. The writings of the Ionians, who were particularly interested in nature, appear to have been lost. Hence, what we know about them derives from statements about them by Plato and Aristotle. However, a late Ionian thinker by the name of Heraclitus distinguished himself from other Ionian scholars by his propensity for debate and controversy.

Heraclitus held a belief in the unity of opposites – the notion that all things come into being through a conflict of opposites – and that change is the true nature of things. According to Heraclitus, nothing would exist without change, while stability in the sense of a lack of change is tantamount to death and non-existence. Heraclitus' followers were known as the Sophists, who took doubt to its ultimate extreme. Consequently, Heraclitus is considered the forefather of skepticism in Greek philosophy.[15]

Before the days of Socrates, a prominent community of Greek philosophers gathered around a renowned teacher by the name of Pythagoras (572-497 BC). Therefore they came to be known as the Pythagoreans. The Pythagoreans are credited with having founded the science of Mathematics. In addition to Mathematics, however, they concerned themselves with astronomy, music and medicine, considering that the most significant traits that characterize this world are order and proportionality. According to the Pythagoreans, numbers and harmony constitute the true nature of existent entities. The Pythagoreans propounded the view that the Earth is round, and that it revolves in an orbit around a centralized fire.[16]

Another philosopher of the same period was Democritus (470-361 BC), who rethought natural science. According to Democritus, existence is essentially material in nature, and bodies consist of infinitesimal, indivisible material particles (atoms). Between these atoms there is a void out of which other bodies emerge. Atoms are in constant motion, colliding and parting in a process that accounts for the various changes in visible objects. Democritus held that the most simple of all entities is the individual essence, or the indivisible part, that the essences and the void are truly existent, and that they are the sole object of knowledge.[17]

It will be noted that the topic of research is what governed the general framework for research methods and ways of thinking in the various phases of Greek history. In the beginning, research moved in the direction of studying the visible aspects of the natural world. The Ionians, the Pythagoreans, Heraclitus and others focused on the basic material component of the cosmos, the things of nature and the changes they undergo. Hence, it should come as no surprise to find that the research activities of that early period were governed by the natural method.

The Sophists' Rhetorical, Dialectical Method

In the fifth century BC the Athenians managed to rout the Persians and regain their independence. Consequently, they achieved sufficient stability to allow for the spread of culture and education. Competition among individuals and groups increased, political and judicial debate flourished, and there emerged a need for oratory, methods of argumentation, and techniques for winning over one's audience. Certain members of the intelligentsia who worked to develop their rhetorical skills were known as Sophists. The term "Sophist," derived from the Greek *sophizesthai*, "to become wise or learned," came to mean "someone who gives intellectual instruction for pay" in this or that science, discipline, or craft. However, it was used most frequently to refer to a teacher of rhetoric in the positive sense of the word. Nevertheless, the Sophists specialized in debate and in marshalling arguments, often specious ones, of relevance to the various questions, issues and situations of the day, and in the use of means of persuasion and rhetorical effect without any real concern for the truth as such. They restricted their efforts to an examination of terms, their meanings, types of issues, arguments and their conditions, and means of perfecting fallacious arguments. They debated well-known philosophical schools, mocked both reason and religion alike, and glorified power and dominance.

Most of Aristotle's trusted works have been compiled, translated into English, and published in a single 1,488-page volume. Beginning with the six books of the *Organon* (Aristotle's logical treatises), the volume includes *Physica* (On Physics), parts of *De Caelo* (On the Heavens), *De Generatione et Corruptione* (On Generation and Corruption), *De Anima* (On the Soul), *De Memoria et Reminiscentia* (On Memory and Reminiscence), *De Somniis* (On Dreams), *Historia Animalium* (The History of Animals), *De Partibus Animalium* (On the Parts of Animals), *De Generatione Animalium* (On the Generation of Animals), *Metaphysica* (Metaphysics), *Ethica Nicomachea* (Nicomachean Ethics), *Politica* (Politics), *Rhetorica* (Rhetoric), and *De Poetica* (Poetics). See Richard McKeon (ed.), *The Basic Works of Aristotle*, New York: Random House, 1941.

The Sophist method and its adherents came to be viewed with contempt after Socrates and his disciples took them on. One of the best-known Sophists was Protagoras (480-410 BC), who was quoted by Plato as saying that "of all things the measure is man, of the things that are, that [or "how"] they are, and of the things that are not, that [or "how"] they are not." In other words, the truth about things is relative to the individual observer, things are in constant flux, and there is no absolute truth or error.[18]

Aristotle's Logic, or The Organon

There are a considerable number of Greek sages and philosophers, such as Socrates, Plato, and Pythagoras, whose thought has had lasting effects on the human experience down the ages. However, of all Greek philosophers and thinkers, Aristotle (384-322 BC) may well be the most mature, and the one who has most profoundly influenced Western thought and human thought overall, especially with respect to the development of methods of research and investigation in philosophy and the sciences.

Aristotle's contributions span a wide variety of fields, including ontology, ethics, politics, natural science, and metaphysics. All of Aristotle's works were marked by a peculiar manner of reasoning which came later to be known as Aristotelian logic, and which rests fundamentally on the method of analogical reasoning. Some researchers maintain that Aristotle's legacy has been badly misunderstood by its expositors, whose critics accuse them of having neglected Aristotle's interest in induction and empirical observation. Nevertheless, the impact left by Aristotelian studies is such that "reading Aristotle is tantamount to gaining an understanding and awareness of the foundation of Western thought in its entirety."[19]

The six treatises of Aristotle dealing with method and logic have been gathered into a single book known as the *Organon*. The six treatises contained in Aristotle's *Organon* are: "Categories," "On Interpretation," "Prior Analytics," "Posterior Analytics," "Topics," and "On Sophistical Refutations."[20] The Greek word *organon* means "organ, instrument or tool"; hence, the title of this work, which deals with instruments or tools of thought which serve to protect reason from error. In his introduction to *The Basic Works of Aristotle*, editor Richard McKeon states:

> The influence of Aristotle, in the first sense as initiating a tradition, has been continuous from his day to the present, for his philosophy contains the first statement...of many of the technical distinctions, definitions, and convictions on which later philosophy and science have been based....Much of the history of civilization in the West can be, and indeed has been, written in the form of a debate in which the triumph of Aristotle in the thirteenth century and the defeat of Aristotle in the Renaissance indifferently herald great intellectual advances.[21]

Abd al-Rahman Badawi notes that the Arabs became familiar with Aristotle exclusively through his *Organon*, as a result of which "they grew accustomed to referring to him simply as 'the master of logic.'"[22]

The European Cultural Hiatus and the Emergence of Islam

The Roman Empire fell heir to the rich intellectual, rhetorical and philosophical legacy of the Greeks. However, the Romans became preoccupied with military adventures both within and without Europe's borders, thereby plunging Europe into a phase of intellectual and cultural decay. This decay accelerated after 285 CE, at which time the Roman state was partitioned into a Western Roman Empire and an Eastern (Byzantine) Roman Empire under Diocletian. Rulers of both Eastern and Western empires instated dictatorial feudal regimes; nor did Christianity's entrance onto the European scene do anything to improve matters, since both rulers and nobility allied themselves with the Church, while the Church adopted Aristotelian logic in its interpretation of religious texts. Research and rational exchange accordingly ground to a halt, and Europe drifted into a sound cultural slumber.

This same period of time witnessed the birth of Islam, which created a stable society which occupied the Levant, Iraq, Persia and Egypt, regions that had previously been home to ancient civilizations. Islam was marked by a positive attitude toward reason and the pursuit of knowledge, stressing the importance of reflection on the created universe and the laws and patterns established by the Creator in objects, events, and natural, psychological and social phenomena. Muslim scholars benefited from the new spirit of liberation in the realms of research and discovery, and drew on existing knowledge by familiarizing themselves with the sciences established by their predecessors from India, Persia and Greece. Most of the Greek legacy was translated into Arabic, and schools and universities were founded [in the Arab-Muslim world]. Europe awakened in the midst of this cultural advance, which had reached it via a variety of channels, including direct contact with the Arab-Muslim world during the Crusades, and cultural exchange in Sicily and Andalusia. Europeans began acquainting themselves with the ancient Greeks' contributions by reading Arabic and Syriac translations of their works. In consequence, they became aware of the methodological developments related to induction and experimentation undertaken by Muslim scholars, particularly in the fields of astronomy, geometry and mathematics. This new awareness contributed significantly to subsequent religious reform movements, and served as a powerful impetus toward more research and experimentation by scholars and scientists. Despite the fierce resistance with which renewal and reform movements were met in Europe's Middle Ages, European societies began in the sixteenth century to witness major achievements in the realm of scientific discovery and industrialization. Such achievements enabled the Europeans to acquire forms of power and mobility which they quickly put to use in colonizing most of the old world (Africa, Asia and Europe) in addition to the discovery and occupation of the Americas.

As will be seen shortly, the history of Europe witnessed a number of important way stations in the evolution of methods in Western thought, including the efforts of thinkers such as Francis Bacon, René Descartes, Augustus Comte, Emile Durkheim, and the post-modernist movements.

Francis Bacon and the New Organon

Francis Bacon (1561-1626 CE) was an English philosopher who lived during a period of Europe's history in which the Greek philosophy founded upon debate and abstract thought was prevalent. During this period numerous scientific discoveries and inventions were made. These include William Harvey's (1578-1657) discovery of the circulatory system, Robert Boyle's (1627-1691) experiments with air pumps, William Gilbert's (1544-1602) experiments in magnetism, the invention of typing, the compass and the rifle, etc. This intellectual atmosphere so strongly committed to the use of scientific and technical tools, as well as the vast variety of experiments being performed on nature, had the effect of moving Bacon decisively away from metaphysics and toward the pursuit of a scientific knowledge that would contribute to the control and domination of nature through the use of the scientific method based on practical experimentation and problem solving. Bacon took the title for his book *The New Organon: or True Directions for the Interpretation of Nature* from Aristotle's *The Organon: The Instrument for Rational Thinking.*

Bacon stressed the need for the progression of science at a time when Aristotle's logic was proving woefully inadequate to this task in the new era. Consequently, *The New Organon* proposed a system of thought that went beyond that of Aristotle, and which was better suited to the progression of knowledge in the scientific era. Where Aristotle's system of argumentation relied on analogical reasoning and was capable of deriving consistent outcomes logically from basic premises, Bacon's logic was designed to inquire into the basic premises themselves. And whereas Aristotle's logic presupposed certainty by relying upon non-negotiable assumptions whose validity could not be questioned, Bacon proposed an inductive system of argumentation that relied on inquiry into the basic evidence found in the natural world. In Bacon's system, the researcher into the sciences gradually moved from basic data which he had compiled by dint of ongoing effort through the use of "the new organ" toward higher levels of probability.[23]

Bacon severely criticized Aristotelian syllogisms, which had led to intellectual stagnation and hindered scientific progress by restricting scientists' freedom to engage in fresh, creative research. In Bacon's system, the process of scientific logic begins with induction and scientific experimentation by means of which the facts are discovered. It then goes on to trace these facts back to universal principles through the use of Aristotelian logic. The facts are then recorded and conveyed to others through the use of explanatory methods and techniques.

Bacon's logic is divided into two parts. The first part, which is negative, undertakes to deconstruct "illusions" which "block men's minds," preventing them from arriving at the truth. So attached are people to these illusions and so influential are they over their thinking that Bacon refers to them as "idols," of which he identifies four kinds, namely, "idols of the tribe," "idols of the cave," "idols of the marketplace" and "idols of the theatre."[24] The second part, which is positive, is a new system capable of discovering the facts as they are. It is a system based on induction, scientific experimentation, and its applications to a number of research topics such as heat, motion, light, scents, power, and others.

René Descartes and his Discourse on Method

René Descartes (1596-1650 CE) was a French philosopher who had been educated in a number of different European countries at a time when the system of logic founded on the Aristotelian syllogism held sway over thought in Europe's religious establishment. So attached was the Church to the Aristotelian system that it would prosecute any scholar who dared to cast doubt on the theories supported by Aristotelian logic, including theories that were purely scientific in nature. Descartes was not satisfied with the Aristotelian education he had received in school, and felt that the knowledge he had acquired lacked consistency and certainty. He noticed that of all the sciences he had studied, mathematics alone was characterized by certainty and precision, and he began wondering how he might develop sciences that were as consistent, unified, and certain as mathematics.

Descartes felt powerless and frustrated due to his inability to formulate a new intellectual scheme that would serve as a solid foundation for all of the sciences. Despite his orderly vision and his earnest striving, he despaired of achieving the goal he had set for himself. Nevertheless, after years of hopelessness, confusion and raucous living, he decided to give up his various preoccupations in life and devote himself entirely to accomplishing the task he had envisioned. He then proceeded to write his *Discourse on Method and Meditations on First Philosophy*.[25] The book consisted of six parts. Part I dealt with a number of considerations relating to philosophy, religion, and the sciences. Part I treated the principles and foundations of the method the author had set out to formulate. Part III treated certain ethical rules derived from his method. Part IV set out to prove the existence of God and the human spirit. Part V was devoted to questions of physics, the movement of the heart, and certain issues relating to medicine and the difference between human beings and animals. And Part VI discussed the requirements of achieving progress in research into nature, and the reasons he had decided to write his book.

In Descartes' view, the Aristotelian method based on syllogisms was incapable of generating new knowledge and, therefore, fruitless. At the same time, Descartes held that experimental induction which relies on sensory experience, and which Francis Bacon had formulated as an alternative to Aristotelian logic, would not lead to coherent, certain knowledge. As for the method which Descartes formulated, it began with doubting the validity of people's beliefs, which consist in mere illusions to which they cling by virtue of what they have grown accustomed to without serious consideration, and by virtue of their unthinking imitation of others. He stated, "I learned not to believe anything too firmly of which I had been persuaded only by example and custom; and thus I little by little freed myself from many errors that can darken our natural light and render us less able to listen to reason."[26]

Descartes' method is based on four principles. The first principle is never to accept as true anything that one does not know to be such, and to avoid biased or hasty judgments. In addition, one should make certain that there is no reason to doubt something's truth or validity. The second principle is to divide each difficulty into as many parts as possible so as to facilitate its resolution. The third principle is to conduct one's thoughts in an orderly fashion, beginning with those objects that are simpler and easier to know "in order to ascend little by little, as by degrees, to the knowledge of the most composite things." And the fourth principle is to go back and make certain that there is no aspect of the difficulty concerned that one has failed to make note of and investigate.[27]

Comte, Descartes and the Positivist Method

Despite the fact that the eighteenth and nineteenth centuries were largely colored by scientific discoveries relating to matter and nature, this period of history also witnessed major developments in the establishment of the social and human sciences, whose pioneers attempted to apply the experimental scientific method to the social sciences. French philosopher August Comte (1798-1857) is credited in the West with founding the discipline of sociology as well as the doctrine of positivism, which rejects all supernatural and metaphysical dimensions. Positivism reinterprets the evolution of human thought and the search for truth in keeping with the "law of three stages." These three stages are: (1) the theological, (2) the metaphysical, and (3) the positive. In the theological stage, religious thought develops from idol worship, to polytheism, to monotheism. In this stage, human reason is dependent on superstitious and mythological interpretations. In the metaphysical stage, which is more mature than the theological stage, reason seeks explanations in abstract or symbolic forces. In the third, positive stage, human reason does not ask why phenomena occur; rather, it asks how they occur with reliance upon the precise description of "objective" events and cases through which it can discern relationships and derive scientific laws that explain all phenomena, natural and social alike.

No less important to the formulation of positivism was the contribution of Émile Durkheim (1858-1917 CE), who, in his book entitled *Rules of Sociological Method*, argued that sociology is a discipline which is subject to the positive method just as other sciences are. Durkheim formulated the science of socialism on the basis of three assumptions. The first assumption is the unity of nature, the second is that social phenomena are part of the objective world of nature, and the third is that these phenomena are subject to natural laws and principles and can therefore be studied in accordance with the scientific method based on induction and experimentation.[28]

Modernism and Post-Modernism

Between the Age of Enlightenment (beginning in the mid-seventeenth century) and the mid-twentieth century, the Western world passed through a historical phase in which a set of beliefs, customs, attitudes and intellectual orientations now referred to as "Modernist" held primary sway. This Modernist period was marked by an absolute confidence in the powers of human reason, and the clear emergence of scientific and technological progress. Western society and culture were largely colored by secularism during this period, with the Christian religion losing confidence in its ability to cope with the real world's day-to-day challenges. Three forms a new religion thus began to emerge. The first of these was faith in a creator God who has nothing to do with the affairs of the universe He made. The second was an individualist piety accompanied, in a rather schizophrenic manner, by intense interest in worldly affairs. And the third was a kind of defensive isolation. These phenomena taken together yielded a situation in which the religious dimension of life in Western society reached a very low ebb.[29]

Some modernist intellectual trends and schools of thought turned into philosophical frameworks and worldviews that gave rise to specific research methods. Scientific rationalism, which emerged in the seventeenth century and took a leading role in the eighteenth century, supplanted metaphysics and religion. Scientific rationalism formulated a secular positivistic philosophy that touted the unlimited potentials of science and the scientific method and human beings' ability to achieve total control over nature. Scientism[30] became a cult of sorts with all the features of a religious sect. Such currents gained additional strength with the transformation of the theory of biological evolution into a philosophical school that proclaimed the continuation of human evolution and progress in a never-ending upward trajectory. Among the dangers of this school of thought was that it justified ethnocentrism and saw war as a law of social life justified by natural forces rather than being a result of people's choices.

Yet even with their rosy optimism, these intellectual currents could not prevent currents of another sort from making their appearance on the European stage. Hence, the eighteenth and nineteenth centuries witnessed the emergence of pessimistic thought trends whose adherents believed that scientific progress had created a bourgeois ideology that had robbed people of certain aspects of their humanity by exalting reason and neglecting intuition, sentiment and emotion. Rationalism thus triggered a backlash in the form of Romanticism, which in turn led to the emergence of psychoanalysis with its emphasis on the subconscious. Marxism erupted in partial response to Capitalism, Nietzsche brought nihilism, Sartre brought existentialism, and Oswald Spengler launched an assault on Eurocentrism, declaring that European civilization would collapse just as civilizations before it had done.

Exercise

Design a chart showing the various stages of the evolution of methodology in Western thought and their intellectual premises.

The spirit of pessimism developed into "ascientific" methods and approaches that purported to represent "the new science" as an alternative to the science associated with modernism. This "new science" has found expression in a variety of currents, schools of thought and methods, all of which fall under the rubric of what has come to be known as "postmodernism." Postmodern thought trends reflect a shared belief that the modernist enterprise suffered from serious defects. Some pioneers of postmodernism focus on the philosophical priority given by modernism to reason centered around the self; others focus on critiques of its moral relativism, while still others highlight the harmful effects of the rationalism that led scientific and technological progress. Academic circles over the past several decades have observed a host of research methods in the humanities, and particularly in the field of sociology, associated with postmodernist philosophical currents such as structuralism, hermeneutics, deconstructionism, formalism, phenomenology, and others.

Third: THE RELATIONSHIP BETWEEN THE CONCEPT OF METHODOLOGY AND THE EVOLUTION OF SCIENTIFIC FIELDS IN ISLAMIC AND WESTERN HISTORY

The concept of methodology in the history of Western thought has been linked primarily to the natural sciences, whereas in the history of

Islamic thought it has been linked for the most part with the sciences dealing with divine revelation. In the West, science has been viewed primarily as a discipline that examines natural substances and phenomena, while the method used by scientists was the scientific method, or more specifically, the experimental scientific method. Most Western historians of science hold that experimental science began in Europe, where it grew and evolved before spreading to North America. It was this science that led to the West's being the geographical locus of the industrial, technological and information revolutions. Nevertheless, one does find historians of science who give credit to other peoples, particularly in the Eastern world, which witnessed the birth of civilizations whose impact on the evolution of the natural sciences would be difficult to ignore. Yet despite this acknowledgment, the discussion remains restricted to the history of the natural sciences alone.

From the Islamic perspective, by contrast, the concept of science has to do with the evolution of human perceptive capacities in all areas of life, including the material, the social, the psychological and the spiritual. The authoritative point of reference for this perspective is the divine revelation, which relates chapters from the story of humankind's evolution in its earliest stages. These chapters make clear that from the time when human beings were first created they have been equipped with the capacity for reflection, thought, and experimentation. In keeping with the divine wisdom, human beings have also been equipped with the understanding and knowledge they need in order to function as God's *khalīfah* on earth. God declares, "Yea, indeed, [O men,] We have given you a [bountiful] place on earth, and appointed thereon means of livelihood for you: [yet] how seldom are you grateful!" (*sūrah al-Aʿrāf* 7:10). God in His wisdom has subjected the earth and everything in and around it to His dominion. As a result, cosmic phenomena take place in an orderly fashion. The laws that govern such phenomena are orderly as well, a fact which makes it easier for human beings to discover them and put them to use. We read in the Qur'an that, "And He has made subservient to you, [as a gift] from Himself, all that is in the heavens and on earth; in this, behold, there are messages indeed for people who think!" (*sūrah al-Jāthiyyah* 45:13). The ability to perceive these realities is a God-given capacity. However, this capacity has grown and developed thanks to the guidance and instruction brought by the prophets, as well as human experience in dealing with and perceiving the links between objects, events, and phenomena in their material, social and psychological dimensions.

One of the first scenes in the story of human beings' creation is the one in which God teaches Adam the names of things, a process by virtue of which Adam is shown to have been given preference over the angels themselves: "And He imparted unto Adam the names of all things; then He brought them within the ken of the angels and said: 'Declare unto Me the names of these [things], if what you say is true'" (*sūrah al-Baqarah* 2:31).[31] Another situation in which direct instruction took place was the one in which God sent a crow to teach Adam's son through a practical demonstration: "Thereupon God sent forth a raven which scratched the earth, to show him how he might conceal the nakedness of his brother's body..." (*sūrah al-Mā'idah* 5:31). Another instructional situation is found in the story about Noah's building of the ark. It was God who taught Noah the scientific principles necessary for the completion of this task, as well as their practical applications. Then Noah carried out the task under God's direct supervision. God said to Noah, "but build, under Our eyes and according to Our inspiration, the ark [that shall save thee and those who follow thee];..." (*sūrah Hūd* 11:37). It was God Almighty who showed Abraham the kingdom of the heavens and the earth as he looked about and observed natural phenomena. God says, "And thus We gave Abraham [his first] insight into [God's] mighty dominion over the heavens and the earth – and [this] to the end that he might become one of those who are inwardly sure" (*sūrah al-Anʿām* 6:75). After granting Abraham this insight and guidance, God commanded him to build in Makkah the first edifice that had ever been constructed on earth for the worship of the one God.

Since the days of Adam, individuals have needed a relatively long time to reach maturity and become capable of bearing responsibility. During this period of instruction and growth, the individual makes use of his God-given instruments of hearing and sight, mind and heart. The data, information, and experiences received via the senses then become the subject of contemplation and reflection. Language, for example, is acquired gradually through a kind of osmosis from the social environment in which the individual lives. Language thus becomes the individual's natural means of communicating with others in his social milieu. No one who has lived his or her entire life in an environment devoid of linguistic interaction with human beings will be able to acquire language, a fact which has been demonstrated through documented cases of children who have grown up in isolation from other human beings.[32] Similarly, there is evidence to confirm that twins who have been raised in separate environments have acquired different languages, customs, and religions.[33]

As the first, newly created human being, Adam had no opportunity to learn things gradually and by osmosis, as it were. Nor was he a child who would need to spend time being prepared to understand the meanings of events and phenomena. Rather, he had been created as a fully developed adult who was capable of understanding and perceiving, and God Almighty had provided him with the knowledge he would need in compensation for what he lacked by way of family and community. Perhaps this is part of the meaning of God's statement that He "imparted unto Adam the names of all things..." (*sūrah al-Baqarah* 2:31).

> Numerous layers of meaning are conveyed by God's statement that He "imparted unto Adam the names of all things."

Religious texts that speak about the origins of humanity testify that from the time when human beings were created they were capable of learning, and that whenever they lost their way or forgot what they had learned, God Almighty would send them messengers and prophets to carry on with the process of instruction and reminder. What we know of human history and the evolution of civilization bears witness to this process. Meanwhile, individuals are born without any type of knowledge whatsoever, after which they begin instinctively at an early age to record the impressions gleaned from hearing, sight, taste, touch, and smell. These impressions and expressions are then organized into what we might describe as realization and consciousness. Unlike other creatures, human beings are able to communicate about their experiences through speech and to record them in a variety of ways, thereby enabling them to pass them from one individual to another, from one generation to another, and from one people or nation to another. It is in this way that cultures and civilizations are formed and perpetuated.

Our God-given instincts, propensities and faculties combine with both the inborn and acquired use of the tools of consciousness and understanding (such as the sense of hearing, sight, and intelligence) to construct methods of thought, research and practice that can help us find answers to our questions and, in so doing, influence our decisions and behavior. Methodology is certainly no newcomer to the human scene; on the contrary, it comes naturally to human beings as entities created purposefully by God and appointed to be God's *khalīfah* on earth. Methodology is a cognitive process peculiar to rational beings, and a practice which is necessary for the continuation of life in all its dimensions.

Methodology in the thought and life of humankind
- a natural instincts,
- a rational property,
- and a practical necessity.

Methodology is a historically recognized phenomenon of which we have written records. Such records bear witness to the ways in which the ancients of various civilizations dealt with the worlds of things, people, and ideas. The remnants of ancient civilizations in China, India, the Fertile Crescent, Pharaonic Egypt, and South America testify to remarkable degrees of development in mathematics, geometry, astronomy, architecture, agriculture, medicine, mining, and the manufacture of tools and instruments required for observation, arithmetical calculations, time measurements, medical treatment, excavation, inscriptions, drawing, and other undertakings that would be easily recognizable to historical museum goers.

Our purpose in linking the concept of methodology with the evolution of the various sciences has been to show that in the sphere of human endeavor, it is difficult to distinguish one realm that is natural and material, a second that is social and human, and still another that is spiritual, psychic and emotional. Indeed, the individual human being is a composite entity composed of reason or mind, spirit, and body, while human populations consist of networks of relationships involving cooperation among families, tribes, peoples, societies and states for the purpose of providing life's necessities such as food, clothing and shelter. Such necessities led to the invention of tools for agriculture, industry, trade, transportation and communication. Such tools were then developed and improved from one age to the next thanks to the combined efforts of scientists from a variety of specializations.

In sum, methodology did not simply spring up suddenly in the context of modern civilizations; nor is it the exclusive product of a particular community or people or a particular era. Every community and nation is entitled to search in its history for the ways in which it has contributed to the development of science and civilization, and to take pride in these contributions. However, it should not, in the process, gainsay the equally significant contributions made by other communities or nations.

CONCLUSION

Every discovery undoubtedly leads in some way or other to those that succeed it, just as later discoveries are dependent on those that preceded them. In fact, all experiences, even negative ones, have some value in guiding human thought toward that what more beneficial and closer to the achievement of its aims.

Nevertheless, the history of humankind has had its ups and downs, and human civilizations have differed from place to place and era to era. Although the divine providence has provided us with apostles and prophets to guide us and draw us away from many a deadly precipice, we have quickly forgotten what we were taught, and lost our way anew. For not long after a prophet leads his people to the worship of the one true God and to the establishment of a society founded on the principles of justice and virtue, you find them drawing pictures of their prophet and chiseling idols in his image to remind themselves of what he did for them. Then they forget the prophet himself and the idol remains. Common sense might lead us to realize the impotence of our idols and the absurdity of worshipping them in our search for the Deity we have lost sight of during times when no prophet has been sent. Yet we still have no compunctions about representing this Deity in the form of a planet, a river, or a cow!

Magical rites may have been a manifestation of the mythical, metaphysical stage of this or that people's evolution. However, we still see peoples in the present day who celebrate rites no less magical, albeit with the use of tools and gadgets proper to the twenty-first century – satellite channels, websites, newspapers and forums. The peoples of the world have not followed the same path in their various communities and environments. In fact, even within the same community you find some individuals, groups and classes adhering to one way of thinking, while other individuals, groups and classes adhere to a way of thinking that differs entirely. Similarly, we might see a member of a modern-day community practice his or her profession in a perfectly orderly and scientific manner only to find that when he goes home, he believes in the same groundless superstitions that prevail in the rest of his community.

Human knowledge originated as a gift from God Almighty by means of which God distinguished human beings from other creatures. When God "imparted unto Adam the names of all things," He gave him the ability to acquire knowledge from its two sources (divine revelation and the created universe) by means of its two instruments (reason and sensory perception). Some writers portray the evolution of research methods as a steadily upward progression. However, the truth is that in every stage of their evolution, human beings have used a variety of methods and means of acquiring knowledge. Adam's first son received some knowledge directly from his father, who in turn had received knowledge from God Almighty. Yet, when he killed his brother, he did not know what to do with him. In this situation, a raven taught him by example how he needed to comport himself in that situation: "...[And Cain] cried out, 'Oh, woe is me! Am I then too weak to do what this raven did, and to conceal the nakedness of my brother's body?' – and was thereupon smitten with remorse" (*sūrah al-Mā'idah* 5:31).

The nations of the world make use of the knowledge available to them in proportion to the degree of advancement they enjoy. When a nation is in a state of backwardness, it fails to realize the value of the cultural heritage it possesses, and is thus unable to employ it to its best advantage. This is the situation in which Europe found itself during its Dark Ages (approximately 500-1000 CE) following the collapse of the Roman Empire both East and West. The nations of Europe failed to see the value of the rich Greek heritage to which they had fallen heir in the fields of medicine, mathematics, philosophy, geometry, literature and poetry. When, by contrast, the Muslims found themselves in a position of cultural ascendency, they saw the value of what they had at their disposal, as well as the knowledge possessed at that time by the Europeans, Indians and others. Hence, they quickly set about to transfer this knowledge to themselves through translation and other means. They sifted through the scientific works that had come into their possession, bringing things to light, editing the texts in their possession, accepting some things and rejecting others, developing and modernizing. When, on the other hand, the Muslims found themselves in a state of backwardness, they were unable to make use of the legacy they had received from their forebears, and failed properly to appreciate the value of the achievements their scholars had made in earlier times. Later, when fortunes changed and Europe has its awakening, the European nations realized the value of the Greek heritage the Muslims had given humanity through their efforts. They also discovered the pioneering developments the Muslims had achieved in the various scientific disciplines, whereas the Muslims themselves were unable to make use of these very same achievements during the time of their own backwardness.

Therefore, it comes as no surprise to find that some of the Muslims' greatest achievements have come to our knowledge through Westerners' discoveries of them. One major Muslim figure whose importance has been brought to light by the West is Ibn al-Haytham (d. 432 AH/1040 CE), who is known to have written upwards of two hundred books in various scientific fields. He is also known for his precise and thorough formulation of the experimental scientific method based on observation, experimentation and proof. Another is Ibn Khaldūn

(d. 808 AH/1406 CE), a pioneering thinker who provided us with crucial keys to the social sciences as they relate to politics, the economy, development, education and psychology. Ibn Khaldūn's greatest contribution in the area of research methodology and ways of thinking lies in his emphasis on the importance of practical, concrete experience (empiricism) for acquiring an understanding of the defining characteristics of things, social laws, and principles of causality.

However, as was pointed out earlier, a comparison between Muslims' own critiques of the Prophetic Sunnah and those undertaken by Orientalists who have attempted to study the hadiths reveals a fundamental, and essentially irreconcilable, difference in approach or method, with the Islamic method being founded upon religious faith, and the Western method being based on a secular, materialist critique of history.[34]

5

Schools of Islamic Methodology

GOALS OF THIS CHAPTER

1. To distinguish between (*wāḥid*) or unitary perspective (one method working at a time) and (*tawḥīdī*) or unifying perspective (several methods working at a time)of Islamic methodology.
2. To demonstrate the importance of *tawḥīdī* methodology for integrating and uniting the various levels of methodological work, from thought about research, to research procedures and regulatory guidelines.
3. To identify the most significant defining characteristics of a number of methodological schools: the rationalist, the mystical, the empirical-scientific, and the juristic-*uṣūlī*.[1]
4. To draw attention to the variety that exists within each of the Islamic methodological schools.
5. To clarify the developmental features of a number of methodological schools in Islamic history.
6. To cite examples of scholars and thinkers representative of each of the Islamic methodological schools.

INTRODUCTION

The basic thrust of this chapter is that Islamic methodology encompasses a number of different approaches and areas of interest which, despite their diversity, are united by the premises that underlie their modes of thought, research, and conduct. It is these shared premises which they appeal to in their efforts to achieve their aims, and which mark their various expressions and formulations.

When we speak in this chapter of "methodological schools," we are referring to the variety of expressions and approaches that exist within the broader framework of Islamic methodology. Islamic methodology, that is, "the methodology of epistemological integration," has taken the form of numerous methodological schools over the course of Islamic history. These schools include, first, the "methodology of reception" that emerged during the lifetime of the Prophet and the methodology of criticism and documentation that accompanied the recording and codification of the Prophet Sunnah. This latter methodology gave rise to the sciences of contestation and validation (*al-jarḥ wa al-taᶜdīl*), causes (*al-ᶜilal*), and derivation of legal rulings from detailed evidence. This latter science coincided with the emergence of the juristic schools, the principles of jurisprudence, Qur'anic exegetical methods, and approaches to dealing with doctrinal issues, all of which underwent changes with the introduction of theology and philosophy and the Sufis' development of the mystical-experiential approach. It should also be remembered that some groups of scholars adhered to the experimental scientific method when dealing with issues that required such an approach.

Islamic civilization embraced all of these methodological schools. Hence, when a Muslim scholar was dealing with a given topic, he would make use of whichever method was required, and in most cases he would combine more than one method. It was, in fact, quite common in many phases of Islamic history for a scholar to acquire encyclopedic knowledge, being well-versed in numerous disciplines. A single scholar might simultaneously be a jurist, an expert in the principles of Islamic jurisprudence, and a hadith scholar as were Imam Mālik and al-Shawkānī. He might be a Qur'anic exegete, a philosopher and a physician as were Abū Bakr al-Rāzī and Ibn Sīnā (Avicenna), a philosopher and a Sufi as were Ibn ᶜArabī, Ibn Ṭufayl and al-Suhrawardī, or a jurist, a theologian and a Sufi as was Abū Ḥāmid al-Ghazālī. Other examples include Abū Ḥayyān al-Tawḥīdī, who was litterateur, philosopher, and Sufi; Al-Ḥasan ibn al-Haytham, who was philosopher, mathematician, and physicist; Ibn Zuhr, who served at once as physician and philosopher, and Ibn Ḥazm, who was jurist, theologian and litterateur. Similarly, Imam al-Ṭabarī combined a knowledge of history, exegesis, and jurisprudence, while Jābir ibn Ḥayyān was both chemist and philosopher.

First: METHOD AS SEEN FROM A UNITARY PERSPECTIVE VS. A UNIFYING PERSPECTIVE

We have drawn a distinction elsewhere between what we term a "one-dimensional discourse" that spurns the type of approach advocated by an Islamic methodology of epistemological integration, and a "monotheistic discourse" which encompasses various forms of reasoned interpretation and methods of investigation, and which aims, in an integrated fashion, to advance the Muslim community toward needed reform.[2] What we have sought to show is that as long as such a discourse proceeds from fixed principles while aiming for the achievement of comprehensive objectives and promoting an open mind and sincere intentions, there is no harm in accommodating various forms of reasoned interpretation and approach, particularly if ample opportunity is given for cooperation and integration, and if these processes involve the review and evaluation of expertise and experience.

At this point we would like to digress slightly in order to build on the notion of a distinction between one-dimensional discourse and *tawḥīdī* discourse. This will be done by means of a distinction between what we are terming a "unitary view" and a "unifying view" of method and approach as they apply to methodological schools.

By "unitary view" we mean a vision according to which at any given time, there is only one approach to thought and research in relation to a given issue, question, or aspect of reality in the natural, social or human spheres. Seen from this perspective, human thought has evolved in a linear fashion, passing out of one phase and into another in such a way that in any given phase of their evolution, human beings have been adopting one approach only and no other. August Comte's three-stage theory of human thought might be viewed as an expression of the unitary vision, since it holds that human beings have passed through three successive stages: the religious-theological phase, the philosophical-metaphysical phase, and the positivist-scientific phase, the last of which represents the arrival of human thought at genuine maturity through the discovery of the scientific experimental method. According to Comte's theory, each stage in the evolution of human thought has been marked by the use of a single approach or method and no other such that when they pass from one stage to the next, they leave behind the single method that characterized the previous stage of their development and replace it with another.

Many scholars and scientists over the past two hundred years have held that the question of how to acquire, test, and employ knowledge has been settled definitively in favor of the scientific experimental method. This method has proved highly effective in enabling us to become acquainted with material objects, natural phenomena and their defining properties, and to discover the laws that govern their composition and conduct. Given its success, the scientific method with its tools and procedures has come to be applied to the topics of social, human, and psychological phenomena as well. The predominant view has been that scientific research is the act of investigating a topic through the use of "the scientific method," and that the scientific method is, to be specific, "the experimental scientific method." It has been generally believed that scientific method or methodology cannot be described in ideological terms. One cannot speak, for example, of an "Eastern" or "Western" scientific methodology. Nor can one speak of a "positivist" or an "Islamic" scientific methodology, the reason being that to add such descriptors to the term "scientific methodology" would be inconsistent with the objectivity and neutrality of those who engage in research in keeping with the scientific method.

However, this view is countered by the Qur'an's own view of method. The Arabic term being rendered here as "method" (*minhāj*) occurs once in the Qur'an, where we read:

> And unto thee [O Prophet] have We vouchsafed this divine writ, setting forth the truth, confirming the truth of whatever there still remains of earlier revelations and determining what is true therein. Judge, then, between the followers of earlier revelation in accordance with what God has bestowed from on high, and do not follow their errant views, forsaking the truth that has come unto thee. Unto every one of you have We appointed a [different] law (*shirʿah*) and way of life (*minhāj*). And if God had so willed, He could surely have made you all one single community:

> but [He willed it otherwise] in order to test you by means of what He has vouchsafed unto you. Vie, then, with one another in doing good works! Unto God you all must return; and then He will make you truly understand all that on which you were wont to differ. (*Sūrah al-Mā'idah* 5:48)

The context of this verse speaks about the nations of the prophets who went before us, affirming that the single religion brought by all of the prophets entailed a different law (*shirʿah*) for each nation. The laws specific to the world's nations share some rulings in common while differing in others. Given that this verse allows for a variety of different laws, it likewise allows for a variety of methods and approaches. It follows, therefore, that we can speak legitimately of an "Islamic method" (*minhāj islāmī*) or an "Islamic methodology" (*manhajiyyah islāmiyyah*). Moreover, within the context of this or that method, there is room for different understandings of the means and tools to be employed in research. All such tools and means are united overall by virtue of their association with Islamic methodology even though they differ in certain details.

Therefore, the researcher who adopts the concept of "*tawḥīdī* methodology" is free to use numerous different methods in his or her attempts to manage the affairs of his life, be they theoretical-scientific or practical in nature, depending on the nature of the topic being investigated and the specific circumstances that impact his or her interactions with the topic, including chronological age, knowledge of the subject, experience in life, and his or her need to look into the topic concerned. The researcher will employ each of these various methods for the purpose it is best suited to achieve, without forgetting that there are other methods that he or she could also use at another time or in another situation. This practice is consistent with the notion of a multiplicity of approaches which we are terming "methodological pluralism." Nor should a researcher forget to combine methods depending on the specific roles they perform. In so doing, the researcher unites different methodological elements and procedures in an integral, self-consistent endeavor to reach his stated aim. This, in sum, is *tawḥīdī* methodology.

The notion of methodological schools occupies a central place in the methodology of epistemological integration, since a discussion of methodological schools will include the notions of plurality, integration and the divine unity as they apply to methods or approaches as opposed to the notion of a single approach. Hence, method in the Islamic vision may be described as "*tawḥīdī*," but not as "unitary."

The term "multiplicity" as it applies to method and methodology refers to the use of whatever methodological methods and techniques will meet the needs represented by the topics and issues calling for investigation, as well as varied research requirements on the level of data, tools, and methods of organization and analysis.

The term "integration" refers to the need in research situations for elements that may belong to numerous distinct approaches. For example, research may present the need for both quantitative and qualitative data, both statistical analysis and inductive thought, both the formation and testing of hypotheses, both induction and deduction (which represent complementary parts of the reasoning process), both descriptive reports of facts and features and normative values and aims, and so on.

As for *tawḥīdī*, it means directing research efforts, which are characterized by multiple elements and integrated functions, toward achievement of the ultimate aim of the research, with every step and phase of the research being connected to every other.

The notion of a unitary methodology, which exalted the experimental scientific method exclusively, remained in the ascendancy throughout the eighteenth and nineteenth centuries. Beginning in the twentieth century, however, it became apparent that the experimental scientific method would be incapable of answering certain questions of a purely scientific nature. The prestige of this method was accordingly undermined, while its positivist philosophical foundations came in for criticism and sometimes outright attacks. Some critics of the empirical scientific method held that it was unsuitable for application to the humanities and the social sciences because of the radical differences between natural and social phenomena, while others argued that the scientific and technological progress that had resulted from the scientific method had produced a materialistic culture founded on rivalry and conflict among individuals while fostering competition among states for influence, power and wealth. Such developments, these critics held, had led to the most destructive wars in human history, environmental degradation, the rise of tyrannical regimes, and a widening gap between social classes and their standards of living.

> After a period of dominance, the notion of a unitary methodology in the West gave way to the notion of a dual methodology, which was supplanted in turn by the notion of integrative methodology.

Rejection of such outcomes contributed to the emergence of the post-modernist philosophies, which developed approaches that were critical of the modernist notions that had relied on the empirical scientific method. The post-modernist approaches revealed the incoherence of the philosophical foundations underlying the empirical scientific method while advocating alternative methods.

In illustration of the notion of methodological integration, we find that the empirical scientific method, whether it was applied to the natural sciences or the humanities, relied until quite recently upon quantitative data which was organized into tables and charts and subjected to statistical analysis. The aim of this process was to arrive at results that could be interpreted based on statistical tests or quantitative descriptions. The value of a given piece of research was measured in terms of the quantitative data it presented and the complexity of its modes of statistical analysis together with the degree of stability, objectivity, and validity that characterized the numerical data. Toward the end of the twentieth century, however, the statistical results of research on social and human issues came in for attack, particularly when these results were not supported by qualitative descriptive data that provided higher levels of validity and significance than the results of statistical analysis. Researchers then began employing methods that relied on qualitative description rather than mere quantification of the relevant features of the research topic. In addition, professional associations promoting qualitative research methodology were established along with specialized scientific journals devoted to the dissemination of qualitative research.

However, the ongoing debate over the advantages of quantitative research, which may provide more precise, fixed descriptions, and qualitative research, which tends to provide greater validity and profundity of meaning, led researchers to see that, in fact, both types of research need to be used in specific situations. It had now become apparent that in the wrong situations, neither type of research is of any benefit, and that there are situations in which both quantitative and qualitative research methodologies need to be employed in a single piece of research. This latter situation falls under the rubric of what is termed "mixed research methodology." Indeed, some writings that fall under the rubric of integrated methodology go beyond the entire quantitative-qualitative dichotomy. Hence, although it is most common to say that one's research philosophy is what dictates the methodology one employs, some recent writings reverse this equation, holding, by contrast, that "Philosophy does not determine the research methodology employed. It's the other way round: methodology determines the philosophy you might employ to explain your approach to undertaking research."[3]

Elements of Tawḥīdī Methodology

1. Ways of thinking,
2. Research procedures, and
3. Research ethics.

The *tawḥīdī* methodology we are advocating is not limited to combining or integrating research methods and tools based on research-related procedural requirements. Rather, it goes beyond this to lay the foundations for an approach that unites the three levels of methodological activity, namely, (1) ways of thinking about the research topic, (2) research procedures relating to data collection and analysis and methods of deriving and interpreting results, and (3) research ethics, that is, criteria governing conduct and research activity which call for fairness, integrity and impartiality in one's search for truth.

The monotheistic methodology unifies the researcher's efforts to derive knowledge from its sources: both from the written revelation, which will guide him to the most suitable and reliable methods and techniques; and from the created universe in its natural, social and psychological dimensions. Similarly, it unifies the researcher's use of the tools available for acquiring, testing and employing knowledge, including both reason and sensory reception. The efforts entailed by the *tawḥīdī* methodology include, then: derivation of knowledge from its sources, the use of knowledge-acquisition tools, and integration of these source and tools.

> The effort involved in methodological activity from a *tawḥīdī* perspective has three aspects: (1) derivation of knowledge from its sources, (2) the use of knowledge-acquisition tools, and (3) integration of these source and tools.

The *tawḥīdī* methodology unifies a researcher's vision as it pertains to how he thinks, how he engages in research, and his conduct in the various fields of knowledge and their specializations. We have a multiplicity of fields at our disposal – the Shariʿah sciences, which revolve around the texts of divine revelation; the social and human sciences, which revolve around the changing social, economic, political, and educational conditions of people's lives; the natural and physical sciences, which examine the distinctive properties of natural substances both living and non-living and the transformations they undergo; and the applied sciences, which assist human beings in living their practical lives and providing health care and means of transport and communication. God has either directly revealed these sciences to human beings or provided them with the capacity to acquire them in order to maintain and enhance their earthly existence. This being the case, the *tawḥīdī* view requires human beings to unite their efforts toward the development of such sciences, since whatever is achieved by this or that individual, nation, or community will ultimately impact, whether negatively or positively, on all other individuals, nations and communities.

It is our hope that Muslim researchers and scientists will work together to meet the challenges placed before them by the *tawḥīdī* methodology: by training themselves in this methodology, applying it to their work, promoting it among others and presenting it to the world community at large, which expects Muslims to demonstrate an effective presence on the world scene by making a tangible contribution to constructing and guiding human civilization.

Second: EXAMPLES OF METHODOLOGICAL SCHOOLS

It is difficult to give a precise description of the methodological practices in which Muslim scholars have engaged within the framework of a given school or to place them within clearly definitive categories, since most Muslim scholars in ages past enjoyed some degree of encyclopedic knowledge, combining knowledge from more than one discipline. In addition, they were actively applying the scientific methods that were consistent with both their faith and the variety of fields in which they were versed.

What follows is a description of a number of the methodological schools that have contributed to shaping the thought and research of Muslim scholars in times both ancient and modern.

(1) *The Rationalist-Scholastic-Philosophical School*

We are combining a discussion of scholastic theologians and philosophers given the overlap that has occurred between these two groups of thinkers over the course of Islamic history with respect to both their research topics and their methods. The methodology represented by this school is marked by the important place it gives to human reason, particularly as it relates to questions of belief. Some Muslim scholars, such as al-Kindī (d. 249 AH/873 CE), Ibn Sīnā (d. 429 AH/1037 CE), and al-Birūnī (d. 440 AH/1048 CE), may be said to have demonstrated a greater affinity for Greek philosophy by dealing with religious doctrine through reliance on reason, while others, such as the Muʿtazilites, the Ashʿarites, and the Maturidites, adhered to the methods familiar to juristic scholars, though they differed in the degree to which they favored reason over revelation or vice-versa. There is, in addition, a third group, including Ibn Taymiyyah (a Ḥanbalī), Ibn Rushd (a philosopher), and Ibn Ḥazm (a Ẓāhirī), who formed a special school of their own which sought to combine reason and revelation based on the conviction that there is essentially no contradiction between them and that we should therefore not have to give either of them priority over the other.

Books of traditional Islamic learning are filled with theological and philosophical debates over the relative authority to be assigned to reason and revelation in the methodology one adopts for deriving doctrinal rulings. Some of these debates have been summarized for us by Dr. Hasan al-Shafi'i,[4] who explains how, when arriving at doctrinal rulings, the Prophet's Companions, their immediate successors, and leading early Muslim thinkers such as al-Ḥasan al-Baṣrī, Jaʿfar al-Ṣādiq, Abū Ḥanīfah and al-Thawrī relied first upon the Qur'an and the Sunnah, then on reason and opinion. In other words, they relied on evidence taken at once from revelation and reason, both of which were recognized sources of authority.[5]

The Muʿtazilites raised reason to the level of sole arbiter in matters relating to divinity and prophethood, while giving revelation sole arbiter status in questions relating to the Qur'an and the Sunnah. However, they gave consideration to evidence based on both reason and revelation in relation to questions the answers to which do not serve as a basis for the validation of prophethood or the validity of Islamic legal rulings. Such questions include, for example, whether God is one, whether one must return something one has received as a trust, or whether it is permissible to benefit from or make use of something that will bring no harm to anyone.

The Ashʿarites agreed with the Muʿtazilites on some points and differed with them on others. The Maturidites took a position somewhere between that of the Ashʿarites and the Muʿtazilites. Dr. al-Shafi'i summarizes the issue of rational investigation in its capacity as a path to doctrinal knowledge, saying:

> Most scholastic theologians of both earlier and later periods, particularly the Ashʿarites, the Maturidis and the Muʿtazilites acknowledged that rational evidence is acceptable in relation to questions of doctrine alongside evidence based on received revelation, and that theological insight may be derived from both reason and revelation. Some of them – that is to say, most of the Muʿtazilites and the late Ashʿarites, Maturidis, and Twelver Shi'is – may have gone to extremes in their reliance on rational evidence and their disparagement of the value of evidence based on revelation for theological inquiry.[6]

After explaining the scholastic theologians' various methods, Dr. Shafi'i draws attention to the criticism these methods received from Abū Ḥāmid al-Ghazālī, a Sufi thinker, Abū al-Walīd ibn Rushd, a rationalist philosopher, and Ibn Taymiyyah, a leading Salafi scholar, all of whom preferred to give priority to Qur'anic evidence. All three of these thinkers viewed Qur'anic evidence as being more effective and rationally persuasive, in addition to the fact that it enjoyed greater religious legitimacy than formal theological arguments. Al-Shafi'i advocates basing methodology anew on the Holy Qur'an, not in order for us to adhere to its teachings based on a traditional, unthinking acceptance but, rather, in order for us to subject our reason to a guidance that turns our attention to the signs God has placed both within our own minds and spirits and in the created universe around us. For only in this way will we be released from the shackles of formalistic, superficial evidence and dialectical complexities into new expanses that augur a true flowering of theological studies.

The Holy Qur'an contains hundreds of verses (*āyāt*, or "signs") which instruct us to engage in rational investigation. Not only do they instruct us to use our reason; they even show us how to use it in establishing doctrine, that is, by relying on revelation as a source of knowledge and on reason as a tool. Being itself an authoritative point of reference, the Qur'an demonstrates the role and functions of reason, making it the focal point of discourse and human responsibility without any need for speculative theological schools. Shaykh Abd al-Halim Mahmud is a contemporary scholar who, after having been thoroughly trained in philosophy, theology and Sufism, chose this kind of Qur'anic focus as the means of defining the place and function of reason. Shaykh Abd al-Halim Mahmud explains his position as follows: "We remain dependent on reason until the [divinely revealed] message has been confirmed. For once the true divine revolution has been substantiated, it is absurd and inconsistent with reason itself, true philosophy, or the method adhered to by the pious ancestors, for us to treat anything else as its equal."[7]

Dr. Hasan al-Shafi'i's discussion is especially important for the way in which it traces the evolutionary phases that were witnessed by rational-theological methodology and its branches. These phases were accompanied by some degree of vacillation as the representative scholars of each school reconsidered and developed their schools' respective arguments and the evidence on which they were based. In illustration of this process, al-Shafi'i cites the evolution that occurred in the Ashᶜarite school. Abū al-Ḥasan al-Ashᶜarī (d. 324 AH/935 CE) began by taking a highly reserved position in which he gave approximately equal weight to reason and revelation. However, in his *Kitāb al-Ibānah ᶜan Uṣūl al-Diyānah* (Clarification of the Principles of the Religion), al-Ashᶜarī came out as a "revelationist" who argued against his former Muᶜtazilite colleagues. In his book, *al-Lumaᶜ* ("Flashes"), by contrast, al-Ashᶜarī restored some degree of balance to his thinking by giving more credence to reason. This relative balance of reason and revelation continued in the thought of al-Bāqillānī (d. 402 AH/1011 CE) in his book *Iᶜjāz al-Qur'ān* (The Miraculousness of the Qur'an). However, signs of a methodological evolution in the form of a growing predilection for reason began to emerge in the thought of Abū Bakr ibn Fūrak (d. 406 AH/1015 CE) and ᶜAbd al-Qādir al-Baghdādī (d. 429 AH/1037 CE). It was around this same time that Imām al-Ḥaramayn al-Juwaynī (d. 419 AH/1028 CE) adopted the Muᶜtazilites' tripartite division of theological issues into (1) issues that can be understood through reason alone, (2) issues that can be understood based on revelation alone, and (3) issues that can only be understood based on reason and revelation together. This rationalist trend continued with al-Ghazālī (d. 505 AH/1111 CE), who also accepted the Muᶜtazilites' tripartite division. After al-Ghazālī, the rationalist approach came to dominate Islamic theology in its entirety. This can be seen in the works of al-Shahrastānī (d. 548 AH/1153 CE). Al-Shahrastānī was followed by al-Rāzī (d. 606 AH/1209 CE), who cast further doubt on evidence derived from revelation and detailed his position in a list of eleven points. Al-Rāzī was succeeded by al-Āmidī (d. 631 AH/1233 CE), who, although he agreed with much of what al-Rāzī had to say, concluded that evidence derived from revelation could yield definitive certainty if it was accompanied by supporting evidence, thereby reestablishing a greater relative balance in Ashᶜarite thought.

Ashᶜarite thought began with Abu al-Ḥasan al-Ashᶜarī's break with the Muᶜtazilah school and his restoration of a more prominent role to revelation in theological matters. Over time, however, Ashʿarite thought evolved methodologically into an acceptance of the Muʿtazilites' division of theological questions into three categories depending on the roles played therein by reason and revelation.

An example Dr. al-Shafi'i cites in illustration of the methodological evolution within one subgroup of the scholastic-theological school may give us a clearer picture of the methodological development of this school as a whole. The reason-revelation question had not been an issue of urgent importance during the days of the Prophet's companions and their immediate successors, although a few early examples of the use of reason can be found among the Khawarij. However, the methodological foundations of scholastic theology as a discipline concerned specifically with doctrine and the principles of religion may have become clearer with the emergence of the Muʿtazilites.

Methodological thought manifested itself in Muslims' use of reason to understand and process the texts of revelation – that is, the text of the Qur'an and the Prophetic Sunnah – as well as in the concern to employ these revealed texts for the purpose of deriving legal rulings in diverse manners. It was these varied ways of deriving legal rulings that paved the way for the appearance of the juristic schools founded by scholars such as Abū Ḥanīfah, Mālik, al-Shāfiʿī, Aḥmad ibn Ḥanbal, and others. However, these scholars saw no need to discuss whether to give priority to reason or revelation, since the Qur'anic methodology to which they adhered made it unnecessary to engage in such debate.

The Muʿtazilites, by contrast, went to extremes in the importance they placed on reason. Abū al-Ḥasan al-Ashʿarī had himself been an adherent of the Muʿtazilah school. However, he later broke with them and established a school of his own which attracted a good number of followers. The Ashʿarite school, as we have seen, rehabilitated the role of revelation without belittling the role of reason. There then came Abū al-Ḥasan al-Māturīdī (333 AH/944 CE), who, building upon the legacy left by Imam Abū Ḥanīfah, formulated a moderate scholastic theological school that struck a balance between the positions taken by the Muʿtazilite and the Ashʿarite schools. These three schools thus share the assumption that there is an opposition of sorts between reason and revelation that requires us to determine which of the two is to be assigned greater authority.

In a subsequent development, certain scholars of the scholastic-theological school relinquished the notion that reason and revelation are somehow inconsistent. Such scholars stressed the need to avoid any appearance of conflict (*dar' al-taʿāruḍ*) between reason and revelation, the importance of agreement between "the correct understanding of revelation and the explicit import of reason," and the need to formulate what one scholar referred to as "the definitive word on the link between wisdom and the Islamic law" (*faṣl al-maqāl fī mā bayn al-sharīʿah wa al-ḥikmah min ittiṣāl*). These and other expressions of the balance and complementarity between reason and revelation served to revive the Qur'anic approach that had been adhered to by early Muslim scholars. This earlier approach entailed engaging in rational inquiry into those matters that call for investigation while avoiding controversial issues that lead to no constructive action, knowledge of which yields no benefit, and ignorance of which does no harm. This newly emerging school was headed by scholars with various orientations such as al-Ghazālī, Ibn Rushd, and Ibn Taymiyyah.

(2) *The Experiential-Sufi School*

This school relies on the distinction between experiential knowledge on one hand and, on the other, the various other types of knowledge that are acquired through revelation, sensory perception or reason. Just as the latter types of knowledge are associated with specific methodological procedures that enable us to acquire knowledge, test it, and put it to use, experiential knowledge is likewise associated with specific methodological procedures. The knowledge that comes via revelation, sensory perception or reason might be described as "acquisition" (*kasb*). Experiential knowledge, by contrast, might be described as an "endowment" (*wahb*). For it is a gift from God Almighty, who grants it to those individuals who strive against their baser nature through worship and the remembrance of God and who continue to ascend to higher and higher levels of purification and consciousness of the Divine until they are in such a state of nearness to God that they merit this divine bequest.

In his article entitled, "The Mystical-Experiential Approach of Islam's Sufis,"[8] Dr. ʿAbd al-Hamid Madkur describes the features that characterize experiential knowledge and expounds the rules and criteria that govern the mystical approach. Dr. Madkur grounds the mystical-experiential approach in Islamic revelation, Islamic law, and reason, making use of the original works of leading Sufi figures. He draws on the writings of Abū Ḥāmid al-Ghazālī, Abū al-Qāsim al-Qushayrī (d. 457 AH/1074 CE), al-Ḥārith al-Muḥāsibī (d. 243 AH/857 CE), al-Ḥakīm al-Tirmidhī (d. 298 AH/910 CE), Muḥyī al-Dīn ibn ʿArabī (638 AH/1240 CE), and Abū Ṭālib al-Makkī (d. 386 AH/996 CE). Dr. Madkur also discusses the ways in which the Sufi heritage was assessed by other scholars such as Ibn Taymiyyah and Ibn al-Qayyim al-Jawziyyah (d. 751 AH/1350 CE). The following is a synopsis of Dr. Madkur's discussion:

In speaking of experiential knowledge, the Sufis have employed a variety of terms, including "inspiration" (*ilhām*), "disclosure" (*kashf*), and "witnessing" (*shuhūd*). They have described their science as being *ladunnī*, meaning, "issuing from the divine presence." The use of this term is based on God Almighty's statement about the upright servant Moses, upon him be peace, whom He describes as "one of Our servants on whom We had bestowed grace from Ourselves and unto whom We had imparted knowledge [issuing] from Ourselves (*ʿallamnāhu min ladunnā ʿilma*)" (*sūrah al-Kahf* 18:65). In speaking of their experiential knowledge, however, the Sufis prefer the term *maʿrifah* (a term used to refer to knowledge of persons) over the word *ʿilm* (the term generally used when referring to a science or academic discipline).[9] This *maʿrifah* – a knowledge associated with inspiration and the heart – does not originate from sensory experience, rational comprehension, or logical syllogisms. Nor does it grow out of studying the Qur'an and the Prophetic Sunnah or learning from a professor or spiritual guide. Rather, the adept arrives at this knowledge by traveling toward God along a path on which he or she "ascends spiritually toward the Divine. Consequently, it is a path marked by way stations through which one passes, or stairs along which one ascends."[10]

This path, which is what Dr. Madkur refers to as the Sufi mystical approach or method, rests on two foundations. The first foundation consists of the upward path or spiritual journey, which is a process of inward struggle and striving marked by renunciation or emptying (*takhliyyah*) and the acquisition of godlike, virtuous traits (*taḥliyyah*). The second foundation is the desired end, or arrival at the knowledge of God Almighty. However, whereas the first foundation is necessary for the realization of the second, the realization of the second does not necessary follow from the first, since the path traveled is a kind of acquisition (*kasb*), that is, a process that depends on human effort, whereas the knowledge sought is an endowment from God (*wahb*). The process of being emptied of one's baser instincts and imperfections and acquiring virtue and godlikeness is a long, rugged path on which the traveler may need a shaykh, that is, a spiritual guide who is knowledgeable of what the soul needs in order to be properly trained up and purified. This training and purification involves a series of strivings in the course of which the traveler ascends by degrees through a number of spiritual stations (*maqāmāt*) beginning with repentance and culminating in oneness with the Divine. These stations have no set order; rather, they differ from one spiritual traveler to another. The effect of these stations manifests itself through spiritual, psychological states (*aḥwāl*) that come over the heart without effort or struggle. Such states include dejection (literally, contraction, or *qabḍ*), expansion (*basṭ*), that is, a state of merriment and spiritual release, joy (*ṭarab*) and sorrow (*ḥuzn*). Describing the link between stations and states, the Sufis say, "the stations are acquired through human effort (*al-maqāmāt makāsib*), while the states are granted as gifts (*wa al-aḥwāl mawāhib*)."[11]

There is a longstanding consensus among both scholars and the population at large that whether we are dealing with religious texts or observing natural phenomena and social-psychological processes, we arrive at knowledge by using our reason, our senses, or a combination of the two. The Sufis do not deny this. However, to these traditional means of acquiring knowledge, all of which are associated with some type of method and discipline, they have added another, non-traditional means of acquiring knowledge. The Sufis have exerted great efforts to ground the mystical-experiential method in the texts of Islamic revelation and law as well as in human reason. In so doing, they have sought to demonstrate that experiential knowledge is an actual possibility, and that the supposition that one can only arrive at true knowledge based on rational evidence acquired and employed in keeping with known methods "is a narrowing of God's wide mercy."[12] In the course of grounding experiential knowledge in religious texts, the Sufis have focused on Qur'anic verses which link human beings' achievement of a deep consciousness of God with the spiritual gifts God grants them. These gifts include discernment, sustenance, light, mercy, guidance, and wisdom, all of which Sufis understand to be types of experiential knowledge: "knowledge acquired without [human] instruction, and insight without experimentation." They also cite texts of the Prophetic Sunnah that speak of the believer's discernment and openness of heart, qualities that the Sufis understand to be the light God shines into the believer's heart. The Sufis also refer in this context to sayings attributed to some of the Prophet's Companions and leading Muslim thinkers about what they term "inspiration without instruction."[13]

In connection with the Sufis' concern to ground experiential knowledge in the Islamic revelation, Madkur offers two observations. The first is that discussions of "inspirational knowledge" are not restricted to the Sufis alone. A number of early Muslim scholars, among them Ibn Taymiyyah and Ibn al-Qayyim al-Jawziyyah, spoke in similar terms about an inspiration-based knowledge from God, who graciously bestows visions, disclosures and inspirations upon whomsoever He wills of His servants. Madkur's second observation is a kind of objection to the Sufis' interpretation of Qur'anic verses which they see as demonstrating the reality and validity of the disclosures and inspirations God gives to those who are conscious of Him. After all, observes Madkur:

> Someone who is conscious of God will be aware of the distinction between truth and falsehood. Indeed, such an individual is committed to truth in his words and deeds alike, avoiding falsehood in everything he does. As for disclosure (*kashf*), it has to do with realities that are beyond the reach of normal human perception; in other words, it is unrelated to realities that are obvious to us, and comes in the form of an outpouring into the believing servant's heart. If such an outpouring indicates anything, it indicates the way in which God grants success to His servants in the choices they make, and not a unique disclosure or inspiration.[14]

As for the Sufis' efforts toward grounding the mystical-experiential method in reason, they have focused around the mind's need for something beyond itself. The physical senses, for example, are necessary in order for the mind to perform its role in the acquisition of knowledge. The mind, or reason, is only capable of operating within certain realms and parameters. Faculties and talents that distinguish some individuals from others, such as the ability to write and enjoy poetry, for example, lie in the realm of subjective experience, a realm that requires us to grant people their personal preferences and tastes. Additionally, the mind can fall into error; hence, it needs a standard or criterion on the basis of which to weigh its thought and ideas rather than being its own standard. This being the case, it is best for us to turn to God for true, inspired knowledge.

The Sufis do not disparage reason as a means of acquiring knowledge of the outer, concrete world in which we live. Indeed, the Sufi, like the rest of us, stands in need of rational knowledge to serve as the external framework for mystical knowledge. However, rational knowledge is insufficient to ensure the well-being of the heart. Consequently, reason acknowledges the existence of another way to gain knowledge and treads another path toward its acquisition; in so doing, it discovers a degree of confidence that may not be possible on the level of rational knowledge alone.

The knowledge to which one gains access through the mystical-experiential method is subjective in nature. In other words, it belongs exclusively to the person who experiences it, having been cast into his or her heart in a way that excludes narration, story, indoctrination and learning. For this reason it has no need of evidence from outside itself. Rather, it is a witness unto itself, and those who deny its existence must simply acknowledge it and concede to it given their inability to acquaint themselves with it directly. It is difficult to give expression to such knowledge in ordinary language, and the experience of it is restricted to those who have "tasted" it. In short, it is impossible to give verbal expression to an experiential state. The rational thinker and the Sufi gnostic (in the simple sense of "knower") may agree on certain ideas. However, there remains an essential difference between them: the difference between head knowledge and heart knowledge! When mystical knowledge is granted, it tends to come suddenly and all at once, without one's having been expecting it or having exerted an effort to obtain it. In this respect, mystical knowledge resembles what happens to a scientist who is engrossed in the study of certain phenomena he is unable to explain. In his frustration, he stops thinking about them for a while and busies himself with something else when, out of the blue, a sudden thought occurs to him, like light dawning in his head, and before him there appears a clear explanation and an integrated vision.

Lastly, Madkur stresses the fact that the mystical-experiential method is integrative in nature. The Sufis disregard neither rational knowledge nor the Islamic legal sciences. However, they look beyond these to another horizon. Hence, if the outcomes of this mystical-experiential approach are consistent with the criteria set by Islamic law and meet the requirements of rationality, they see no reason to reject them, especially in view of the fact that this approach is linked with the desire for spiritual ascent and moral refinement. Certain aspects of human needs are more fully met through this approach, which helps to meet the requirements of the methodological integration to which contemporary minds aspire.

(3) *The Scientific-Empirical School*

Chapter Four of this book, which treats the development of research methods in Islamic thought and Western thought,[15] presents examples of the ways in which the scientific-empirical method has manifested itself in the Islamic world as well as the phases of its development in the West.

It should be noted here that the scientific-empirical method in Islamic history has not been applied exclusively to research on matter, its physical and vital properties and its chemical transformations. Nor has it been restricted to practical applications of this method to industry, agriculture, medicine and the like, as can be seen today in the nano-sciences and other applied fields. Rather, it has also encompassed legal rulings pertinent to these sciences and their applications. The scientific-empirical method has likewise been applied to the logical and rational requirements of social and historical studies as well as field observations and practical experiments. All of these "worlds" created by "the Lord and Cherisher of the worlds" – the physical universe from the vastest expanses to the minutest of its elements and particles, the world of human society with its peoples, tribes and cultures, and the world of individual human beings with their souls, spirits, minds, and hearts, their agonies and their hopes – were created with masterly precision and are subject to unvarying laws that can be discovered and put to practical use. The integrative features of the scientific empirical method – which involves employing the procedures best suited to the nature of the research topic, be they field observations, practical experiments, quantitative measures, or various inductive processes – are likewise inherent to the distinctively Islamic understanding of this method.

The phrase "scientific method" is clearly associated with "science." The term "science" as used within the Islamic perspective, based both on its etymology (being derived from the Arabic root ^{c} – *l* – *m*, meaning "to know") and its use in scholarly terminology, means "knowledge" in the unqualified sense. As such, it includes ways of thinking about all topics whatsoever, methods of researching them, and their practical applications. In the West, by contrast, the term "science" has been used to refer specifically to the study of material phenomena within the fields of physics, chemistry and other "exact sciences." And whereas the scientific-empirical method has specifically to do with acquiring knowledge about the physical nature of things, the methodology of epistemological integration requires the use of the scientific-empirical method in whichever situation calls for it, just as it uses other methods in whatever situations require them.

The scientific method as understood and applied within the Islamic framework means documentation and proof in keeping with the maxim: "If you are transmitting information, strive for accuracy, and if you are making a claim, provide proof." Accuracy of transmission was associated with the sciences of narration (the Hadith sciences, for example), while proof was associated with research. The proof provided might be rational and logical, or sensory and empirical. Hence, within the Islamic framework the scientific method has been employed equally in the natural and applied sciences, the social and human sciences, and the sciences of Islamic law. Islamic classification of the sciences in the past, being based on criteria that differ from those that are prevalent today, was characterized by pairs that brought together virtually all known disciplines. Sciences were classified, for example, as "praiseworthy" or "blameworthy," "sciences of ends" or "sciences of means," "this-worldly sciences" or "other-worldly sciences," "sciences of revelation" or "sciences of the cosmos." The term "jurisprudence" (fiqh) was used to refer to the desired understanding in relation to all topics of study. Hence, one had a "jurisprudence of rites of worship" (*fiqh al-ʿibādāt*) and a "jurisprudence of transactions" (*fiqh al-muʿāmalāt*), the latter of which encompassed much of what falls today under the rubric of the social sciences, such as economics, sociology, education, psychology, political science, and the like.

As for the methodological authority to which appeal was made, it found its locus in the texts of the Holy Qur'an and the Prophetic Sunnah as well as the reasoned interpretations put forward by early Muslim scholars. It was thus a *tawḥīdī*, integrative point of reference that included methods of research, investigation and the pursuit of knowledge, as well as methods of application, practical use, and practice. The Islamic methodology that served as a guide to research stressed the importance of making use of sensory perception, reason, examination, reflection and contemplation in the search for the patterns and laws that govern events and explain natural, social, and historical phenomena. It was by means of such thought processes that scholars read religious texts and came to conclusions concerning practical realities and human nature as manifested in individuals and society. Moreover, such processes were carried out in an integrated fashion that made use of both divine revelation and the created universe, both reason and sensory perception.

Application of the scientific method from an Islamic perspective necessarily involves taking a firm stance against any hindrances to sound thinking and research. Such hindrances might take the form of haphazard behavior which is inconsistent with the methodical procedures called for by the scientific method, or practices that become commonplace by virtue of inherited custom without attempts to put their validity to the test. Such situations are reflected in the Qur'anic account of people's defense of idol worship on the grounds that "...we found our forefathers doing the same!" (*sūrah al-Shuʿarā'* 26:74) or "...We found our forefathers agreed on what to believe – and, verily, it is but in their footsteps that we follow!" (*sūrah Zukhruf* 43:23). Such practices might be based, as in the days of the Prophet, on superstition, myth, or incorrect interpretations.

It is true, of course, that methodological theorization had begun with the recording of the oral accounts that formed the Prophetic Sunnah and the earliest interpretations of the Qur'an. The theorization process continued with the development of the principles of jurisprudence, the principles of religion, theology, linguistics, and history, after which it came to include all other sciences as well, including physics, chemistry, astronomy, medicine, mechanics, and so on. However, the few writings that dealt specifically with methodological theorization tended to restrict themselves to discussions of leading scholars and the methods they had used in the pursuit of knowledge and instruction. Add to this the fact that methodological theorists saw no need to explicate the Qur'anic frame of reference for systematic thinking and practice, since scholars and writers at that time assumed its validity as a matter of course. Nevertheless, many of the books that make up the Islamic heritage begin with a chapter entitled, "The Book of Knowledge (Science)," or include a chapter with a similar title such as "On encouraging the pursuit of knowledge and an exposition of its virtues."[16] Such a chapter generally includes references to Qur'anic verses and Prophetic hadiths that promote the pursuit of knowledge, detail the virtues of students and teachers, and describe the journey entailed by the pursuit of knowledge, pedagogical methods and techniques, research procedures designed to acquire knowledge on particular topics and ways of testing and applying such knowledge. There were, in addition, books that specialized in these various topics, including debate, dialectics, theology, jurisprudence, and Sufism.[17]

It need not be considered a shortcoming in the Arabic Islamic heritage that it has bequeathed us no books specializing in the scientific empirical method. Nor have other heritages handed such books down to us. As succeeding generations of thinkers and scholars in various specializations accumulate greater and greater experience and expertise down the generations and glean experience and expertise from other peoples, human thought grows and develops. If methodological thought had been served in the Islamic heritage as it has been in the Western heritage, we would discover that certain texts from the Islamic heritage are of equal, if not greater, value than the writings of Newton and Descartes, who, benefitting from the accumulation of methodological knowledge and expertise that was available to them in their time, were able to lay a theoretical foundation for methodological activity and research.

(4) *The Juristic-Uṣūlī School*

We have combined the juristic and *uṣūlī* methods, both of which focus on the actions of human beings in their capacity as servants of God who are accountable to Him for their conduct, into a single school. Ibn Khaldūn states in his *Muqaddimah*:

> Jurisprudence (*fiqh*) is knowledge of God's rulings or edicts pertaining to the actions of His servants, who are accountable to Him for what they do. Such rulings, which specify whether a given action is obligatory, prohibited, recommended, undesirable, or permitted, are derived from the Qur'an and the Prophetic Sunnah and the evidence contained therein. The process of deriving legal rulings from this evidence is referred to as jurisprudence.[18]

Jurisprudence emerged with Islam's earliest beginnings, and had two sources: the Qur'an and the Prophetic Sunnah. Islam is a set of doctrines, moral principles, and practical rulings which were revealed in the form of the Qur'an to the Prophet Muhammad, who then communicated them to the people around him. Such doctrines and principles would also come at times from the Prophet himself in the form of legal rulings, verdicts, and answers to questions. During the era immediately subsequent to the death of the Prophet, his Companions would respond to events and newly arising situations by offering reasoned interpretations of the texts of the Qur'an and the Sunnah; these interpretations then became a third source of Islamic jurisprudence. During the second and third centuries AH, many non-Arab peoples entered Islam and the Islamic state extended its rule over a vast geographical area. Consequently there arose new problems and situations, which required that Muslim scholars offer new interpretations of the Qur'an, the Sunnah and the views of the Companions in order to rule on previously unfamiliar issues, some actual and some hypothetical. It was at this stage that juristic rulings began to be compiled into books, and the interpretations offered by these second and third-century scholars became a fourth source of juristic input.

Juristic writings proliferated to the point where they made up a significant percentage of Muslim scholars' output over the centuries that followed, and a variety of juristic writing styles and approaches emerged. Ibn Ashur mentions two approaches to juristic writing. The first of these approaches involves mentioning specific issues and questions and their types followed by the relevant rulings. This approach is found in al-*Mudawwanah*, which is based on the jurisprudence of Imam Mālik, and in *al-Jāmi*ᶜ by Muḥammad ibn al-Ḥasan al-Shaybānī (d. 241 AH/805 CE), a student of Abū Ḥanīfah's. The second approach to juristic writing involves touching first on juristic universals and related principles followed by a listing of specific questions and issues as we find in *al-Dhakhīrah fī al-Fiqh al-Mālikī* (A Treasure of Mālikī Jurisprudence) by Shihāb al-Dīn al-Qarāfī (d. 684 AH/1285 CE)[19] and *Qawā*ᶜ*id al-Aḥkām fī Iṣlāḥ al-Anām* (Principles Underlying Juristic Rulings for the Good of Mankind)[20] by al-ᶜIzz ibn ᶜAbd al-Salām (d. 660 AH/1261 CE).

However, the science of jurisprudence suffered a setback as a result of uncompromising attachment to this or that particular juristic school and an insistence on deriving legal rulings solely on the basis of a single school's teachings while ruling out evidence or considerations that might argue in favor of alternative rulings. These developments led to a ban on any sort of innovative interpretation of Islam's religious texts and disregard for the higher aims and intents of Islamic law. Devoting most of their attention to rulings pertinent to Islamic rites of worship, jurists frequently lacked knowledge in areas they needed to be well-versed in if they were to derive the soundest possible legal rulings.[21] Negative developments such as these are certain to have contributed to the backward state in which the Muslim ummah has found itself over the past few centuries.

There was no need to spell out the principles of jurisprudence during the lifetime of the Apostle, nor in the era of the Companions following his death. However, subsequent mixing of Arabs and non-Arabs within the developing Muslim ummah generated a need to establish grammatical rules to assist non-Arab Muslims in understanding and correctly pronouncing religious texts. This development coincided with a dispute that arose between "the people of the hadith," or simply, Traditionists (*ahl al-ḥadīth*), who relied exclusively on the literal import of the hadiths, and "the people of independent reasoning" (*ahl al-ra'y*),[22] who based their rulings on reasoned, innovative interpretation (ijtihad). There was, in addition, a growing tendency to argue from religious texts in capricious, tendentious ways. It thus became necessary to set down rules governing the use of textual evidence and conditions for drawing conclusions from such evidence. It was these grammatical rules and regulations for how to reason from textual evidence that came to be known as the science of the principles of jurisprudence (*ᶜilm uṣūl al-fiqh*).

The field of jurisprudence began small, then gradually expanded, passing through a series of stages in the process. The first Muslim scholar to write about the principles of jurisprudence was Imam al-Shāfiᶜī (d. 204 AH/819 CE). Al-Shāfiᶜī's work was followed by a number of other works that reflected varying methodologies. The method adhered to by scholastic theologians was first to establish the rules governing the principles of jurisprudence and research relating thereto by means of theoretical discussion and logical proofs. Ḥanafī jurists likewise would begin by specifying the juristic rules they believed their forebears to have used as a foundation for their interpretations. A third group adhered to a method that combined elements of the first two methods just described; in other words, they took care to define rules and establish proofs, after which they would apply them to subsidiary juristic questions. Representatives of this latter group include Tāj al-Dīn al-Subkī (d. 771 AH/1369 CE), author of *Jamᶜ al-Jawāmiᶜ*. It should be borne in mind that the principles and rules of jurisprudence are nothing but tools and methods, not texts of divine revelation.[23]

The discipline of the principles of jurisprudence developed to the point where some scholars described it as "the greatest, most illustrious, and most beneficial of the Islamic legal sciences."[24] Most books dealing with the principles of jurisprudence were slanted toward a particular juristic school of thought, with each scholar marshalling lengthy arguments in support of his own school; examples of scholars who adopted this approach include al-Bāqillānī and al-Ghazālī. Other scholars, such as al-Qarāfi and Ibn al-Ḥājib, kept their expositions brief and concise. However, just as there were factors that delayed the progress of the science of jurisprudence (*ʿilm al-fiqh*), the field of the principles of jurisprudence (*ʿilm uṣūl al-fiqh*) was likewise set back by various factors. Such factors included an excessive preoccupation with logic, grammar, linguistics and theology that had nothing to do with the science per se and which added nothing of value on the practical level, and the discussion of irrelevant issues and questions which al-Shāṭibī, for example, judged to be of no use to scholarship. There was also a lack of consistency between "roots" and "branches," that is, between the situations in response to which original juristic rulings had been issued (the "roots," or *uṣūl*), and later situations the rulings on which were based on comparisons or analogies with the original ones (the "branches," or *furūʿ*), because the codification of the principles of jurisprudence came after the definition of the branches. Other factors that prevented the field of jurisprudence from progressing included a disregard for the higher aims of Islamic law and what is termed "the closing of the door to ijtihad," that is, an unofficial ban on the use of independent reasoning and innovative interpretation, which significantly undermined Muslims' use of their intellectual powers and the quality of Islamic life overall.

Despite such signs of backwardness in the juristic sciences, efforts toward reform in the field did not come to a complete halt. In fact, a number of scholars made appreciable efforts toward this end. In this connection, mention might be made of Muḥammad ibn ʿAlī al-Shawkānī (d. 1250 AH/1834 CE), who composed a number of works that contributed to progress in juristic thought. Such works include his *al-Darārī al-Muḍī'ah fi Sharḥ al-Durar al-Bahiyyah* and *al-Sayl al-Jarrār al-Mutadaffiq ʿalā Ḥadā'iq al-Azhār* on comparative jurisprudence, and his *Irshād al-Fuḥūl ilā Taḥqīq al-Ḥaqq min ᶜIlm al-Uṣūl* on the principles of jurisprudence. Al-Shawkānī, whose work heralded the end of the backwardness and stagnation that had afflicted the field of jurisprudence, formulated an integrated vision of scholarly reform which consisted of a theory of renewal based on three methodological foundations: (1) prohibition of blind imitation of one's forebears and the call to independent reasoning and innovative interpretation, (2) a thorough exploration of the science of the principles of jurisprudence, and (3) revitalization of the methodology adhered to in juristic studies.[25]

Juristic method (*al-manhaj al-fiqhī*) and the method associated with the principles of jurisprudence (*al-manhaj al-uṣūlī*) can thus be integrated, since they both address a single theme. Juristic method is no longer restricted to the work of imams and muftis who rule on issues of personal piety, such as rites of Islamic worship, daily transactions, and personal status; rather, it goes beyond these to the work of judges and lawyers in all areas of relevance to the protection of human rights and resolution of conflicts.

The discipline of the principles of jurisprudence lends itself to integration given the fact that it is a science in which, in the words of one Muslim thinker, "reason has been mingled with revelation, and which involves examination of both evidence and the rulings to which it points. As such, it has been a significant aid toward understanding the Book of God and the words and actions of the Messenger of God."[26]

According to Ali Sami al-Nashshar, the way of thinking adopted by Imam al-Shāfiᶜī in the course of formulating the principles of jurisprudence was scientific and philosophical in nature. In support of this view al-Nashshar cites Imam Aḥmad ibn Ḥanbal, who is reported to have said, "Al-Shāfiᶜī was a philosopher in four respects: in respect to language, the variety in people's points of view, meanings, and jurisprudence."[27] Al-Nashshar points out that the rules governing the *uṣūlī* method are consistent with the rules governing scientific experimental induction, particularly the law of effective causes (*qāᶜidat al-ᶜillah*) and the law of constancy (*qāᶜidat al-iṭṭirād*, according to which as long as a given cause is present, so is its ruling, and vice-versa), as well as the methods for identifying effective causes (*masālik al-ᶜillah*) – that is, isolation of the effective cause (*al-sabr*), restricting the range of a cause's anticipated qualities (*al-taqsīm*), elimination of irrelevant causes (*al-ṭard*), consistency of effective causes (*al-dawarān*), and ascertaining the effective cause (*taḥqīq al-manāṭ*). In this connection the author quotes a statement by al-Qarāfī according to which many of the laws governing the science of medicine are confirmed through experimentation, which is an expression of the juristic principle of consistency of effective causes (*al-dawarān*).[28]

The *uṣūlī* method consists of rules which regulate the process of ijtihad for the purpose of deriving legal rulings relevant to rites of worship and day-to-day transactions and of relating more effectively to the Qur'an and the Prophetic Sunnah. This being the case, Hadith scholars and other thinkers and researchers are of the view that this same method may be activated, developed and revitalized so as to provide guidelines for the contemporary propagation of Islam, shape religious awareness, base Islamic jurisprudence on a proper understanding of aims and priorities, and manage the Muslim community's affairs while achieving its best interests in the various areas of its life. Based on his observation of a number of experiments in the renewal of the *uṣūlī* method, one scholar posits that "the science of the principles of jurisprudence is one of the most important factors contributing to the revitalization of thought and knowledge in the Muslim community."[29]

CONCLUSION

Our aim in this chapter has been to give a brief overview of what we term "methodological schools." Our focus has been four of the methodological schools representing Islamic methodology. All of these schools demonstrate a commitment to the general principles and ideals of Islamic methodology, deriving their data from the same sources (the written Islamic revelation and the created universe) and employing the same tools (reason and sensory perception), albeit with differing degrees of emphasis on this or that source or tool. Hence, though numerous and varied, all of these schools embody the methodology of epistemological integration from the Islamic perspective. It will be clear from our discussion here that none of these schools serves as a substitute for any of the others except in relation to the purpose for which it is being adhered to and the person who has chosen to associate himself with it. We have chosen to describe the phenomenon of multiplicity and variety in Islamic methodology in terms of a *tawḥīdī* perspective, which adopts integration as its fundamental approach, as opposed to a unitary or one-dimensional perspective, which only sees truth in a single school.

We have found that every one of these schools adopts the methodology of epistemological integration. As such, none of them adopts an extreme, one-sided position on any given issue. The adherents of the scholastic-theological school, for example, disagreed over the degree to which we should rely on reason as opposed to revelation. However, none of the parties to this disagreement supported exclusive reliance on either reason or revelation, for to take such an exclusive position would have set them outside of the Islamic fold. Rather, most adherents of the scholastic-theological school took positions that fell somewhere along the middle range of the continuum between total reliance on reason and total reliance on revelation; some leaned toward greater reliance on reason, others leaned toward greater reliance on revelation, and still others relied almost equally on both.

Similarly, scholars belonging to this or that methodological school differ in terms of the ways they practice their school's traditions and carry out its procedures, as well as the positions they take. Hence, there are sub-schools within each of the larger schools. As we saw in the case of the rationalist-scholastic school, the positions taken by the Muʿtazilites, the Ashʿarites, and the Maturidites on the matter of reason and revelation differ, though not always or in every respect. Rather, their positions are more or less similar on some issues, while diverging on others. Similarly, we find significant variation among the positions taken by different adherents of the mystical-experiential school. Differences of position within this school are represented by major representative figures such as al-Ghazālī, al-Ḥārith al-Muḥāsibī, al-Qushayrī, Muḥyī al-Dīn Ibn ʿArabī, and so on.

As in the case of human knowledge, no methodological school has emerged fully formed. Each of them began with a distinctive experience or insight on the part of some scholar who then went on to introduce a method of investigation, research, and treatment of intellectual or theological issues. Each of these scholars came to have students and disciples who then developed the approach he had initiated until it was fully formed and exhibited those features that distinguished it from other methods and approaches. The practices of this or that methodological school have sometimes ramified to form sub-schools. Hence, the maturation of a method and the integration of its various elements does not necessarily mean that it has stopped growing, developing and changing. On the contrary, the law of change and development governs all of these schools. It may also happen that different schools' orientations become more similar over time, and that certain elements in a given school's perspective merge with elements in the perspective of some other school with the result that they come together, causing still other schools to be born.

6

Sources and Tools of Methodology

GOALS OF THIS CHAPTER

1. To explain what is meant by "sources" and "tools" in the context of a discussion of Islamic methodology.
2. To identify the primary sources of knowledge in the Islamic worldview, and to justify limiting them to written revelation (the Qur'an and the Prophetic Sunnah) and the created world.
3. To identify the primary tools of knowledge in the Islamic worldview and to justify restricting them to reason and sensory perception.
4. To clarify the concept of integration in relation to the aforementioned sources and tools of knowledge within the context of Islamic methodology.
5. To derive a model for epistemological integration.
6. To distinguish between tools of thought and tools of research.
7. To identify the place of the tools used in currently prevailing research methods within Islamic methodology.
8. To distinguish between tools for data collection, analysis, and interpretation.
9. To clarify the place of instinct or inborn human nature in the process of epistemological integration from the Islamic perspective.

INTRODUCTION

Sources and tools are linked directly with practical method and its associated procedures. In what follows, we will be discussing the sources and tools of methodology (as opposed to method) because, in its capacity as "the science of methods," methodology governs the process of choosing methods and putting them to use. It is our hope that the act of linking sources and tools within a single context will aid the transition from theoretical conceptualization of the elements of methodology to the practical implementation of methods. No discussion of sources will be clear without mention of the tools that are used to glean knowledge from these sources; hence, the profound interpenetration between sources and tools.

This chapter presents a discussion of the terms "source" and "tool" and concepts of relevance to each. It distinguishes between sources and tools in the areas of thought and research, and identifies the primary and secondary sources from which Muslims draw knowledge, rulings, and data, as well as the principle tools Muslims employ in order to obtain data and information from their sources in order to arrive at what we have termed the "epistemological integration equation."

First: THE CONCEPT OF "SOURCE"

The Arabic term for "source," that is, *maṣdar*, is derived from the trilateral root *ṣ – d – r*. The noun *ṣadr*, derived from the same root, means the beginning of something or its front part,[1] while the verbal noun *ṣudūr*, which bears the sense of coming out, exiting or departing, is used in contrast to the word *wurūd*, which refers to the act of coming or entering. This meaning is illustrated in the verse of the Qur'an that reads, "...They answered, 'We cannot water [our animals] until the herdsmen drive [theirs] home (*ḥattā yuṣdira al-ruʿāh*)'..." (*sūrah al-Qaṣaṣ* 28:23), that is, until they depart with their herds after having brought them to drink. Another illustration is found in *sūrah al-Zalzalah* 99:6, "On that day will all men come forward, (*yawma'idhin yaṣduru al-nāsu*...)...to be shown their [past] deeds." In other words, they will come out of their graves. According to one reading of the phrase, people will come to Earth, then depart Earth to the site of the resurrection, while according to another, they will come to the site of the resurrection for an accounting, then come away to receive either reward or punishment.[2] Another meaning of the word *ṣadr* (plural, *ṣudūr*) is the chest or breast, which contains the heart as the site of understanding.

Thus we read, "...Verily, it is not their eyes that have become blind – but blind have become the hearts that are in their breasts (*fī al-ṣudūr*)!" God Almighty knows "all that the hearts (*al-ṣudūr*) would conceal" (*sūrah al-Hajj* 22:46), while someone who recites the Qur'an might call out to God, saying, "O my Sustainer! Open up my heart (*ishraḥ lī ṣadrī*!" (*sūrah Ṭā Hā* 20:25). Hence, the term *ṣadr* is also used to refer to one's inner sense of things.[3]

The term *maṣdar* in Arabic can also refer to the verbal noun from which the verb is said to have been derived.[4] (According to the Basrah linguistic school, the verbal noun or *maṣdar* can function as a verb since it is the verb's source. The Kufan school disagrees, however, saying that the verbal noun is derived from the verb.) Arab grammarians have classified verbal nouns into numerous types.[5]

In the fields of geography and environmental sciences, the word "source" (*maṣdar*) is used to refer to the location or site from which various sorts of materials are taken; we speak, for example, of surface and underground sources of water. In the field of economics we speak of imports (*wāridāt*) and exports (*ṣādirāt*), while merchandise sold on the market comes from a source (*maṣdar*) that produced it and/or exported it (*ṣaddarahā*). When discussing research methods, we speak of sources and references in the form of books, periodicals and other written materials from which the researcher obtains his or her data and information and which generally appear in footnotes or endnotes and the work's bibliography. In sum, we find the term "source" (*maṣdar*) and its derivatives being used in numerous epistemological fields.

The term "source" is used when speaking of jurisprudence and its origins (the sources of Islamic legislation). The sources of Islamic legislation are the Holy Qur'an, the Prophetic Sunnah, and independent reasoning (ijtihad) in its dual branches of analogical reasoning (*qiyās*) and consensus (ijmaᶜ). In the science of the principles of jurisprudence, they are viewed as primary sources on which the majority of scholars agree. To these we might add subsidiary sources which are the subject of debate among scholars, such as juristic preference (*istiḥsān*), presumption of continuity (*istiṣḥāb*), blocking of pretenses (*sadd al-dharā'iᶜ*), revealed laws that preceded the law of Islam (*sharᶜu man qablanā*), the saying of a single Companion (*qawl al-ṣaḥābī*), established practice (*al-ʿādah al-muḥkamah*), etc. These sources of legislation are sources for the derivation of legal rulings. As for the methodology for arriving at these rulings from their sources, it is a science founded upon reason, confidence in the reliability of these sources, and the necessity of turning to them and drawing on them. These sources, therefore, are the foundations of the methodology by means of which reason derives the practical rulings that provide Muslims with guidance in their thought and behavior.

When we need something, we think of the source from which we can obtain it. If we are at home and want some water, we might get it from the kitchen faucet, for example, or from a bottle in the refrigerator. However, the tap water in the kitchen comes from a prior source, such as the municipal water reservoir, which in turn comes from a prior source, such as a river, a lake, an Artesian well, or a water desalination plant. In other words, in addition to the original source for the water, there are a variety of subsidiary or secondary sources.

If someone is faced with a question having to do with a woman's right to dispose of her husband's estate after his death when she has several dependent children by her late husband, the source of the answer to this question might be a book on inheritance laws in Islam, or a scholar who can answer the question for her directly. However, the scholar who has given her an answer to this question, or the author of the book he has consulted, will both have grappled with this juristic question through reliance on previous academic sources, such as books on jurisprudence and the principles adopted by a particular juristic school. Moreover, the writings that have emerged from this school will themselves rely, albeit in part, on a previous and more original source, viz., particular texts from the Holy Quran and the Prophetic Sunnah. Hence, although the person faced with this issue will have obtained an answer directly, either from the author of the book he has consulted or a judge or mufti, these subsidiary sources will have obtained their knowledge from prior sources, including books by earlier scholars who relied for their expertise on the primary source represented by the Islamic revelation.

Similarly, if a given country's minister of education should need an epistemological basis on which to make a decision concerning whether to centralize or decentralize his educational administration, he may find what he needs in books dealing with the subject of educational administration. Such books might explain the advantages and disadvantages of centralization and decentralization respectively and the situations to which this or that system is best suited. Having read such books, he can use his reason to choose the system that seems most appropriate to his country's particular circumstances in light of the experiences of the various countries described in these books. Hence, these books serve in this case as references and resources for his decision-making.

The minister might resort to convening dialogue sessions and hosting discussions among groups of stakeholders, including high- and mid-level administrators, school directors, teachers, parents, and others. He might assign a researcher or team of researchers to ascertain the views of the target groups through opinion polls, questionnaires, interviews, etc. He might then analyze the data from the research done and draw conclusions that would form a basis for deciding which type of educational system to adopt. In this case, the source for his decision-making is the information he has received from the community that will be directly affected by the decision to be made. Hence, he is applying the principle of consultation (*shūrā*) and popular participation in decision-making. In a situation such as this, the information will have been accessed through scientific research that makes use of the best suited methods and tools for collecting and analyzing data and drawing conclusions based on such data.

What we are talking about here is not a legal ruling concerning what is or is not permissible. Rather, we are dealing with an action that is essentially permissible, and concerning which a decision is to be made in light of an assessment of what will best serve people's interests. In the course of making this decision, our hypothetical minister of education aims to make use of his own and others' previous experience while taking into consideration what those concerned – the majority of them, at least – consider best suited to them.

Of note here is that we only arrive at the source of the knowledge that needs to be acquired by means of appropriate tools and established practices. Moreover, many of the details that are taken into consideration have to do with the religious nature of the community, its intellectual leanings, its cultural priorities and its worldview. Nevertheless, the person engaged in studying all these details benefits not only from the previous experiences of his own community, but, in addition, from the experiences of other communities. In so doing, he employs the outcomes of his thought and systematic investigation as a means of serving people's interests and meeting their needs.

Second: SOURCES OF METHODOLOGY

There is a significant overlap between the sources from which we obtain knowledge, of whatever sort it happens to be, and on the basis of which we derive legal rulings; and the sources of our research methodology and our way of thinking. This should come as no surprise, since there is a science of legal rulings which we derive from specific sources (the science of jurisprudence, for example), and there is, in addition, a method for deriving this science from the aforementioned sources (the science of the principles of jurisprudence).

In the Qur'an one finds knowledge about God, the angels, the prophets and human history, as well as about the creation of objects, living beings, phenomena, and events. It contains knowledge (science) about the world beyond the realm of human reason and sensory perception as well as about the visible, perceptible world. Hence, if we talk about the sources for these types of knowledge, the Qur'an will certainly be one of them.

The Holy Qur'an is likewise a source from which legal rulings are derived, since from the Qur'an we obtain rulings having to do with what is permissible and prohibited, financial transactions, rules governing social conduct, inheritance, and so on.

(1) *Revelation as a Source of Knowledge*

The Islamic worldview draws a clear distinction between two sources from which practical guidance can be sought. These two sources, as we have seen, are revelation and the created world. By "revelation" we mean the message which God Almighty revealed to His Prophet Muhammad and which he communicated to others, then clarified to them in word and deed. This revealed message includes what might be termed "the explicit revelation," that is, the Holy Qur'an, and the "hidden revelation," that is, the Prophetic Sunnah, or the words and actions by means of which the Prophet clarified the meanings of the Qur'an, applied its rulings, and made specific that which in the Qur'an is stated in more general terms.

Nevertheless, the term "revelation" (Arabic, *waḥy*) as used in the Qur'an itself can refer to messages God communicates to chosen individuals in ways that we may or may not understand. It may come, for example, in the form of an inspiration, a thought that occurs to them, or a dream. Thus God declares, "And so, [when he was born,] We inspired [thus] the mother of Moses: (*awḥaynā ilā ummi mūsā*): 'Suckle him [for a time], and then, when thou hast cause to fear for him, cast him into the river, and have no fear and do not grieve – for We shall restore him to thee, and shall make him one of Our message-bearers!'" (*sūrah al-Qaṣaṣ* 28:7). The term *waḥy* can refer to messages that God communicates to other creatures as well. Thus we read, "And [consider how] thy Sustainer has inspired the bee (*awḥā rabbuka ilā al-naḥl*): 'Prepare for thyself dwellings in mountains and in trees, and in what [men] may build [for thee by way of hives]'" (*sūrah al-Naḥl* 16:68).

The divine revelation has been written down with the greatest of accuracy, precision and faithfulness on the level of its chapters (*suwar*), verses (*āyāt*), words (*kalimāt*) and letters (*ḥuruf*). One chapter thus begins by saying, "A divine writ [is this], with messages that have been made clear in and by themselves, and have been distinctly spelled out as well – [bestowed upon you] out of the grace of One who is Wise, All-Aware" (*sūrah Hūd* 11:1). Elsewhere we read: "And this, too, is a divine writ which We have bestowed from on high – blessed, confirming the truth of whatever there still remains [of earlier revelations] – and [this] in order that thou mayest warn the foremost of all cities and all who dwell around it. And those who believe in the life to come do believe in this [warning]; and it is they who are ever-mindful of their prayers" (*sūrah al-Anʿām* 6:92). God speaks of the Qur'an thus: "*Alif. Lām. Mīm.* This divine writ – let there be no doubt about it – is [meant to be] a guidance for all the God-conscious" (*sūrah al-Baqarah* 2:2); "*Alif. Lām. Rā'.* A divine writ [in this – a revelation] which We have bestowed upon thee from on high in order that thou might bring forth all mankind, by their Sustainer's leave, out of the depths of darkness into the light: onto the way that leads to the Almighty, the One to whom all praise is due" (*sūrah Ibrāhīm* 14:1); "*Ṭā. Sīn. Mīm.* These are messages of the divine writ, clear in itself and clearly showing the truth" (*sūrah al-Shu*ᶜ*arā'* 26:1-2); "*Alif. Lām. Rā'*. These are messages of the divine writ, full of wisdom" (*sūrah Yūnus* 10:1); and "*Alif. Lām. Mīm. ād.* A divine writ has been bestowed from on high upon thee – and let there be no doubt about this in thy heart – in order that thou mayest warn [the erring] thereby, and [thus] admonish the believers:" (*sūrah al-A*ᶜ*rāf* 7:1-2).

The Holy Qur'an serves as the origin for the overall perceptions that govern the Muslim's perspective on the Creator, the creation, the life of this world, and the life of the world to come. Similarly, such perceptions govern the Muslim's view of human nature, the purpose of human existence, the realm beyond human perceptions, and the world of reason and sense perception. The Qur'an is the source that generates Islamic legal rulings on rites of worship, day-to-day transactions, ethical standards, and the criteria for human thought that order the ways in which human beings understand and respond to things, ideas, and events.

In relation to principles of belief, practical rulings, regulations governing individual behavior, reports concerning nations that lived in the past, and educational methods, the revelation embodied in the Qur'an and the Sunnah is a direct source of knowledge, particularly those verses and accounts which specify actions that are praiseworthy, intentions that are good to act upon, and actions that are mandatory or recommended. Such texts might also have to do with actions that a person should refrain from, including those that are simply undesirable and those that are utterly forbidden.

However, some texts do not serve as a direct source of knowledge or rules for living. Rather, such texts represent a source of general guidance, universal principles, worldview, and higher authority that sketch out patterns of human conduct in all areas of life. Texts such as these serve as a call to strive for progress within the parameters of earthly causes and effects to discover natural laws and put them to use for the purpose of bearing our God-given responsibilities and achieving progress in a variety of fields. Such fields include historical research (to discern laws and patterns of historical development that serve as lessons for us in the present), sociological research (to reveal social patterns that enable us to understand human nature and social interactions), research in the physical sciences (to discover the laws of physics, chemistry, etc.), educational research, and so on. Texts such as these help us to reflect on the affairs of our lives, the environment in which we live, and our relationships with others. Then, in light of the texts' guidance, we can weigh the various options before us and choose those that are most in keeping with the intents of the Islamic religion, most likely to achieve our aims, and least likely to involve undue hardship.

As for the Prophetic Sunnah, which we have termed "the hidden revelation," it is a companion to the Holy Qur'an. Muslims hold that all of God's messengers and prophets are infallible with respect to the messages they deliver from God, including their practical rulings and instructions on how to lead a life of godliness and integrity that will ensure people blessing both in this life and the life to come. The accounts that make up the Prophetic Sunnah cover a broad range of topics relating to the various areas of human life, and they serve a variety of purposes. Some accounts clarify the meaning of the Qur'an, others detail Qur'anic statements that are general in nature, while still others show how the Prophet applied Qur'anic teachings in ways that provide us with practical guidance or serve as a practical example for us to follow in this or that area of life. For this reason, Muslim scholars developed methods for properly understanding the narratives of which the Prophetic Sunnah consists. Such scholars identified numerous forms of guidance that can be derived from the life of the Prophet, including legislation, instruction, the description of virtues and praiseworthy customs, etc.

(2) *The Created World as a Source of Knowledge*

The second source of human knowledge in relation to methodology and other epistemological realms is the world, that is, the created universe, of which we can distinguish three different levels:

1. The natural, material world ranging from microscopic entities to vast, far-flung galaxies that can only be seen with the aid of powerful telescopes.
2. The social world, which includes human beings' lives as peoples, tribes, societies, communities and nation-states; family relationships, social relationships, and international relations; and the systems and laws that define people's rights and obligations.
3. The psychological world, that is, the realm of the individual human being on the level of mind and spirit, life and death, health and illness, knowledge and ignorance, thought and emotion, feelings and responses; how one thinks, how one's abilities grow and develop, how one ages and deteriorates, why and how one loves and hates. For although human beings are only tiny entities within the natural world, each of them contains within himself/herself an entire world of great vastness and complexity. As the fourth rightly guided caliph, ʿAlī ibn Abī Ṭālib, once said:

> The cure you seek is within you, but you sense it not,
> The illness that afflicts you is from you, but you see it not.
> You claim that you are but a miniscule entity,
> Though the cosmos in all its vastness is contained within you.[6]

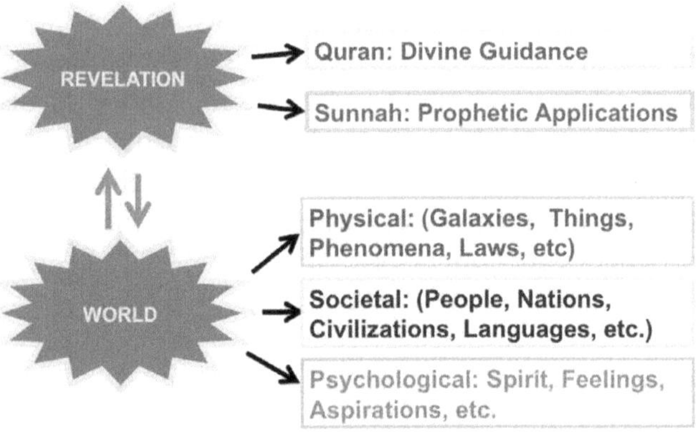

The information we obtain about the entities, events and phenomena in the world falls on a variety of planes. Some information will be a simple description, be it quantitative or qualitative; other information will be a compound description of an object, phenomenon or relationship, that is, a description accompanied by the articulation of a law or equation. Still other information will take the form of an explanation for the existence of certain things or phenomena, or a prediction that this or that phenomenon will occur with regularity given specified conditions.

(3) *Integrating Written Revelation and the Created World as Sources of Knowledge*

It is difficult to imagine boundaries separating written revelation and the created universe as sources of knowledge. After all, the Holy Qur'an declares the texts of its own verses, be they read from a page or recited, to be a source of knowledge. However, it declares the signs of God in the visible creation to be a source of knowledge as well. God Almighty is both the One who sent the written revelation down from on high and the One who created the physical universe. To God alone belongs all sovereignty. That is to say, God is the ultimate source of all the means of guidance He provides and in relation to all human affairs. Human beings "read" what is visibly displayed before them of the created universe, including the material, natural world, the social world, and the psychological world. They witness it, ponder it, measure it, calculate it, test it and put it to use.

Human beings are among God's creations, and God has brought them to completion in successive stages. Hence, anyone who ponders this act of God is bound to exclaim, "Hallowed, therefore, is God, the best of artisans!"[7] God Almighty commanded the Prophet, saying, "Read in the name of thy Sustainer, who has created – created man out of a germ-cell!" (*sūrah al-ʿAlaq* 96:1-2). This "reading" of God's signs in the created world, from the depths of people's souls to the vast horizons of the cosmos, leads the individual to the one Creator.

According to Imam Fakhr al-Dīn al-Rāzī, may God have mercy on him, "It has been related that ʿUmar ibn al-Khayyām was once reading the *Almagest*[8] to his instructor, ʿUmar al-Abharī. A certain jurist then asked him, 'What are you reading?' to which ʿUmar replied, 'I am explaining a verse from the Qur'an which reads, "Do they not look at the sky above them – how We have built it and made it beautiful and free of all faults?" (*sūrah Qāf* 50:6). I am explaining how the sky was built.' And he was correct in what he said, because whoever delves more deeply into the mysteries of God's creations will be more aware of God's majesty and greatness."[9]

There is, as we have noted, another kind of reading as well. For after saying to the Apostle, "Read in the name of thy Sustainer, who has created – created man out of a germ-cell!, Read – for thy Sustainer is the Most Bountiful One who has taught [man] the use of the pen – taught man what he did not know!" (*sūrah al-ᶜAlaq* 96:1-5). When we read what has been written in a book, that is, what has been written with a pen (whether literally or figuratively), it is because God has taught us how to write with the pen, that is, how to record the various types of knowledge we have acquired. Among the types of knowledge we have been given is what is contained in the book hidden from all eternity in the "preserved tablet," then bestowed from on high on God's Messenger: "[it is] a revelation from the Sustainer of all the worlds" (*sūrah al-Ḥāqqah* 69:43). God commanded the Prophet, "And convey [to the world] whatever has been revealed to thee of thy Sustainer's writ..." (*sūrah al-Kahf* 18:27), "...for We have sent thee but as a herald of glad tidings and a warner, [bearing] a discourse which We have gradually unfolded, so that thou might read it out to mankind by stages, seeing that We have bestowed it from on high step by step, as [one] revelation" (*sūrah al-Isrā'* 17:105-106). The Prophet's coming was an answer to the supplication made long before by Abraham and Ishmael, who prayed, saying, "O our Sustainer! Raise up from the midst of our offspring an apostle from among themselves, who shall convey unto them Thy messages, and impart unto them revelation as well as wisdom, and cause them to grow in purity: for, verily, Thou alone art almighty, truly wise!" (*sūrah al-Baqarah* 2:129).

The Qur'an (which means, "reading" or "recitation") thus consists of two complementary, integrated readings, each of which helps to complete the other. It is thus essential that we combine these two readings in order to obtain the wisdom and guidance we need. The two readings complete each other when the written revelation is read in order better to understand and relate to the created world, and when the created world is "read" in order better to understand and relate to the written revelation.

Let us turn now to some examples of the way in which these dual readings – the reading of the written revelation and the reading of the cosmos – complement and correct one another. God Almighty declares, "And it is He who has spread the earth wide and placed on it firm mountains and running waters, and created thereon two sexes of every [kind of] plant; and it is He who causes the night to cover the day. Verily, in all this there are messages indeed for people who think!" (*sūrah al-Raʿd* 13:3). In his commentary al-Qurṭubī (d. 671 AH) states, "This verse is a response to those who claim that the earth is spherical...." He goes on to quote statements by Ibn al-Rāwundī and others concerning the composition and movement of the Earth, then comments on them with the words, "Both Muslims and the recipients of the earlier revelations [the Jews and Christians] are of the view that the Earth is a flat expanse which remains still rather than moving [in an orbit], and that whatever movement occurs in it generally takes place as a result of earthquakes."[10]

Al-Qurṭubī relied for his understanding of this verse on the knowledge that prevailed in his day concerning the Earth's shape, composition, and movement. He even went so far as to scorn Ibn al-Rāwundī and others for claiming that the Earth was spherical, rotated on its axis and revolved around the Sun. Al-Qurṭubī supported his position by noting that it was consistent with the prevailing understanding among Muslims, Christians and Jews. Today, of course, we know that the Earth is in fact spherical, that it spins on its vertical axis counterclockwise (as seen from the North Pole), that it makes one revolution on its axis every twenty-four hours, and that it makes one revolution around the sun every 365 days (one solar year). Much of this knowledge is now virtually beyond doubt, being supported by empirical evidence, and is shared by Muslims, Christians, Jews, and others all over the world. As for the Qur'anic statement that God "has spread the earth wide," and which al-Qurṭubī cited in refutation of those who claimed that the Earth was spherical, we now have a different way of understanding what it means. The Earth does not appear to be spherical when we look at the part of it that surrounds us; nor can we feel it spinning. Moreover, the Earth is so large by comparison with those of us who live on it that we cannot see beyond the horizon. However, things need to be the way they are in order for us to live stable lives on Earth.

Other Examples:

Try to cite other examples from the Islamic heritage of Qur'anic verses or hadiths our understanding of which has changed due to a reexamination of our surroundings or a rethinking of issues in light of new information and discoveries. For just as the sciences of the ancients served as a tool for understanding religious texts, our present-day sciences perform a similar role.

Consequently, we can excuse al-Qurṭubī and other commentators who, in their day, did not have access to sufficient scientific data to realize that the Earth is round and that it revolves around the Sun. At the same time, we have no choice but to disagree with their interpretations of Qur'anic verses such as those that speak of God spreading the expanse of the Earth wide (*sūrah al-Nāziʿāt* 79:30), or according to which God "causes the night to flow into the day, and causes the day to flow into the night" (*sūrah al-Zumar* 39:5), or "covers the day with the night in swift pursuit" (*sūrah al-Aʿrāf* 7:54). Our present-day knowledge of natural phenomena is far greater than that which was available to al-Qurṭubī and those whose views he depended on for his understanding of things. From this it can be seen that the import of a Qur'anic verse is not restricted to what its words were understood to mean in a given age or period of history, nor does it stop at the boundaries of the knowledge that was available to this or that exegete during the age in which he lived. Rather, this meaning is capable of expanding to accommodate the new understandings God grants to human beings and which harmonize more fully with contemporary empirical knowledge of natural phenomena and the laws that govern them. Moreover, the fact that Ibn al-Rāwandī, who was known to be a freethinker and a libertine, stated a certain opinion does not necessarily mean it was mistaken for the simple reason that he rebelled against Islamic traditions. Contemporary scholars and scientists in many different countries might be classed as atheists and deniers of the truth about God. They are, nevertheless, highly respected scholars in their respective fields and specializations. Hence, their immoral lifestyles and their unbelief does not prevent them from arriving at scientific truths, concepts and principles in relation to the natural world, sociological patterns, psychological processes, and so on.[11]

Another example of the need to combine the two readings – the reading of the written revelation and of the natural world – can be seen in relation to a hadith concerning the undesirability of using water that has been exposed at length to the sun for ritual ablutions. This hadith was narrated on the authority of the Mother of the Faithful ʿĀ'ishah, may God be pleased with her, in numerous versions of differing degrees of reliability. The content of the hadith is found in a tradition passed down on the authority of ʿUmar ibn al-Khaṭṭāb, may God be pleased with him.[12] The hadith is cited because it treats the question of why this practice would be deemed undesirable. We read that,

> allowing ablution water to be exposed to the sun for a long period of time is undesirable given two conditions. The first condition is that it be exposed to the sun in containers made of metals such as copper, iron or lead, because, if the sun affects these metals, a fetid odor as of greasy meat develops over the surface of the water, which causes leprosy. This does not occur, by contrast, when the water is sunned in containers made of gold or silver. Nor is it undesirable for the water to be exposed to the sun if it is in containers made of pottery or other substances. The second condition for the undesirability of allowing ablution water to be exposed to the sun for long periods is that the exposure take place in extremely hot climates. If it takes place in moderate or cool climates, the practice is not undesirable because the effect of the sun on the water in the containers will be far less pronounced, and the question of whether to use the water for ablutions can be referred to a physician....The undesirability here will be either definitive, in which case one receives a reward from God for refraining from using such water for ablutions, or non-definitive, in which case there is no reward for refraining from using it for ablutions, since it is purely a medical matter.[13]

A third example has to do with the legal ruling on photography and visual representation in general. There are sound hadith recorded by al-Bukhārī and Muslim that prohibit pictorial and three-dimensional representations on the grounds that they are attempts to simulate the act of creation, and due to a proposed similarity between the act of placing them in people's homes and the placement of idols in people's homes in pre-Islamic days. Hence, until quite recently, Muslim scholars prohibited visual representations. Such prohibitions also included sculptures and other three-dimensional representations, and drawings done by hand. However, the increasingly widespread use of photographs for supporting documents and identification, the use of photocopy machines, and the growing need for photographs for a variety of purposes, had the effect of stripping photographs of their association with reverence and adoration and, therefore, idol worship. These developments also made it far less likely that the person doing the photography would be attempting to simulate the act of creation. Hence, scholars began issuing legal rulings permitting photography out of necessity. This was followed by rulings that permitted photography under virtually all circumstances provided it was not accompanied by other practices forbidden in Islam, such as photographing nudity, or allowing a man to be alone with a potentially marriageable woman for the purpose of taking photographs.

Third: METHODOLOGICAL TOOLS

The way in which we are presenting methodological tools may differ from the way they are generally presented in research literature, which tends to restrict itself to techniques and procedural methods used in data collection, such as laboratory experiments, questionnaires, interviews and the like. Contemporary research literature also presents detailed discussions of ways to ensure that one's research tools provide reliable measurements that are consistent from one researcher to another and from one instance to another. Such literature also provides instructions on how to use these tools and implement research procedures. This type of knowledge is certainly very useful, and if one learns it well and is trained in its use, it may help to correct some of the shortcomings that plague research practices in so many of our universities and research institutions.

The aforementioned research literature should be accessed and mastered whenever necessary. In addition, however, we want to expand the range of methodological tools that will help to connect the research questions from which we begin, the research procedures we implement, and the research outcomes at which we arrive. These tools only perform their role fully when they draw a firm connection between the researcher who has chosen a given tool, the way in which the tool is used, and the research topic that takes shape through the way in which the tool is used. It should be remembered that we resort to the use of tools in order to reveal information that was previously unknown to us and which would not be immediately obvious to us. Hence, the "subjective value" of a given tool lies in its ability to "decipher the symbols of phenomena...by gaining access to the secrets that lie hidden within them." This task will never be accomplished unless the appropriate tool is chosen for the desired purpose. As for the "added value" of a tool, it has to do with the researcher's ability to make maximal use of the tool he or she has chosen.[14]

It will be noted that our presentation of the topic of methodological tools also includes the major concepts, general entry points, "intellectual-ideological schools of thought, grand theories and explanatory models which the research employs as methodological tools, not only in order to compile research material and basic data but, in addition, in order to organize, analyze and explain such data, then use the resultant knowledge as an epistemological or ideological tool."[15]

For example, Dr. Sayf al-Din Abd al-Fattah has organized his presentation of methodological tools based on four approaches. The first approach is centered around the aims and intentions of Islamic law as set forth by Imam Abū Isḥāq al-Shāṭibī (d. 791 AH/1388 CE), which provides us with elements on the basis of which to describe, analyze, interpret and evaluate political phenomena, both local and international. The second approach, which we might term the "ship" approach, centers around the hadith in which the Messenger of God illustrated the nature of public responsibility and social cohesion by describing a group of people who find themselves on a ship at sea and observing that if any member of the group were to do damage to the ship, everyone would perish.[16] The third approach is a conceptual one which employs concepts in their capacity as systems for the analysis of interrelated social phenomena. As for the fourth approach, it is based on Thomas Kuhn's notion of an epistemological model as a tool for analyzing the scientific community's prevailing intellectual paradigms, which serve as research-related traditions and ways of thinking.[17]

The Tools of Reason and Sensory Perception

Just as the written revelation and the cosmos are the only two methodological sources – all other sources being traceable back to these two – so also are reason and sensory perception the only two methodological tools, since they serve as the basis for all other tools.

A tool is a means of fulfilling an intention or attaining a goal. If a well is a source of water, then buckets and pumps are tools for obtaining the water. Similarly, the eye is a tool for seeing, the ear is a tool for hearing, and the heart is a tool for reflecting, comprehending and understanding. God declares, "And most certainly have We destined for hell many of the invisible beings and men who have hearts with which they fail to grasp the truth, and eyes with which they fail to see, and ears with which they fail to hear. They are like cattle – nay, they are even less conscious of the right way: it is they, they who are the [truly] heedless" (*sūrah al-Aʿrāf* 7:179). A staff is also a kind of tool: "He [Moses] answered: 'It is my staff; I lean on it; and with it I beat down leaves for my sheep; and [many] other uses have I for it'" (*sūrah Ṭaha* 20:18). So also is awareness, or the mind: "And so We propound these parables unto man: but none can grasp their innermost meaning save those who [of us] are aware" (*sūrah al-ʿAnkabūt* 29:43).

The Arabic word *ʿaql*, translated as "mind" or "reason," is a verbal noun related to the process of intellection and reflection. God Almighty says, "Do you bid other people to be pious, the while you forget your own selves – and yet you recite the divine writ? Will you not, then, use your reason (*afa lā taʿqilūn*)?" (*sūrah al-Baqarah* 2:44); "We said: 'Apply this [principle] to some of those [cases of unresolved murder]: in this way God saves lives from death and shows you His will, so that you might [learn to] use your reason (*laʿallakum taʿqilūn*)" (*sūrah al-Baqarah* 2:73); and "Verily, in the creation of the heavens and of the earth, and the succession of night and day: and in the ships what speed through the sea with what is useful to man: and in the waters which God sends down from the sky, giving life thereby to the earth after it had been lifeless, and causing all manner of living creatures to multiply thereon: and in the change of the winds, and the clouds that run their appointed courses between sky and earth: [in all this] there are messages indeed for people who use their reason" (*li qawmin yaᶜqilūn*)" (*sūrah al-Baqarah* 2:164). The function of the mind, or reason, is to reflect, to contemplate, and to learn. Thus God Almighty declares, "And so We propound these parables unto man: but none can grasp their innermost meaning save those who [of us] are aware" (*sūrah al-ᶜAnkabūt* 29:43).

The term *ᶜaql* is used in the Qur'an in the same sense of the term *rushd*, that is, discernment and awareness of what is right. God Almighty says, "And, indeed, long before [the time of Moses] We vouchsafed unto Abraham his consciousness of what is right (his *rushd*); and We were aware of [what moved] him" (*sūrah al-Anbiyā'* 21:51). God states, "And test the orphans [in your charge] until they reach a marriageable age; then, if you find them to be mature of mind (if you find them to have *rushd*), hand over to them their possessions..." (*sūrah al-Nisā'* 4:6). The opposite of *rushd* is *ḍalāl*, that is, a failure to follow the right path even though one remembers the end toward which one ought to be aiming, and *ghayy*, which is a failure to follow the right path while forgetting the end one is should be striving for.

As for sensory perception, it is the use of the five known senses: the sense of sight, the sense of smell, the sense of hearing, the sense of touch, and the sense of taste. (Is there is a sixth sense?) Sensation is the ability to record the physiological effect of an object or event perceived on the sensory tool or organ. As for the meaning or significance of a physical sensation, this is conveyed when mental perception takes place, that is, when the mind interprets the sensation and attributes to the entity perceived the qualities and the defining characteristics appropriate to it. Perception via the eye is vision together with the ability to distinguish the size, color, and shape of the entity seen. Perception via the ear is hearing and the ability to distinguish sounds, including their quality and tone, whether they are loud or soft, a beautiful tune or a cacophonous roar, a human voice or the sound of a bird. Sounds also have names. Referring to the sense of hearing, God

Almighty asks, "...how many a generation have We destroyed before their time – [and] canst thou perceive any one of them [now], or hear any whisper of them?" (*sūrah Maryam* 19:98).

The unaided human senses can benefit from instruments or devices which broaden these senses' normal range of operation. The naked eye, for example, can only see within certain limits. It can see neither very tiny objects, nor objects that are extremely far away. However, instruments such as microscopes and telescopes can enable the eye to see both. Advanced microscopes enable the eye to see very minute details, while advanced telescopes enable it to see bodies that are extremely distant with far greater clarity. Such instruments enable the eye to do much more than merely note things' presence or distinguish them from other things by their proper names and functions. In addition, they enable the eye to distinguish numerous identifying characteristics such as dimensions (length, width, depth), colors of varying degrees of intensity, both primary and secondary, regular and scattered, as well as regular shapes, both two-dimensional (triangles, circles, etc.) and three-dimensional (spheres, cylinders) and irregular shapes.

Modern vision tools have become capable of distinguishing objects and identifying their many qualities and defining characteristics by means of something called a "magic eye." This "magic eye" picks up signals which stand for particular things and which call up a record of their numerous defining features because they have been programmed into the eye itself. You may have seen lines printed on the various types of merchandise displayed in supermarkets and other retail outlets. When the cashier wants to know the price of a given item, all he or she has to do is pass the item over the magic eye, which reads the item's name, determines its price, and adds it to the prices of the other things you have bought. The cashier then gives you a receipt that lists the prices of everything you bought and the total amount you owe for them. And all this takes place within a matter of a few moments.

Similarly, there are computers which can recognize the person using them based on the person's thumbprint or eye when it is presented to a magic eye mounted in the computer's screen. Once this recognition has taken place, the computer allows the individual to access and use the computer's programs. You also may have seen how an employee in this or that institution is able to open the doors to certain offices by inserting a special card into a magic eye, which recognizes the card's owner by picking up the data saved on the card, then allows him or her entry. These cards are now used as keys to houses and hotel rooms.

When cameras were first invented they could "see" a person's features, then record an image of him or her. Cameras then evolved from the use of light-sensitive film which, when developed in the proper manner, yielded images in black and white, to film that could pick up colored images. Then came digital cameras which require no film but, rather, can and store images instantaneously, and motion picture recorders whose digitally stored images can be easily transferred to microscopic chips, floppy disks or compact discs, each of which is capable of storing vast numbers of images and sounds.

All of these are examples of vision tools that far surpass the capabilities of the unaided human eye, thereby expanding our range of vision and the ways in which it can be put to use in thought, research and numerous practical spheres of life.

A similar story could be told about instruments that assist the human ear in picking up sounds in far greater detail and in far broader ranges than it could do otherwise; and the same goes for the other human senses. However, perception or sensation (Arabic, *iḥsās*, *ḥass*) is not limited to the material or physical realm alone. These terms can also be applied to knowledge,[18] or to awareness of something on the level of the heart, the mind, or the psyche. It is in this sense that the word *aḥassa* is used in the Qur'anic verse that reads, "And when Jesus became aware of (*aḥassa*) their refusal to acknowledge the truth, he asked...." (*sūrah Āl ʿImrān* 3:52).[19]

How do Reason and Sensory Perception Operate in Relation to Revelation?

When we read a verse of the Qur'ān, we attempt to understand the meanings of its words on the levels of both ordinary and technical usage, and what they mean in relation to the various other terms used in the Qur'an. We then attempt to understand the meaning of the verse within its immediate context and overall context. The principle of structural unity in the Qur'an, which requires that the Qur'an be allowed to interpret itself, is a basic methodological determinant in dealing with the Holy Quran as a source of knowledge. When reading the Qur'an we may also need to familiarize ourselves with the way the Prophet explained specific verses, in which case we will be making use of available commentaries and hadith collections.

Some verses of the Qur'an consist of explicit legal rulings having to do with matters that touch on essential parts of Islamic practice, such as financial transactions or social relations. Verses such as these may not be the subject of a great deal of research and review due to the clarity of their meaning. Nevertheless, reflecting on passages such as these may enable us to arrive at new wisdom in light of current events and newly gained expertise in the natural, social, and psychological sciences. Much of what is being written today on the miraculousness of the Qur'an as it pertains to scientific knowledge grows out of this type of reflection.

However, there are other Qur'anic verses which lend themselves to deeper and more prolonged reflection, and in connection with which God may open up new understandings to the thoughtful reader, revealing meanings that may never have occurred to either his forebears or his contemporaries. After all, the Qur'an is generous, ever-giving, and its wonders never cease. When reading verses such as these, we have less reason to be content with the explanations offered by early Muslim exegetes or hadith scholars, and more reason to interpret these passages in light of recent human experience of relevance to the text concerned. If the passage in question has to do with human experience in this earthly life, whether on the level of natural phenomena, social life, or psychological matters, we are called upon to give careful thought to the Qur'anic text and its various meanings in an attempt to acquire information about natural phenomena, social realities or inner experience of relevance to the text by the use of the appropriate tools and on the appropriate levels.

The verse we are reading might have to do with matters that lie beyond the realm of human sense perception. For example, it might contain statements about events that are to occur on the Day of

Resurrection and the accounting that follows it, be it easy or difficult, and whether it leads to lasting bliss in Paradise or miserable chastisement in Hell. In this case, the topic of contemplation in relation to the meanings of the verse lies beyond earthly human experience. Nevertheless, the divine revelation given to us in the Qur'an is a message to human beings, not to the angels. Consequently, the meanings of the words we find in the Qur'an are inevitably linked to human experience and can only be understood in light of it. Hence, God declares:

> And so they say, "[O Muḥammad,] we shall not believe thee till thou cause a spring to gush forth for us from the earth, or thou have a garden of date-palms and vines and cause rivers to gush forth in their midst in a sudden rush, or thou cause the skies to fall down upon us in smithereens, as thou hast threatened, or [till] thou bring God and the angels face to face before us, or thou have a house [made] of gold, or thou ascend to heaven – but nay, we would not [even] believe in thy ascension unless thou bring down to us [from heaven] a writing which we [ourselves] could read!" Say thou, [O Prophet:] "Limitless in His glory is my Sustainer! Am I, then, aught but a mortal man, an apostle?" Yet whenever [God's] guidance came to them [through a prophet:] nothing has ever kept people from believing [in him] save this their objection: "Would God have sent a [mere] mortal man as His apostle?" Say: "If angels were wa alking about on earth as their natural abode, We would indeed have sent down unto them an angel out of heaven as Our apostle." (*Sūrah al-Isrā'* 17:90-95)

Even when communicating to us about realities that lie beyond the realm of human sense perception, the Qur'an speaks in terms of concrete earthly human experience: "[And can] the parable of the paradise which the God-conscious are promised – [a paradise] wherein there are rivers of water which time does not corrupt, and rivers of milk the taste whereof never alters, and rivers of wine delightful to those who drink it, and rivers of honey of all impurity cleansed, and the enjoyment of all the fruits [of their good deeds] and of forgiveness from their Sustainer: – can this [parable of paradise] be likened unto [the parable of the recompense of] such as are to abide in the fire and be given waters of burning despair to drink, so that it will tear their bowels asunder?" (*sūrah Muḥammad* 47:15). Rivers, water, milk, wine, honey and fruits are all things that human beings know from their concrete experience of them. At the same time, these entities are not the realities they will encounter in Paradise, however similar to them they might seem to be:

> But unto those who have attained to faith and do good works give glad tiding that theirs shall be gardens through which running waters flow. Whenever they are granted fruits therefrom as their appointed sustenance, they will say, "It is this that in days of yore was granted to us as our sustenance!" – for they shall be given something that will recall that [past]. And there shall they have spouses pure, and there shall they abide. (*Sūrah al-Baqarah* 2:25)

For what we encounter in Paradise are realities that no eye has seen, nor ear heard, nor human heart conceived.

In sum, it is difficult, if not impossible, to make a neat separation between the function of the physical senses and that of the mind, or reason, in understanding the possible meanings to be found in the texts of the divine revelation. Rather, the working principle is that of integration and complementarity.

How do the Mind and the Senses Function in the World?

"Read in the name of thy Sustainer, who has created – created man out of a germ-cell!" (*sūrah al-ʿAlaq* 96:1-2). The kind of "reading" being referred to in these verses takes place by putting our senses to use through observation, qualitative description, assessment, quantitative calculation, and the discovery of relationships, laws and patterns by noticing the regularity of phenomena and events. This is followed by a process of predicting events and phenomena and the willingness to adjust our behavior in keeping with such predictions. We then put our minds to work formulating theories to explain the phenomena that we have observed within the parameters of a comprehensive, God-centered worldview. In light of such a worldview, we see these efforts as a way of investing the powers God Almighty has granted us as *khulafā'* (vicegerents) on earth.

In order to develop a method of relating to the Holy Qur'an as a source of knowledge, we need to draw a distinction between two ways of conceptualizing the relationship between the Qur'an and the realities people face. According to the first conceptualization, the Qur'an was revealed to the Prophet within the context of a particular reality and set of circumstances in which people were faced with specific issues and problems. Seen from this perspective, the verses of the Qur'an were a response to the issues of that day and provided answers to its questions. As for the second conceptualization, it relates the Qur'an to the realities we face today, and which – quite naturally – present us with our own issues, problems and questions. However, we tend not to read the Qur'an in order to receive the guidance we need in order to solve our problems. Rather, we are content most of the time to read the Qur'an for the sake of a reward we hope to receive, to find textual support for the juristic rulings we have learned, or in order to experience the solace and tranquility it brings us. All of these motives for reading the Qur'an are good, of course. However, unless we try to establish a connection between the Qur'an and the issues, problems and questions that face us in our present-day lives, we will never discover its methodological and epistemological value.

In order to develop a method for relating to the Qur'an as a source of knowledge, we need to approach it with specific problems that require solutions, crises we hope to overcome, and questions that need answers. And of these we certainly have plenty in our day! However, we have grown accustomed to taking our problems to experts when we are unable to solve them for ourselves. In most cases, the experts spend a significant amount of time and effort studying the problem and familiarizing themselves with its background, history, extent, causes, surrounding circumstances and the like before suggesting a way to resolve it. The difficulty we face in cases such as these is primarily methodological in nature, since it has to do with our inability to take the first step involved in any research effort, viz., to define the problem and to formulate it in a manner that leads the way to all of the subsequent steps that must be taken in our search for answers and solutions.

In order to define a problem, we need to understand the context in which the problem is occurring. This context may have to do with material objects and natural phenomena, with social and international relations, or with psychological issues relating to the individual and his or her changing states and conditions. This reality – this context – is a source of knowledge concerning the details of the problem calling for a solution. When did the problem begin? How did it become visible? What is the extent of it? What are the circumstances that surround it in terms of place, time, and people? These are some of the questions that need to be asked. As we ask the necessary questions, we will find that we need to review records of relevance to the problem, to analyze the data found in records, pictures and documents, to meet with concerned individuals in order to poll their views and attitudes, and to analyze our findings for consistency or inconsistency. The process may also require the use of instruments that broaden the range of our unaided human senses, such as blood type tests, gene analyses, and so on.

The world around us on its various levels – physical, social, and psychological – is something that we have no choice but to study and understand. This process of studying and understanding the facts is what has come to be termed "the jurisprudence of reality." In order to engage properly in this type of jurisprudence, reality needs to be studied with the aid of the appropriate methods and tools. For only then will we be able to effect the needed interaction between our reality and the Qur'an so that we can correct what needs correcting, resolve our problems, and cope successfully with our crises.

In sum, the proper reading of the written revelation takes place through the use of both our reason and our senses in order to link the written revelation to the world, while the proper reading of the world takes place through the use of both our reason and our senses in order to link the world to the written revelation.

Fourth: TOOLS OF THOUGHT, RESEARCH AND CONDUCT

Methodological tools can be classified as either tools of thought, tools of research, or tools of conduct. It is difficult to draw distinct lines between these three domains, which are interrelated and overlapping. Moreover, although the term "tool" may not be equally appropriate in all three realms, a discussion of this sort provides an occasion to affirm the importance of distinguishing between the methodology of thought, the methodology of research, and the methodology of conduct or practice. For although thought can take place without research, no research can take place without thought. As for conduct or practice, many patterns of behavior are pursued as a matter of mere habit, and are thus not accompanied by a great deal of thought. Other patterns of behavior, however, most certainly require thought of varying degrees of difficulty and depth.

The term "tools of thought" or "thinking tools" is sometimes applied to the mental operations one engages in while dealing with a particular issue in order to arrive at a desired outcome. Such operations include quantitative description or measurement, summarization, expansion or extrapolation, addition, classification, reordering, hypothesizing, and so on. Some teaching and training programs use exercises that develop specific thinking skills. These exercises, which involve operations such as cause identification, prioritization, presentation of evidence, and so on, take the form of a paper or set of papers which the trainee reads, after which he or she completes certain procedures in order to solve a problem or respond to a question.

There is a fair amount of semantic overlap between the terms "thinking tools," "types of thought" and "thinking skills." This overlap becomes apparent in a number of well-known training programs that aim to develop thinking skills. Maltesian physician and psychologist Edward de Bono has developed programs of this sort known as "CoRT," "Six Thinking Hats," and others. These programs aim to develop the skills people need in order to engage in certain types of thinking. There is a similar semantic overlap between "thinking tools," "ways of thinking," "thinking styles" and "thinking aids." Much of the literature of relevance to these various categories has to do with human development training programs which have come to enjoy a growing market in recent years.

Exercise

Design a training situation in which trainees search for examples of human development programs that make use of thinking tools, methods, and styles. This can be followed by a discussion of trainees' experiences with these programs.

Thinking tools include the things people do in order to organize and clarify their thoughts: by linking ideas, for example, or by expressing them through representative drawings or shapes. When ideas are linked to such drawings and shapes, abstract notions become tied to concrete figures, which renders them clearer and easier to remember, teach, review, test and critique. Someone might, for example, make reference to a close or necessary association between two things by placing his or her index finger and middle finger together, by moving his hand in a straight line to indicate a straight road, in a zigzag line to indicate a crooked road, and so on. Thinking tools need not be sensory or concrete in nature. In some cases they might be purely ideational or abstract, as when the tool is a familiar idea that one uses to refer to or speak about an unfamiliar one. However, one of the most commonly used thinking tools throughout the world is the practice of citing illustrative examples, where the example cited links the idea being discussed with a mental image of something known in the sensory, material realm, or of familiar social relationships or feelings.

This approach is used repeatedly in the Qur'an, which frequently clarifies ideas for its hearers and readers by means of examples drawn from the fates of bygone nations, natural phenomena and events, or human experiences and feelings. All of these examples are taken from the earthly realm in which we live in order to illustrate moral principles and truths or describe events that will take place on the Day of Resurrection. Such examples are also found frequently in the Prophetic hadiths, since the Messenger of God often resorted to the use of concrete examples in communicating with others.

Exercise

One or more situations could be set up in which trainees recall verses from the Holy Qur'an or accounts from the Prophetic Sunnah in which concrete examples are cited. These examples can then be discussed in terms of how they function as thinking tools, what they are designed to communicate, and their meaning.

Research Tools

Research tools can best be discussed by distinguishing among the three levels at which they operate: (1) research data collection, (2) research data analysis, and (3) research data interpretation.

Most of the literature published in books on research methods concerns itself with tools for collecting data from its sources. The discussion revolves around quantitative and qualitative data, the use of tests as a tool for measuring student achievement, the use of questionnaires as a tool for gathering facts from individuals who make up a study sample, the use of opinion polls as a means of determining what position on a given issue or set of issues is adopted by a community or representative sample thereof, attitude assessment criteria, document and record analysis, interviews, participatory observation, content analysis, etc. Books on research methods describe ways of constructing each type of tool, the cases and situations for which they are suited, conditions for their use, as well as their advantages and disadvantages. Even more importantly, they describe how to ascertain how reliable, consistent and objective a given research tool is prior to using it.

Which data collection tool one chooses for one's research depends on what question one is trying to answer, the type of data that needs to be collected, the nature of the members of the community involved, the size of the sample, the nature of the decision or decisions that will be made based on the outcomes of the research, as well as other conditions relating to the way in which the research process will be managed, and relevant ethical and psychological considerations. Such topics are treated in numerous works on research methods, so they need not be discussed any further in this context.

Data analysis tools have to do with quantitative (statistical) analytical procedures, qualitative analytical procedures, or a mixture of the two. There are books which deal specifically with each of these three types of data analysis and the research for which they are best suited.

In research that involves the use of quantitative data, the data are analyzed through the use of statistical methods or tools. These include: (1) descriptive statistics, which involves the use of frequency tables, central tendency measures, data curves, measures of association, change criteria, bar graphs, percentages, statistical ranking, and others; (2) analytical statistics, which calls for the use of statistical tests having to do with correlation, differences between averages, variance analyses, covariance analyses, and others; and (3) nonparametric statistics, such as chi square, t-tests, the Wilcoxon rank-sum test, and others. In the past, arithmetical procedures and algebraic formulas of varying degrees of complexity were used in order to perform such statistical tests, and the resulting analyses were quite time-consuming. Now, however, computer programs are able to perform the statistical analysis in a matter of a few seconds once the data has been organized and properly entered.[20]

As for research involving qualitative data, the data being employed will be descriptive. As such, it will take the form of observations recorded in various ways (responses the researcher has recorded while conducting interviews or during participatory observations and other forms of written narrative; audio or audiovisual recordings of dialogues or narratives, documents, observation forms, etc.). There are specialized references that detail techniques for analyzing this type of data, including procedures for converting the data from raw material into material capable of being systematically analyzed. It is usually necessary to choose units for analysis best suited to the type of research being done, with the units of analysis generally being on the order of partial thoughts and observations concerning the contexts and patterns in which such ideas appear.

Qualitative data analysis might, for example, take the form of what is termed conversation analysis, which looks at the forms of verbal interaction that take place in a particular environment or social context. The analysis aims to examine the indicators of the interaction needed in order to preserve the existing social order, and any indicators that disturb this order. The analysis involves observing verbal and nonverbal communication, both direct and indirect, in search of messages that lay hidden within the communication, and noting sequences of events and varying patterns of emotional intensity. The topic of interest in the observation and analysis may be the content of the discourse rather than its form, the purpose being to reveal the attitudes and cultural, racial or political biases and prejudices contained in the discourse, and the way in which the discussion of a particular topic has been structured. Alternatively, the topic of analysis might be the type of communication, which is then classified under one or more of a number of communication patterns that are customary in the culture of the local community, such as, for example, irony, sarcasm and ridicule, gossip and slander, debate, threat, optimism, etc.

Qualitative analysis is essentially inductive in nature, its aim being to move from partial facts and data to the formulation of a general conclusion or theory that goes beyond the original givens. The process of analyzing qualitative data is distinguished by the fact that it takes place in the course of data collection rather than after the data collection has been completed. The researcher arrives at a tentative conclusion during a particular phase of his/her observations. He/she then tests this conclusion by making further observations, which will either support the initial conclusion or lead the researcher to modify it in whole or in part. Qualitative data analysis is also distinguished by the fact that it is selective and eclectic in nature. Hence, it is not defined ahead of time, nor are decisions about it made in advance. Rather, the researcher chooses specific tools of analysis when and if they are seen to be needed.

The process of analyzing qualitative data involves two distinct strategies which nevertheless go hand in hand. The first strategy entails deconstructing the larger body of qualitative data and reorganizing it into sets which are easy to compare and link with the research questions being proposed. The second strategy is that of contextual interpretation, that is, explaining the data within an overall, consistent context that establishes the connection between the overall narrative and its specific events. These two strategies are sometimes combined in the presentation of the research results. For example, the results might be presented in the form of conceptual schemes or maps, matrices, or figures and tables that show the links among the various elements of the theoretical structure that has been arrived at.[21]

Theorists working on the topic of research in the social and human sciences have noticed that reliance on research that is strictly quantitative or strictly qualitative does not necessarily lead to the best results, and that some situations and topics call for the use of both types of research together. In cases such as these, the researcher chooses some elements from quantitative research and others from qualitative research in keeping with the requirements of the situation or topic at hand.

Recent years have witnessed the emergence of books devoted to what are termed mixed research methods.[22]

As for the tools used to interpret research results, they can be likened to those used in interpreting the Holy Qur'an. Interpreting the Qur'an entails efforts to arrive at an understanding of the meaning of Qur'anic texts through the use of a number of exegetical tools, including language, occasions of revelation (*asbāb al-nuzūl*), the principle of abrogation according to which some Qur'anic verses abrogate others (*al-nāsikh wa al-mansūkh*), and others. Some researchers make use of certain linguistic concepts on the basis of which they attempt to understand the meaning of the Qur'anic text. In an attempt to explain the meanings of foreign names (or, at least, names that are suspected of being foreign) in the Qur'an, one researcher made use of six linguistic concepts or phenomena to which he referred as "exegetical tools," namely, synonymy (*al-tarāduf*), opposition (*al-taqābul*), Arabization (*al-taʿrīb*), translation (*al-tarjamah*), correspondence (*al-mushākalah*), and general context (*al-siyāq al-ʿāmm*).[23] This researcher's thesis was that the Qur'an explains such foreign names within the context of the verses in which they occur, and that by the use of the aforementioned exegetical tools we can comprehend the Qur'an's explanation of these names.

Many Qur'anic exegetes these days make use of modern sciences as tools for understanding the meanings of the Qur'an. The culture of modernism and post-modernism has developed categories of thought that are of great value for the work of thinkers and philosophers. Some of these categories have become methodological entry points for understanding and interpreting both phenomena and texts. Others have developed into integrated theories or schools of thought that govern the work of thinkers in terms of the way they understand what they wish to understand, particularly written texts, be they religious, poetic, literary or historical in nature. Hermeneutics, for example, is now an interpretive tool that gives the reader the meanings he or she wants from the text regardless of what the text's own writer intended!

Little has been written on tools for the interpretation of test results. However, such tools tend to be latent within both a researcher's attitudes and worldview, and the research situation or environment. After all, no one begins the research process with a blank slate. Rather, he or she comes to the research with already existing knowledge about the topic to be investigated. He or she will also have expectations and desires concerning the results the research may yield. The researcher will know, for example, that specific results were yielded by a study in the past for particular reasons, while similar results were not yielded by another study for other reasons.

An example of research-result interpretation within a particular frame of reference can be found in the area of educational evaluation. When, for example, we have the results of an evaluation of the performance of a particular group of learners, we interpret these results within what is termed an evaluation frame of reference. Three types of evaluation frames of reference may be identified:

1. *Criterion-referenced evaluation*, which identifies a particular target level of performance on the basis of which results are evaluated, such as setting 60 percent as the minimum passing score on an academic test.
2. *Norm-referenced evaluation*, in which the basis for judgment is a comparison with the mean performance of a standard group. In this case, results are evaluated based on the degree to which a given score deviates (by points or fractions of a point) from the [statistical] norm.
3. *Self-referenced evaluation*, in which the individual is compared to himself or herself. That is, the individual's performance at a given time is compared to what it was at a previous time. The degree or percentage of change is noted, as well as how regular or even such change is.

Results might be interpreted in light of a given confidence interval and test of significance. The confidence interval (CI) is a statistical tool used in measuring the availability or nonavailability of sufficient statistical evidence to reject the null hypothesis.[24] The confidence interval may be set at 1 percent, 5 percent, or as high as 10 percent depending on the nature of the decisions which the researcher or the society will be making in light of the research results. The size of the confidence interval will, quite naturally, also depend on the research domain. In the exact sciences, for example, it would be difficult to allow for even a one-percent chance of error. In the social and human sciences, on the other hand, it might be possible to allow for as much as a five-percent chance of error. In fact, a ministry of education might be willing to risk embarking on a new policy or making some other education-related decision based on research results with a ten-percent chance of error for particular economic or social reasons.

Just as theories or theoretical models are constructed in light of research results, they then become explanatory tools in subsequent studies. Economic researchers, for example, explain some of the economic phenomena they observe in their research based on knowledge they already possess about economic practices and market mechanisms. Researchers in other fields also depend for their interpretations on prior knowledge of this sort.

When doing qualitative research, we will of course need tools of a qualitative rather than statistical nature for interpreting our research results. One reason for this is that qualitative research aims at gleaning information that is linked to the researcher's own worldview.[25] Interpreting the results of such research also calls for a significant degree of intuition and creativity, and an exceptional ability to link research outcomes with the cultural background of the community or society in which the study is being done, including its social customs, economic practices, ethical values and standards, religious frames of references, etc. Reference was made earlier to the strategy of story-telling or the use of examples and parables, which is a methodological tool employed frequently in the Qur'an and the Prophetic Sunnah. Stories, parables and examples might be used as tools for interpreting research results as well.

Fifth: A MODEL FOR EPISTEMOLOGICAL INTEGRATION

The epistemological integration model is an attempt to summarize and link everything that can be understood about the sources and tools of knowledge from an Islamic perspective. This model is made up of two parts: sources and tools. Epistemological integration within the Islamic worldview emerges on three levels: integration of sources, integration of tools, and integration of sources and tools together.

Seen from an Islamic perspective, methodology has two sources: written revelation and the created world. Hence, any and all epistemological and methodological approaches must seek to integrate these two sources. As creations of God, human beings have no choice but to relate to the created realm around them on its three levels – the natural world, the social world, and the psychological world. Human beings relate to these worlds regardless of their religious and intellectual frames of reference. However, as someone who believes in the written revelation embodied in the Qur'an, the Muslim is both answerable to God and equipped with the God-given ability to relate to the world in light of the guidance the divine revelation, which directs us to develop a God-centered awareness of the world and respond to it accordingly.

This, then, is the true nature of integration between the written revelation and the created world as sources of knowledge and sound methodology.

Similarly, methodology seen from an Islamic perspective has two tools to work with: reason and sensory perception. The senses cannot perform their intended function without reason, just as reason cannot function properly outside the realm of concrete reality. As we have seen, even the most abstract concepts are conceptualized by the human mind in terms of sensory experience, and the Qur'an urges human beings not to exert any effort in connection with realities to which they have no access. As God Almighty declares concerning himself, "...there is nothing like unto Him, and He alone is All-Hearing, All-Seeing" (*sūrah al-Shūrā* 42:11). Hence, there is no need to think about the divine Essence. Rather, it is sufficient for human beings to think about the creatures that point to the attributes of their Creator.

This, then, is the true nature of epistemological integration between reason and the senses as tools of knowledge and sound methodology.

The epistemological integration equation makes clear that deriving knowledge from the written revelation requires not only reason, but sensory perception, just as deriving knowledge from the created world requires not only sensory perception, but reason as well. This is what we mean by epistemological integration between sources and tools.

The diagram below is an attempt to illustrate these three types of integration:

Epistemological Integration Model

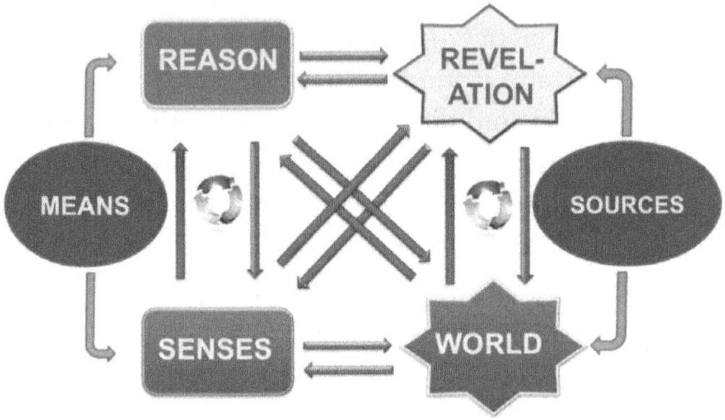

The inborn nature with which God has endowed human beings and other created beings has an important role to play in our understanding of the complementary nature of the sources and tools of knowledge. It helps us to understand God's purposes in creation and guides our thoughts and actions as God's *khalīfah* on earth toward achievement of these purposes. The written revelation in its capacity as a source of guidance ("...there shall, none the less, most certainly come unto you guidance from Me:..." – *sūrah al-Baqarah* 2:38), and reason in its capacity as a tool for understanding the purposes of the revelation ("And in the succession of night and day, and in the means of subsistence which God sends down from the skies, giving life thereby to the earth after it had been lifeless, and in the change of the winds: [in all this] there are messages for people who use their reason" – *sūrah al-Jāthiyyah* 45:5) complement one another in people's efforts to understand and apply the messages brought by this revelation. God Almighty knows best what human beings truly need in his earthly life, and has thus given us a place on earth and means of sustenance: "...We have given you a [bountiful] place on earth, and appointed thereon means of livelihood for you: [yet] how seldom are you grateful!" (*sūrah al-Aʿrāf* 7:10). Anything that disturbs the ecological balance of land, sea, and air prevents the Earth from fulfilling its God-given purposes.

Hence the use of biological, chemical and nuclear weapons, for example, whose destructive effects linger for hundreds and thousands of years, does nothing but corrupt the Earth. The ways in which this corruption manifests itself are evident to us based on observation, experimentation, and measurement, as well as our awareness of the pristine state in which the world existed before all this destruction began.

Our inborn moral awareness leads us to strive for justice, promote human rights and treat one another with integrity and equity, for it is in these ways that human beings' best interests are served. As for practices such as cheating others out of what is rightfully theirs, it corrupts relations between people, causing injustice, violating people's rights and causing people to harbor growing resentment and hatred in their hearts: "...Give, therefore, full measure and weight [in all your dealings], and do not deprive people of what is rightfully theirs; and do not spread corruption on earth after it has been so well ordered: [all] this is for your own good, if you would but believe" (*sūrah al-Aʿrāf* 7:85). The Qur'an explicitly commands us to demonstrate concern for others' welfare and forbids us to act in a niggardly fashion. It warns those who act in this way of a severe chastisement to come, since this type of conduct spreads corruption on earth. Armed with the mental capacities we have been given and the input we receive through our senses, we can understand the Qur'anic text by reflecting on examples of altruism and of selfishness, whose forms differ from one time and place to another but whose essence remains the same. Our God-given moral compass works together with the tools of knowledge to enable us to understand the messages conveyed by the written revelation, which is our source and authoritative point of reference; it also assists us in making practical distinctions between cases of altruism and selfishness, righteousness and evil.

As applied to the sexual relationships that serve people's true interests, our inborn moral compass leads us to strive for love and affection that nurture peace of mind and protect both husband and wife from temptations to satisfy their sexual urges outside their marital bond. Marital relations help to preserve the species through childbirth, while enabling people to carry on their family names and enter into fruitful, cordial relationships with other families, thereby forming tribes and entire peoples and nations while reinforcing a cohesive social fabric. Any sexual relationship that deviates from the God-given norm by taking place outside of marriage or between two members of the same sex brings corruption on earth, imbalance in both individual psychological makeups and the social structure, and destruction to social relationships. The written revelation is a moral authority that commands us to exercise sexual restraint with everyone other than our spouses; our reason helps us discern the wisdom inherent in this command, while our God-given moral compass helps us to distinguish between the sound relationships that serve people's true interests, and corrupt relationships that violate human interests and bring destruction, hardship, and social and psychological harm in their wake.

Such considerations highlight the need for us to deepen our understanding of the divinely intended order of things so that we can integrate sources and tools of knowledge with ever increasing efficacy.

CONCLUSION

It will be clear from the foregoing that the two sources of human knowledge within the Islamic framework – the written divine revelation and the created world – complement one another in enabling human beings to access greater and greater knowledge. It is true, of course, that God Almighty, being the One who bestows revelation from on high and being Creator of the World, is ultimately the sole Source of all knowledge. The term "revelation" as we are using it here refers to both the Holy Qur'an and the Prophetic Sunnah, which are viewed as the highest revealed authority for all human knowledge, while the term "created world" is understood to include the three distinct but interrelated domains of: (1) the natural world, that is, the realm of physical entities, (2) the social world, that is, the world of people as individuals, families, peoples, tribes, language groups, cultures and civilizations, and (3) the psychological world, that is, the world of the human soul as mind/reason, spirit, thought and behavior, including what we know of these realities and what we do not, and the full range of emotions that the individual experiences, both good and evil.

As the locus of the knowledge we are discussing, human beings have been brought into this world to be God's *khalīfah* on it, where the world itself is made subservient to them. When human beings were brought into the earthly realm, there descended with them the Revealed guidance they would need in order to fulfill their purpose of being *khalīfah*. This world with its three domains is the subject of the written revelation that guides people in their strivings to develop and populate the Earth and to live meaningfully and prosperously. It goes without saying, then, that this world is likewise a source of knowledge for human beings.

The same can be said about the tools of knowledge, since it would be impossible for human beings to manage their earthly affairs with nothing but abstract, disembodied reason. After all, the senses are the avenues by means of which the mind achieves understanding and awareness of both the messages of divine guidance and facts about the world in which we live.

The mind's God-given function, which is to discern the meanings of the divine revelation and to glean and understand facts about the world, lies at the heart of the divine purpose for creation. The function of the senses, which is to make the meanings of the divine revelation and the facts about the world easily accessible to the mind, is likewise God-given and central to the divine purpose for the created realm. Consequently we might say that just as the two sources of knowledge (revelation and the created world) are inherently complementary, so also are the two tools of knowledge (reason and sensory perception).

We have, additionally, the capacity to develop secondary sources of knowledge, as well as sophisticated devices that enable us to acquire more and more know-how, both theoretical and practical. And as we continue to progress to higher levels of understanding we should pray, "...O my Sustainer, cause me to grow in knowledge!" (*sūrah Ṭā Hā* 20:114).

7

Methodological Principles and Values

GOALS OF THIS CHAPTER

1. To clarify the meanings of the terms "principles" and "values" in the context of a discussion of Islamic methodology, and to highlight the reciprocal, complementary relationship between them.
2. To discuss the levels of methodological principles.
3. To identify the principles of Islamic methodology in the realms of thought, research, and conduct.
4. To identify the principles that are derived from the higher Islamic values of monotheism (*tawḥīd*), purification (*tazkiyah*), and societal development and prosperity (*ʿumrān*).
5. To explain the importance and various manifestations of *tawḥīd* in thought and life.
6. To explain the importance of purification on the levels of both individual thought and behavior and the building up of society, its systems, and its forms of governance.
7. To explain the normative value of the Qur'anic concept of civilization (*ʿumrān*), which serves as a guide for developmental efforts and achievements on the levels of the individual, the society, and the ummah.

INTRODUCTION

In this chapter we will attempt to define the concepts of "principle" and "value" within the Islamic intellectual framework in general, and within the framework of Islamic methodology in particular. Although each of these two terms has its own distinct meaning, they nevertheless overlap significantly on the level of semantics and usage. The overlap is so great, in fact, that the terms "principle" and "value" are used synonymously or interchangeable in many writings, and one of the two terms will sometimes be defined with reference to the other. One author might speak, for example, of "the principles and values upon which [this or that] movement is based...," or speak interchangeably of "the principle of monotheism" and "the value of monotheism." Similarly we might read that "by 'foundational principles' we mean the set of valucs that are derived from Islam's primary source...." This should come as no surprise, since both principles and values are viewed as guidelines and standards on the basis of which we make judgments concerning the power and validity of ideas and the soundness of the behavior to which these ideas give rise.

Islam's central higher values – monotheism (*tawḥīd*), purification, and development/prosperity/civilization – are both complementary and comprehensive. As a result, numerous secondary principles can be derived from any one of them. This higher value system can thus be viewed as a set of universal principles which govern the process of epistemological integration. For example:

1. The value of monotheism (*tawḥīd*) yields the principles of creation, the complementary of this world and the next, the complementary of the written revelation and the created world, the complementarity of reason and sensory perception, the epistemological integration model, and so on.
2. The value of purification (*tazkiyah*) yields the principles of: the complementarity of body, mind and spirit; the complementarity of the individual and society; the complementarity of knowledge and action, etc.

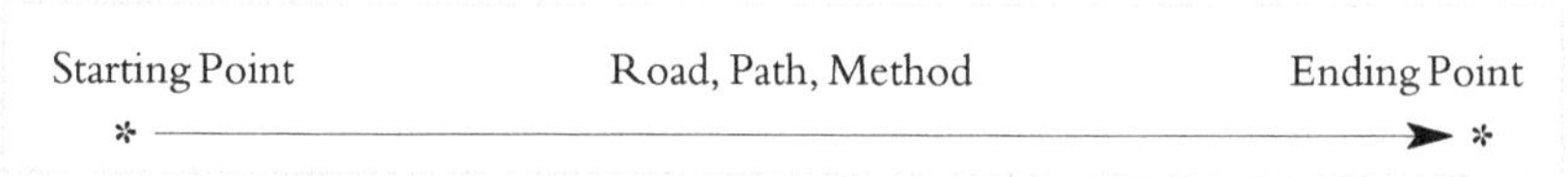

3. The value of civilization, societal development and prosperity (*ʿumrān*) yields principles such as the complementarity of life's social requirements (agriculture, industry, trade, communication, etc.), the complementarity of epistemological fields (the sciences of revelation, the humanities, the natural sciences, and the technical sciences), and the complementarity of utility and enjoyment.

We hope to show in what follows that each of these three elements of the higher value system serves as a foundation for a number of secondary values, and is manifested in numerous practical expressions of Islamic life. It might be noted here that in our discussion of *tawḥīd*, we have avoided a doctrinal or theological treatment of this value; in discussing the value of purification, we have omitted its mystical-experiential aspect; while in our discussion of societal development and prosperity, we have avoided their cultural aspects. In so doing, our intention is not to disparage these emphases, each of which is of great significance within its own proper context. However, as we have noted on more than one occasion, each of these three values has a universal quality that manifests itself in all of life's dimensions, not in a particular dimension to the exclusion of others.

What is the Relationship Between the Principles of Islam and the Principles of Methodology?

- "Know, then, that there is no deity save God..."
  (*Sūrah Muḥammad*, 47:19)
- "...produce your evidence if you truly believe in your claim."
  (*Sūrah al-Naml*, 27:64)

If we start with a principle, where do we end? We should reach the ends we hope to achieve, goals after their realization, the form in which applications and practices emerge, or one's final verdict on a given issue or question.

What are the ideas that would not be considered principles? They include things such as the essential elements of the Friday prayer, for example, or a wife's share of her deceased husband's estate when she has borne him no children.

First: AN INTRODUCTION TO THE PRINCIPLES OF METHODOLOGY

(1) *"Principle" as Term and as Concept*

The noun "principle" (Arabic, *mabda'*, plural, *mabādi'*) as it is used in discussions of Islamic methodology is a modern term. There is no reference in either the Qur'an or the Prophetic Sunnah to the technical sense of this word as it is used today. The noun *mabda'*, which is derived from the verb *bada'a*, meaning "to begin," is not found in the Qur'an. However, the Qur'an does use numerous forms of the verb *bada'a*, all of which speak in one way or another of the commencement of an action. Most Qur'anic verses in which some form of the verb *bada'a* appears couple this verb with its opposite, that is, *aᶜāda*, meaning "to bring back" or "do again." We read, "God creates [man] in the first instance, and then brings him forth anew:..." (*sūrah al-Rūm* 30:11). The verse reads literally, "God begins the creation" (*Allāhu yabda'u al-khalqa*), "then creates again" (*thumma yuᶜīduhu*). Similarly we read, "...as We brought into being the first creation, so We shall bring it forth anew..." (*sūrah al-Anbiyā'* 21:104), which reads literally, "As We began the first creation" (*kamā bada'nā awwala khalqin*), "we will create again" (*nuᶜīduhu*). We are told, "...As it was He who brought you into being in the first instance (*kamā bada'akum*), so also [unto Him] you will return (*taᶜūdūn*)" (*sūrah al-Aᶜrāf* 7:29), and "...He begins the creation of man (*bada'a khalq al-insān*) out of clay" (*sūrah al-Sajdah* 32:7). The phrase *bādiya al-ra'y* (*sūrah Hūd* 11:27), translated by Abdullah Yusuf Ali as "in judgment immature," refers to someone who forms a point of view in haste, without careful thought or examination. Similar uses of the root *b-d-'* are found in the Prophetic Sunnah. According to one saying of the Prophet, "Islam began as a stranger (*bada'a al-islāmu gharīban*), and as it was in the beginning, it will become a stranger once again (*wa sa yaᶜūdu kamā bada'a gharīban*). Blessed, then, are the strangers."[1] One of the beautiful names of God mentioned in the Prophetic Sunnah is *Al-Mubdi' Al-Muᶜīd*, derived from the Qur'anic description of God as the One "Who creates from the very beginning, and He can restore (life)" (*sūrah al-Burūj* 85:13, Abdullah Yusuf Ali).

When used as a technical term, the word "principles" appears in a variety of contexts. Depending on the context, the word "principles" can refer to information, beliefs, postulates, assumptions, premises, constants, or relationships between the concepts that define the theories and conclusions that can be tested and proven. The word "principles" can refer to governing values that guide behavior and standards for regulating and evaluating conduct. Similarly, it can refer to the foundations of an intellectual edifice, a religious belief, a practical course of action, and so on.

The term "principles" can also be used with varying degrees of generality or specificity. We might speak, for example, of principles of religion, principles of science, principles of thought, principles of research, principles of behavior, etc. The principles of Islam are its five well-known pillars, while the principles of faith consist of six pillars.[2] The principles of chemistry are the fundamental topics of this science. In other words, a book with a title "Principles of the Science of Chemistry" will most likely be an introduction to the science of chemistry, or the fundamental information from which students commence their study of this field. They may then go on to study the same discipline at higher levels and in greater depth and detail.

On the level of a specific book, principles may consist of the set of axioms or assumptions upon which the author bases his or her writing. The principles that contribute to the formation of a book on research methods, for example, might include the assumptions that research is a highly beneficial, worthwhile intellectual and professional activity; that development of research skills is critical to any profession; and that the process of learning research methods need not be daunting or tedious.

A principle might also be the scientific foundation, such as a scientific theory or a natural law, on the basis of which a particular device functions. The principle for the operation of a remote control device, for example, is the electrical contact that takes place between the remote control and another device via infrared rays without the use of any wiring. The remote control device in this case works together with some other device (a television, for example) by aiming the rays being emitted by the remote control at an electronic eye located in the television, which receives the rays and responds by opening or closing the electrical current, changing the channel, reducing or increasing the volume, etc. In the case of a natural phenomenon such as thunder, twilight, solar or lunar eclipses, etc., its underlying principle will be its scientific foundation, which consists in facts, theories and laws that enable us to understand how the phenomenon in question takes place.

In the realm of human conduct, a principle is the foundation for one's actions or a fundamental doctrine. For example, an ethical or moral principle is a type of commitment. Someone who is committed to a particular position in relation to his or her behavior or point of view is said to be a person of principle, since it is the principle in which the person believes that brings about the commitment in question. Such a person will accept or reject an idea or a course of action on the basis of principle, as a result of which his or her position on the matter will be nonnegotiable. In a situation in which a person lacks complete information on the idea or course of action concerned, he or she might make a tentative decision based on principle, with the decision being subject to review once more information is available, or once the idea or course of action has been examined in greater detail.

As we have seen, the Arabic word translated as "principle," namely, *mabda'*, is derived from the verb *bada'a*, meaning a starting point of some kind. The existence of a starting point requires, of course, the existence of some kind of ending point, as well as a road or path that connects the two points. Movement or change proceeds from the beginning point, then continues in the direction of an end point or goal. The path or road that connects the beginning and ending points is referred to in Arabic as a *manhaj*, which, as we have seen, is also applied to a method or approach. In order to reach the goal or finish line, one must commit himself or herself firmly to the appropriate *manhaj*, that is, path or method.

Given our definition of "methodology" as a science which concerns itself with ways of thinking, research methods, and patterns of behavior, it follows that, like other sciences, the science of methodology will have associated principles. The principles of methodology are the topics that constitute the basics of the science, that is, its major facts and concepts, how it began and developed, its theories, and its practical applications. Therefore, the main themes of the methodology sessions and workshops organized by the IIIT reflect the principles of the science of methodology: methodological concepts and other relevant notions, the evolution of the concept of methodology, the sources, tools, and schools of methodology, how methodology is applied to the various scientific fields, and so on.

(2) *How Principles Relate to Methodological Issues*

Intellectual reform (which includes both the reform of thought and the Islamization of knowledge) is a necessary condition for the cultural advancement of the Muslim ummah. Moreover, such reform requires that we define an Islamic methodology which is capable of achieving the desired aims. In applying Islamic methodology it will be necessary to proceed on the basis of fundamental principles, without which our vision will be blurred, our ideas will be unorganized, the character of the Muslim community will be tarnished, and its members will lack the impetus they need to move forward.

The methodology of which we are speaking is an action we engage in, an effort we make. Hence, it must begin with a conceptualization of where it will lead, it must arise out of the beliefs we hold, and it must adhere consistently to the standards, criteria and values that reflect these beliefs. In the context of a discussion of Islamic methodology, what we mean by "principles" are the premises on the basis of which the methodology proceeds in the realm of thought, research and conduct, to which it appeals in its efforts to reach its goals, and which lend their distinctive mark to its expressions and formulations.

The principles of methodology fall on a number of levels, of which we refer here to two: the level of the general or universal, and the level of the partial and specific. On the general level these principles have to do with the pillars of Islam, the pillars of faith and higher values, or *Maqāṣid*, while on the partial, specific level, they take the form of rules, standards and defining features of thought or research activity that aims to acquire, test and employ knowledge, or criteria for regulating and guiding conduct. The principles of methodology on the first level are well known. As for the specific level, it includes the following:

1. *Thought-related* methodological principles call for thinking to be universal, comprehensive, orderly, causal, aims-oriented, strategic, and practical.

2. *Research-related* methodological principles have to do with documentation (which should be done with honesty, integrity, and objectivity) and evidence (which should be practical, rational, and consistent with written revelation). These principles can be summed up in the motto: "If you are transmitting information, strive for accuracy, and if you are making a claim, provide proof."

3. *Conduct-related* methodological principles have to do with (a) intention, (b) adherence, and (c) creativity. On the level of intention, the researcher is expected to undertake his/her work for God's sake with a pure heart and a clear conscience. On the level of adherence, one is expected to follow a path that is tried and true, thereby aiming to reach one's goal in the most efficient manner possible, to emulate the example set forth by the Prophet, and to act collectively when this would serve one's community's best interests. On the level of creativity, one is expected to strive for greater and greater wisdom, to go beyond what has already been achieved when possible, to do good for others in the awareness of the divine presence, and to master whatever one undertakes.

(3) *Principles of Islamic Methodology*

In what follows we will make brief mention of a number of Islamic methodological principles, the content of which will have become sufficiently clear from the discussions contained in earlier chapters. Numerous other writings have also presented them in detail. (See in particular the works of Dr. Taha Jabir Alalwani, AbdulHamid AbuSulayman, Nadiya Mustafa, and Sayf al-Din Abd al-Fattah.) The Muslim undertaking research in a given area will be expected to:

1. Strive for internal consistency and harmony between his/her Islamic worldview, the epistemological system to which he/she adheres, and this system's methodological elements.

2. Adopt the Qur'an as his/her final authority, the concept of the Qur'an's structural unity, and the Prophetic Sunnah as a clarification and application of the Qur'anic message on the level of both facts and precepts.

3. Combine the readings of both the word of God i.e., the Revealed text, and work of God, i.e. the created world, undertaking both of them in light of God's oneness (*tawḥīd*) and the complementarity of sources that forms the basis for the epistemological integration model.

4. Apply the Islamic system of higher methodological values – that is, the triad of monotheism (*tawḥīd*), purification (*tazkiyah*) and societal progress and prosperity (*ʿumrān*) as the sources of all other Islamic principles and values on the levels of both theory and practice.

5. Apply the fundamentals of the Islamization of knowledge, which calls for competence, comprehension, and the aspiration to stretch existing boundaries by striving for continual progress toward human perfection.

Second: THE BASICS OF METHODOLOGICAL VALUES

The aforementioned tripartite system of higher values within Islamic methodology will be discussed in some detail, for three reasons.

First: Because this system is an all-encompassing framework for Islamic methodology.

Second: In order to emphasize these values as standards and regulations that govern all other methodological principles, whether on the general level of thought, theory and doctrine and belief, or on the concrete level of practice and procedure as they pertain to thought, research and conduct.

And third: In order to broaden the domain of action known as the ethics of scientific research method and to tie it into the overall goals and approaches of Islamic methodology.

(1) *Monotheism (Tawḥīd): The First Foundation of the Triad of Governing Values*

In his view of Qur'anic guidance and the major principles to which it gives rise in what he terms "the system of governing values," Taha Jabir Alalwani defines its elements as the three value-based concepts of monotheism (*tawḥīd*), purification (*tazkiyah*), and societal development and prosperity (*ʿumrān*).3 In Alalwani's view, these three values together constitute an aims-based frame of reference which reveals God's purposes for creation. They are also a normative value system which gives rise to all of the other primary and secondary values in the Islamic religion. At the same time, however, this value system is an expression of the true nature of things, not something extraneous that is imposed on them from without.

These three values are intimately linked. The first value – *tawḥīd* – is an absolute truth to which we are led naturally by contemplation and reflection on the nature of things. Affirmation of *tawḥīd* frees human beings from the states of confusion, anxiety and lostness that grow out of all other ways of conceiving God and the universe. The second value, that of *tazkiyah*, entails a process of bringing the human soul to a higher plane and purging society of all forms of corruption and perversity, and cleansing people's wealth by distributing it more justly among the members of the community and putting it to more beneficial use. These are all processes that bring about greater peace of mind while promoting a sense of responsibility and social solidarity and building a society with unified, cohesive structures and systems. As for *ʿumrān*, it requires efforts to put human potentials in a way that enables human beings to fulfill their purpose as *khalīfah* on earth by developing human civilization to its fullest potential. In short, this triad of higher values brings together the elements of the Islamic worldview as it relates to God, human beings, and the world.

Islamic doctrine places central importance on affirmation of the divine oneness. Seen from the Islamic perspective, this affirmation is of intrinsic value, with all other values being derived from it. The entire world is subject by its very nature to the requirements of the divine unity. Hence, if human beings want to be in harmony with the world, they have no choice but to be purified from within by turning to God alone in worship. Allah Almighty is the Lord of mankind as he is the Creator and Sustainer (*tawḥīd al-Rubūbiyyah*). He is the Sovereign King of mankind, who has the right to order and legislate (*tawḥīd al-Ḥākimiyyah*). He is the God of Mankind who is the only one to be worshipped (*tawḥīd al-Ulūhiyyah*).[4] It is human beings as *khalīfah* on Earth who stand in need of purification and reform. This purification and reform take place as we submit ourselves to the divine guidance by caring for all of God's creatures and managing their affairs. Hence, purification is both the end and means of societal development and prosperity; as such, it is an inseparable part of a sound, thriving social structure.

Despite the integrated, interconnected nature of the Islamic value system's three elements, they are not necessarily of equal importance, since the divine unity, or *tawḥīd*, remains the most central and fundamental of them all. It is *tawḥīd* that ensures continuity between human efforts in this world and reward or retribution in the world to come. Indeed, the affirmation of God's oneness has always been the foundation of the divinely revealed religion and God's message to His apostles and prophets. As God Almighty declared to the Prophet, "… before thy time We never sent any apostle without having revealed to him that there is no deity save Me, [and that,] therefore, you shall worship Me [alone]!" (*sūrah al-Anbiyā'* 21:25). Utterance of the words, "There is no god but God, and Muhammad is the Messenger of God" is the way in which one enters Islam and commences the erection of its five pillars by affirming the religion on the level of doctrine, worship and lifestyle. The aforementioned dual testimony of faith defines the six pillars of faith[5] and releases people's God-given intellectual and psychological potentials by enabling them to achieve the proper balance between material and spiritual concerns. It frees them from the illusions so rampant in human society, planting their feet in the certainty of true knowledge. When the pillars of faith have been affirmed, believers are established as brothers and sisters who build a single community whose members work to achieve advancement, prosperity and true human *khilāfah* on Earth.

Affirming God's oneness involves more than simply fulfilling the basic requirements of faith and submission to God. Rather, it goes beyond these to the level of inward goodness, where the mind, the heart, and one's entire physical being are released to achieve ever advancing levels of purity as one is freed from the effect of the misconceptions that arise from *shirk* – association of partners with God – on the levels of both belief and behavior.

Elsewhere[6] I have treated the subject of the divine oneness as it is presented in the Holy Qur'an and the Prophetic Sunnah, tracing the various ways in which this topic has been dealt with throughout the history of the Muslim community. The present discussion will be limited to a particularly noteworthy treatment of this topic which stresses the impact of affirming the divine oneness on the individual and society in their spiritual and material dimensions alike. The work to which I refer, entitled *Al-Tawhid: Its Implications for Thought and Life*,[7] was written by the late Ismaʿīl al Fārūqī (d. 1986), a pioneering scholar and thinker of the Islamization of knowledge school.

Al-Tawhid: Its Implications for Thought and Life is distinguished for the way in which it views *tawḥīd*, or affirmation of God's oneness, as the most central and significant value of the Islamic religion and the source of virtually all other Islamic values as well. The book presents an overview of the various ways in which the value of *tawḥīd* has been manifested in all areas of life. A serious modern attempt to revive and reactivate scholastic theology, *Al-Tawhid: Its Implications for Thought and Life* links scholastic theology to the movement of history and to Muslims' legitimate longings for cultural advancement in the modern age. The book does a superb job of presenting the methodology of epistemological integration, a methodology which the author himself adhered to, thereby consolidating the link between the Islamic authority underlying this methodology and its manifestations in thought, scientific and academic research, and the cultural practices of both individual Muslims and the Muslim ummah.

Beginning with the reality being experienced at present by the Muslim ummah, al Fārūqī discusses *tawḥīd* as a value that governs all areas of Muslims' lives on both the individual and collective levels. His aim is to present a vision of existence that will help young Muslims to progress along the path of true reform, and to analyze the concepts of Islam in such a way that they serve as a measuring rod for reform programs. *Tawḥīd* is the essence and heart of Islam; as such, it is both the launching pad for reform and its defining content. Hence, all thirteen chapters of al Fārūqī's book have to do with *tawḥīd*, which, lying at the heart of all divinely revealed messages, provides the standard for judging history, the realm of the unseen, ethics, the social system, economic and political systems, the family, the world order, and even aesthetics. The special merit of al Fārūqī's book is that every one of its chapters affirms the centrality of the divine oneness as a standard for evaluating and discussing that chapter's theme.

Al Fārūqī shows the way in which the *tawḥīdī* worldview integrates and combines the philosophical, epistemological and practical dimensions of a culture. Without burdening the reader with conceptual overload as sometimes happens in traditional writings on Islamic philosophy and scholastic theology, al Fārūqī aims throughout to promote the reform of Islamic thought and the contemporary Islamic reality.

The following are examples of the way *tawḥīd* serves as the source of other values in all realms of human life.

(a) *Manifestations of Tawḥīd in the Social System: The Nuclear Family and the Muslim Ummah*[8]

The teachings of Islam encompass all aspects of life, while the task of acting as God's *khalīfah* focuses primarily around the ordering of social life and relations in accordance with God's commands. Such commands are not limited to family affairs, but go beyond them to include rulings on financial and economic transactions, affairs of state and governmental administration, judicial rulings, and laws intended to ensure justice, all of which touch on the social dimension. Rulings on rituals of worship and individual ethics make up only a small proportion of Islamic legislation. It should also be borne in mind that many rulings on those rituals are social in nature, having to do with practices such as the distribution of zakah and the major and minor pilgrimage to Makkah, i.e., Hajj and Umrah, while others, such as ritual prayer and fasting, impact the social dimension in effect as well.

The ethical guidance Islam provides gives concrete form to the moral trust human beings bear as *khalīfah* in this world. Human beings can only bear their God-given trust in the context of a social system, in which ethical values might be likened to a spirit that rules relationships. Such relationships include, for example, the processes of buying and selling, in which people cooperate in providing for their basic needs. It is in social interactions such as these that integrity, honesty, and trustworthiness come into play. If there were no society, such ethical values would be meaningless. Moreover, the concrete measures designed to regulate people's behavior differ from one society to another and from one time period to another. These differences illustrate the dialectical relationship bet-ween the essence of an ethical value and the practical, concrete forms this value takes.

The Islamic social system, being founded upon the belief in God's oneness, views the family as the foundational unit of society and stresses the importance of promoting and strengthening family ties. In this respect the Islamic social system differs from all other systems. Communism, which attempted to do away with the role of the family, worked to undermine family ties and relationships, while the spirit of individualism in the West has damaged family cohesiveness to the point where the family is on the verge of dying. Similarly, anthropological theories that view relationships among people as analogous to those that exist among animals have encouraged people to believe that there are no significant differences between animals and human beings, which has in turn undermined the honorable role assigned to the family. Hence, given the intimate connection between the family and human culture, human civilization is in danger of disintegrating.

It is significant, therefore, that the Qur'an contains numerous detailed laws and legal rulings pertaining to marriage, divorce, the nursing of infants, and inheritance – all of which have to do with the family – whereas in all other areas, it contents itself with general principles and only the occasional detailed ruling.

The Muslim family continues to preserve a number of its distinctive characteristics thanks to its adherence to rulings of Islamic law, all of which arise from the doctrine of *tawḥīd*, or the oneness of God. The reason for this is that the purpose for the creation of human beings was to perfect the ethical side of the human will via the actions of human beings' themselves. This process takes place on four levels: the individual self, the family, the tribe or nation, and the Muslim community at large. The first two levels are self-evident. As for the third level, it derives its value entirely from the fourth level, since, if tribal and international relations restrict peoples' cooperation with each other to those who belong to the same race, whose skin is the same color, and who speak the same language, this does nothing but destroy human dignity, generate a spirit of superiority and entitlement, and lead to conflicts and wars.

As for the community whose existence is based on the doctrine of God's oneness, it is also based on harmony with people's inborn nature and what this nature requires, namely, relationships marked by good will, compassion, and shared responsibility. The basic unit for building such relationships is the family, which consists of a husband and a wife and the relationships to which their marriage gives rise with in-laws, children, grandchildren, and so on. These familial relationships involve a network of responsibilities to which reference is made in Qur'anic phrases such as *ūlū al-arḥām*, which is translated variously as "kindred by blood" and "closely related" (its literal rendering being, "those who share in wombs") and *dhawū al-qurbā* – literally, "those marked by nearness" – and which is translated as "near of kin" or simply "kin." These phrases are often used in relation to legal rulings whose purpose is to order social relationships and to ensure that they are sound, healthy and stable. Such rulings are rendered effective by virtue of people's faith in God's oneness. For unless a society adopts the family within its legal framework, the manifestations of the principle of *tawḥīd* will not be evident in human society.

The extended Muslim family does not rely on the notion of financial autonomy for the man and the woman, the husband and the wife. Rather, it is founded on cooperation and mutual support which make it possible to marry at an early age. The children in the family live with its older members, and a single household will embrace at least three generations. Such a household is a place where cultural norms, customs and traditions are passed down naturally from one generation to another, and children are raised on long-established values. Love, good will, and compassion are freely exchanged in an atmosphere that deepens empathy, affection, and respect. This type of family atmosphere nurtures the various expressions of normal life with its joys and sorrows, laughter and tears, seriousness and banter, and shared sacrifice, and life within such a household is marked by an optimistic view of the future. All these phenomena serve to promote the psychological health that every one of us needs. As for the nuclear family, its choice is based on a materialistic view of life and the world in which the husband and wife attempt to flee from God-given social responsibilities. In reality, however, they bear even greater responsibilities that fill their lives with hardship and burdens, not to mention the fact that such a life does not require them to develop greater psychological maturity (and hence, psychological health) or a deepened sense of their own humanity.

Islam sets down a clearly defined concept of the family, which is the building block of the larger community of faith. In addition, it offers a clearly defined concept of the larger community of faith. The Arabic word ummah, being translated here variously as "the Muslim community" or "the larger community of faith," is a uniquely Islamic term which points to a reality that is linked to Islam's vision of the world. The term ummah differs from the terms *mujtamaᶜ* (society), and *jamāᶜah* (group) in terms of its linguistic denotations and its idiomatic significance. It is difficult to convey the full meaning of the Arabic term ummah in translation, since it refers neither to a specific people (*shaᶜb*), nor to a state (*dawlah*), nor to a national or ethnic group or tribe (*qawm*). The term ummah is not linked to any particular place or geographical boundaries. Nor is it tied to ethnic origin, nationality, or political affiliation. Rather, all human beings on earth either belong already to this ummah, or community of faith, or are invited to join it.

The unity of the Muslims or ummah is a religious and ethical unity, not a unity of biology, ethnic origin, language or politics. This is why the Prophet referred to the Jews of Madinah as an ummah despite the fact that they formed part of the society of Madinah and shared with the Muslims of the city in the same geographical, linguistic, political and cultural milieu. In other words, it is religious identity which defines the concept of ummah. Nevertheless, the existence of political, geographical, ethnic and linguistic unity supports and reinforces an ummah's religious unity. After all, it is those nearest to us in all these respects who have the greatest claim on us. At the same time, these various types of unity are not the basis for the ummah's makeup and identity. They are defining characteristics which exist of necessity, and some of which may be outside of our control. However, membership in an ummah in the religious sense is something we consciously decide on, and which comes about by virtue of a deliberate individual choice. Consequently, it cannot be forced upon us from without.

(b) *Manifestations of Tawḥīd in the Political Order*[9]

As a central value in Islam, affirmation of the divine unity is the source of other Islamic values as well. It content is reflected in all realms of thought and life, from the political system to aesthetic and artistic values. The divine unity is manifested most fundamentally in the unity of the Muslim community, or ummah, which is a basic condition for fulfillment of the purposes of human *khilāfah* in the political realm, as elsewhere. In other words, the ummah is the major formative unit of the Islamic political system. If unity is an attribute of God Almighty, this calls for the unity of the community of faith associated with God's religion. As God has declared, "Verily, [O you who believe in Me], this community of yours is one single community, since I am the Sustainer of you all: worship, then, Me [alone]!" (*sūrah al-Anbiyā'* 21:92).

As we have seen, the concept of ummah is a uniquely Islamic one characterized by a universality that goes beyond ethnicity, color, language, and location. Similarly, it transcends political authority, and in this way it enables Muslims to carry out their religious obligations while at the same time enjoying their legitimate rights anywhere on earth. Such individuals can adhere to the civil laws of the society in which they reside as long as these laws allow them to carry out their Islamic religious obligations. In such a situation, by virtue of their ethical conduct, Muslims can be an example that draws others to their religion, encouraging others to embrace Islam and, in so doing, to join the Muslim community. If, on the other hand, Muslims are not free in the country where they reside to practice their Islamic faith, they have the option of emigrating to some other country where they will be free to do so: "And he who forsakes the domain of evil for the sake of God shall find on earth many a lonely road, and well as life abundant..." (*sūrah al-Nisā'* 4:100).

The Prophet's Companions and their immediate successors demonstrated great interest in the sayings and actions of the Prophet. This interest was a reflection of the nature of the Islamic religion itself and the historical movement that was produced by the application of Islamic principles. For the Islamic religion is, first and foremost, a practical, realistic, applied religion, not a utopian, pie-in-the-sky preoccupation with things that can never be. The details of the Prophet's life helped his Companions and those who succeeded them to move from the realm of abstract, theoretical understanding into realms that would translate this understanding into concrete action. Practical details are the ways in which the values of the religion express themselves. They also perform an educational function in that they make such values easier to grasp.

The Islamic understanding of the ummah, or Muslim people, has three distinguishing features. First, the Muslim ummah is one in its worldview, which consists of an awareness of the values that shape the divine will and the ability to discern how these values apply to new and changing situations, problems and questions. It is this ability that gives Islamic values an ongoing vitality and effectiveness. Second, the Muslim community is one in its readiness to translate the values that determine what ought to be into concrete practices on the level of individuals, groups, and leadership in such a way that the members of the Muslim ummah work together toward their desired aims. Third, the Muslim ummah is one in its practical orientation and creativity, both of which are needed in order for its members to be *khalīfah* on earth. In other words, the Muslim ummah strives together for the legitimate enjoyment of the blessings of this world, including a prosperous life and a sense of individual and collective security. This striving includes efforts to prevent the spread of ignorance, poverty, and disease or, at the very least, to minimize their impacts. These three distinguishing features are thus indicative of the Muslim ummah's consensus in terms of vision, will, and action.

The affirmation of God's oneness expressed in the testimony that "there is no god but God" means, among other things, that the divine guidance is valid for everyone everywhere, that the Muslim ummah is the foundation for human togetherness, and that the concept of ummah differs from non-Islamic religious concepts in that it gives the followers of other religions the right to come together on the basis of their own religion; in fact, it urges them to do so. The ummah integrates the followers of these other religions into Muslim society while allowing them to retain their own religious identities and institutions. The constitution of a Muslim society must convey to all that they are invited to enter Islam or, at the very least, to enter Islam's protection, while continuing to protect their rights as religious minorities and promote an environment of peace. This global feature of the affirmation of God's oneness is thus an open invitation to peace. It does not necessarily ensure people's entry into Islam. However, it does guarantee the establishment of peaceful relations in the context of which human freedom and dignity are nourished and maintained via mutual understanding, neighborliness, and cooperation in the areas of the economy, society, thought and culture. To deprive people of freedom is to violate their human dignity. Hence, every member of a Muslim society should enjoy complete freedom to choose his or own religious affiliation.

When the world is imbued with ethical values, God's will is done, and human beings' care for and preservation of this world become a form of worship. Every one of God's creatures is an instrument for the perfect fulfillment of God's will. However, human beings are creatures upon whom a special honor has been bestowed. As such, they possess the ability and the will to fulfill the divine will. They are not in an existential predicament from which they have no ability to escape; hence, they do not need a rescuer or savior. Rather, all they need is to carry out their duties, and once they have done this, their value will increase in proportion to their achievements. Affirmation of the divine oneness is likewise an affirmation that it is God's will for blessing to come to all human beings. Ethical action possesses the same value regardless of people's customs, the color of their skin, or where they live. Hence, an ethical life is of universal value, and is societal in nature.

(c) *Manifestations of Tawḥīd in the Economic System*[10]

In al Fārūqī's view, the value-based dimension that follows from the testimony that "there is no god but God" is among the most significant manifestations of *tawḥīd* in Islam. The will of God Almighty possesses ultimate value, and everything else derives its value from this will. People's worship of God Almighty is a fulfillment of the divine will, which is what gives true value to time and place. The divine purpose for creating the world was to build a world filled with values through human beings' possession of the divine worldview and the ethical action with which they fill their lives. As human beings are mindful of all the things around them, every one of which is of cosmic value, they perceive their obligation to preserve, improve, and beautify this world. All human beings are equal, and no one surpasses any other except by virtue of good works (consciousness of God). Similarly, all things in this world operate in keeping with God's laws, and their value is enhanced by their being put to beneficial use by human beings in their endeavors to help the world fulfill its God-given potential.

As a religion that declares God's oneness, Islam affirms the need for a balanced relationship between the material and the spiritual. By virtue of this affirmation, Islam seeks to bring benefit and blessing to human beings everywhere by striving to make beneficial use of the Earth's resources, by providing for people's material needs, and by promoting integrated development. Any and all spiritual progress or advancement must be accompanied by material improvement as well (and vice-versa), because, if there is no balance between the material and spiritual dimensions, the order of life will be disturbed.

The economic system in Islam is based on two principles. According to the first principle, no individual or group has the right to exploit others. According to the second principle, no individual or group has the right to impose an economic blockade on others or deny them access to merchandise or services. Ibn Khaldūn made clear that principles such as these are universal social laws. Human beings are civic by nature. In other words, human life requires some sort of a collectivity in order for there to be cooperation and integration between individuals and communities with interconnected, shared interests. Hence, the Prophet did away with the arrangements that had been in place among the various tribes of the Arabian Peninsula in order to facilitate transportation, travel, migration and free trade. Similarly, the second Caliph, ʿUmar ibn al-Khaṭṭāb abolished all customs border checkpoints in order to ease the movement of persons and merchandise among the various territories of the Islamic state. Indeed, trade between the various Islamic administrative districts and the Byzantine Empire remained unfettered even in times of hostility and armed conflict.

Belief in the divine oneness is likewise reflected in the general principles operative in an Islamic economy. It has manifested itself, for example, in Muslims' work ethic and Islamic principles of production. One such principle stipulates that one should produce more than one consumes, offer more services than one uses, and give the world during one's lifetime more than one has received. Another Islamic principle of production stipulates that agricultural and industrial production should be geared toward what will most benefit consumers without doing harm to the resources of which human beings have been made *khalīfah*. A third such principle stipulates that if one is given use of something that belongs to someone else, one should always return it to its owner in the same or better condition than it was when one first received it. A fourth principle requires that products be untainted in any way, and that services be rendered in an entirely honest and straightforward manner, not for fear of detection by surveillance institutions but, rather, out of a desire to abide by the noble ideals that arise from belief in *tawḥīd*, by a God-given aspiration to do good, and the inward satisfaction that comes from doing the divine will and anticipating a goodly reward in the life hereafter.

With respect to the ethics of production and consumption, belief in *tawḥīd* gives rise to a number of principles. These include a positive attitude to material consumption, in other words, an awareness of the value of material things and the importance of meeting one's fundamental material needs, yet not to the point of wastefulness and extravagance. Surplus production in an Islamic economy is to be reinvested in order to increase production, enrich the Muslim ummah, and contribute to social services and other good causes in the hope of winning God's favor and demonstrating compassion and solidarity with those in need. There are numerous possible ways of spending funds in order to meet basic needs on the levels of the individual, the society, and the state. On the level of the individual, one is required to support his family and distribute the zakah he owes among the individuals and groups specified in the Qur'an.[11] Individual Muslims may also extend voluntary charity to whoever else they feel moved to assist. When a Muslim dies, whatever wealth he or she has left is distributed according to a highly precise and equitable system. On the level of the state, there is an ample treasury which is supplied from specific sources, including public properties and zakah funds that exceed people's needs. Non-zakah funds collected from the wealthy, through various types of taxes, for example, is spent by the government to strengthen and protect the Muslim ummah by spearheading production and investment projects in agriculture, industry, and services. Out of the proceeds of such enterprises the state pays the salaries of the military and government employees, builds roads, opens schools and hospitals, and so on.

The ethics of an Islamic economic system as they apply to work, production and consumption promote positive attitudes, responsibility and equity, thereby helping to achieve material and spiritual well-being for the members of society.

(d) *Manifestations of Tawḥīd in the Aesthetic Realm*[12]

In keeping with Islam's emphasis on strict monotheism (*tawḥīd*), Muslim artists developed the art of embellishment. They then developed this art into a form of abstract representation known as "Arabesque," which extends infinitely in all directions until it is disconnected from the material nature of things and is transformed into nothing but a field of vision. With their various forms, including the intricate interlacing of shapes and letters, Arabesque and Arabic calligraphy convey a highly developed awareness of the transcendent. Even when Muslim artists use the forms of plants, animals, or human beings in their drawings, they shape them in such a way that they transcend materiality. Muslim artists thus turn their linguistic and literary heritage into a panorama of meanings and ideas by projecting their aesthetic values onto the interiors and exteriors of buildings. In this way, *tawḥīd* becomes the key to explaining and interpreting the works of Muslim artists whose view of the universe has been transformed by Islam into elements that transcend geographical location, language, or ethnicity.

The absence from Islamic culture of art forms that involve the representation of persons – such as sculpting, drawing, painting, and drama – has been an expression of the absolute commitment to the divine oneness and the refusal to attribute any quality that might be associated with creatures to God the Creator. The absence of these art forms has thus been an attempt to avoid any sort of *shirk*, or association of partners with God, by fostering a constant awareness of the divine transcendence and hence, the impossibility the Divine's being embodied in any way. Attempts to represent God in any sort of natural form, even in the form of a human being, are viewed by Islam as superficial and naïve, incapable of symbolizing the All-Transcendent One who deserves to be recognized as totally Other than the finite creation. Muslims' realization that God Almighty cannot be represented in any kind of material, visible form is, in fact, the most sublime aesthetic value to which human beings can attain, since no physical creature can represent God in His transcendence and perfection. The Qur'an's declaration concerning God Almighty that "...there is nothing like unto Him..." (*sūrah al-Shūrā* 42:11) embodies the most perfect awareness of beauty.

Al Fārūqī holds that seen in light of the doctrine of *tawḥīd*, art might be likened to an attempt to read into nature an essence that is not there, and to give this essence the visible form best suited to it. However, rather than being found in Nature, this essence exists above and beyond Nature, because it belongs solely to Nature's transcendent Creator. This pre-existing essence, which is the object of aesthetic experience and perception, is the aspect of beauty that stirs human emotions and lifts them beyond material forms which, in and of themselves, are devoid of all true value.

Al Fārūqī describes representative art as the expression of the inexpressible, which is, of course, an impossibility! However, Muslim artists have approached this impossible task through what al Fārūqī terms "the Islamic artistic genius," and "Islamic artistic breakthroughs." The example al Fārūqī cites of this phenomenon is that of a Muslim artist who represents a plant or a flower in a manner that differs entirely from the way in which an individual plant or flower would actually appear. Instead, the artist presents infinitely repeated images of the plant or flower, thereby canceling out its individuality and driving its natural attributes out of human consciousness. The aesthetic depiction of the infinite and inexpressible through the repetition of the object being depicted is an attempt to convey nonverbally a message similar to that contained in the verbal formula, "There is no god but God." The genius of the Arabic language and Arabic poetry were both sources of great pride to the Arabs of the pre-Islamic era. The revelation of the Qur'an then brought Arabic to new heights which created for the Arabs, then for the entire Muslim community after them, new standards of beauty that found sublime expression on the levels of visible form, sound, and profound universal meanings.

In concluding our discussion of the doctrine of the divine oneness we wish to emphasize two points. The first is that Muslim scholars are in unanimous agreement that *tawḥīd* is the very cornerstone of Islam, that gives Islamic civilization its identity. Utterly central to the Islamic worldview, *tawḥīd* serves as the source of Islamic values that find concrete expression in virtually all aspects of Islamic life, from thought and rational investigation, to the political, social and economic systems, to the realm of aesthetics and Muslims' approach to the various art forms. The second point is that *tawḥīd* is the foundation for the unity of knowledge, which serves in turn as the foundation for epistemological integration in the Islamic worldview, and in Islamic methodology and practice.

Tazkiyah, "Purification" in Islam's Governing System of Values

In the Islamic perspective, a divinely revealed religion has no meaning without an affirmation of a single Creator, nor without a process by which to purify human beings who, as God's creatures, need to be empowered to bear the trust involved in being *khalīfah* on Earth. It is human beings who are addressed by the revelation that has been sent down from on high by the One Creator, who believe in the Creator's unity, who acknowledge themselves as His servants, and who strive accordingly to use their mental and physical capacities to better the Earth and human life. And it is through such striving that human beings purge themselves, their possessions, and their relationships of all that is unworthy of God's blessing.

Our purpose in this discussion is to arrive at an epistemological perspective on purification, *tazkiyah*, which occupies an important place in the Qur'anic value system. The object of purification and reform is human beings who – as individuals, groups, and members of the wider ummah – are accountable before God for the way they dispose of what they have been entrusted with on Earth. Since human beings live on both a material plane and a spiritual plane, the process of purification likewise takes place on both these planes. Reform must advance human beings along the path of purification; otherwise, it is devoid of value. *Tazkiyah* is both the end served by human development and the means by which development takes place. More than a matter of individual feelings, emotions or scruples, *tazkiyah* is also a vital element of social development.

A discussion of *tazkiyah* will touch on the various meanings of the term *tazkiyah* as it is used in the Holy Qur'an, the place occupied by the concept of *tazkiyah* in the thought and practice of Muslim ascetics, mystics and warriors, as well as *tazkiyah* as a fundamental purpose of divine revelation.

Purification-Related Terms and Concepts in the Holy Qur'an

Derivatives of the Arabic root *z – k – w* occur fifty-nine times in the Qur'an. These include *zakā, zakkā, azkā, zakiyyan, zakāh,* and others. The term zakah – which connotes purification, blessing and growth – occurs thirty-two times in reference to the portion of a Muslim's wealth that he or she is required to spend on needy members of the Muslim society, and four times in the sense of praise and commendation. The word *tazkiyah* occurs four times in reference to one of the four purposes of the divine revelation, while the remaining occurrences refer to processes such as purging, advancement, development, and increased goodness and benefit. In what follows we will discuss selected passages that serve to clarify a number of the specific meanings conveyed by the term *tazkiyah* in the Qur'an.

Purification of the Individual

An individual is purified by entering into faith. God Almighty once reminded the Prophet that a certain blind man who had approached him in search of understanding "...might perhaps have grown in purity" (*sūrah ʿAbasa* 80:3). It is by seeking self-purification that one avoids the fires of hell: "For, distant from it shall remain he who is truly conscious of God: he that spends his possessions [on others] so that he might grow in purity" (*sūrah al-Layl* 92:17-18). Those who strive for self-purification bring great benefit to themselves. Thus did God Almighty explain to the Prophet, "...thou canst [truly] warn only those who stand in awe of their Sustainer although He is beyond the reach of their perception, and are constant in prayer, and [know that] whoever grows in purity, attains to purity but for the good of his own self, and [that] with God is all journeys' end" (*sūrah Fāṭir* 35:18). Someone who is characterized by faith, goodness, righteousness and loyalty may be described as "an innocent human being," that is, a pure soul or "a soul endowed with purity" (*nafs zakiyyah*), (*sūrah al-Kahf* 18:74 and *sūrah Maryam* 19:19). The longest oath sworn by God in the Holy Qur'an has to do with purification of the soul:

> By the Sun and his [glorious] splendour;
> By the Moon as she follows him;
> By the Day as it shows up [the Sun's] glory;
> By the Night as it conceals it;
> By the Firmament and its [wonderful] structure;
> By the Earth and its [wide] expanse;
> By the Soul and the proportion and order given to it;
> And its enlightenment as to its wrong and its right;
> Truly he succeeds that purifies it,
> And he fails that corrupts it! (*Sūrah al-Shams*, 91:1-10)

God Almighty swears in this passage of the Qur'an by a number of His creation – the sun, the moon, the day, the night, the heavens and the earth, and the human soul. Given the sheer number of entities by which the Almighty has sworn, there can be no doubt that the declaration whose truth He has sworn to must be of great import. And indeed, the truth to which the Almighty has sworn is that those who purify their souls will meet with success, and that those who corrupt their souls will meet with failure: "Truly he succeeds that purifies it [the soul], and he fails that corrupts it!" Purification of the soul involves avoiding sinful acts that would incite God's displeasure and performing works of righteousness that merit His favor. As for corruption of the soul, it comes about by succumbing willfully to the temptation to act unrighteously, which prevents one's soul from progressing spiritually and thereby experiencing blessing and growth in goodness.

The human soul that either prospers due to having undergone purification or is cast into the abyss of loss and despair due to having allowed itself to be corrupted represents the entire human being – body, mind and spirit. A "soul" may be either an individual human being or a human collectivity. Human beings possess various forms of wealth by divine proxy. In other words, this wealth has been entrusted to them by its Owner, who is God Almighty. They also live in a God-given environment over which God has appointed them *khalīfah* who are responsible for using their God-given wealth to develop the Earth to the fullest and build human civilization. However, the focal point of purification is the human psyche, the seat of emotion, caring and feeling, which brings about the ascent and progress of the restless inner self, "...for, verily, man's inner self does incite [him] to evil,..." (*sūrah Yūsuf* 12:53; cf. *sūrah al-Maʿārij* 70:19). After hearing the accusing voice of conscience, the soul continues to grow in purity until it becomes fully pleasing to God in every respect and worthy to hear the Almighty address it with the words, "Return thou unto thy Sustainer, well-pleased [and] pleasing [to Him]; enter, then, together with My [other true] servants – yea, enter thou My paradise!" (*sūrah al-Fajr* 89:28-30).

Purification of the Feelings and Social Relations

Derivatives of the word *tazkiyah* are often used in the sense of a cleansing and elevation of the emotions and of social relations. When, for example, a husband and wife divorce, there is a tendency for people to succumb to feelings of hatred and bitterness where there had once been love and affection. Such feelings might prompt the woman's family to forbid her to return to her husband even in situations where the husband and wife wish to be reunited. However, God makes it clear in the Qur'an that reconciliation is best for everyone, and that reestablishing harmony and goodwill in their marriage will bring greater purity to their hearts than continuing to harbor doubt and suspicion. The issue, then, has to do with the promotion of thoughts and feelings that will purify people's hearts, strengthen relationships, and reinforce systems that are beneficial to society. God Almighty says:

> And when you divorce women, and they fulfill the term of their *ʿIddah* [waiting period], do not prevent them from marrying their [former] husbands if they mutually agree on equitable terms. This instruction is for all amongst you who believe in God and the Last Day. That is [the course making for] most virtue and purity amongst you (*dhālika azkā lakum*). And God knows, and ye know not. (*Sūrah al-Baqarah,* 2:232)

According to Ibn Ashur, the phrase translated here as "[the course making for] most...purity amongst you" means that a wife's return to her husband,

> will be most conducive to a life of purity on both her part and his, more likely to preserve both her honor and his, as well as being most conducive to goodness and blessing for everyone concerned. The term *azkā* ("purer") refers to increase and abundance. This is because they [the wives' families] had been hindering them from returning to their husbands out of a zeal to prevent their reputation from being tarnished. However, God informs them that allowing the woman to be reconciled to her husband will do more to protect their honor, since it will help to preserve the goodwill between the families who been brought closer through the ties of marriage. Hence, if, by hindering a divorced woman from being reunited to her husband, her family is attempting to ward off harm or prevent injustice, their

decision to allow her to return to her husband is an act of magnanimity and pardon by means of they seek to mend what needs mending.[13]

The phrase "most conducive to your purity" (*azkā lakum*) or "most conducive to their purity" (*azkā lahum*) recurs in contexts in which a given practice might cause offense or harm. For example, refraining from asking to be received as a guest in someone's house out of respect for others' privacy, refraining from looking unduly at members of the opposite sex, and refraining from sexual relations in the wrong situations in order to preserve one's own and others' honor, all result in the purification of both one's conscience and one's outward conduct. As a result, one's whole being is lifted to a higher plane and one becomes more aware of God's surveillance of everything one thinks and does. We are told, for example, "...if you find no one within [a house], do not enter it until you are given leave; and if you are told, 'Turn back', then turn back. This will be most conducive to your purity (*huwa azkā lakum*); and God has full knowledge of all that you do" (*sūrah al-Nūr* 24:28). And, "Tell the believing men to lower their gaze and to be mindful of their chastity: this will be most conducive to their purity (*dhālika azkā lahum*) – [and] verily, God is aware of all that they do" (*sūrah al-Nūr* 24:30).

Purification of Wealth

With regard to the term zakah, which refers to one of the five pillars of Islam and a uniquely Islamic religious obligation, Ibn Ashur holds that prior to the revelation of the Qur'an the word zakah was never used in the sense of wealth spent for God's sake, and that it is only in the Qur'an that we find the word used in this way.[14] As a pillar of the Islamic religion, zakah is on a par with the testimony that "there is no God but God," ritual prayer, fasting the month of Ramadan, and making the major pilgrimage to Makkah. A unique mainstay of the overall social system, zakah functions to purify the individual Muslim of niggardliness by helping him or her not to become too attached to his or her wealth; at the same time it honors the rights of the community and its members. Zakah is of great importance to the economic system, since the act of collecting money is looked upon in Islam as a form of worship. Zakah, which consists of a specified portion of the individual's wealth which is given to the community, only comes into force when the individual has full possession of the wealth concerned and is therefore free to dispose of it as he/she sees fit due to his/her having earned it through honest labor. Zakah is levied on production, agricultural yield, industry and trade, and is associated with specific times and amounts. It is due on wealth that exceeds a particular amount and must have been in its owner's possession for an entire year. It is also associated with specific times of the year, such as the harvest season ("...give [unto the poor] their due on harvest day..." – *sūrah al-Anʿām* 6:141). As for the amount due, it may be 2.5 percent, 5 percent, 10 percent, or 20 percent depending on the type of wealth in question and the type of work performed in order to acquire it. The percentage of wealth spent on society's interests might be as much as 100 percent in the case of energy resources that cannot be held as private property.

Zakah is a guaranteed means of bringing blessing and increase: "And [remember:] whatever you may give out in usury so that it might increase through [other] people's possessions will bring [you] no increase in the sight of God – whereas all that you give out in charity, seeking God's countenance, [will be blessed by him:] for it is they, they [who thus seek His countenance] that shall have their recompense multiplied!" (*sūrah al-Rūm* 30:39). So, whoever is looking for a kind of commerce that is guaranteed to multiply his wealth, let him give of his wealth in the form of zakah.

God Almighty has promised to be with His people. "And God said: 'Behold, I shall be with you!'..." (*sūrah al-Mā'idah* 5:12). What a marvelous Companion to have! However, God's companionship is tied to certain conditions, one of which is one's willingness to distribute one's wealth in charity, that is, zakah: "...If you are constant in prayer, and spend in charity (zakah), and believe in My apostles and aid them, and offer up unto God a goodly loan,..." (*sūrah al-Mā'idah* 5:12). God's companionship is a great blessing, one that guides us and protects us. However, it is also conditional, since it requires that we,

> obey Him by conducting ourselves according to His conditions...and that we base our economic life on an approach that guarantees that wealth will not simply be

> passed back and forth among the wealthy, lest wealth amassed in the hands of a few lead to economic depression due to the masses' inability to purchase and consume. In such a situation the wheel of production will grind to a halt, or, at the very least, become painfully slow, leading to luxury and opulence on the part of some, hardship and deprivation on the part of others, and corruption and imbalance in the society at large...All these evils are prevented by *zakāh*. They are prevented by God's approach to the distribution of wealth and economic management...[15]

The contemporary Islamic economic order rests on usurious interest, and most people would have a hard time conceiving of a valid system based on any other practice. Zakah has become little more than a form of individual altruism which could never serve as the basis for a modern economy. Hence, people in our day have lost their sense of what zakah is and could be, since they have never witnessed the implementation of a truly Islamic economy.

Purification of the Community of Faith as a Purpose of Divine Revelation

Derivatives of the root *z – k – w* occurring in four verses of the Qur'an refer to purification as an explicit purpose of the divine revelation, particularly the divine revelation given to the seal of the prophets, Muhammad. These four verses read as follows:

> "O our Sustainer! Make us surrender ourselves unto Thee, and make out of our offspring a community that shall surrender itself unto Thee, and show us our way of worship, and accept our repentance: for, verily, Thou alone art the Acceptor of Repentance, the Dispenser of Grace! O our Sustainer! Raise up from the midst of our offspring an apostle from amongst themselves, who shall convey unto them Thy messages, and impart unto them revelation as well as wisdom, and cause them to grow in purity (*yuzakkīhim*); for, verily, Thou alone art Almighty, truly Wise!" (*Sūrah al-Baqarah*, 2:128-129)

> Even as We have sent unto you an apostle from among yourselves to convey unto you Our messages, and to cause you to grow in purity (*yuzakkīkum*), and to impart unto you revelation and wisdom, and to teach you that which you knew not. (*Sūrah al-Baqarah* 2:151)

Indeed, God bestowed a favour upon the believers when he raised up in their midst an apostle from among themselves, to convey His messages unto them, and to cause them to grow in purity, and to impart unto them the divine writ as well as wisdom – whereas before that they were indeed, most obviously, lost in error. (*Sūrah Āl ʿImrān*, 3:164)

He it is who has sent unto the unlettered people an apostle from among themselves, to convey unto them His messages, and to cause them to grow in purity, and to impart unto them the divine writ as well as wisdom – whereas before that they were indeed, most obviously, lost in error. (*Sūrah al-Jumʿah*, 62:2)

The first passage cited here contains a supplication that was uttered by Abraham, upon him be peace, in which he asked God to make his offspring into a nation or community submitted to God, and to send them an apostle who would be one of their own. The apostle that Abraham asked God Almighty to send would come to accomplish four tasks: (1) to convey God's messages to his people, (2) to impart revelation to them, (3) to give them wisdom, and (4) to cause them to grow in purity. As for the other three passages, they speak of the way in which God graciously answered the prophet Abraham's supplication by sending His Messenger, Muhammad and by bringing the Muslim ummah into existence. In this connection two observations are in order. The first observation is that purification is mentioned in Abraham's prayer as the fourth task or purpose which the coming apostle was to accomplish, whereas in the other three passages cited above, purification is listed immediately after that of conveying God's messages. The second observation is that the purification spoken of was to take place within the Muslim ummah for whom God's prophet Abraham had prayed. In the second passage cited above, God addresses this community directly, while in the third and fourth, He speaks of them in the third person as "believers" and as "an unlettered people" respectively. Hence, it will be seen that neither purification nor any of the other three purposes the Apostle was sent to fulfill had to do with disciplining the individual, building individual character, or refining or elevating individual consciousness, sentiments, or emotions. However, although the Qur'anic passages addressing human beings as agents who are accountable to God are generally addressed to a plurality they nevertheless include all units of that plurality, from the individual to the family to the tribe and beyond, since the aim of divine revelation ultimately is to purify all of human civilization.

These four Qur'anic passages set forth a program for educating the Muslim community. This program consists of four principle components which work together to build up the community, define its image, and determine its defining characteristics. The first component of the divinely-inspired program is that of conveying God's signs. It should be remembered that the word translated as "signs" here is the same used in Arabic to refer to verses of the Qur'an (*āyāt*). Hence, "conveying [God's] signs" (*tilāwah al-āyāt*) can also be understood as "reciting [God's] verses." This process involves wiping out illiteracy or "unletteredness" on its various levels, from the inability to read and write to ignorance in the realms of learning and culture, and elevating those to whom such recitation is addressed to a plane on which they experience the dignity of being honored by God by virtue of reciting His revelation and benefitting from its content. The second component is purification, which encompasses the dimensions of refinement, purgation, blessing, increase and abundance. The third component is that of imparting revelation, that is, conveying its content to people on the levels of knowledge and moral guidance. And the fourth component is instruction in wisdom, that is, teaching others the content of the revelation in such a way that it bears fruit on the level of both word and deed, acquiring greater spiritual discernment and insightfulness, and developing the ability to weigh matters properly by understanding both their causes and their purposes.

Purification as Understood by the Schools of Renunciation (Zuhd), Mysticism (Taṣawwuf) and Struggle (Jihad)

During the early days of Islam, some of the Prophet's Companions chose to adopt a lifestyle of asceticism. Later, as some classes of Muslim society became increasingly worldly and as ongoing political strife became the order of the day, the tendency toward asceticism developed into a kind of isolation from society, and the associated practice developed into what came to be known as Sufism. Sufism was marked by the renunciation of the passing satisfactions of this earthly life and regular engagement in acts of piety in pursuit of greater nearness to God Almighty. As time went on, these forms of self-purification and personal piety took on a collective quality as like-minded practitioners gathered into distinct groups whose members committed themselves to the teachings of a defined leadership and particular patterns of behavior in the areas of worship and *dhikr*, or invocation of the Divine, as well as in their manner of relating to each other as members of a spiritual community. Eventually there grew up a specialized vocabulary having to do with Sufi thought and practice with the result that some Sufi terms, while appearing to mean one thing to the layperson, might bear another, esoteric meaning to members of the Sufi brotherhood or its spiritual leaders. An example of such terminology is what came to be known in certain Sufi orders as the tripartite system of *takhallī* – *taḥallī* – *tajallī*. The term *takhallī* refers to the abandonment of sinful actions, while *taḥallī* means taking on certain virtuous, godly qualities. Steady commitment to both *takhallī* and *taḥallī* may enable the aspirant to enter a state of spiritual transparency and psychological transport to which Sufis refer as *tajallī*, in which the aspirant experiences the divine presence descending upon him and manifesting itself within him.

However, some Sufi practices became associated with terms and forms of behavior that were viewed as unacceptable innovations, while other practices having to do with asceticism and advancement along the path of self-purification remained with the realm of orthodoxy. Some Sufi orders engaged in armed conflict against the enemies of Islam, while others worked to propagate the Islamic faith in numerous regions of Africa and Asia.

As one might expect, *tazkiyah* is associated with various forms of struggle, or jihad. There is the inward struggle against one's baser self. This type of struggle is referred to in God Almighty's declaration that "But as for those who strive hard in Our cause – We shall most certainly guide them onto paths that lead unto Us: for, behold, God is indeed with the doers of good" (*sūrah al-ʿAnkabūt* 29:69). There is the struggle that involves sacrificing personal comfort, possessions, and sometimes one's very life. This type of struggle in spoken of in the Qur'an's reference to "Those who believed, and adopted exile, and fought for the faith, with their property and their persons, in the cause of God,..." (*sūrah al-Anfāl* 8:72, Abdullah Yusuf Ali). In addition, there is a struggle that involves the sacrifice of one's wealth; the Qur'an speaks approvingly of the person who "...spends his possessions [on others] so that he might grow in purity" (*sūrah al-Layl* 92:18).

It thus becomes clear that on the individual level, purification has to do with feelings, thoughts, intentions, attitudes, and personal conduct. Those who strive for self-purification are promised success in the true sense of the word. *Tazkiyah* also takes place on the level of the social life. Hence, the Prophet who was sent to Mankind helps people to grow in purity by improving relations between people and reforming social and economic systems. *Tazkiyah* also takes place in relation to people's wealth and possessions. The zakah which the Muslim is required to distribute among the needy is a means of purifying the individual who distributes the wealth, the wealth of the individual, and the wealth of the society as a whole; this is a process that brings both blessing and increase. The various meanings of the term "*tazkiyah*," which complete and complement one another, encompass everything the Muslim might contemplate, everything he or she might strive to learn about through study and research, and everything he or she strives to achieve in this world and the next. These, then, are the three spheres of Islamic methodology: thought, research, and conduct.

ʿUmrān, Societal Development and Prosperity in the Islamic Value System

If *tawḥīd*, the affirmation of the divine unity, has fundamentally to do with the Islamic vision of the God who creates and orders the universe, and if *tazkiyah*, or purification, has to do with the Islamic view of human beings as creatures with God-given responsibilities and tasks, then *ʿumrān*, or societal development and prosperity, has to do with the Islamic view of human beings' function as *khalīfah*. In keeping with this worldview, human development and prosperity constitute a normative standard, i.e., a value, on the basis of which the value of life is measured both individually and collectively. It is also a normative standard for evaluating and correcting the development efforts and achievements of the individual, community or nation.

As we have stated before, the values of *tawḥīd, tazkiyah* and *ʿumrān* are intimately linked. Taken together, they constitute an integrated system which forms the foundation for the methodology of epistemological integration. *Tawḥīd* is the most significant fact of existence. The divine unity is a reality with intrinsic value out of which other realities proceed. The entire cosmos is subject by nature to the requirements of the divine unity. This is why, if human beings wish to be in harmony with the universe, they must strive for self-purification by worshipping God alone and submitting to God's guidance in relation to how they manage their affairs and relate to other creatures. Purification is both the means and the end of human development and prosperity; as such, it lies at the very heart of the social structure.

This tripartite system of values makes up an authoritative frame of reference in relation to which we can discern God's purpose in creation. It likewise serves as a normative system of values that yields all of the primary and secondary values in the Islamic religion. At the same time, however, it should be remembered that it is an expression of the true nature of things, not an external frame of reference which is imposed on things from without.

We will be discussing the value of *ʿumrān* in the sense of prosperous human development (civilization) from a juristic perspective, i.e., *fiqh al-ʿumrān*, and the link between this "value" and the life God desires for human beings. Jurisprudence is simply what God Almighty has to say about people's actions: which actions merit God's favor, which actions God forbids, and which actions He exhorts us to avoid, the aim throughout being to ensure people's well-being and spare them undue hardship. Prosperous societal development constitutes a value that governs our understanding of human striving in this earthly life, particularly the striving of society as a whole as this relates to systems of administration and public affairs. Societal development manifests itself in the material aspects of our lives, including buildings and roads, agriculture and industry. It also manifests itself in the emotional and spiritual aspects of our lives, including ways of maintaining security, upholding justice, and engaging in collective consultation. The task of society's influential and wealthy stratum, including its rulers, is to serve the interests of the ordinary members of society, while the task of society at large is to pray for God to grant blessing and strength to those in positions of influence.

During the days when the Muslims heeded "the jurisprudence of prosperous human development" (*fiqh al-ʿumrān*), their lives were filled with blessing. Institutions of learning spread far and wide and God opened up to them the treasures of heaven and earth. They enjoyed an abundance of all that they needed, and thanks to the advanced, refined civilization they propagated, they were sought out by other nations. When, conversely, Muslims disregarded this same jurisprudence, they grew weak. Their power and authority waned, their empire crumbled, and they were vanquished by their foes. Their negligence and inattention were revealed in a lack of ambition and a preference for a life of ease and indolence. At times these weaknesses were exacerbated by writings that promoted unwholesome notions which had no claim to being valid understandings of Islamic law. Such writings promoted a disdain for the life of this world, a denial of its value, and a refusal to involve oneself in its affairs. The result was a tendency to neglect society's affairs and a failure to protect people's interests and rights or demonstrate a sense of belonging to the Muslim ummah.

We will commence our discussion of *ʿumrān* with an examination of this term's use in the Holy Qur'an. We will then look at the link the Qur'an draws between the population and development of the Earth, the nature of the life to which this leads, and the fate that awaits human beings thereafter. The discussion will be concluded with a reference to the pioneering work of Ibn Khaldūn, who drew inspiration from Qur'anic guidance for the creation of a new discipline which he termed "the science of human development" (*ʿilm al-ʿumrān al-basharī*).

ʿUmrān in the Language of the Qur'an

Derivations of the triliteral root *ʿ - m – r* occur twenty-five times in the Qur'an. Three of these are in the form of a proper noun:

> Behold, God raised Adam, and Noah, and the House of Abraham, and the House of ʿImrān above all mankind. (*Sūrah Āl ʿImrān* 3:33)

> And [We have propounded yet another parable of God-consciousness in the story of] Mary, the daughter of ʿImrān, who guarded her chastity, whereupon We

> breathed of Our spirit into that [which was in her womb], and who accepted the truth of her Sustainer's words – and [thus,] of His revelations – and was one of the truly devout. (*Sūrah al-Taḥrīm*, 66:12)

> when a woman of [the House of] ᶜImrān prayed, "O my Sustainer, Behold, unto Thee do I vow [the child] that is in my womb, to be devoted to Thy service. Accept it, then, from me: verily, Thou alone art All-Hearing, All-Knowing!" (*Sūrah Āl ᶜImran*, 3:35)

The root ᶜ – *m* – *r* occurs three times in reference to the rite of minor pilgrimage or "pious visit" (*ᶜumrah*) to the Sacred Mosque in Makkah. Unlike the major pilgrimage (hajj), which can only be performed during a particular month of the year, the minor pilgrimage can be performed at any time, as a result of which the Sacred Mosque in Makkah is filled with pilgrims all year round, ᶜ – *m* – *r*: "And perform the pilgrimage (hajj) and the pious visit (*ᶜumrah*) [to Makkah] in honour of God; and if you are held back, give instead whatever offering you can easily afford..." (*sūrah al-Baqarah* 2:196).

The root ᶜ - *m* – *r* occurs three times in connection with visiting and maintaining mosques:

> It is not for those who ascribe divinity to aught beside God to visit or tend (*yaᶜmurū*) God's houses of worship, the while [by their beliefs] they bear witness against themselves that they are denying the truth. It is they whose works shall come to nought, and they who in the fire shall abide! Only he should visit or tend (*yaᶜmuru*) God's houses of worship who believes in God and the Last Day, and is constant in prayer, and spends in charity, and stands in awe of none but God: for [only such as] these may hope to be among the right-guided! Do you, perchance, regard the [mere] giving of water to pilgrims, and the tending of the Inviolable House of Worship (*ᶜimārat al-masjid al-ḥarām*) as being equal to [the works of] one who believes in God and the Last Day and strives hard in God's cause? These [things] are not equal in the sight of God. And God does not grace with His guidance people who [deliberately] do wrong. (*Sūrah al-Tawbah* 9:17-19)

Another use of the root ᶜ - *m* –*r* is as an adjective describing a house of worship: "Consider Mount Sinai! Consider [God's] revelation, inscribed on wide-open scrolls. Consider the long-enduring house [of worship] (*al-bayt al-maᶜmūr*)!" (*sūrah al-Ṭūr* 52:1-4).[16]

In three other places the same root occurs in the sense of settling on land and cultivating it, constructing dwellings and castles, and establishing a settled community after having lived a nomadic existence. God speaks of peoples who dwelled on the land for a long time, built up strength, tilled the land and extracted its minerals:

> Have they, then, never journeyed about the earth and beheld what happened in the end to those [deniers of the truth] who lived before their time? Greater were they in power than they are; and they left a stronger impact on the earth, and built it up (*ʿamarūhā*) even better than these [are doing] (*akthar mimmā ʿamarūhā*); and to them [too] came their apostles with all evidence of the truth: and so, [when they rejected the truth and thereupon perished,] it was not God who wronged them, but it was they who had wronged themselves. (*Sūrah al-Rūm* 30:9)

This may be a reference to the people of ʿĀd to whom the prophet Hūd was sent, who constructed edifices on the heights and built castles and fortresses. God addresses these people, saying, "Will you, in your wanton folly, build [idolatrous] altars on every height, and make for yourselves mighty castles, [hoping] that you might become immortal? And will you [always], whenever you lay hand [on others], lay hand [on them] cruelly, without any restraint?" (*sūrah al-Shuʿarā'* 26:128-129). They thought mistakenly that they would dwell in their land for all time.

The root ʿ – *m* – *r* occurs once in the sense of "life," where God Almighty swears by the life of His Prophet, saying, "Verily, by thy life [*la ʿamruka*] (O Prophet), in their wild intoxication, they wander in distraction, to and fro" (*sūrah al-Ḥijr* 15:72, Abdullah Yusuf Ali). As for the remaining occurrences of this word, they all refer to the passage of time in a human being's life: "Nay, We have allowed these [sinners] – as [We allowed] their forebears – to enjoy the good things of life for a great length of time:... (*ḥattā ṭāla ʿalayhim al-ʿumur*)..." (*sūrah al-Anbiyā'* 21:44). "And God has created you, and in time will cause you to die; and many a one of you is reduced in old age to a most abject state (*ilā ardhal al-ʿumur*), ceasing to know anything of what he once knew so well. Verily, God is All-Knowing, infinite in His power!" (*Sūrah al-Naḥl* 16:70).

The passage of time is necessary for us to be able to accomplish tasks and reach goals we have set for ourselves. It is a factor in the individual's physical, psychological and spiritual growth and the emergence of certain defining characteristics. Similarly, it is necessary for time to pass in order for society to achieve various levels of development and cultural formation. Malek Bennabi proposed an equation that combines the elements of civilization, and which clarifies the role played both by human effort in bringing together material causes and by the passage of sufficient time for cultural institutions and apparatuses to develop. According to Bennabi, however, the combination of these three elements – people + soil + time – does not necessarily result in a civilized state of affairs. Rather, such a result calls for a degree of spiritual energy, or a spark capable of activating these elements in such a way that they are capable of performing their function in cultural advancement.[17]

The opposite of the term *ʿumrān* as it is used in the Qur'an is corruption, killing, bloodshed, destruction, ruin, annihilation, and desolation. All of these terms as used in the Qur'an are set in contrast to life's proceeding in harmony with the laws and patterns God has established in the universe such that houses of worship are filled with worshippers who invoke God's name, and people live in keeping with God's guidance. The Qur'anic term *ʿumrān* thus yields a variety of interrelated and overlapping meanings which together form a semantic field populated by complementary denotations and connotations. The following are among the meanings conveyed by the word *ʿumrān*:

ʿUmrān as the State of Life

As the years of a person's life pass, his or her life comes to completion. As we read in *sūrah al-Shuʿarā'* 26:18, "[But when Moses had delivered his message, Pharaoh] said, 'Did we not bring thee up among us when thou wert a child? And didst thou not spend among us years of thy [later] life (*ʿumrika*)?" The individual begins his life in his mother's womb, then emerges into this world. When death comes, his life on earth comes to an end. He then finds himself in the womb of the Earth until Resurrection Day, at which point he is raised to another, eternal, life. Each of us begins his or her earthly life as a newborn. He then becomes a young child who has yet to reach puberty. After he has reached his peak in terms of both mental and physical prowess, he continues to age until he reaches his nadir, or what the Qur'an refers to as "a most abject state."

Just as an individual has a definable lifespan, so does a community. The community witnesses the passage of years and generations, and as it does so it retains its life in terms of presence, authority and stability in a specific mode of being. If its life comes to an end, its identity and power dissolve and vanish. The homes that had once stood erect become nothing but tumble-down, abandoned shells: "Behold, then, what all their scheming came to in the end: We utterly destroyed them and their people, all of them; and [now] those dwellings of theirs are empty, [ruined] as an outcome of their evil deeds. In this, behold, there is a message indeed for people of [innate] knowledge" (*sūrah al-Naml* 27:51-52). With the passage of time one's life may lose its value if one fails to respond to God's invitation to a true, genuine vitality: "O you who have attained to faith! Respond to the call of God and the Apostle whenever he calls you unto that which will give you life;..." (*sūrah al-Anfāl* 8:24). Unless people respond to this call of God, their lives will not be complete, filled with truth, blessing and righteousness. As a consequence, their lifetimes will lack true value; in fact, they will have been spent in falsehood and futility.

Developing and prospering the Earth is linked directly to life on Earth – on land, on the sea, and in the air – and to the preservation of living beings in all these spheres. Consequently, it also entails avoiding the destruction of life, whether directly, or indirectly by destroying, depleting, or tainting the resources and environments upon which life depends. The process of developing and prospering the Earth on which we and other creatures live thus involves making sound use of all that God has deposited on our Planet – on its land, in its seas, oceans, lakes and rivers, and in its atmosphere – be it in the form of living creatures, natural phenomena and cycles, or sources of energy.

ʿUmrān As Living and Settling in a Particular Place

The term *ʿumrān* conveys the sense of settling in a particular place and making it one's home; hence, it requires that one abandon a life of nomadic wandering through deserts and steppes, till the land, construct dwellings and build factories to meet the requirements of a settled life. This type of settled existence is what one finds in villages and cities as opposed to a life of desert wandering. The prophet Joseph, upon him be peace, is recorded in the Qur'an as having stated that when his father Jacob's family gave up their Bedouin existence and moved to the city, this was a blessing and grace from God. He said, "...O my father! This is the real meaning of my dream long ago, which my Sustainer has made come true. And He was indeed good to me when He freed me from the prison, and [when] He brought you [all to me] from the desert after Satan had sown discord between me and my brothers..." (*sūrah Yūsuf* 12:100). There may, of course, be some degree of development and prosperity in the deserṭ, whether of a material or a spiritual nature. However, it differs from the development and prosperity one finds in urban areas. This is because a desert or steppe might be inhabited at one time, then become desolate wasteland that no one makes his home. The Qur'anic meaning of words derived from the root ᶜ – *m* – *r*, namely, to dwell in, to inhabit, or to tend, can be seen in the use of the adjectives *ᶜāmir* and *maᶜmūr*, both of which mean populated, filled to capacity, prosperous, thriving, civilized, and so on, and the noun *al-maᶜmūrah*, which refers to the inhabited world.[18] Similarly, when it is said that *ᶜumrān* has spread in this or that country, it means that it is filled with populous areas where people have built homes and taken up residence in them.

ᶜUmrān as Material Development and Prosperity

Material development and prosperity have to do with the concrete aspects of civilization resulting from the knowledge and experience that accumulate over time as we observe the regularity in the universe, discover the laws that govern objects and events, and acquire the ability to predict events' occurrence. These advances lead in turn to the ability to avail ourselves of the opportunities such knowledge provides while avoiding the dangers it heralds. The application of newly acquired knowledge enables human beings to make better use of the Earth's resources, construct buildings, build roads, bridges and factories, produce merchandise and improve means of transport and communication. And now with the existence of digital, virtual worlds and their associated developments and inventions, people can meet, converse, and exchange information, the arts and products of various sorts without leaving their homes!

Another aspect of material development and prosperity is realized through tilling and cultivating arable land and improving means of livelihood to the point where every square meter of arable land in is productive use and every able-bodied adult enjoys gainful employment, as well as modern edifices and facilitated means of transport and communication. It is to this type of development that the Qur'an refers in *sūrah al-Rūm* 30:9 when, by way of reprimand, it asks, "Have they, then, never journeyed about the earth and beheld what happened in the end to those [deniers of the truth] who lived before their time? Greater were they in power than they are; and they left a stronger impact on the earth, and built it up (*ʿamarūhā*) even better than these [are doing] (*akthar mimmā ʿamarūhā*)..."

Signs of material development and prosperity can be seen both on land and sea; at the same time, however, such development has been accompanied by signs of corruption and destruction to which the Qur'an makes reference when it states, "[Since they have become oblivious of God,] corruption has appeared on land and in the sea as an outcome of what men's hands have wrought: and so He will let them taste [the evil of] some of their doings, so that they might return [to the right path]" (*sūrah al-Rūm* 30:41). In order to avoid such destruction, we must cease engaging in practices such as burying nuclear and radioactive waste or dumping it into the sea, and pass and enforce laws that regulate the pollutants that are released into the air by automobiles and factories.

ʿUmrān as Intellectual and Cultural Development and Prosperity

The non-material side of human civilization is advanced as people gain experience in ordering their social and economic affairs, including the passage of laws and establishment of systems that regulate and manage relations among people living in the same location. Such advances give rise to cultures and subcultures and the crystallization of customs and traditions as people willingly submit to the authority of an administration or government for the sake of ensuring security and stability. The powers with which God has blessed human beings over other creatures, including even the angels (who, unlike Adam, were not taught the names of all things) may be part of the process by which God has enabled the human race to establish itself on Earth and, thereby, carry out the task of developing and prospering the Earth not only in the material sense, but in the spiritual, cultural sense as well.

Just as God commends those who seek to tend and maintain houses of worship, He reprimands those who seek to harm or destroy them: "Hence, who could be more wicked than those who bar the mention of God's name from [any of] His houses of worship and strive for their ruin,...?" (*sūrah al-Baqarah* 2:114). In His wisdom God Almighty has established certain patterns of human behavior which serve to preserve diversity among us. One of these patterns may be seen in the way in which different groups of people are allowed by God, when conflicts arise among them, to defend and protect God's houses of worship as places to remember and extol His name. The Qur'an reminds us that "...if God has not enabled people to defend themselves against one another, [all] monasteries and churches and synagogues and mosques – in [all of] which God's name is abundantly extolled – would surely have been destroyed [ere now]..." (*sūrah al-Ḥajj* 22:40). In other words, it is God who enables believers to confront their enemies, thereby helping to preserve and protect the facilities they have constructed for His worship and the remembrance of His name.

Other such patterns include the practice of coming together in support of systems and laws which order people's affairs, accepting the rule of an elected leader who seeks out the counsel of experts who have likewise been elected by the population, and establishing a judiciary whose representatives serve society by ruling on people's disputes and upholding their rights.

Still another pattern of this sort is the fact that people differ in the amount of knowledge they possess, as a result of which those with less knowledge seek out those with more. This process leads to the establishment of schools and universities, training centers, institutes, and centers devoted to study, research, and problem-solving. These and similar phenomena are manifestations of progress in the spheres of thought, culture, education and administration. People rightly take pride in such progress, vying with each other for distinction in various fields of knowledge and being classified on the basis of their specializations.

One of the established patterns and unchanging laws that have been observed in the rise and fall of the Earth's civilizations is that a country's prosperity or ruin, the pleasantness or misery of its life, is simply the outcome of its inhabitants' practices. The Qur'an relates the stories of nations that had reached advanced levels of material and spiritual success, but who were not grateful to God for the blessings they had received. Instead of acknowledging their achievements as gifts from God, they dealt unjustly with both themselves and others, and as a consequence, the laws God implanted in the workings of the universe led to their downfall and destruction. Such countries were brought to ruin together with the evidences of civilization and development that were devoid of life and spirit. The mansions and castles they built are still standing. However, they are empty of their unjust inhabitants, whose material prosperity proved of no use to them. As for the manifestations of cultural and development that related to the use of water, they are still usable, but they no longer have anyone to use them and benefit from them. They stand as monuments to the advances their inventors and artisans had achieved; however, they are also witnesses to these people's failure to preserve their progress or give thanks for their blessings: "And how many a township have We destroyed because it had been immersed in evildoing – and now they [all] lie deserted, with their roofs caved in! And how many a well lies abandoned, and how many a castle that [once] stood high!" (*sūrah al-Ḥajj* 22:45).

The destruction these peoples witnessed did not take the form of a devastating earthquake that leveled their edifices to the ground, for example. Nor was it because they no longer had access to means of subsistence such as vital water supplies ("...We made out of water every living thing? Will they not, then, [begin to] believe?" – *sūrah al-Anbiyā'* 21:30). Rather, these people were overtaken by destruction even though the products of their material development and prosperity remained intact and their means of subsistence remained available in abundance. This fact may provide an explanation for the difficulties being faced by some present-day Arab and Islamic societies, whose countries exhibit numerous signs of material prosperity, but whose members are content to lead lives of indolence, consumption and dependency. Such people lack the strength to ward off the assaults of their enemies, the productivity they need to achieve self-sufficiency, the just governmental policies needed to provide them with stability and security or nurture a sense of belonging to their society and the resultant motivation to preserve and protect its foundations, and just economic systems that would provide people with jobs while ensuring that state funds are spent on high-priority areas and necessities such as local agricultural and industrial production.

Situations such as these have made life for most people a kind of perdition and emptiness. Rather than being filled with fruitful labor, reform efforts, generosity, hope, and creative contributions that enable them to be pioneers in contemporary culture or, at the very least, to take part effectively in and make distinctive contributions to this culture, their lives are filled with grumbling, complaining, envy, resentment, hostility and name-calling. As a consequence, they have despaired of any possibility of reform, since they see themselves as irretrievably lost and dying.

ᶜUmrān as Development, Prosperity and Life

The act of preserving life is linked in the Qur'an to that of giving life, or bringing to life. Hence we read that "..if anyone slays a human being – unless it be [in punishment] for murder or for spreading corruption on earth – it shall be as though he had slain all mankind; whereas, if anyone saves a life, it shall be as though he had saved the lives of all mankind (*aḥyā al-nāsa jamīᶜan*, literally, given life to all people)" (*sūrah al-Mā'idah* 5:32). The acts of preserving life and affirming its value and sacredness are ways of developing and prospering the Earth, while taking life is an act of corruption. Al-Iṣfahānī may have derived his definition of the word *ᶜumur* (meaning "lifetime") from the phrase *ᶜumrān al-ḥayāh*, which might be rendered "thriving life," or the notion of a person's body being filled with vitality (*ʿumrān badan al-insān bi al-ḥayāh*).[19] The Arabic word *istiʿmār*, rendered in English as "colonization," refers in essence to a process of striving for development and prosperity, since it is derived from the same root as the nouns *ʿumrān* (populousness, prosperity, thriving civilization), *iʿmār* (the act of populating and developing) and *taʿmīr* (the act of populating, prolonging life, repairing, reconstructing). It is through striving for development and prosperity on Earth that human beings act as *khulafāʾ* (plural of *khalīfah*), ("Behold, thy Lord said to the angels, 'I will create a vicegerent on earth'..." – *sūrah al-Baqarah* 2:30, Abdullah Yusuf Ali). The opposite of striving for development and prosperity and acting as *khulafāʾ* is the act of wreaking destruction on Earth, and the most terrible form of such destruction is the act of taking human life.

When the individual undertakes to be *khalīfah* on Earth, a task that includes working for human development and prosperity, he or she is engaging in a task that will enrich his or her life in this earthly sphere. After the individual dies, blessing will be extended to others as well based on the ongoing charity he or she had given during his days on earth, knowledge he or she left to posterity, or righteous offspring who pray for him or her. The Prophet is reported to have said, "When a servant of God dies, his work on Earth is over with the exception of three things: ongoing charity, knowledge from which others can benefit, and righteous children who will pray for him,"[20] not to mention the abundant, never-ending existence he will enjoy in the afterlife. This task extends to the entire human race, passing from one generation to the next and one nation to another as long as the human race endures. However, if this prosperous development is tainted with corruption, people's lives on Earth will become nothing but error and distress: "But as for him who shall turn away from remembering Me – his shall be a life of narrow scope; and on the Day of Resurrection We shall raise him up blind" (*sūrah Ṭa Ha* 20:124). Development and prosperity in the true sense require that we live in accordance with divine guidance, which means goodness and blessing both in this life and the life to come, whereas corruption leads to a straitened existence both in this life and the life to come.

As we have seen, a positive response to God's call to develop and prosper the Earth leads to life (cf. *sūrah al-Anfāl* 8:24), whereas a refusal to answer this call leads to corruption and death. The person who rejects this call is one who, "...whenever he prevails, he goes about the earth spreading corruption and destroying [man's] tilth and progeny: and God does not love corruption" (*sūrah al-Baqarah* 2:205). The fruits of such a person's corruption will affect not only him, but what the Qur'an refers to as people's "tilth and progeny," that is, the land on which everyone lives and its suitability for agricultural use, as well as future generations. On the collective level the same is true: If a nation or state refuses God's call to seek right guidance and act as a steward on Earth – shedding blood by waging unjust wars, hindering people's efforts to earn their keep via agriculture or otherwise, and squandering the Earth's resources and filling the Earth with poisons and pollutants – the outcome will be the destruction of tilth and progeny all over the world unless other nations take it upon themselves to restrain this rogue state. After all, the Earth upon which human beings have been placed as *khulafā'* is like a ship on which all of us are passengers. If it sinks, everyone on it sinks, the bad and the good alike. Their ultimate reckoning, of course, remains with God, who will judge all in His perfect knowledge, compassion and justice.

A good life in this world thus results from personal happiness, peace of mind, overall blessing, an atmosphere of goodwill among people, an overall sense of security, an openness to knowing one another and working together, and the availability of the resources required for a life of ease and satisfaction. These things are made possible when people engage in righteous action and demonstrate practical concern for reforming whatever needs to be improved or corrected: "As for anyone – be it man or woman – who does righteous deeds, and is a believer withal – him shall We most certainly cause to live a good life; and most certainly shall We grant unto such as these their reward in accordance with the best that they ever did" (*sūrah al-Naḥl* 16:97). If, on the other hand, people's lives together are tainted by corruption and the desire to seek their own narrow interests at others' expense, the result will be lostness, misery and privation. This principle applies on all levels: that of the individual, the community, and the human race as a whole. As for the good life in the world to come, it involves a better reward and a better outcome, one that results from having developed and prospered the earthly realm through righteous action and efforts toward reform.

People's lives in this world are only complete when they work together to manage their affairs. As we have seen, people are communal by nature, and do not thrive in isolation from one another. Rather, the individual lives within a family whose life is ordered by rulings, relationships, and responsibilities, while families come together in groups, tribes, peoples and nations. Families are sometimes spread out among different communities and states. They may develop ties of cooperation and beneficial exchange in times of peace, whereas, in times of rivalry and conflict, hostilities may surface between them. People's lives are marked by various living patterns in relation to food, drink, attire, type of dwelling, and modes of transport and communication. Each individual has his or her own life trajectory and story, one that will be marked by wealth or poverty, health or illness, knowledge or ignorance. Each nation also has its own history, which will be characterized by nomadic wanderings or urban settlements, backwardness or progress, sciences and industries, and so on. Those who wish to record the lives and histories of individuals and nations will need a proper understanding of the nature of human civilization and the laws that govern its evolution, since only then will they be able to document events and facts and test narratives for validity and reliability on the level of both their content and the individuals on whose authority they were passed down.

People's lives on this Earth have a purpose. God created human beings for a specific end, which is to worship Him: "...I have not created the invisible beings and men to any end other than that they may [know and] worship Me" (*sūrah al-Dhāriyāt* 51:56). In order for us to understand the meaning of worship as the purpose for our existence, God revealed the following words: "Behold, thy Lord said to the angels: 'I will create a vicegerent on earth'..." (*sūrah al-Baqarah* 2:30, Abdullah Yusuf Ali). Hence, what worship means is for us to act as *khulafā'*, that is, as vicegerents, by developing and prospering the Earth on which He has placed us. As the prophet Ṣāliḥ reminded the people of Thamūd, "...He brought you into being out of the earth, and made you thrive (*istaʿmarakum*) thereon..." (*sūrah Hūd* 11:61). Human beings' concern in this earthly life should be to cause the Earth to thrive just as God has caused them to thrive on the Earth. For while other creatures render God worship and praise by submitting instinctively to His laws, human beings must do so by conscious choice just as they choose consciously to believe in the divine unity.

The Earth existed before we did. Then we were created in order to be *khalīfah* on the Earth. This is why God holds us accountable for what He has given us. He says, "Yea, indeed, We have given you a [bountiful] place on earth, and appointed thereon means of livelihood for you:..." (*sūrah al-Aʿrāf* 7:10). "Are you not aware that God has made subservient to you all that is in the heavens and all that is on earth, and has lavished upon you His blessings, both outward and inward?..." (*sūrah Luqmān* 31:20). Hence, we are accountable to God for what we do as *khulafā'* on Earth. This is what true worship entails, and this is the purpose for which we were made.

ʿUmrān as Expounded by Ibn Khaldūn

Ibn Khaldūn (d. 808 AH/1406 CE) grasped many more aspects of the concept of *ʿumrān* than his predecessors had, though few thinkers who came after him built on his discussion of it. Ibn Khaldūn wrote a book on history entitled, *Kitāb al-ʿIbar wa Dīwān al-Mubtada' wa al-Khabar fī Akhbār al-ʿArab wa al-ʿAjam wa al-Barbar wa man ʿĀṣarahum min Dhawī al-Sulṭān al-Akbar* (The Book of Lessons to be Gleaned From Accounts Concerning the Arabs, the non-Arabs and the Berbers and Their Most Influential Contemporaries). However, Ibn Khaldūn's introduction to this tome was destined to be better known to posterity than the book itself. Even though it is simply an introduction to a book on history – a field of study that was well-established in his time – it nevertheless contains chapters on a variety of topics which, long after Ibn Khaldūn's time, developed into independent disciplines in their own right, and to which present-day researchers in the social and human sciences continue to devote their efforts.

What Ibn Khaldūn did was to take the Qur'anic concept of *ʿumrān* – civilization, human development and prosperity – and make it into a new science that concerns itself with people's lives, the various changes and transformations they undergo, and the relationships and institutions that come into existence as a consequence. Ibn Khaldūn referred to this new science as science of *ʿilm al-ʿumrān*: "the science of human development and prosperity," "the science of civilization" or what we now know as sociology. Announcing the birth of this new field of study and setting forth its methodology, Ibn Khaldūn invited those who came after him to complete the work he had begun by researching the relevant topics and issues, saying:

> It is our intention (now) to stop with this First Book, which is concerned with the nature of civilization (*ṭabīʿat al-ʿumrān*) and the accidents that go with it...perhaps some later (scholar), aided by the gifts of a sound mind and of solid scholarship, will penetrate into these problems in greater detail than we did here. A person who creates a new discipline does not have the task of enumerating (all) the (individual) problems connected with it. His task is to specify the subject of the discipline and its various branches and the discussions connected with it. His successors, then, may gradually add more problems until the discipline is (completely) presented. "...God knows, whereas you do not know." [*sūrah al-Baqarah* 2:216][21]

In introducing his *Muqaddimah*, Ibn Khaldūn moves from history – which is a report of events – to the subject of history, which is world civilization and the various conditions it has witnessed. He states:

> It should be known that history, in matter of fact, is information about human social organization, which itself is identical with world civilization (*ʿumrān al-ʿālam*). It deals with such conditions affecting the nature of civilization, as, for instance, savagery and sociability, group feelings, and the different ways by which one group of human beings achieves superiority over another. It deals with royal authority and the dynasties that result (in this manner) and with the various ranks that exist within them. (It further deals with) the different kinds of gainful occupations and ways of making a living, with the sciences and crafts that human beings pursue, and with all the other institutions that originate in civilization through its very nature.[22]

The aim of this discipline is to change the purpose of history-writing from that of narrating reports and hunting down curiosities to the establishment of "a normative method for distinguishing right from wrong and truth from falsehood in historical information by means of a logical demonstration that admits of no doubts." Consequently, he continues, "(The subject) is, in a way, an independent science. (This science) has its own peculiar object, that is, human civilization (*al-ʿumrān al-basharī*) and social organization. It also has its own peculiar problems, that is, explaining the conditions that attach themselves to the essence of civilization, one after the other."[23]

The fluctuating circumstances and successive tragedies Ibn Khaldūn witnessed in his lifetime may have contributed to his desire for a time of seclusion in Ibn Salamah Castle (west of modern day Alger), where he could devote himself to study and reflection and record his conclusions concerning the state in which the Muslim community found itself in his day. From this period of study and reflection, Ibn Khaldūn deduced certain laws governing human civilization as they pertain to human psychology, the history of nations and civilizations, geographical environments, government and politics, economics and wealth, principles of social organization, educational curricula, and so on.

One of the divinely ordained patterns to be observed in human societies is that in the course of human advancement, people develop a tendency to immerse themselves in luxury and ease, which undermines the society's strength and cohesiveness and leads eventually to its collapse as a civilization. It is then succeeded by a more youthful nation marked by greater unity and esprit de corps. This nation, like the one that preceded it, reaches a peak; it maintains this peak for a period of time, then gives way to a successor. As God reminds us in the Qur'an, "If misfortune touches you, [know that] similar misfortune has touched [other] people as well; for it is by turns that We apportion unto men such days of fortune and misfortune:..." (*sūrah Āl ʿImrān* 3:140). Hence, no matter how long a state, nation or empire endures, it is destined eventually to fall prey to a spirit of sloth and decadence which brings it in turn to a phase of weakness and imminent collapse.

Ibn Khaldūn possessed a distinctive understanding of history and social organization and how these relate to the natural world and the laws of existence. This understanding set Ibn Khaldūn apart from others who had treated these subjects before him. Human society had been the subject of reflection and investigation on the part of other thinkers prior to Ibn Khaldūn, among them Plato, Aristotle, al-Fārābī and Augustine. However, the theoretical and philosophical conceptualizations that had colored these other thinkers' efforts remained disconnected from the realities of human life and society. These other thinkers' approach had been prescriptive or normative in nature in they set out to determine what society *ought* to be like rather than how it actually *is*. Ibn Khaldūn, by contrast, relied in his study of society on what happens in reality, basing his observations on his practical experience with society. Hence, although he did not disregard what society ought to be like in the ideal, neither did he allow himself to be confined within an abstract philosophical framework or point of view. Instead, he approached his subject realistically, with an awareness of divine guidance as he understood it to be set forth in the Qur'an. As a consequence, Ibn Khaldūn combined descriptive reports with normative declarations. He talked about the concrete, observable world without disregarding the world of the unseen, and he recognized the authority of reason without forgetting the authority of divine revelation.

However, the most important distinguishing feature of Ibn Khaldūn's approach to the study of human civilization is his insistence that we can only understand the nature of civilization if we have first understood the laws and defining characteristics of human organization. The reason for this insistence on Ibn Khaldūn's part is that what actually happens in human society takes place in accordance with God-given laws and patterns which resemble those that govern the material universe. Therefore, it is necessary to study social facts and events in keeping with an organized method that reflects reality as it is. Ibn Khaldūn asserted that "the normative method for distinguishing right from wrong in historical information on the grounds of (inherent) possibility or absurdity is to investigate human social organization, which is identical with civilization. We must distinguish the conditions that attach themselves to the essence of civilization as required by its very nature...."[24] Therefore, when Ibn Khaldūn identified the subject matter of sociology, or "the science of civilization" and the issues it addresses, he concluded by saying, "Thus, the situation is the same with this science as it is with any other science, whether it be a conventional or an intellectual one."[25]

Ibn Khaldūn's words might be understood as a call to present-day advocates of reform and change in Muslim societies to study the laws that govern change both in people's minds and hearts and in social conditions. Such a study and the knowledge it might yield of natural laws and patterns would then form the basis for reform efforts. After all, real change does not take place through limited personal experiences, the so-called expertise of shallow-minded individuals who get ahead by happenstance, or slogans bandied about without well-thought-out, practical programs regardless of how valid these slogans might be in and of themselves. Change will not take place as a result of the hopes of well-meaning individuals, however heartfelt they may be. Nor will it come about in response to believers' prayers, however loudly they raise their voices in supplication! Rather, change will only take place in response to concrete, determined human effort based on a methodology that integrates knowledge of the laws of the universe, the causes that operate in the world, concrete reality and its requirements, and application of principles and values that will guide and purify human striving.

In the course of creating the discipline of sociology, Ibn Khaldūn was not merely following in other scholars' footsteps, be they Muslims or adherents of other religions. Rather, he undertook this enterprise based on the realization that what earlier scholars had accomplished was not sufficient to provide a thorough understanding of human civilization and the mechanisms of transformation and evolution in human beings' lives. It was this realization that led Ibn Khaldūn to devote himself for a period of four years to sustained reflection, reading, and writing until, by the end of his stay in Ibn Salamah Castle, west of modern day Alger, he had completed both *Kitāb al-ʿIbar* and the chapters that make up the *Muqaddimah*, which contains the foundations of modern sociology. What he accomplished in these two works was a prodigious feat of creativity which he himself praised, saying:

> It should be known that the discussion of this topic is something new, extraordinary and highly useful. Penetrating research has shown the way to it....In a way, it

> is an entirely original science. In fact, I have not come across a discussion along these lines by anyone....We, on the other hand, were inspired by God. He led us to a science whose truth we ruthlessly set forth.[26]

Hence, the science Ibn Khaldūn was inaugurating involves more than simply studying the known laws of change; rather, it goes beyond this to a rational examination of these known laws in order to determine how they are related to the topics of study and their extent in space and time. It is a process that calls for the same genius as that demonstrated by Ibn Khaldūn himself in his own day and age. It may also call for the concerted efforts of numerous researchers working both individually and in teams so that their knowledge and expertise can be integrated. Given these conditions, they may be able to revise positions that require revision and help society to solve its many problems.

The Qur'anic understanding of civilization in the sense of human development and prosperity – *ʿumrān* – is thus a universal concept that combines and integrates a variety of elements. These elements include: the ways in which human beings develop and prosper the Earth, the process by which people's lives develop and prosper through righteous action and material advances, and the refinement and purification of people's hearts through God-consciousness and hope in God's mercy and forgiveness. The meaning of human civilization in the sense of development and prosperity is reinforced by an awareness of their opposites. The life that is promoted through human development is opposed to death, while righteousness and edification are opposed to destruction, ruin and perdition. Similarly, our understanding of human development is reinforced by an awareness of the origin from which it springs, that is, a faith grounded at once in the heart and the mind, and a determination to base one's life on concrete adherence to divine guidance. The outcome that springs from this source is a life of prosperity both in this world and the next:

> If the followers of the Bible would but attain to [true] faith and God-consciousness, We should indeed efface their [previous] bad deeds, and indeed bring them into gardens of bliss; and if they would but truly observe the Torah and the Gospel

> and all [the revelation] that has been bestowed from on high upon them by their Sustainer, they would indeed partake of all the blessings of heaven and earth. Some of them do pursue a right course; but as for most of them – vile indeed is what they do! (*Sūrah al-Mā'idah* 5:65-66)

> Yet if the people of these communities had but attained to faith and been conscious of Us, We would indeed have opened up for them blessings out of heaven and earth: but they gave the lie to the truth – and so We took them to task through what they [themselves] had been doing. (*Sūrah al-Aʿrāf* 7:96)

The Qur'an's emphasis on *ʿumrān* as a source of material benefits may be a means of gaining a hearing from individuals who crave this type of outcome. For whereas rational discussion and logical analysis may be gateways to faith for some, the promise of "the blessings of heaven and earth" in the sense of material abundance, a handsome livelihood and a life of ease may serve better to entice other individuals to enter the fold of faith. Once inside the fold, peace of mind and certainty follow as the fruit of the sweetness of faith. The generous, noble Qur'an addresses different types of people in different ways out of compassion for them in their varied states, and in the hope that all will benefit. The differences that exist among people require these varied forms of address.[27] Some people benefit most from a message that addresses itself to the conscience and the emotions; others benefit more from a discourse that focuses on the physical senses and practical benefits. Hence, Qur'anic discourse reflects a varied yet integrated methodology that speaks to one and all.

CONCLUSION

The subject of this chapter has been methodological principles and values. We have noted the semantic overlap between the terms "principle" and "value," and we have seen that the principles of methodology (*mabādi' al-manhajiyyah*) are the premises on which Islamic methodology bases its thought, research, and conduct. It is these principles to which Islamic methodology appeals in its efforts to achieve its aims, and which are reflected in its various expressions and formulations. We have posited that one of these principles is the adoption of a system of ruling values or ideals. This tripartite value system – consisting of the divine unity (*tawḥīd*), purification (*tazkiyah*), and human development and prosperity (*ʿumrān*) – governs the Islamic methodology of epistemological integration. Being a comprehensive, integrated value system, it is possible to derive numerous secondary principles from each of its three primary components.

These three components – affirmation of the oneness of God the Creator; purification of people's lives on the level of the individual, the group and the wider ummah; and human civilization identified as the process by which people develop and improve the various dimensions of their lives – constitute a system of values which the Muslim ummah needs to adopt as a basic constituent of its approach to thought, knowledge and conduct. At the same time, we need to deepen our understanding of this value system through additional studies and research, then work to derive secondary value systems which can be transferred from the realms of personal piety and the Islamic legal sciences to that of the humanities and the social and the physical sciences. This achieved, we can then apply these principles in such a way that Muslim communities become beacons of right guidance for other societies of the world.

Concluding Remarks

First: STEPS TOWARD ACHIEVING EPISTEMOLOGICAL INTEGRATION

(1) *Defining the Concept of Integration*

The term "integration" has as many meanings as it does contexts. The most commonly occurring meaning of the Arabic term *takāmul*, translated frequently as "integration," is an encyclopedic breadth of knowledge spanning numerous fields or disciplines as opposed to knowledge that is restricted to one field or specialization alone. The second most common meaning associated with the term *takāmul* pertains to the various sciences' need for each other in order to develop, mature, and apply their principles in practical contexts.

In the present context we are using the term "integration" in connection with what we have termed "the epistemological integration model." This model is based on three levels of complementarity or interdependence: (1) interdependence between the two sources of knowledge, viz., the created world and revealed word; (2) interdependence between the two tools of knowledge, namely, reason and sensory perception, and (3) interdependence between sources and tools. The term "integration" has also been associated with the process of combining our readings of the written revelation and the created world. In the context of the Islamization of knowledge and the reform of contemporary Islamic thought, epistemological integration requires that we:

- Possess adequate knowledge of Islam's principles and aims,
- Develop a methodology suited to the application of these principles or aims,
- Employ this methodology to understand and relate to contemporary sciences,

- Form a modern-day Islamic character which is solid and effective,
- Enable the Muslim ummah at large to make distinct contributions to human civilization and provide it with the guidance derived from divine revelation.

(2) *Relating to the Aims and Contents of the Various Sciences Rather Than Focusing Exclusively on Their History*

The aforementioned definition of epistemological integration assumes that we are prepared to go beyond the current approach to teaching the Islamic legal sciences. The current pedagogical approach involves presenting Islamic doctrines, rites of worship and practices as they were viewed and understood in the past. However, what we present about Islam needs to be taught in a manner that relates it to present-day reality and the tasks that face the Muslim in this present-day context. For only then will we be capable of the kinds of distinctive achievements that will place us in the lead among the nations of the world.

(3) *Interrelated Conditions for Achieving Epistemological Integration*

In order to achieve epistemological integration, four conditions must be met:

First: Those involved in the enterprise of epistemological integration must be so thoroughly versed in the Islamic worldview that it serves as an authoritative point of reference with respect to their way of understanding and relating to ideas. What this means, among other things, is a thorough grasp of the Islamic disciplines of direct relevance to the topic of research, be it on the level of texts from the Qur'an and the Sunnah, or on the level of early Muslim scholars' interpretations of these texts in the context of their own times, places, and circumstances. It also means the ability to reinterpret such texts in light of discoveries that have been made over the ages, and new understandings of the aims of these texts and how they apply to different times, places, and conditions.

Second: Those striving for epistemological integration should have such a firm grasp of contemporary academic disciplines of relevance to the topic of research. In other words, their thinking about this topic should proceed from the point at which human knowledge and experience have arrived. They must have a good understanding of relevant facts, concepts, principles and theories, including the philosophical premises of modern sciences and the historical and sociological backdrop to these sciences' emergence, formulation and application.

Third: Those engaged in epistemological integration will need to develop the critical and analytical vision required to recognize the elements of doctrinal-ideological assertions and intellectual points of reference as they relate to human experience and practice, be it traditional and Islamic, or contemporary and humanistic. This type of critical analysis will make it possible to examine such experience and practice, related schools of thought, and their authoritative points of reference, then make fair judgments on the various components of these practices and the role they play individually. This type of critical, analytical vision is necessary in order to achieve the most comprehensive possible understanding of research questions. It is likewise crucial for identifying areas that require more thorough study and research, revising research priorities, developing scientific projects and planning their implementation. In the process of carrying out tasks such as these, assistance can be sought from individuals with relevant specializations, whether in the Islamic sciences per se, or in other fields.

Fourth: If the three aforementioned conditions have to do with the effort required for proper understanding, the fourth condition has to do with surpassing what has been attained in the past. By "surpassing" we do not mean disregard. If we were expected to disregard earlier processes of mastering both Islamic foundations and contemporary human knowledge and expertise, these processes would not be included among the basic conditions for epistemological integration. Rather, what we mean by "surpassing" is the act of moving beyond the experiences of both past and present to a creative process of building a new future guided by both divine revelation and our knowledge of the laws and patterns exhibited in the physical, social and psychological worlds. The future envisioned in the Islamic perspective is not a return to some past reality. Rather, it is a leap forward in which the Muslim mind creates a reality no less significant than the one it created during the early days of Islam, at which time the guidance contained in the divine revelation, together with Muslims' action based on this guidance, led to the emergence of a new culture and civilization that constituted an unprecedented human achievement.

The woes that have been inflicted on us by materialistic civilization have brought the human race nearly to the breaking point. Hence, human beings in our time are in dire need of the kind of creative leap that would reshape modern civilization, put its achievements to proper use, and harness its resources and potentials for the good of all. Once this leap occurs, Muslims will be strangers on Earth the way they were in Islam's earliest beginnings. However, these "strangers" will accomplish what the first generation of Muslims accomplished before them: they will modernize the concept of religion and religiosity, take on the task of *khalīfah* on Earth, and develop and prosper the Earth by basing their lives on truth, justice and peace.

Second: DEFINING FEATURES OF THE METHODOLOGY OF EPISTEMOLOGICAL INTEGRATION IN THE REALM OF THOUGHT

People are thinkers by nature; hence, thought is a defining characteristic of human beings. A person's approach to thought – his or her way of thinking – is thus the most significant area of his or her methodology, since thought is the foundation for whatever follows it by way of research, practice, or individual or collective action. An Islamic methodology of thought is marked by a set of defining characteristics which are interrelated and complementary. Seen from an Islamic perspective, thought is:

1) *Purpose-oriented*; in other words, it achieves understanding of a revealed text in light of the wise purpose for which it was revealed in the context of particular concrete realities and circumstances.

2) *Comprehensive*; that is, it is based on an inclusive worldview which locates particular issues in their wider contexts, giving each of them its proper place and significance in relation to times, places, and circumstances.

3) *Orderly*, in that it connects events, phenomena and outcomes with their causes and governing universal Divine laws.

4) *Practical*, since it views everything in terms of how it relates to concrete reality while investigating all possible scenarios in search of solutions to existing problems.

5) *Strategic, predictive and positive*, focusing on ways of constructing the future and achieving cultural advancement for the Muslim ummah.

Third: THE METHODOLOGY OF EPISTEMOLOGICAL INTEGRATION IN THE REALM OF RESEARCH

It would be inconceivable to engage in research in isolation from thought processes; hence, a methodology of epistemological integration applicable to research will include elements of relevance to thought. One of the thought-related elements of such a methodology is identification of research priorities.

Identifying research priorities enables the researcher to choose the issues that are most worthy of investigation in a particular society and a particular set of circumstances. Research is not an end in itself. Rather, it is a means of acquiring the knowledge necessary to solve problems, answer questions, and improve performance levels. Therefore, not everything that is worth researching in one society would be worth researching in another. Moreover, issues that were investigated and sciences that were recorded by Muslim scholars of the past need not be researched or recorded again, since these scholars' contributions consisted of interpretations of divine revelation and the way in which its guidance was to be applied to the issues of their own day. These earlier scholars fulfilled the responsibility that was theirs in their day and in the contexts of their own societies given the knowledge that was available to them. What is required of contemporary scholars, then, is to think creatively about the ways in which the guidance provided by divine revelation is to be applied to the issues and problems we face in our own day. After all, divine revelation is a spring so vast that it will never be exhausted no matter how many come to drink from it, and no matter how often. Similarly, it is equally valid in all times and places, and its guidance is ongoing,

It cannot be said that the scholarship of the past left nothing else to be done.

Hence, preoccupation with reviving the Islamic heritage by, for example, editing, annotating and abridging manuscripts for publication in order for people in our day to benefit from them is not a substitute for the establishment of new disciplines derived from the texts of the Qur'an and the Sunnah. If the Muslim ummah and its scholars are no longer capable of making ongoing contributions to the Islamic heritage by engaging in independent reasoning and intellectual creativity, this indicates a serious lack of vitality that will undermine Muslims' ability to hold their own in the larger community of nations by contributing to its intellectual and cultural advances. The Messenger of God warned, in fact, that the Muslim ummah would find itself in this condition some day.

It should be borne in mind that the academic disciplines recognized by Muslims are by no means restricted to what have come to be called the Islamic legal sciences (*al-ᶜulūm al-sharᶜiyyah*), and which concern themselves with recording, documentation, exegesis, and derivation of legal rulings from authoritative religious texts. Rather, they also include what are known today as the natural sciences, the applied, practical sciences, and the social and human sciences. These sciences need not be derived from the texts of written revelation. Rather, they are based on the study of the nature of things, events and phenomena in light of the God-given physical, social and psychological laws that govern them.

The texts of the Qur'an constitute a source of general guidance for us in our strivings to attain, test and use knowledge for the purpose of achieving human development and the betterment of life on Planet Earth. Based on the guidance they derive from the Qur'an, Muslim scholars or researchers will be prepared to undertake whatever scientific activity is required by the subject under investigation, such as familiarizing themselves with others' work and viewpoints or doing observation and experimentation. And in all such situations, they will be careful to employ the most appropriate and effective methods and tools.

Fourth: HOW THE METHODOLOGY OF EPISTEMOLOGICAL INTEGRATION MANIFESTS ITSELF IN CONDUCT

An Islamic approach to conduct requires integration of various worlds: the world of persons, the world of ideas, the world of things, and other worlds as well, since both thought and research span a variety of realms. In Chapter Seven we made brief reference to the ruling principles of methodology in the realm of conduct. We identified three interrelated and complementary principles that serve to regulate behavior in a systematic way, namely, intention (*niyyah*), adherence (*ittibāʿ*), and creativity (*ibdāʿ*). When we set out to apply these principles, we do not permit ourselves to be ruled by mere custom or habit, opportunism, or blind imitation of others.

Human conduct is associated with the outward, practical aspect of action. However, this outward, visible aspect is, in reality, a direct outcome of an action that is subtle and unseen. This subtle, unseen action includes the processes of reflection and cogitation, examination of alternatives and choices, contrasts and comparisons in the course of which an individual arrives at a decision with which he or she feels comfortable and forms an intention to take a certain course of action. This kind of inward conduct is an action undertaken by the heart or conscience. In the case of a Muslim who has the desire to apply an Islamic methodology, these inward processes represent a predisposition to seek God the Creator. In other words, they reflect a kind of God-consciousness, which motivates the individual to seek what will please God and merit divine favor and reward, while avoiding what would displease God and incite divine wrath and chastisement.

Such an individual may take into consideration the experiences of others, in which case he or she follows a path that is tried and true, and which is more or less guaranteed to lead him or her to the desired end. Hence, there is no need in this situation for trial and error. Rather, it involves conscious, insightful adherence to a well-established approach in which the individual's conduct conforms to the path set forth by the Prophet. Such adherence is an affirmation of one's belonging to Muslim society and the Muslim ummah. However, it is not blind dependency or rigid, stereotypical responses at a minimal level of performance. Rather, it is an ongoing effort to overcome obstacles, advance, grow, and create out of a desire for wisdom and true virtue.

In conclusion, we will need to clarify the ways in which a "methodological culture" will impact the qualifications of the integrated Muslim scientist or scholar, particularly university professors, who realize that systematic (methodological) thinking is a fundamental element of their academic persona and overall identity. In their specialized academic culture they are scholars, while in their social milieu they are reformers, as well as educators of present and future generations. It is university professors in particular who engage in systematic thinking as a means of defining things and making distinctions, systematic research as a professional activity, and systematic behavior as a daily commitment. These things take place spontaneously, however, since methodological thinking and acting have become an integral part of them.

And God Almighty knows best.

APPENDIX

PLANNING A TRAINING PROGRAM ON THE METHODOLOGY OF EPISTEMOLOGICAL INTEGRATION

The material we will be presenting in this appendix is not a complete training program in the methodology of epistemological integration, nor is it intended as a training manual on this topic. Rather, it is an invitation to the reader of this book, and to the trainer who may benefit from it in preparing for a course or courses on this topic, to reflect on a number of the requirements for drawing up a complete training program or manual.

The suggestions presented below came out of several training courses which were organized and implemented by the author on the topic of this book under the auspices of the International Institute of Islamic Thought.

FIRST: COURSE REQUIREMENTS

The document outlining course requirements is of great importance, and must be sent to participants long enough before the course's commencement for them to do the necessary preparation. The period of time allowed for participant preparation depends on the nature of the course, the amount of material to be covered in it, and the number and type of tasks participants are requested to carry out before the course begins. In order to ensure that most of the course time is taken up with discussion and training rather than with reading and presentation, the document should include deadlines for completion of the aforementioned tasks. Course preparation on the part of the participants will require deliberate, thoughtful reading of the basic course materials, as well as sufficient familiarity with any additional material provided. Participants are expected to have completed all preparations, including all readings and all activities in the preparation program, before the course begins.

The course requirement document should contain the following elements:

1. Information about the course participants: their number, what countries they come from, their specializations and experience

2. Complete copies of required and recommended reading material to be covered in the training course.

3. Pre-Course Activities

a) Participants will do a careful, critical reading of the required course materials and familiarize themselves adequately with supplemental materials.

b) Participants will answer the questions and complete the exercises that accompany the required course materials, and prepare to present and discuss them at the appropriate points in the course sessions.

c) Each participant will choose some relevant academic material which he or she expects to be beneficial for other participants. He or she will then send the material to the course administrator by a specified date.

d) Each participant will decide on a research project in his or her area of specialization and in the development of which he or she can apply the experience and expertise he or she has acquired in the course. The participant will complete the project later for publication in a refereed journal, or as part of a volume containing the contributions of all course participants. He or she should send the title of his or her proposed project to the course administrator by a specified date.

e) Each participant will suggest three titles for high-priority research projects in his or her area of specialization to which he or she believes the content of the course ought to be applied. The participant will then send these three titles to the course administrator by a specified date.

f) Each participant will choose one of the topics to be treated in the course and prepare to help lead the session in which this topic will be discussed. He or she will develop a number of training situations of relevance to this topic, then send in the topic he or she would like to help lead the discussion of by a specified date.

4. Course Activities

Each participant will:

a) Review the elements of the topic for each session, and prepare to take an active part in each session's activities.
b) Write a one-page (250-word) summary of the most important ideas and skills contained in the session's activities. Summaries will be written either during the session concerned or at its conclusion, and will be submitted in the morning of the day following the relevant session.
c) Identify the styles of participation he or she observes during the sessions. Participation styles will include, in particular: individual thinking, team work, and general participation.
d) Develop a research plan which he or she will complete and prepare for publication by adding new elements to its content over the course of the training sessions. The research plan prepared prior to and during the course should come to a minimum of 2, 500 words.
e) Develop plans for the three research projects he or she views as research priorities in his or her area of specialization. Each research plan should consist of a minimum of 250 words. In addition to the title of the research, the plan should include a paragraph on the idea and importance of the topic, related questions, the methodology to be employed in implementing it, and the most important outcomes the participant expects to be achieved through said research. The aim of this activity is to produce a list of high-priority potential research projects. This list, which will be three times longer than the course participant roster, will be distributed among participants during the course's concluding session.
f) Respond to the questions on the two evaluation forms which participants will receive upon arrival together with their training

package. The questions on these two evaluations forms, one of which is quantitative in nature, and the other, qualitative, may be answered gradually as the course progresses, or during the course's concluding session.

5. Post-Course Requirements

Participants will be expected to:

a) Organize communication among themselves through email groups in order to exchange expertise, experiences, materials, and achievements of relevance to the issues dealt with in the course.
b) Work to completion on the research project, then prepare it for publication. Participants will be given a grace period of two to four months to complete their papers, which should come to approximately 10,000 words in keeping with the requirements of most academic journals, and send them to the course administrator. The research papers may either be published in refereed journals, or collected into a single volume for publication by the institution that sponsored and organized the training course.

6. Structure of the Course Program

   The course structure should specify the total number of hours of which the program will consist, including an approximation of the number of hours needed to prepare for the course and complete post-course assignments, in addition to the number and times of sessions to be attended each day, and the nature of evening activities.

7. Course program details, that is, a list of the topics to be discussed in the course sessions.

8. Introduction cards with identical or similar formats should be provided for participants. Cards should be sent out to participants well in advance of the course's commencement so that course organizers can prepare a file that enables participants to get better acquainted with each other, and which should be ready for

distribution during the course's opening session, or even before the beginnings of the course. The material used to introduce each participant should consist of 50-75 words, and include the following:

Name:	______________
Highest qualification:	______________
Specialization:	______________
University:	______________
City:	______________
Year:	______________
Position:	______________
Place of work:	______________
Number of books published:	______________
Number of papers published:	______________
Areas of one's research:	______________
Most important achievements:	______________
Nature of current academic and practical interests:	______________

SECOND: THE TRAINING PACKAGE

The training package is a set of materials which have been prepared beforehand to place in participants' hands from the beginning of the course. These materials consist of the following:

1. Course brochure. This brochure will generally contained an advertisement for the course and an invitation to participate in it. It contains the basic idea behind the course, its aims and themes, the nature of the activities it will involve, and how to contact the institution organizing the course or the person who will serve as the trainer.

2. Course material. Course material consists of the required and recommended readings and exercises that were sent to participants prior to the course. Required course material generally consists of a

book or pamphlet, or selected chapters of one or more books which will be the focus of discussions and training activities. As for the recommended materials, they will also consist of a book or a chapter from one or more books which the course organizers recommend to those who wish to read more widely on the theme of the course.

3. The course program, which specifies the times and topics of the various course sessions, and opening and closing session activities.

4. A course requirement card containing a listing of what the trainee is expected to do in completion of the course. This includes pre-course preparations, course activities, and assignments to complete following the course's conclusion. This card will have been sent to participants before the course's commencement; however, it is also placed in the training package upon their arrival for follow-up purposes.

5. A participant introduction card, which is a brief bio of the individual participant consisting of seven elements: the participant's highest qualification, his/her academic specialization, the nature of his/her current employment, her/her most notable achievements (books and papers published, prizes, etc.), his/her current areas of interest, his/her email address, and a personal photo. The information should be limited to 50-75 words so that it will fit onto a single card, which will be distributed among the other participants at the start of the course.

6. Trainee course evaluation forms. These forms have a double purpose. First, they help course organizers to determine how successful they have been – in participants' eyes – in achieving the goals of the training course, and what aspects of the course need to be improved in the future. Second, these forms give participants an opportunity to review the elements and requirements of the course and how much they have benefitted from them. It is preferable that participants be provided with three different course evaluation forms: a form for evaluating training sessions (the number of forms in the

training package should equal the number of sessions included in the course schedule), and two final evaluation forms, one quantitative and the other qualitative.

7. Trainee self-evaluation form: This form contains information which the trainee records himself about his attendance of sessions, performance of assignments, the topics he feels he has mastered and the topics he feels he needs to expend more effort in order to master, to what extent he feels he would be capable of organizing a similar course, and the score (out of 100) he would give himself on the extent to which he realized the overall course aims.

8. The certificate which is awarded at the conclusion of the course to every participant who has completed its requirements.

9. Course session training cards: Although the trainer is expected to prepare the training card for each session, it is preferable that he not include training cards for all the sessions in the training package. This is because each group in the evening activities is asked to cooperate in preparing a training card for one of the sessions that was organized that same day, and every participant individually is asked to prepare a training card for another session the following evening. The reason for this is that one of the course aims is to teach participants to prepare training cards. Each card contains the following four elements: a) the aims of the session, which are directly related to the session's topic and to one of the course's overall aims, b) key concepts of the session, c) the most important outcomes of the session, which are recorded in the form of meaningful sentences or conceptual formulations of the information and activities needed in order to develop the skills and attitudes the session is intended to develop, and d) the session's training situations and activities, including the name and type of each activity or situation, its duration, requirements for its implementation, and its manner of implementation.

THIRD: TRAINING SITUATIONS

Different training situations are associated with different aims, assume different practical forms, and take various amounts of time to implement. The following are examples of training situations and activities:

1. Thinking Alone and in Pairs

One possible purpose of this activity is to ensure that every one of the trainees is engaged in thinking and reflection independently of others, and that his or her thinking and understanding of the topic at hand is not being influenced by the intellectual environment being shaped by the attitudes and opinions of other speakers taking part in the discussion. Most people – though not all – are influenced in their attitudes by whichever point of view happens to prevail, and which is defined by speakers' orientations. If the prevailing trend is to accept a certain point of view, the individual will tend to be more accepting of it, and if the prevailing attitude is one of rejection, the individual will be more likely to reject it. Another purpose this activity serves is to open the way for precise, clear, well-defined linguistic expression by having each individual trainee write out the answer to a particular question, since in most cases, one's written language is more precise, clear and eloquent than one's spontaneous, unplanned speech.

a) The form taken by the training situation in this case is that of individual activity, including individual thinking, independent reflection, and expressive writing. The trainer asks each of the trainees to write, without consulting with anyone, a specified number of words (twenty, for example) in answer to a question within a specified time frame (60 seconds, for example). The trainer asks a number of trainees to read aloud what they have written, then comments on the variety and richness in the directions they took in their thinking and the positive value of this variety. Each trainee is encouraged to observe the direction his or her thought took and the degree to which his or her thinking differed from that of the other participants, as well as the need to note things he or she had not noted before. Individual thinking is conducive to abstraction and objectivity in seeking the truth. Consequently, this training situation may be more important for the individual than it is for the group. Trainees may be asked to write to themselves without there being any need to inform others of where their thinking has led. Instead of sharing what they have written with others, trainees keep what they have written and compare it later with what they wrote in another situation, noting the development in their thought about the topic concerned. This kind of training can help to remind people of their direct, individual responsibility before God Almighty. For every one of us will come before God as an individual, and will be judged individually for the things he or she did on Earth: "[On the Day of Judgment,] every human being will be held in pledge for whatever [evil] he has wrought" (*sūrah al-Muddaththir* 74:38), and will be alone responsible for his doings: "...no bearer of burdens shall be made to bear another's burden..." (*sūrah al-Isrā'* 17:15). When we think in this way, we realize that we have no choice but to be objective and diligent in seeking the truth.

b) The purpose might, alternatively, be to create opportunities for cooperation in thinking between two individuals. This training situation gives each pair of participants a certain length of time (120 seconds, for example) to exchange opinions on the possible answer to a question, after which one of them mentions this answer to the larger group. This kind of dual thinking generates a degree of candor. The purpose, however, is not to demonstrate the strength of either paired partner before others, since it is not a public debate. Rather, its purpose is to enable both partners to contribute to the effort needed to arrive at a position that both of them agree on. The trainer can ask each participant to form a team with the person to his right, then discuss an issue within a specified time period. (In order to prevent the same pairs from working together every time, the trainer can ask participants in one situation to work with the person to their right, and in a subsequent session to work with the person to their left.)

The importance of thinking both individually and in pairs is alluded to in the Qur'anic passage that reads, "Say: 'I do admonish you on one point: that ye do stand up before God, – (It may be) in pairs, or (it may be) singly, – and reflect (within yourselves): your Companion is not possessed: he is no less than a warner to you, in face of a terrible Penalty'" (*sūrah Saba'* 34:46). Translation Abdullah Yusuf Ali.

2. Thinking as a Team

Despite the importance of thinking individually and in pairs in some situations, other situations require that we broaden the circle of dialogue to include a larger group. The need to form teams becomes evident when it is necessary to give each trainee more time to participate in the discussion of a given topic, when a group of trainees is being asked to arrive cooperatively at a shared opinion or stance on a given topic, or when there is a need to provide training in giving expression to a single shared point of view or a variety of points of view. Some topics are composed of numerous particulars and elements to which justice cannot be done in a single discussion. When this sort of topic is to be treated, trainees can be divided up into a number of groups (3-5 groups consisting of 4-6 members each). Members of each team are then asked to discuss a single element of the topic and reach whatever conclusions they can. One member of each group is then assigned to summarize these conclusions in front of everyone.

This type of training situation is of significant practical value, as will be seen from the following example. Let us suppose that there are twenty trainees and that the topic to be discussed consists of four elements. If the trainer wants to give each of the trainees one minute to express his opinion, then the time required to discuss each element comes to 20 minutes. Discussing all four elements on the level of the entire group would take 80 minutes. However, this is a fairly long time period which may not be available, not to mention the fact that an open discussion might lead people's thoughts in a particular direction while preventing trainees' thinking from moving in other directions. The alternative to this approach is to divide the trainees into four groups of five, each of which discusses one of the four elements of the topic. Each team is given ten minutes, during which time its members formulate a shared perspective. At the end of the ten minutes, all participants gather in a single session, and each group is given one minute to summarize the position it has reached. In this way the participants' vision of the topic under consideration, including each of its four elements, is formulated in a short period of time, which allows time for the discussion of other topics as well.

Formation of teams does not necessarily mean that the teams must all be discussing different topics. In fact, all four teams can be discussing the same topic simultaneously, after which one member of each team summarizes the outcome of his or her group's discussion for the larger group. In this way, each individual participant has much more time to express his or her opinions and thoughts and to share information. It also allows the various teams to take different directions in discussing the topic at hand without their individual members being unduly affected by the overall mood or trend that might color the conversation in the event of an open, all-group discussion.

In situations where it is necessary to explore the possible arguments or evidence in support of varying points of view on the topic being considered, a debate on the topic might be organized between two or more teams.

3. Open (all-group) Discussions

Discussion of a given topic may also be opened up to all trainees at once. The trainer may, for example, present some particular experience or practical piece of information in the form of a story, chart, or sketch to which he draws everyone's attention, then allow a specific amount of time for comments and questions. It is preferable for the presentation time not to be so long that the session turns into a lecture, nor for the discussion time to be prolonged to the point where all the time is taken up with expression of opinions, rejoinders, and counter-rejoinders. Consequently, not all participants will be expected to contribute to this type of discussion. It will suffice for the trainer to feel that he has received enough input to enable him to move on to another topic or training situation. However, the trainer should be careful to give as many trainees as possible the opportunity to speak, and not to allow certain participants to dominate the discussion at others' expense, or at the expense of other aspects of the topic being treated.

It should be remembered, of course, that training of this sort involves a significant degree of reflection on what is being presented and discussed so that the trainee can digest the information he or she is taking in, take a stance on it, incorporate it into his or her epistemological frame of reference, and reorganize his or her individual experience, expertise and perspective on the basis of the new input being received. The time the trainee spends in this type of reflection is no less important than the time he or she spends in conversation with others.

There are various ways of leading group discussions. The discussion might be launched on the basis of a question raised by the trainer or one of the trainees. Then, rather than receiving a single answer or a single formulation of that answer, the trainer opens up the conversation in order to obtain a variety of answers, or ways of formulating a given answer. The trainer might pose a problem calling for a solution or a task needing to be implemented, in which case the discussion may take the form of a brainstorming session in which participants call on their varied knowledge and experience in their efforts to solve the problem posed or implement the task at hand.

FOURTH: NOTES ON THE CONCEPT OF TRAINING

The concept of training, as opposed to that of teaching or instruction, has been associated with a number of negative or mistaken notions. The following are examples:

- Teaching or instruction is associated with adult intellectual awareness and maturity, whereas training is thought of in connection with the immaturity of the child, or the lack of awareness of an animal.
- Training is associated with the acquisition of applied or practical skills, while teaching is associated with information and ideas.
- Some teaching styles are restricted to listening and passive reception on the part of learners, while training styles are devoted to active learner participation.

The reality, however, is otherwise. Teaching can be addressed to both children and adults; it can also involve active participation. It may also entail helping learners to acquire information, skills, and attitudes. Otherwise, it is not good teaching. Conversely, training might consist of a series of lectures in which the trainee is simply a passive recipient. When this happens, however, the training cannot be described as good. Hence, both instruction and training practices may be good or bad. Since the context of the present discussion is that of training, we will focus on what we view as good quality training.

We will bypass discussion of familiar practices in many so-called "training programs" or "training courses" in which most activities are limited to lectures with the use of certain teaching aids, particularly the PowerPoint slides presentation, PPT.

Like teaching, training entails providing learners with information and skills and helping them to form new orientations and attitudes. Training focuses information pertinent to a particular topic and the inculcation of positive attitudes toward acquisition of relevant skills. After all, every skill, be it practical and applied, or mental and intellectual, rests on an epistemological foundation or information base.

A researcher, for example, must acquire the ability to formulate research questions in a manner that calls for particular types of data and whose language is tied directly to the problem to be investigated. This ability in turn requires information about the conditions and specifications which research questions have to meet. A training program relating to research skills might present examples of good research questions, then allow trainees to deduce from these examples the conditions and specifications such questions meet. He might then present trainees with examples of research questions that do not meet such specifications and conditions and lead a discussion on how they might be improved. Lastly, the trainer might lead participants in a discussion of questions they themselves have written on research topics of their own choice, and have them develop these questions until they conform more closely to the required specifications. The point of significance in this example is the fact that there are specifications and conditions which good research questions must meet. This information could be presented directly in the form of a brief lecture; it could, alternatively, be conveyed through a written text or deduced through a discussion of examples such as those described above.

People tend to be personally motivated to participate in paid training programs out of a desire to increase their knowledge and develop their abilities and skills. Consequently, a trainee can be expected to attend such programs out of a sense of personal interest, a belief in the aims the program is designed to achieve, and a seriousness that justifies the effort, time and expense required to complete it.

NOTES

PREFACE

1 *Al-Manhajiyyah al-Islāmiyyah* (Islamic Methodology) was later published in two volumes by IIIT in cooperation with Dār al-Salām in Cairo.

2 Ahmed Fouad Pasha, et. al., *Al-Manhajiyyah al-Islāmiyyah* (Islamic Methodology), (Cairo: The International Institute of Islamic Thought and Dār al-Salām, 2010).

3 *Islāmīyat al-Ma'rifah: al-Mabādī' wa Khiṭṭat al-ʿAmal wa al-Injāzāt* (The Islamization of Knowledge: General Principles, Plan of Action, and Achievements), (Herndon: The International Institute of Islamic Thought, 1986).

4 Al-Tayyib Zayn al-Abidin, ed., *Al-Manhajiyyah al-Islāmiyyah wa al-ʿUlūm al-Sulūkiyyah wa al-Tarbawiyyah: Aʿmāl al-Mu'tamar al-ʿlamī al-Rābiʿ li al-Fikr al-Islāmī fī Jāmiʿat al-Kharṭūm* ("Islamic Methodology and the Behavioral and Educational Sciences: Proceedings of the Fourth International Conference on Islamic Thought at the University of Khartoum"). (Herndon, Virginia: IIIT, 1990).

5 Nasr Muhammad Arif, ed., *Qaḍāyā al-Manhajiyyah al-Islāmiyyah: Aʿmāl Mu'tamar Qaḍāyā al-Manhajiyyah fī Jāmiʿat al-Amīr ʿAbd al-Qādir bi Qusantina, 1989* ("Issues of Islamic Methodology: Proceedings of the Conference on Issues of Methodology at the Emir Abedkader University at Qusantina, 1989"), (Herndon, VA.: The International Institute of Islamic Thought, 1996).

6 Muhammad Amarah, *Malāmiḥ al-Manhaj al-Islāmī* (Features of Islamic Method), (Cairo: The International Institute of Islamic Thought and al-Azhar University, 1990).

CHAPTER I

1 C. P. Snow, *The Two Cultures* (London: Cambridge University Press, 1993).

2 See al-Khaṭīb al-Baghdādī, Aḥmad ibn ʿAlī ibn Thābit, *Iqtiḍā' al-ʿIlm al-ʿAmal* (Knowledge Calls for Action), ed. Muhammad Nasiruddin al-Albani, (Damascus: Al-Maktab al-Islamī, Fifth Edition, 1984).

3 Ernest Boyer, *Scholarship Reconsidered: Priorities of Professoriate* (Princeton, NJ: Carnegie Foundation for the Advancement of Teaching, 1990), p. 19.

4 See Allen Utke, "The (Re)unification of Knowledge: Why? How? Where? When?" in G. Benson, R. Glasberg, and B. Griffith, *Perspectives on the Unity and Integration of Knowledge* (New York: Peter Lange, 1998), p. 4.

5 Ibid., p. 20. One should beware of the conclusions to which such scientific discourse might lead in its pessimism vis-à-vis the achievements of modernity, or its optimism vis-à-vis the promises of post-modernism. As I see it, Islamic methodology neither views all of modernism's achievements as evil, nor all the promises of post-modernism as good.

6 C. H. Lai and Azim Kidawi, eds., *Ideals and Realities: Selected Essays of Abdus Salam*, Third Edition, (World Scientific, 1989), pp. 465-466. See also: http://www.nobelprize.org/nobel_prizes/physics/laureates/1979.

7 Paraphrased from Ahmed Fouad Pasha, *Falsafat al-ʿUlūm bi Naẓrah Islāmiyyah* (Philosophy of Science from an Islamic Perspective), First Edition, (Cairo: Self-published, 1984), pp. 47-50.

8 Muzaffar Iqbal, *Islam and Science* (Aldershot, UK: Ashgate Publishing LMT, 2002), pp. 293-294.

9 Ismaʿīl al Fārūqī, "Islamization of Knowledge: Problems, Principles and Prospective," in *Islam: Source and Purpose of Knowledge* (Herndon: IIIT, 1988), pp. 13-63.

10 Sardar and his group have taken the Arabic-Persian word *ijmālī* (meaning "comprehensive, inclusive, all-embracing"), which occurs in Jalaluddin al-Rumi's *Diwan-i Shams*, and transliterated it into English to reflect the holistic nature of their approach. See Ziauddin Sardar, *Explorations in Islamic Science* (London: Mansell Publications, 1989), pp. 154-172.

11 ʿAbd al-Majid al-Najjar, *Mabāḥith fī Manhajiyyat al-Fikr al-Islāmī* (Studies in the Methodology of Islamic Thought), (Beirut: Dār al-Maghrib al-ʿArabi, 1992), p. 66.

12 Sardar, *Explorations in Islamic Science*, p. 155.

13 Seyyed Hossein Nasr, *The Need for a Sacred Science* (New York: State University of New York Press, 1993), p. 54.

14 Osman Bakar, *Classification of Knowledge in Islam: A Study in Islamic Philosophy of Science*, (Kuala Lumpur, Malaysia: Institute for Policy Studies, 1992), p. 270.

15 J. P. Moreland and William Lane Craig, *Philosophical Foundations for a Christian Worldview* (Downers Grove, Ill.: InterVarsity Press, 2003), p. 595. See also John Schwarz, *The Complete Guide to the Christian Faith* (Minneapolis, MN: Bethany House Publishers, 2001), p. 184.

16 Isma^cil R. al Fārūqī, *Al-Tawhid: Its Implications for Thought and Life*. Reprint. (Herndon, VA: IIIT, 2000).
17 Ibid., pp. 10-15.
18 Ibid., p. 17.
19 Ibid., p. 43.
20 Ibid., p. 44.
21 Ibid., p. 51.
22 Seyyed H. Nasr, *An Introduction to Islamic Cosmological Doctrines* (New York: State University of New York Press, 1993), pp. 280-281.
23 Seyyed H. Nasr, "The Cosmos and the Natural Order," in S. H. Nasr, ed., *Islamic Spirituality I: Foundations*, vol. 19 of *World Spirituality: An Encyclopedic History of the Religious Quest* (London: Routledge and Kegan Paul, 1987), p. 350.
24 Ibid., p. 73.
25 Osman Bakar, *Tawhid and Science: Essays on the History and Philosophy of Islamic Science* (Kuala Lumpur, Malaysia: Secretariat for Islamic Philosophy and Science, 1991), p. 62.
26 Ibid., pp. 74-75.
27 Ali Shariati, *Al-Insān wa al-Islām* (Humanity and Surrender to God), translated by Abbas al-Tarjuman (Beirut: Dār al-Rawḍah, 1992), p. 29.
28 Sayyid Qutb, *Khaṣā'iṣ al-Taṣawwur al-Islāmī wa Muqawwimātuhu* (Distinguishing Features and Components of Islamic Conceptualization), part I. Reprint. (Kuwait: International Islamic Federation of Student Organizations (IFSO), 1983), p. 7.
29 Abu Bakr Muhammad Ahmad Ibrahim, *Al-Takāmul al-Ma^crifī wa Taṭbīqātuhu fī al-Manāhij al-Jāmi^ciyyah* (Epistemological Integration and Its Applications in University Curricula), (Herndon, VA: The International Institute of Islamic Thought, 2007), p. 1.
30 Ibid., p. 121.
31 Ibid., p. 101.
32 AbdulHamid AbuSulayman, *The Qur'anic Worldview: A Springboad for Cultural Reform* (London and Washington: The International Institute of Islamic Thought, 2011), p. 35.
33 *Khilāfah*: Stewardship, vicegerency, successorship. Office of the head of the Muslim state. Also the designation of the political system of the Muslim state after the noble Prophet. The author prefers to use *khalīfah* on earth, rather than God's *khalīfah*. The meaning of *khalīfah* reminds us that Mankind have the trust and responsibility of establishing a social-political order, full of

justice and good life to fulfil the will of God. English words such as steward or vicegerent may not bring the essence of *khalīfah*.

34 Taha Alalwani, "Al-ʿAql wa Mawqiʿuhu fī al-Manhajiyyah al-Islāmiyyah," (Reason and Its Place in Islamic Methodology), *Majallat Islāmīyat al-Ma'rifah*, no. 6, September 1996, pp. 36-39.

35 Ibid., p. 11.

36 AbuSulayman, *The Qur'anic Worldview*, p. 124.

37 Ibid., p. 123.

38 Wan Mohd. Nor Wan Daud, *The Concept of Knowledge in Islam and Its Implications for Education in a Developing Country* (London: Mansell, 1989), p. 67.

39 For more detail on the integration of sources and tools of knowledge, see the discussion of the epistemological integration equation in Chapter Six, "Sources and Tools of Methodology."

40 Abū al-Walīd ibn Rushd, *Faṣl al-Maqāl fī mā Bayn al-Ḥikmati wa al-Sharīʿah min al-Ittiṣāl* (The Definitive Word on the Link Between Wisdom and the Divinely Revealed Law), ed. Muhammad Abid al-Jabiri (Beirut: Markaz Dirāsāt al-Waḥdah al-ʿArabiyyah (Center for Arab Unity Studies), 1997), pp. 85-88.

41 Abū Ḥāmid al-Ghazālī, *Jawāhir al-Qur'ān wa Duraruhu* (Gems and Pearls of the Qur'an), (Beirut: Dār al-Jīl, 1988), pp. 26-27.

42 Abū al-ʿAbbās Taqiy al-Dīn ibn Taymiyyah, *Dar'u Taʿāruḍ al-ʿAqli wa al-Naql* (The Case Against Contradiction Between Reason and Revelation), ed. Muhammad Rashad Salim (Riyadh: King Muhammad Bin Sa'ud University, 1979), vol. 1, p. 147.

43 See Thomas Tritton, "Integrated Learning: Passing Fad or Foundation for the Future?" in Antonio Damasio, et al. (eds), *Unity of Knowledge: The Convergence of Natural and Human Sciences* (New York: The New York Academy of Sciences, 2001), p. 272.

44 Edward O. Wilson, *Consilience: The Unity of Knowledge* (New York: Vintage Books, 1999), p. 294.

45 Muhammad Abdus Salam, "Gauge Unification of Fundamental Forces," Nobel lecture, December 8, 1979. See http://www.nobelprize.org/nobel_prizes/physics/laureates/1979/salam-lecture.html?print=1.

46 William J. Broad, "Why They Called It the Manhattan Project," *The New York Times*, October 30, 2007.

47 Charles Murray and Catherine Cox, *Apollo: Race to the Moon* (Clearwater, FL: Touchstone Books, 1990).

48 Ibn Rushd, *Faṣl al-Maqāl*, p. 25.

Notes

CHAPTER 2

1 In the course of researching how consistent Muslim scholars down the centuries have been in their use of the terms *minhāj*, *manhaj* and *nahj* in the titles of their books, I discovered that these three terms were used interchangeably in the title to the same book over the course of several centuries. The original title of the book was *Minhāj al-Ṭālibīn wa ᶜUmdat al-Muftīn* by Imam Abū Zakariyyā Yaḥyā ibn Sharaf al-Nawawī (d. 676 AH/1277 CE). Approximately three centuries later the book was retranscribed, and in the margins one finds the book, *Manhaj al-Ṭullāb* by Shaykh Zakariyyā al-Anṣārī (d. 936 AH/1529 CE). Three more centuries passed, at which time the word *manhaj* was abbreviated to *nahj* in the title, *Nahj al-Ṭālib ilā Ashraf al-Maṭālib* by Aḥmad Ibn Muḥammad al-Jawhari (d. 1215 AH/1800 CE). One cannot help but note the evolution of the word in the title from *minhāj* to *manhaj* to *nahj*.

2 Abū al-Faḍl Jamāl al-Dīn ibn Manẓūr, *Lisān al-ᶜArab* (Beirut: Dār Ṣādir and Dār Beirut, no date), vol. 2, p. 383.

3 Abū ᶜAbd Allāh Muḥammad ibn Aḥmad al-Anṣārī al-Qurṭubī, *Al-Jāmiᶜ Li Aḥkām al-Qur'ān* (Beirut: Mu'assasat Manāhil al-ᶜIrfān, no date), vol. 6, p. 211 in commentary on the phrase quoted above from *sūrah al-Mā'idah* 5:48, "Unto every one of you have We appointed a [different] law (*shirᶜah*) and way of life" (*minhāj*).

4 Abū al-Fidā' Ismāᶜīl Ibn Kathīr, *Tafsīr al-Qur'ān al-ᶜAẓīm* (An Explanation of the Noble Qur'an), (Cairo: ᶜĪsā al-Bābī al-Ḥalabī, no date), vol. 2, p. 66.

5 Ibid.

6 Abdullah Yusuf Ali's translation, *The Holy Qur'an: Text, Translation and Commentary* (New York, NY: Tahrike Tarsile Qur'an, Inc., 1987).

7 ᶜAlī Ibn ᶜAbd al-Kāfī al-Subkī, *Al-Ibhāj fī Sharḥ al-Minhāj: Sharḥ Minhāj al-Wuṣūl ilā ᶜIlm al-Uṣūl* by ᶜAbd Allāh Ibn ᶜUmar al-Bayḍāwī (Beirut: Dār al-Kutub al-ᶜIlmiyyah, 1995), vol. 1, p. 3.

8 Abd al-Munim al-Hafni, *Al-Muᶜjam al-Shāmil li al-Muṣṭalaḥāt al-Falsafiyyah*. Reprint. (Cairo: Maktabat Madbūlī, 2000), p. 849.

9 Michael Agnos, ed., *Webster's New World College Dictionary*, Fourth Edition) (Foster City, CA: Webster's New World, 2001), p. 906. See also the *Oxford Illustrated American Dictionary* (New York: Oxford University Press, 1998), p. 515.

10 Faris Ishta, "Madkhal ilā al-Manhajiyyah fī al-ᶜUlūm al-Ijtimāᶜiyyah" (An Introduction to Methodology in the Social Sciences), *Majallat al-ᶜUlūm al-Ijtimāᶜiyyah* (Lebanese University, 1991), vol. 1, no. 1, pp. 33-47.

11 *Al-Muᶜjam al-Falsafī* (Cairo: Majmaᶜ al-Lughah al-ᶜArabiyyah, 1979, p. 196.

12 Abd al-Rahman Badawi, *Al-Mawsūᶜah al-Falsafiyyah* (Beirut: al-Mu'assasah al-ᶜArabiyyah li al-Dirāsāt wa al-Nashr, 1984), p. 475.

13 Abd al-Rahman Badawi, *Manāhij al-Baḥth al-ᶜIlmī* (Scientific Research Methods), (Cairo: Dār al-Nahḍah al-ᶜArabiyyah, 1963), p. 5.

14 Abū Ḥāmid al-Ghazālī, *Tahāfut al-Falāsifah* (The Incoherence of the Philosophers), ed. Sulayman Dunya (Cairo: Dār al-Maᶜārif, no date), p. 5.

15 Muḥammad ᶜAlī al-Fārūqī al-Tahānawī, *Kashshāf Iṣṭilāḥāt al-Funūn*, ed. Lutfi Abd al-Badi(Cairo: al-Hay'ah al-Miṣriyyah li al-Kitāb, 1972), vol. 1, pp. 5-6.

16 Faris Ishta, *Introduction to Methodology in the Social Sciences*, pp. 46-47.

17 Fathi Malkawi and Ahmad Odeh, *Asāsiyyāt al-Baḥth al-ᶜIlmī fī al-ᶜUlūm al-Insāniyyah wa al-Tarbawiyyah* (Foundations of Scientific Research in the Humanities and Educational Sciences), (Irbid: Dār al-Kindī, Second Edition, 1993), Chapter Four entitled, "Classification of Educational Research Papers" (*Taṣnīf al-Buḥūth al-Tarbawiyyah*).

18 Sayyid Ahmad Uthman, *Al-Dhātiyyah al-Nāḍijah: Maqālāt fī mā Warā' al-Manhaj* (Mature Subjectivity: Essays in Metamethod), (Cairo: Maktabat al-Angelo al-Miṣriyyah), 2000, p. 15.

19 Ahmed Fouad Pasha, *Dirāsāt Islāmiyyah fī al-Fikr al-ᶜIlmī* (Islamic Studies in Scientific Thought), (Cairo: Dār al-Hidāyah, 1997), p.12.

20 Fuad Kadim Miqdadi, "Maqūlāt fi Fahm al-Khiṭāb al-Thaqāfi al-Taghrībī" (Toward an Understanding of Westernizing Cultural Discourse), *Risālat al-Thaqalayn*, Eleventh Year, no. 41, 2002, pp. 4-14.

21 It is hoped that my comments in this connection will confirm the importance of doing specialized studies of the practices that embody some Muslim thinkers' methodological orientations, and other specialized studies of the positivist methodologies which aim to deconstruct the Islamic religious structure and bring about religious reform in Islam after the manner in which this took place in European Christianity. In illustration of the former trend, see Ibrahim Salim Abu Hlaywa, *Ṭaha Jābir al-ᶜAlwānī: Tajalliyāt al-Tajdīd fī Mashrūᶜihi al-Fikrī* (Taha Jabir Alalwani: Manifestations of Renewal in His Intellectual Enterprise), (Beirut: Markaz al-Ḥaḍārah li Tanmiyat al-Fikr al-Islāmī, 2011), and of the latter trend, Adunis, as detailed in Abd al-Qadir Muhammad Mirzaq, *Mashrūᶜ Adūnīs al-Fikrī wa al-Ibdāᶜī: Ru'yah Maᶜrifiyyah* (Adunis' Intellectual and Creative Enterprise: An Epistemological Vision), (Herndon, Virginia: The International Institute of Islamic Thought, 2008).

22 The question of methodology took center stage in the paper al Fārūqī presented at the Second International Conference on the Islamization of Knowledge in Pakistan in 1982. This paper, which was written jointly by al Fārūqī and AbdulHamid AbuSulayman, was later to become the basis for IIIT's official working document. It was published under the title, "The Islamization of Knowledge: General Principles and Action Plan."

23 Isma^c^īl al Fārūqī, "Islamization of Knowledge: Problems, Principles and Prospective," in *Islam: Source and Purpose of Knowledge* (Proceedings of Selected Papers of the Second Conference on Islamization of Knowledge, Pakistan, 1982), (Herndon, VA: IIIT, 1983), pp. 15-63.

24 Ibid., p. 33.

25 Ibid., p. 35.

26 Ibid., pp. 38-52.

27 AbuSulayman and al Fārūqī shared similar views on the question of methodology in Islamic thought. The two men worked together to found the Association of Muslim Social Scientists in the United States in 1972, and the International Institute of Islamic Thought in 1981, where both have served alternately as president and director.

28 Taha Jabir Alalwani, *Islamic Thought: An Approach to Reform*, translated from the Arabic by Nancy Roberts (London and Washington: The International Institute of Islamic Thought, 2006), pp. 62-90.

29 These six focal points are mentioned frequently in Alalwani's lectures and writings. I heard him explain these in detail for the first time when I was overseeing the printing of the aforementioned working paper in 1994, and I suggested that he expand on the topic. However, it was not until the training course organized by IIIT at Al-Jazīrah University in the Sudan in December 1995 that these themes were treated in detail and used as a foundation for practical training. See Taha Jabir Alalwani, *Al-Jam^c^ bayn al-Qirā'atayn: Qirā'at al-Waḥy wa Qirā'at al-Kawn* (Combining the Two Readings: Reading Revelation, and Reading the Universe), (Cairo: Dār al-Shurūq al-Dawliyyah, 2006), pp. 59-66, where he states, "This task [the task of combining the two readings] can only be undertaken by those who have both a knowledge of the Qur'an and sufficient knowledge of the sciences to be able to discover the methodological overlap between the Qur'an, the wider universe, and human beings. Consequently, Qur'anic method is based on the following foundations..." He then proceeds to explain these foundations, which consist of the aforementioned six focal points.

30 Taha Jabir Alalwani, *Ma^c^ālim fī al-Manhaj al-Qur'ānī* (Landmarks Along the Qur'anic Path), (Cairo: Dār al-Salām), 2010, p. 68.

31 Ibid., p. 69.
32 Ibid., p. 77.
33 Ibid., pp. 82-89.
34 Ibid., pp. 148-150.
35 Ibid.
36 Ibid.
37 Taha Abd al-Rahman, "Fī Taqwīm al-Manhajiyyah al-Manṭiqiyyah li ᶜIlm al-Kalām min Khilāl Mas'alat al-Mumāthalah fī al-Khiṭāb al-Kalāmī" (On the Evaluation of Scholastic Theologians' Logical Methodology Based on the Question of Analogy in Scholastic Theological Discourse), in *al-Manhajiyyah al-Islāmiyyah wa al-ᶜUlūm al-Nafsiyyah wa al-Tarbawiyyah* (Islamic Methodology and the Psychological and Educational Sciences), ed. Al-Tayyib Zayn al-Abidin, (Herndon: IIIT, 1992), vol. II, pp. 203-243.
38 Taha Abd al-Rahman, *Tajdīd al-Manhaj fī Taqwīm al-Turāth* (Updating Approaches to the Evaluation of the [Islamic] Heritage), (Beirut: al-Markaz al-Thaqāfī al-ᶜArabī, 1994), pp. 19-20.
39 Taha Abd al-Rahman, *Fī Uṣūl al-Ḥiwār wa Tajdīd ᶜIlm al-Kalām* (On the Principles of Dialogue and the Revitalization of Scholastic Theology). Reprint. (Beirut: al-Markaz al-Thaqāfī al-ᶜArabī, 2000), p. 4.
40 Ibid., p. 71.
41 Ibid., pp. 145-158.
42 Taha Abd al-Rahman, *Tajdīd al-Manhaj fī Taqwīm al-Turāth*, p. 13.
43 Ibid., p. 421.
44 Taha Abd al-Rahman, *Al-Qawl al-Falsafī Kitāb al-Mafhūm wa al-Ta'thīl (Fiqh al-Falsafah 2)* (Philosophical Talk: The Book of Concepts and [Their Proper] Grounding), *The Jurisprudence of Philosophy* (2), (Beirut: al-Markaz al-Thaqāfī al-ᶜArabī, 1999), pp. 12-17.
45 Ibid., pp. 429-433.
46 Ahmad al-Raysuni, *Al-Fikr al-Maqāṣidī: Qawāᶜiduhu wa Fawā'iduhu* (Aims-Based Thought: Its Guiding Principles and Its Benefits), Pocketbook Series no. 9, published by *al-Zaman* Newspaper, (Casa Blanca, 1999).
47 Ibid., p. 99.
48 Ibid., p. 103.
49 Ahmad al-Raysuni and Muhammad Jamal Barut, *Al-Ijtihād: Al-Naṣṣ al-Wāqiᶜ al-Maṣlaḥah* (Innovative Interpretation: Text, Reality, Benefits), *Silsilat Ḥiwārāt al-Qarn* (Damascus: Dār al-Fikr, 2000), pp. 20-25.
50 Ibid., p. 154.
51 Ibid.

52 The term *uṣūlī* is being used in the sense of "relating to the principles of jurisprudence, or *uṣūl al-fiqh*."

53 Al-Raysuni and Barut, *Al-Ijtihād*, pp. 147-150.

54 Ahmad al-Raysuni, *Naẓariyyat al-Taqrīb wa al-Taghlīb wa Taṭbīqātuhā fī al-ʿUlūm al-Islāmiyyah* (The Theory of Persuasion and Preference and Its Applications to the Islamic Sciences), (Miknas, Morocco: Maṭbaʿat Muṣʿab, 1997), pp. 514-515.

55 Ahmad al-Raysuni, *Al-Kulliyāt al-Asāsiyyah li al-Sharīʿah al-Islāmiyyah* (Basic Universals of Islamic Law), (Rabat: Ḥarakat al-Tawḥīd wa al-Iṣlāḥ, 2007), p. 127.

56 Ahmad al-Raysuni, *Al-Shūrā fī Maʿrakat al-Binā'* (Amman, Jordan: IIIT and Dār al-Rāzī, 2007), p. 5. Published in English as *Al-Shura: The Qur'anic Principle of Consultation, A Tool for Reconstruction and Reform*, tr. Nancy Roberts (London: IIIT, 2011).

57 Brian Godawa, *Hollywood Worldviews: Watching Films With Wisdom and Discernment* (Downers Grove, Ill.: InterVarsity Press, 2002), p. 16.

58 Sayyid Qutb, *Khaṣā'iṣ al-Taṣawwur al-Islāmī wa Muqawwimātuhu* (Distinguishing Features and Components of Islamic Conceptualization), Part I. Reprint. (Kuwait: International Islamic Federation of Student Organiztions (IFSO), 1983), p. 7.

59 Mention should be made in this connection of the notable efforts exerted by participants in the "International Relations Project" under the supervision of Dr. Nadiya Mustafa. The project also benefitted from the participation of a number of professors of International Relations and Political Science at the University of Cairo. IIIT published the outcomes of this project in twelve volumes, while the researchers themselves have published numerous books and papers of relevance to the same. This project and its outcomes have helped bring about a notable shift in contemporary Islamic political jurisprudence. They have also helped toward development of an Islamic methodology for dealing with issues of relevance to political thought, international relations and the social sciences, and training sessions have been organized for the purpose of applying this methodology to Islamic traditional sources. See Nadiya Muhammad Mustafa and Sayf al-Din Abd al-Fattah, *Dawrat al-Minhājiyyah al-Islāmiyyah fī al-ʿUlūm al-Ijtimāʿiyyah: Ḥaql al-ʿUlūm al-Siyāsiyyah Numūdhajan* (A Course on Islamic Methodology in the Social Sciences: The Case of Political Science), (Cairo: IIIT and Markaz al-Ḥaḍārah li al-ʿUlūm al-Siyāsiyyah, 2002).

60 AbdulHamid AbuSulayman, *Azmat al-Irādah wa al-Wijdān al-Muslim: al-Buʿd al-Ghā'ib fī Mashrūʿ Iṣlāḥ al-Ummah* (Crisis in Muslim Thought and

Sentiment: The Missing Dimension of the Enterprise to Reform the Muslim Community), (Damascus: Dār al-Fikr, 2005), p. 54.

61 AbdulHamid AbuSulayman, *Crisis in the Muslim Mind*, translated by Yusuf Talal Delorenzo (Herndon, VA: The International Institute of Islamic Thought, 2004), p. 44.

62 Ibid., p. 33.

63 Thomas Kuhn, *The Structure of Scientific Revolutions*, Second Enlarged Edition (Chicago: University of Chicago Press, 1970), p. xi.

64 Ibid., p. 4.

65 Ibid, pp. 111-135.

66 Edwin Hung, *Nature of Science: Problems and Perspectives* (Belmont, CA: Wadsworth Publishing, 1996).

67 Abdelwahab Elmessiri, *Riḥlatī al-Fikriyyah fī al-Budhūr wa al-Judhūr wa al-Thamar: Sīrah Ghayr Dhātiyyah wa Ghayr Mawḍūᶜiyyah* (My Journey of Thought into Seeds, Roots, and Fruits: An Account Neither Subjective nor Objective), (Cairo: al-Hay'ah al-ᶜĀmmah li Quṣūr al-Thaqāfah, 2000), p. 276.

68 Ibid., p. 279.

69 Nasr Arif, *Naẓariyyāt al-Siyāsah al-Muqāranah wa Manhajiyyat Dirāsat al-Nuẓum al-Siyāsiyyah al-ᶜArabiyyah: Muqāranah Ībistimūlūjiyyah* (Theories of Comparative Politics and the Methodology of Studying Arab Political Systems: An Epistemological Comparison), (Leesburg, VA: University of Islamic and Social Sciences, 1998), p. 45.

70 Fathi Malkawi, ed., *Naḥwa Binā' Niẓām Maᶜrifī Islāmī* (Toward the Construction of an Islamic Epistemological System), (Amman, Jordan: IIIT, 2000). See in particular the article contributed by the late Abdelwahab Elmessiri entitled, "Fī al-Dars al-Maᶜrifī" (On the Epistemological Lesson), pp. 41-60.

71 This equation represents an innovative interpretation of the way in which to define the basic elements that make up the Islamic system from a theoretical, philosophical point of view. However, a number of those to whom the chapters of this book were presented in the context of training courses on the topic of "the methodology of epistemological integration" have suggested the possibility of distinguishing other systems within the Islamic worldview. Such systems might include, for example, the system of rites of worship, the system of transactions, etc., which are of great importance on the practical level. Some course participants have suggested that the equation might be, for example, "The Islamic system = the belief system + the knowledge system + the value system + the system of rites of worship + …."

As we see it, however, the criterion of classification is what determines the nature of the elements that make up the whole, as well as the degree of their autonomy or integration. Different versions of the equation might include: "Islam = law (*shir*ᶜ*ah*) + way of life (*minhāj*)," or "Islam = doctrine + Islamic law + ethics," or, "Islam = Islamic law + the truth" or "Islam = rites of worship + transactions + ethics," etc.

72 Ali Shariati, *al-Insān wa al-Islām*, p. 29.

CHAPTER 3

1 We read in *sūrah al-Ḥāqqah* 69:11-12, "[And] behold: when the waters [of Noah's flood] burst beyond all limits, it was We who caused you to be borne [to safety] in that floating ark, so that We might make all this a [lasting] reminder to you all, and that every wide-awake ear might consciously take it in."

2 Abū ᶜĪsā Muḥammad Banī ᶜĪsā ibn Sūrah al-Tirmidhī, *Al-Jāmi*ᶜ *al-Ṣaḥīḥ*, edited and annotated by Ahmad Muhammad Shakir (Beirut: Dār al-Kutub al-ᶜIlmiyyah, no date). *Kitāb al-*ᶜ*Ilm* (Book of Knowledge), the section entitled, "On encouraging others to convey what they have heard," vol. 5, hadith no. 2657, p. 33. The hadith reads, "ᶜAbd al-Raḥmān ibn ᶜAbd Allāh ibn Masᶜūd related that his father had said, 'I heard the Prophet say, "God will prosper one who, after hearing something from us, passes it on to others just as he heard it, for many a person who passes on what he has heard has greater understanding than one who merely hears."'" Another version of the same hadith reads, "God will prosper one who hears what I have said, heeds it, memorizes it, and conveys it to others, for many who convey learning to others convey to those with [even] greater understanding than they" (hadith no. 2658 from the same source cited earlier in this note).

3 Muna Abd al-Munim Abu al-Fadl, *Naḥwa Minhājiyyah li al-Ta*ᶜ*āmul ma*ᶜ*a Maṣādir al-Tanẓīr al-Islāmī: Bayn al-Muqaddimāt wa al-Muqawwimāt* (Toward a Methodology for Dealing with the Sources of Islamic Theorization: Basic Principles and Component Elements), (Cairo: IIIT, 1996), p. 8.

4 Ibid., p. 11.

5 Ibid., p. 29.

6 Nasr Muhammad Arif, ed., *Qaḍāyā al-Manhajiyyah fī al-*ᶜ*Ulūm al-Islāmiyyah wa al-Ijtimā*ᶜ*iyyah: A*ᶜ*māl Mu'tamar al-Manhajiyyah al-Mun*ᶜ*aqidah fī al-Jazā'ir, 1989* (Issues Pertaining to Methodology in the Islamic and Social Sciences: Proceedings of the Conference on Methodology Convened in Algeria, 1989), (Cairo: IIIT, 1996), p. 10.

7 Abd al-Karim Bakkar, *Tajdīd al-Wa*ʿ*ī* (Renewal of Consciousness), Silsilat al-Riḥlah ilā al-Dhāt ("Journey to the Self" Series), no. 2, (Damascus: Dār al-Qalam, 2000), pp. 9-23.

8 After the defeat of June 1967, a number of noted thinkers and men of letters abandoned their erstwhile loyalty to the existing ruling regimes and political leaders of the day, since it had become apparent to them that their political leaders had misled the masses, as well as those in the political and intellectual vanguard. It was as though even these leaders had been in a state of unconsciousness. Hence, this historic defeat brought about a "return of consciousness" (ʿ*awdat al-wa*ʿ*ī*), a phrase which served as the title to a book written by Tawfiq al-Hakim (Cairo: Dār al-Maʿārif, 1972), as well as a number of poems written by Nizar Qabbani following the selfsame defeat.

9 Sayf al-Din Abd al-Fattah, *Ḥawla al-Manhajiyyah al-Islāmiyyah: Muqaddimāt wa Taṭbīqāt* (On Islamic Methodology: Basic Principles and Applications), a paper presented at the Third Training Course on Islamic Methodology, held at the office of the International Institute of Islamic Thought, Amman, Jordan, 12-17 November 1998, p. 4.

10 Muhammad Abul al-Fath al-Bayanuni, *Al-Madkhal ilā* ʿ*Ilm al-Da*ʿ*wah: Dirāsah Manhajiyyah Shāmilah li Tārīkh al-Da*ʿ*wah wa Uṣūlihā wa Manāhijihā* (Introduction to the Science of the Islamic Call: A Methodological Study of the History of the Call, Its Principles, and Its Methods). Reprint. (Beirut: Mu'assasat al-Risālah, 1993).

11 Muhammad Surur Zayn al-Abidin, *Manhaj al-Anbiyā' fī al-Da*ʿ*wah Ilā Allāh* (The Prophet's Approach to Inviting [Others to Faith in] God), (Birmingham, UK: Dar al-Arqam, 1992).

12 Jasim ibn Muhammad ibn Muhalhal al-Yasin, *Al-Kalimāt al-Manhajiyyah min Kalām Shaykh al-Islām Ibn Taymiyyah* (A Guide to Islamic Methodology Gleaned from the Writings of Ibn Taymiyyah), (Kuwait: Mu'assasat al-Kalimah, no date).

13 Salman ibn Fahd al-Awdah, *Maqālāt fī al-Manhaj* (Articles on Method), Ann Arbor, Michigan: al-Tajammuʿ al-Islāmī fī Amrīkā al-Shamāliyyah (The Islamic Alliance of North America), Silsilat Rasā'il al-Tajdīd (The Renewal Message Series), no. 2, 1999.

14 Taha Jabir Alalwani, *Source Methodology in Islamic Jurisprudence.* A Revised English Edition by Yusuf Talal Delorenzo and Anas S. Al-Shaikh-Ali) (London and Washington: The International Institute of Islamic Thought, 2003), p. 1.

15 Abd al-Rahman ibn Zayd al-Zunaydi, *Manāhij al-Baḥth fī al-*ʿ*Aqīdah al-Islāmiyyah fī al-*ʿ*Aṣr al-Ḥāḍir: Dirāsah li Manāhij al-Fikr al-Islāmī al-Mu*ʿ*āṣir wa*

li al-ʿAnāṣir al-Manhajiyyah fī Dirāsat Uṣūl al-Dīn (Research Methods of Relevance to Islamic Doctrine in the Modern Age: A Study of Approaches to Contemporary Islamic Thought and the Methodological Components of the Study of the Principles of [the Islamic] Religion), (Riyadh: Markaz al-Dirāsāt wa al-Iʿlām, Dār Ishbīlyā (Seville House), 1998), pp. 5-6.

16 Yusuf al-Qaradawi, *Approaching the Sunnah: Comprehension and Controversy,* translated by Jamil Qureshi (London and Washington: IIIT, 2006), p. 11.

17 Abd al-Jabbar Said, "Manhajiyyat al-Taʿāmul maʿa al-Sunnah al-Nabawiyyah (The Methodology for Relating to the Prophetic Sunnah), *Islāmiyyat al-Maʿrifah,* Year 6, Issue no. 18, Fall 1999, pp. 53-88.

18 Nur al-Din al-Eter, *Manhaj al-Naqd fī ʿUlūm al-Ḥadīth* (A Critical Approach to the Hadith Sciences). Reprint. (Damascus: Dār al-Fikr, 1979), p. 8.

19 Hammam Abd al-Rahim Said, *al-Fikr al-Manhajī ʿInd al-Muḥaddithīn* (Methodological Thought Among Hadith Scholars), Doha, *Silsilat Kitāb al-Ummah,* no. 16, Muharram 1408 AH, pp. 17 and 107.

20 Ibrahim Bidhun, "Al-Kitābah al-Tārīkhiyyah al-Islāmiyyah: Bayna al-Ṭarīqah wa al-Manhaj" (Islamic Historical Writing: Manner and Method), *al-Maʿhad* (a quarterly cultural journal issued by the Arab-Islamic Studies Institute in London), Year 1, no. 1, January 1999, pp. 9-15.

21 Abd al-Majid al-Najjar, *Mabāḥith fī Manhajiyyat al-Fikr al-Islāmī* (Studies in the Methodology of Islamic Thought), (Beirut: Dār al-Gharb al-Islāmī, 1992), p. 7.

22 Ali al-Ghazyawi, *Madkhal ilā al-Manhaj al-Islāmī fī al-Naqd al-Adabī* (Introduction to the Islamic Approach to Literary Criticism), Silsilat Kitāb Daʿwat al-Ḥaqq (The Invitation to the Truth Book Series), no. 6, al-Muḥammadiyyah, Morocco: Ministry of Islamic Endowments, 2000.

23 Al-Shahid al-Bushaykhi, "Mushkilat al-Manhaj fī Dirāsat Muṣṭalaḥ al-Naqd al-ʿArabī al-Qadīm" (The problem of Method in the Study of Ancient Arabic [Literary] Criticism and its Terminology), *Majallat al-Muslim al-Muʿāṣir,* no. 14, January-April 1990, pp. 55-56.

24 Taha Abd al-Rahman, *Al-ʿAmal al-Dīnī wa Tajdīd al-ʿAql* (Religious Action and Renewal of the Mind), Beirut: Al-Markaz al-Thaqafī al-ʿArabī, 1997, pp. 9-10.

25 AbdulHamid AbuSulayman, *Crisis in the Muslim Mind,* p. 126.

26 AbdulHamid AbuSulayman, "Maʿārif al-Waḥī: al-Manhajiyyah wa al-Adā'" (The Sciences of Revelation: Methodology and Performance), *Islāmiyyat al-Maʿrifah,* First Year, no. 3, pp. 85-109.

27 Jafar Shaykh Idris, "Qaḍiyyat al-Manhaj ʿInd al-Sayyid Quṭb fī "Maʿālim fī al-Ṭarīq" (The Issue of Method in Sayyid Qutb's 'Maʿālim fī al-Ṭarīq'), in

The Proceedings of the Seminar on "Directions in Contemporary Islamic Thought" held in Bahrain, Riyadh: Maktab al-Tarbiyah al-ʿArabī li Duwal al-Khalīj, 1985, pp. 531-546.

28 Taha Jabir al-Alwani, *Issues in Contemporary Islamic Thought.* Compiled from the *American Journal of Islamic Social Sciences* (London and Washington: IIIT, 2005), p. 11.

29 Ibid., pp. 247–249.

30 Abd al-Fattah, *On Islamic Methodology*, pp. 5-6.

31 Abd al-Majid al-Najjar, *ʿAwāmil al-Shuhūd al-Ḥaḍārī* (Factors in Cultural Contributions), (Beirut: Dār al-Gharb al-Islāmī, 1999), vol. 2, pp. 39-71.

32 Muhammad Rashid Rida, "Manāfiʿ al-Awrubbiyīn wa Maḍārruhum fī al-Sharq – al-Istibdād (3)" [Benefit and Harm from Europeans in the East – Tyranny (3)], *Majallat al-Manār,* vol. 10, no. 4, 1315 AH, pp. 279-284. See in particular pp. 282-283, where the author states, "The greatest benefit the people of the East derived from the Europeans was the realization of what government ought to be. They even began rushing to replace governments whose actions had been dictated by law and a process of consultation with totalitarian regimes whose management was assigned to single individuals. Some of them, such as Japan, achieved their aims in their entirety. Others have begun to do so, such as Iran, while still others, like Egypt and Turkey, are still striving to do so...Let no Muslim say that this type of government is a principle of our religion and that we derived it from the Holy Qur'an and the examples set by the rightly guided caliphs. Rather, we gleaned it from our contact with Europeans and from observing Westerners' ways. Were it not for our emulation of these people, no Muslim would ever have thought that this [type of tyrannical rule] originated in Islam, nor would the first people to call for its establishment have been religious scholars in Istanbul, Cairo and Marrakesh, most of whom still support the tyrannical rule of individuals."

33 An example of this methodological defect may be seen in the evolution of fatwas relating to women in Western societies who embrace Islam and whose husbands remain non-Muslim. Scholars were previously in the habit of issuing the traditional ruling on such cases – namely, to require the woman to separate from her husband – without any attempt to research relevant texts or historical precedents. When increasing numbers of such cases emerged and numerous questions began to be raised, some of the scholars who had previously been quick to adopt the traditional ruling began to hesitate, having become convinced that the traditional ruling produces undue hardship. In consequence, such scholars began searching for and

appealing to historical precedents. Once they had found such precedents, they began justifying their call for a new fatwa based on general principles governing the ways in which Islamic legal rulings are derived, even though, in fact, it was the discovery of the historical precedent that, most cases, had led them to adopt the new fatwa.

34 The funds that are collected in taxes on tobacco products amount to 173 times more than those spent on anti-smoking campaigns. The most important of the strategies governments have adopted to curb smoking is to raise taxes which, in some countries, come to 75 percent of the price of a pack of cigarettes. See World Health Organization, *WHO Report on the Global Tobacco Epidemic* (Geneva, Switzerland: WHO, 2009), pp. 56-62.

35 Ibid., p. 12.

36 The aforementioned WHO report points out a number of facts relating to the dangers of smoking and the types of toxic substances found in tobacco. It includes substantial data on various states' responsiveness to WHO recommendations to provide smoke-free environments, particularly for children. It bears noting, however, that the majority of the Arab and Islamic countries appear to be less concerned than other states to curb smoking, and that the amounts spent on tobacco in these countries is greater than those spent on education and health.

CHAPTER 4

1 Juristic preference involves giving human interests and the higher aims of Islamic Law that prove to have more powerful evidence priority over the results of *qiyās*, or analogical deduction.

2 N. J. Coulson, "European Criticism of Hadith Literature," in A. F. L. Beeston, et. al. (eds.), *Arabic Literature to the End of the Umayyad Period*, (Cambridge: Cambridge University Press, 1983), pp. 317-321.

3 Muwaffaq al-Dīn Abū al-ʿAbbās Aḥmad ibn al-Qāsīm ibn Abī 'Uṣaybiʿah, *ʿUyūn al-Anbā' fī Ṭabaqāt al-Aṭibbā'* (Noteworthy Reports on the Various Classes of Physicians), annotated by Nizar Rida, (Beirut: Dār Maktabat al-Ḥayāh, no date), p. 522.

4 Ibid., pp. 522-523. In his introduction to the passage quoted above, Ibn Abī 'Uṣaybiʿah states, "I copied something Ibn al-Haytham had written by hand concerning what he had done, and classifications he had made of the sciences of the ancients up to the end of the year 417 [AH]. He wrote, 'Ever since I was a boy I have been skeptical of these people's varying beliefs, and the way each group clings to its own point of view. I was suspicious of them

all, convinced within myself that Truth is one, and that differences of opinion over it must arise from the paths we take to reach it. In search of the Truth I delved into all manner of opinions and beliefs, but it got me nowhere. I discovered no path to the Truth or to clear certainty. What I discovered was that I can only arrive at the Truth by means of opinions whose constituent elements are sensory input, and which are formed based on rational considerations. [In sum,] I only found it through the things affirmed by Aristotle.'"

5 Ali Sami al-Nashshar, *Manāhij al-Baḥth ᶜind Mufakkirī al-Islām* (Muslim Thinkers' Research Methods), Second Edition, (Alexandria: Dār al-Maᶜārif, 1965), p. 373.

6 Abū Bakr Muḥammad ibn Zakariyyā al-Rāzī, *Kitāb al-Shukūk ᶜalā Kalām Fāḍil al-Aṭibbā', Jalīnūs, fī al-Kutub allatī Nusibat ilayhi* (Reservations Concerning Statements Made by the Illustrious Physician Galen in Those Books Attributed to Him), edited and introduced by Muhammad Labib Abd al-Ghani, (Cairo: Dār al-Kutub wa al-Wathā'iq al-Qawmiyyah, 2009), pp. 166-167.

7 Ibrahim Madkur, *Fī al-Falsafah al-Islāmiyyah: Manhaj wa Taṭbīquhu* (On Islamic Philosophy: Method and Application). Reprint. (Cairo: Dār al-Maᶜārif, 1983), Part I, p. 21.

8 Was it ignorance or nationalist hubris that led a prominent scientist and philosopher the likes of Francis Bacon to slight the scientific contributions of other peoples and understate their significance and depth? Bacon declared, "Nearly all the sciences we have come from the Greeks. Additions made by Roman, Arabic or more recent writers are few and of no great significance; such as they are, they rest on a foundation of Greek discovery." (Francis Bacon, *The New Organon*, (Cambridge, UK: Cambridge University Press, 2000), p. 58).

9 Yusuf Karam, *Tārīkh al-Falsafah al-Yūnāniyyah* (The History of Greek Philosophy). Reprint. (Cairo: Committee on Writing, Translation and Publication, 1966), p. 1 (author's preface).

10 Ibn Abī 'Uṣaybiᶜah, *ᶜUyūn al-Anbā' fī Ṭabaqāt al-Aṭibbā'*, pp. 11-38.

11 Abū al-Ḥasan ᶜAlī ibn al-Ḥusayn ibn ᶜAlī al-Masᶜūdī, *Murūj al-Dhahab wa Maᶜādin al-Jawhar* (Meadows of Gold and Its True Essence), introduced and explained by Mufid Qamihah, (Beirut: Dār al-Kutub al-ᶜIlmiyyah, 1985), Part 1, pp. 74-84.

12 Ibid., p. 236.

13 Nadim al-Jisr, *Qiṣṣat al-Īmān bayn al-Falsafah wa al-ᶜIlm wa al-Qur'ān* (The Story of Faith: From Philosophy, to Science, to the Qur'ān). Reprint.

(Beirut: al-Maktab al-Islāmī, 1969), p. 36.

14 Hans-Georg Gadamer, *Bidāyat al-Falsafah* (The Beginning of Philosophy), trans. Ali Hakim Salih and Hasan Nazim, (Beirut: al-Kitāb al-Jadīd, 2000), p. 6.

15 Karam, *History of Greek Philosophy*, pp. 10-19.

16 Ibid., pp. 21-26.

17 Ibid., pp. 38-41.

18 Ibid., pp. 44-49.

19 Mustafa al-Nashshar, *Naẓariyyat al-ʿIlm al-Arisṭiyyah: Dirāsah fī Manṭiq al-Maʿrifah ʿind Arisṭu* (The Aristotelian Theory of Science: A Study in Aristotle's Logic of Knowledge). Reprint. (Cairo: Dār al-Maʿārif, 1995), p. 12.

20 Richard McKeon (ed.), *The Basic Works of Aristotle* (New York: Random House, 1941), pp. 1-217.

21 Ibid., p. xi.

22 *Manṭiq Arisṭū* (Aristotle's Logic), edited and introduced by Abd al-Rahman Badawi, (Beirut: Dār al-Qalam, 1980), Part 1, p. 30.

23 Lisa Jardine, from the Editor's Introduction to Francis Bacon, *The New Organon* (Cambridge, UK: Cambridge University Press, 2000), p. xii.

24 Bacon, *The New Organon*, p. 40.

25 René Descartes, *Discourse on Method and Meditations on First Philosophy*, translated by Donald A. Cress, Fourth edition, (Indianapolis, IN: Hackett Publishing Company Inc.), from the editor's preface, pp. vii-viii.

26 Ibid., p. 6.

27 Ibid., p. 11.

28 Ala Mustafa Anwar, *Al-Tafsīr fī al-ʿUlūm al-Ijtimāʿiyyah: Dirāsah fī Falsafat al-ʿUlūm* (Interpretation in the Social Sciences: A Study in the Philosophy of Science), (Cairo: Dār al-Thaqāfah, 1988), pp. 109-196.

29 Stephen Haynes, *Professing in the Postmodern Academy* (Waco, Texas: Baylor University Press, 2002), pp. 34-35.

30 The term "scientism" is used to refer to belief in the universal applicability of the scientific method, and the view that empirical sciences constitute the most authoritative worldview to the exclusion of other viewpoints.

31 We read in the previous verse about how, upon learning that God was about to create human beings and allow them to inherit it, the angels objected, claiming that human beings would spread corruption on earth and be shedders of blood, thereby implying that they were superior to human beings (*sūrah al-Baqarah* 2:30).

32 Douglas K. Candland, *Feral Children and Clever Animals: Reflections on Human Nature* (New York: Oxford University Press, 1995).

33 Nancy L. Segal, *Indivisible by Two: Lives of Extraordinary Twins* (Cambridge, Mass.: Harvard University Press, 2007).

34 N. J. Coulson, "European Criticism of Hadith Literature," pp. 317-321.

CHAPTER 5

1 The term *uṣūlī*, derived from the noun *uṣūl*, meaning foundations or principles, refers to anything relating to the principles of jurisprudence (*uṣūl al-fiqh*).

2 Fathi Hasan al-Malkawi, Editorial in the journal, *Islāmiyyat al-Maᶜrifah*, no. 64, April 2011, pp. 5-13.

3 David Plowright, *Using Mixed Methods: Frameworks for an Integrated Methodology* (Thousand Oaks, CA: Sage Publications Ltd., 2011), p. 181.

4 Hasan Abd al-Latif al-Shafii, "Al-ᶜAqīdah wa al-ᶜAql fī al-Fikr al-Islāmī: al-Dalīl al-ᶜAqlī wa Makānatuhu fī al-Buḥūth al-Iᶜtiqādiyyah" (Doctrine and Reason in Islamic Thought: Rational Evidence and its Place in Doctrinal Studies) in Ahmed Fouad Pasha, et. al., *Al-Manhajiyyah al-Islāmiyyah*, pp. 523-557.

5 Ibid., p. 535.

6 Ibid., p. 526.

7 Ibid., p. 549.

8 Abd al-Hamid Madkur, "Al-Manhaj al-ᶜIrfānī al-Dhawqī ᶜind Ṣūfiyyat al-Islām" (The Mystical-Experiential Approach of Islam's Sufis) in Ahmed Fouad Pasha, et. al., *Al-Manhajiyyah al-Islāmiyyah*, part 1, pp. 559-587.

9 Ibid., p 562.

10 Ibid., p. 564.

11 Ibid., p. 569.

12 Ibid., p. 571.

13 Ibid., p. 573.

14 Ibid., p. 575.

15 See Chapter Four, "Evolution of the Concept of Method in Islamic and Western Thought."

16 See, for example, the book by al-Ḥāfiẓ al-Mundhirī entitled, *Al-Targhīb wa al-Tarhīb* (The Carrot and the Stick, or Motivation and Deterrence). Book I of this work's first volume is entitled, "The Book of Knowledge: On Motivating Others to Pursue Knowledge, to Acquire It and to Teach It, and the Merits of Scholars and Students." The first book of the Quarter on Rites

of Worship in al-Ghazālī's famed *ʿIḥyā' Ulūm al-Dīn* (Revival of the Sciences of Religion) is entitled, "The Book of Knowledge." This book consists of seven sections, the first of which is entitled, "The Merit of Knowledge, Instruction and Learning and Evidence Thereof in Divine Revelation and Reason." Similarly, Section Six of Ibn Khaldūn's *Al-Muqaddimah* (Prolegomenon) bears the title, "On the Sciences and Their Types, on Knowledge and Means of Acquiring It, and the States Through Which One Passes in Connection Thereto."

17 Abū ʿUmar Yūsuf Ibn ʿAbd al-Birr, *Jāmiʿ ʿIlm al-Bayān wa Faḍlihi* (A Compendium on Rhetoric and Its Merits), ed. Abi al-Ashbal al-Zuhayri, (Riyadh: Dār Ibn al-Jawzī, 1994), two volumes.

18 ʿAbd al-Raḥmān Ibn Khaldūn, *Al-Muqaddimah*, ed. Abd al-Wahid Wafi, expanded and revised edition, (Cairo: Dār Nahḍat Miṣr, 2004), Part 3, p. 947.

19 *Al-Dhakhīrah fī al-Fiqh al-Mālikī* (A Treasure of Mlikī Jurisprudence), ed. Muhammad Hajji, 14 vols., (Beirut: Dār al-Gharb, 1994). In this book the author outlines numerous juristic principles, each of which he lists under its appropriate category along with relevant branches.

20 *Qawāʿid al-Aḥkām fī Iṣlāḥ al-Anām* (Principles Underlying Juristic Rulings for the Good of Mankind), ed. Nazih Kamal Hammad and Uthman Jumah Amīriyyah, First Edition, (Damascus: Dār al-Qalam, 2000 CE/1421 AH).

21 For more details see Muhammad al-Tahir ibn Ashur, *A Laysa al-Ṣubḥ bi Qarīb: al-Taʿlīm al-ʿArabī al-Islāmī* (Does the Morning Not Draw Nigh?: Arabic-Islamic Education). Reprint. (Tunis: Dār Saḥnūn and Cairo: Dār al-Salām, 2007), pp. 174-179.

22 The term *Ahl al-Ḥadīth* is a term that came to be applied to the jurists of Madinah, while the term *Ahl al-Ra'y* was used to refer to the jurists of Iraq, one of whose principle representatives was Abū Ḥanīfah.

23 See ʿAbd al-Wahhāb Khallāf, *ʿIlm Uṣūl al-Fiqh* (The Science of the Principles of Jurisprudence), Eighth Edition, (Cairo: Maktabat al-Daʿwah al-Islāmiyyah, no date), pp. 17-20.

24 Ibn Khaldūn, *Al-Muqaddimah*, p. 960.

25 Halimah Bukrushah, *Maʿālim Tajdīd al-Manhaj al-Fiqhī: Unmūdhaj al-Shawkānī* (Signs of a Revitalized Juristic Method: The Case of al-Shawkānī), (Doha, Qatar: Ministry of Religious Endowments), *Kitāb al-Ummah*, Issues no. 90-91 for the months of Rajab and Ramadan, 1423 AH, p. 291.

26 Abū al-Qāsim Muḥammad ibn Aḥmad ibn Jazī, *Taqrīb al-Wuṣūl ilā ʿIlm al-Uṣūl* (Toward a Proper Understanding of the Principles of Jurisprudence),

edited, with commentary, by Abd Allah al-Jaburi, (Amman, Jordan: Dar al-Nafaes, 2002), p. 25.

27 Ali Sami al-Nashshar, *Manāhij al-Baḥth ʿInd Mufakkirī al-Islām* (Research Methods Among Muslim Thinkers), (Cairo: Dār al-Salām, 2008, pp. 60-61).

28 Ibid., p. 97.

29 Musfir ibn Ali al-Qahtani, *Athar al-Manhaj al-Uṣūlī fī Tarshīd al-ʿAmal al-Islāmī* (The Effect of the Uṣūlī Method on the Systematic Organization of Islamic Action), (Beirut: al-Shabakah al-ʿArabiyyah li al-Abḥāth wa al-Nashr, 2008), p. 125.

CHAPTER 6

1 ʿAlī ibn Muḥammad al-Jurjānī, *Kitāb al-Taʿrīfāt* (Book of Definitions), ed. Ibrahim al-Abyari, (Beirut: Dār al-Kitāb al-ʿArabī, no date), p. 174.

2 Fakhr al-Dīn al-Rāzī, *al-Tafsīr al-Kabīr*, or *Mafātīḥ al-Ghayb* (The Great Commentary, or Keys to the Unseen), vol. 32, ed. Imad al-Barudi, (Cairo: al-Maktabah al-Tawfīqiyyah), p. 61.

3 Muhammad al-Tahir ibn Ashur, *Tafsīr al-Taḥrīr wa al-Tanwīr* (Editing the Right Meaning and Enlightening the New Mind in Interpreting the Holy Book), (Tunis: al-Dār al-Tūnisiyyah li al-Nashr, 1984), Part 3, p. 139.

4 Al-Jurjānī, *Kitāb al-Taʿrīfāt*, p. 277.

5 Muḥammad ʿAbd Allāh Jamāl al-Dīn ibn Hishām al-Anṣarī, *Awḍaḥ al-Masālik ilā Alfiyyat Ibn Mālik* (The Clearest Path to [an Understanding of] Ibn Mālik's 'Alfiyyah'), New Revised Edition, (Sidon-Beirut: al-Maktabah al-ʿAṣriyyah, 1966), vol. 3, pp. 179ff.

6 ʿAlī ibn Abī Ṭālib, *Dīwān Amīr al-Mu'minīn wa Sayyid al-Bulaghā' wa al-Mutakallimīn ʿAlī ibn Abī Ṭālib* (Collected Poems of the Prince of the Faithful and Master of Eloquence, ʿAli ibn Abī Ṭālib), compiled and arranged by Abd al-Aziz al-Karam, (Cairo: Maktabat al-Karam, 1963), p. 57.

7 God Almighty declares, "Now, indeed, We create man out of the essence of clay, and then We cause him to remain as a drop of sperm in [the womb's] firm keeping, and then We create of the drop of sperm a germ-cell, and then We create out of the germ-cell an embryonic lump, and then We create within the embryonic lump bones, and then We clothe the bones with flesh – and then We bring [all] this into being as a new creation: hallowed, therefore, is God, the best of artisans!" (*sūrah al-Mu'minīn* 23:12-14).

8 A second-century mathematical and astronomical treatise on the apparent motions of the heavenly bodies, written in Greek by Claudius Ptolemy.

9 Fakhr al-Dīn al-Rāzī (died 606 AH), *Tafsīr Mafātīḥ al-Ghayb*, vol. 2, p. 481.

10 Abū ʿAbd Allāh Muḥammad ibn Aḥmad al-Anṣārī al-Qurṭubī (died 671 AH), *Al-Jāmiʿ li Aḥkām al-Qur'ān* (Compendium of the Provisions of the Qur'an), (Beirut: Dār al-Kutub al-ʿIlmiyyah, 1988), vol. 5, Part 9, p. 184.

11 It should be noted that al-Rāzī who lived in the sixth century before al-Qurṭubī has stated clearly that "it has been proven by evidence that the earth is spherical, how it is possible to deny that?!" See: Muhammad Ibn ʿUmar al-Rāzī, *Al-Tafsīr al-Kabīr*, (The Big Interpretation), (Beirut: Dār al-Fikr, 2005), vol.7, p.7, interpretation of *sūrah al-Raʿad* no 13.

12 The hadith was narrated by al-Dāraquṭnī with a sound chain of narrators. It was also narrated by Imam al-Shāfiʿī on the authority of ʿUmar ibn al-Khaṭṭāb. See Taqī al-Dīn Abū Bakr Muḥammad al-Ḥusaynī al-Dimashqī, *Kifāyat al-Akhyār fī Ḥall Ghāyat al-Ikhtiṣār*) (a commentary on Abū Shujāʿ's book on Shāfiʿī jurisprudence entitled *Ghāyat al-Ikhtiṣār*), part 1, ed. Ali Abd al-Hamid Baltaji and Muhammad Wahbi Sulayman, (Damascus: Dār al-Khayr, 1994), p. 12.

13 Ibid.

14 Sayf al-Din Abd al-Fattah, "Al-Manhajiyyah wa Adawātuhā min Manẓūr Islāmī" (Methodology and Its Tools from an Islamic Perspective), in Pasha, et. al., *Al-Manhajiyyah al-Islāmiyyah*, p. 657.

15 Muhammad Muhammad Amziyan, *Manhaj al-Baḥth al-Ijtimāʿī bayn al-Waḍʿiyyah wa al-Miʿyāriyyah* (Social Research Method: Positivism vs. Normativity), (Herndon, VA: IIIT, 1991), p. 129.

16 The hadith reads as follows: "We were told by Abū Nuʿaym, who was told by Zakariyyā, 'I heard ʿĀmir say that he heard al-Nuʿmān ibn Bashīr, may God be pleased with him, say that he heard the Prophet say, "Those who adhere to the limits set by God and those who violate them might be likened to a group of people who cast lots on a ship. Some of them rode above deck, and some of them in the hull. Those who were riding in the hull, whenever they wanted a drink of water, would pass by those who were riding above deck and say, 'If only we could make a hole in our part of the ship [, we could have water to drink] without doing harm to those above us!' If they had been allowed to carry out the idea in their minds, everyone on the ship would have perished, whereas if they had been restrained, they would all have been saved."''' See Muḥammad ibn Ismāʿīl al-Bukhārī, *Ṣaḥīḥ al-Bukhārī*, ed. Abu Suhayb al-Karmi, Riyadh: Bayt al-Afkār al-Dawliyyah li al-Nashr wa al-Tawzīʿ, The Book of Partnership and Association (*kitāb al-sharikah*), the section entitled, "Is it permissible to cast lots on distributions

(*hal yuqra*[c] *fī al-qismah wa al-istihām fīhā*)?," 1419 AH/1998, hadith no. 2493, pp. 471-472.

17 Sayf al-Din Abd al-Fattah, "Al-Manhajiyyah wa Adawātuhā min Manẓūr Islāmī," in Pasha, et. al, al-*Manhajiyyah al-Islāmiyyah*, Part 2, pp. 657-660.

18 Al-Qurṭubī, *Al-Jāmi*[c] *li Aḥkām al-Qur'ān*, Part 2, p. 97. Citing scholars such as al-Zajjāj and Abū [c]Ubaydah, al-Qurṭubī argues that the Arabic verb *aḥassa*, meaning "to feel" or "to perceive," also means "to know" or "to find," that is, to be aware of something's existence via the senses.

19 Ibn Kathīr understands this phrase to mean that Jesus "sensed his hearers' determination not to believe," Ibn Kathīr, *Tafsīr al-Qur'ān al-*[c]*Aẓīm* (Cairo: Dār Iḥyā' al-Kutub al-[c]Arabiyyah, [c]Īsa al-Bābī al-Ḥalabī, no date), Part 1, p. 365.

20 Fathi Malkawi and Ahmad Abu Awdah, *Asāsiyyāt al-Baḥth al-*[c]*Ilmī fī al-Tarbiyyah wa al-*[c]*Ulūm al-Insāniyyah*, p. 257.

21 Uwe Flick, *An Introduction to Qualitative Research*, Fourth Edition, (Los Angeles: Sage, 2009), pp. 147-180.

22 Charles B. Teddlie and Abbas Tashakkori, *Foundations of Mixed Methods Research: Integrating Quantitative and Qualitative Approaches in Social and Behavioral Sciences* (Los Angeles: Sage, 2009).

23 Rauf Abu Sadah, *Min I*[c]*jāz al-Qur'ān* ([Examples of] the Miraculousness of the Qur'an), (Cairo: Dār al-Hilāl, 1993-1994).

24 According to the null hypothesis, the results obtained from the research experiment could be attributable to chance. Rejecting the null hypothesis thus means that the research results were not due to chance, but, rather, to a causal connection between the variables being tested.

25 G. B. Rossman and S. F. Rallis, *Learning in the Field: An Introduction to Qualitative Research*, Second Edition, (Thousand Oaks, CA: Sage, 2003), pp.35-36.

CHAPTER 7

1 Muslim ibn al-Ḥajjāj al-Nīsābūrī, *Ṣaḥīḥ Muslim*, edited by Abu Suhayb al-Karmi, (Riyadh: Bayt al-Afkar al-Dawliyyah li al-Nashr wa al-Tawzī[c], 1988), p. 83, "Book of Faith," hadith no. 150.

2 Based on *sūrah al-Baqarah* 2:285, the six pillars of faith – or, rather, the six entities in which one must believe – are God Almighty, God's angels, the revealed messages God has sent to humankind, God's messengers and apostles, the Day of Judgment, and divine foreordainment, both good and evil.

3 Taha Jabir Alalwani, *Al-Tawḥīd wa al-Tazkiyah wa al-*[c]*Umrān* (Monotheism,

Purification, and Societal Development and Prosperity), (Beirut: Dār al-Hādī, 2003).

4 This is a reference to the last chapter in the Holy Qur'an, *sūrah al-Nās* 114:1-6: "Say: I seek refuge in the Lord of mankind, The King of mankind, The God of mankind, From the evil of the sneaking whisperer, Who whispereth in the hearts of mankind, Of the jinn and of mankind." English translation of the Holy Qur'an by Mohammed Marmaduke Pickthall.

5 See Note 2 above.

6 Fathi Malkawi, *ʿĀlam al-Qiyam fī al-Ru'yah al-Manhajiyyah al-Islāmiyyah* (The World of Values in the Islamic Methodological Perspective), forthcoming.

7 Ismaʿīl R. al Fārūqī, *Al-Tawhid: Its Implications for Thought and Life*. Reprint. (Herndon, VA: IIIT, 2000).

8 Ibid., Chapters 7, 8 and 9, pp. 85-139.

9 Ibid., Chapter 10, pp. 141-155, and Chapter 12, pp. 185-193.

10 Ibid., Chapter 11, pp. 157-183.

11 *Sūrah al-Tawbah* 9:60 lists eight specific purposes for which zakah funds may be spent.

12 Al Fārūqī, *al-Tawḥīd*, Chapter 13, pp. 195-215.

13 Muhammad al-Tahir ibn Ashur, *Tafsīr al-Taḥrīr wa al-Tanwīr* (Editing the Right Meaning and Enlightening the New Mind in Interpreting the Holy Book), (Tunis: Dār Saḥnūn li al-Nashr wa al-Tawzīʿ, 1997), Part 2, p. 428.

14 Ibid., Part 1, p. 12.

15 Sayyid Qutb, *Fī Ẓilāl al-Qur'ān* (In the Shadows of the Qur'an), (Cairo: Dār al-Shurūq, 1978), vol. 2, part 6, p. 857.

16 There are different views concerning what the term "house" refers to in this passage, with some holding that it refers to the much-frequented Sacred Mosque in Makkah, and others holding that it is a reference to the heart of the believer, or to an abode in heaven filled with angels.

17 Malek Bennabi, *Shurūṭ al-Nahḍah* (Conditions for Renaissance), trans. Abd al-Sabur Shahin and Umar Kamil Misqawi, (Damascus: Dār al-Fikr, 1979), p. 44.

18 Given our scientific knowledge at present, Earth is the only planet populated by human beings.

19 Al-Rāghib al-Iṣfahānī, *Muʿjam Alfāẓ al-Qur'ān al-Karīm*, edited by Ibrahim Shams al-Din, (Beirut: Dār al-Kutub al-ʿIlmiyyah, 1997), entry on *ʿumur*.

20 Muslim ibn al-Hajjāj al-Nīsābūrī, *Ṣaḥīḥ Muslim*, Kitāb al-Waṣiyyah (Book of Bequests), section on what reward a human being will receive after death, (Beirut: Dār Ibn Ḥazm, 1995), hadith no 1631, p. 1016.

21 ʿAbd al-Raḥmān Ibn Khaldūn, *Muqaddimat Ibn Khaldūn*, edited by Ali Abd al-Wahid Wafi, (Cairo: Maktabat Nahḍat Miṣr, p. 1213), Part 3. The English translation is that of Franz Rosenthal, "Concluding Remarks," p. 26, http://www.scribd.com/doc/23552951/al-Muqaddimah-or-the-Prolegomena-to-History#outer_page_824.

22 Ibid., p. 329; Rosenthal, Book One of *Kitāb al-ʿIbar*, website op. cit., p. 1.

23 Ibid., p. 332; Rosenthal, website, op. cit., pp. 7-8.

24 Ibid., p. 332; website, op. cit., pp. 7-8.

25 Ibid., p. 332; website, op. cit., p. 8.

26 Ibid., pp. 333-335; website, op. cit., pp. 8, 10.

27 Abd al-Majid al-Najjar, "Al-ʿUmrān wa al-Īmān" (Human Development and Faith), *Majallat Islāmiyyat al-Maʿrifah*, year 2, issue 8, April 1997, pp. 40-84.

BIBLIOGRAPHY

References in Arabic

Abd al-Fattah, Sayf al-Din. *Ḥawla al-Manhajiyyah al-Islāmiyyah: Muqaddimāt wa Taṭbīqāt* (On Islamic Methodology: Basic Principles and Applications). A paper presented at the Third Training Course on Islamic Methodology, held at the office of the International Institute of Islamic Thought. (Amman, Jordan, 12-17 November 1998).

Abd al-Rahman, Taha. "Fī Taqwīm al-Manhajiyyah al-Manṭiqiyyah li ʿIlm al-Kalām min Khilāl Mas'alat al-Mumāthalah fī al-Khiṭāb al-Kalāmī" (On the Evaluation of Scholastic Theologians' Logical Methodology Based on the Question of Analogy in Scholastic Theological Discourse), in *al-Manhajiyyah al-Islāmiyyah wa al-ʿUlūm al-Nafsiyyah wa al-Tarbawiyyah* (Islamic Methodology and the Psychological and Educational Sciences). Ed. al-Tayyib Zayn al-Abidin. (Herndon: IIIT, 1992).

__________. *Tajdīd al-Manhaj fī Taqwīm al-Turāth* (Updating Approaches to the Evaluation of the [Islamic] Heritage). (Beirut: al-Markaz al-Thaqāfī al-ʿArabī, 1994).

__________. *Al-ʿAmal al-Dīnī wa Tajdīd al-ʿAql* (Religious Action and Renewal of the Mind). (Beirut: al-Markaz al-Thaqāfī al-ʿArabī, 1997).

__________. *Al-Qawl al-Falsafī; Kitāb al-Mafhūm wa al-Ta'thīl (Fiqh al-Falsafah 2)* (Philosophical Talk: The Book of Concepts and [Their Proper] Grounding), *The Jurisprudence of Philosophy* (2). (Beirut: al-Markaz al-Thaqāfī al-ʿArabī, 1999).

__________. *Fī Uṣūl al-Ḥiwār wa Tajdīd ʿIlm al-Kalām* (On the Principles of Dialogue and the Revitalization of Scholastic Theology). Reprint. (Beirut: al-Markaz al-Thaqāfī al-ʿArabī, 2000).

Abu al-Fadl, Muna Abd al-Munim. *Naḥwa Minhājiyyah li al-Taʿāmul maʿa Maṣādir al-Tanẓīr al-Islāmī: Bayn al-Muqaddimāt wa al-Muqaw-wimāt* (Toward a Methodology for Dealing with the Sources of Islamic Theorization: Basic Principles and Component Elements). (Cairo: IIIT, 1996).

Abu Hlaywa, Ibrahim Salim. *Ṭaha Jābir al-ʿAlwānī: Tajalliyāt al-Tajdīd fī Mashrūʿihi al-Fikrī* (Taha Jabir al-Alwani: Manifestations of Renewal in His Intellectual Enterprise). (Beirut: Markaz al-Ḥaḍārah li Tanmiyat al-Fikr al-Islāmī, 2011).

Bibliography

Abu Sadah, Rauf. *Min Iʿjāz al-Qur'ān* ([Examples of] the Miraculousness of the Qur'an). (Cairo: Dār al-Hilāl, 2 vols, 1993-1994).

AbuSulayman, AbdulHamid. *Azmat al-Irādah wa al-Wijdān al-Muslim: al-Buʿd al-Ghā'ib fī Mashrūʿ Iṣlāḥ al-Ummah* (Crisis in Muslim Thought and Sentiment: The Missing Dimension of the Enterprise to Reform the Muslim Community). (Damascus: Dār al-Fikr, 2005).

__________. *Crisis in the Muslim Mind.* Translated by Yusuf Talal Delorenzo (Herndon, VA: IIIT, 2004).

__________. *The Qur'anic Worldview: A Springboad for Cultural Reform* (London and Washington: The International Institute of Islamic Thought, 2011).

________. "Maʿārif al-Waḥī: al-Manhajiyyah wa al-Adā'" (The Sciences of Revelation: Methodology and Performance). *Islāmiyyat al-Maʿrifah,* First Year, no. 3, pp. 85-109.

Alalwani, Taha Jabir. *Islamic Thought: An Approach to Reform.* Translated from Arabic by Nancy Roberts (London and Washington: The International Institute of Islamic Thought, 2006).

__________. *Issues in Contemporary Islamic Thought.* Compiled from the *American Journal of Islamic Social Sciences* (London and Washington: The International Institute of Islamic Thought, 2005).

__________. *Source Methodology in Islamic Jurisprudence.* A Revised English Edition By Yusuf Talal Delorenzo and Anas S. Al-Shaikh-Ali (London and Washington: IIIT, 2003).

__________. *Al-Tawḥīd wa al-Tazkiyah wa al-ʿUmrān* (Monotheism, Purification, and Societal Development and Prosperity). (Beirut: Dār al-Hādī, 2003).

__________. *Maʿālim fī al-Manhaj al-Qur'ānī* (Landmarks Along the Qur'anic Path). (Cairo: Dār al-Salām, 2010).

__________. *Al-Jamʿ bayn al-Qirā'atayn: Qirā'at al-Waḥy wa Qirā'at al-Kawn* (Joining the Two Readings: Reading Revelation, and Reading the Universe). (Cairo: Dār al-Shurūq al-Dawliyyah, 2006).

__________. "Al-ʿAql wa Mawqiʿuhu fī al-Manhajiyyah al-Islāmiyyah" (Reason and Its Place in Islamic Methodology), *Majallat Islāmiyyat al-Maʿrifah,* no. 6, September 1996, pp. 36-39.

Amarah, Muhammad. *Malāmiḥ al-Manhaj al-Islāmī* (Features of Islamic Method). (Cairo: The International Institute of Islamic Thought and Azhar University, 1990).

Amziyan, Muhammad Muhammad. *Manhaj al-Baḥth al-Ijtimāʿī bayn al-Waḍʿiyyah wa al-Miʿyāriyyah* (Social Research Method: Positivism vs. Normativity), (Herndon, VA: IIIT, 1991, p. 129).

Anwar, Ala Mustafa. *Al-Tafsīr fī al-ʿUlūm al-Ijtimāʿiyyah: Dirāsah fī Falsafat al-ʿUlūm* (Interpretation in the Social Sciences: A Study in the Philosophy of Science). (Cairo: Dār al-Thaqāfah, 1988).

Bibliography

Arif, Nasr Muhammad, ed. *Qaḍāyā al-Manhajiyyah fī al-ᶜUlūm al-Islāmiyyah wa al-Ijtimāᶜiyyah: Aᶜmāl Mu'tamar al-Manhajiyyah al-Munᶜaqidah fī al-Jazā'ir, 1989* (Issues Pertaining to Methodology in the Islamic and Social Sciences: Proceedings of the Conference on Methodology Convened in Algeria, 1989). (Cairo: IIIT, 1996).

__________. *Naẓariyāt al-Siyāsah al-Muqāranah wa Manhajiyyat Dirāsat al-Nuẓum al-Siyāsiyyah al-ᶜArabiyyah: Muqāranah Ībistimūlūjiyyah* (Theories of Comparative Politics and the Methodology of Study-ing Arab Political Systems: An Epistemological Comparison). (Leesburg, VA: University of Islamic and Social Sciences, 1998).

Aristotle. *Manṭiq Arisṭū* (Aristotle's Logic). vol. 1. Edited and introduced by Abd al-Rahman Badawi. (Beirut: Dār al-Qalam, 1980).

Al-Awdah, Salman bin Fahd. *Maqālāt fī al-Manhaj* (Articles on Method). Ann Arbor, Michigan: al-Tajammuᶜ al-Islāmī fī Amrīkā al-Shamāliyyah (The Islamic Alliance of North America), Silsilat Rasā'il al-Tajdīd (The Renewal Message Series), no. 2, 1999.

Badawī, ᶜAbd al-Raḥmān. *Manāhij al-Baḥth al-ᶜIlmī* (Scientific Research Methods). (Cairo: Dār al-Nahḍah al-ᶜArabiyyah, 1963).

__________. *Al-Mawsūᶜah al-Falsafiyyah*. (Beirut: al-Mu'assasah al-ᶜArabiyyah li al-Dirāsāt wa al-Nashr, 1984).

Bakkar, Abd al-Karim. *Tajdīd al-Waᶜī* (Renewal of Consciousness), Silsilat al-Riḥlah ilā al-Dhāt ("Journey to the Self" Series), no. 2. (Damascus: Dār al-Qalam, 2000).

Al-Bayanuni, Muhammad Abul al-Fath. *Al-Madkhal ilā ᶜIlm al-Daᶜwah: Dirāsah Manhajiyyah Shāmilah li Tārīkh al-Daᶜwah wa Uṣūlihā wa Manāhijihā* (Introduction to the Science of the Islamic Call: A Methodological Study of the History of the Call, Its Principles, and Its Methods). Reprint. (Beirut: Mu'assasat al-Risālah, 1993).

Bennabi, Malek. *Shurūṭ al-Nahḍah* (Conditions for Renaissance). Translated by ᶜAbd al-Sabur Shahin and Umar Kamil Misqawi. (Damascus: Dār al-Fikr, 1979).

Bidhun, Ibrahim. "Al-Kitābah al-Tārikhiyyah al-Islāmiyyah: Bayna al-Ṭarīqah wa al-Manhaj" (Islamic Historical Writing: Manner and Method). *Al-Maᶜhad* (a quarterly cultural journal issued by the Arab-Islamic Studies Institute in London), Year 1, no. 1, January 1999, pp. 9-15.

Al-Bukhārī, Muḥammad ibn Ismāᶜīl. *Ṣaḥīḥ al-Bukhārī*. Ed. Abū Suhayb al-Karmi. (Riyadh: Bayt al-Afkār al-Dawliyyah li al-Nashr wa al-Tawzīᶜ, 1419 AH/1998).

Bukrushah, Halimah. *Maᶜālim Tajdīd al-Manhaj al-Fiqhī: Unmūdhaj al-Shawkānī* (Signs of a Revitalized Juristic Method: The Case of al-Shawkānī). (Doha, Qatar: Ministry of Religious Endowments, *Kitāb al-Ummah*, Issues no. 90-91 for the months of Rajab and Ramadan, 1423 AH).

Al-Bushaykhi, al-Shahid. "Mushkilat al-Manhaj fī Dirāsat Muṣṭalaḥ al-Naqd al-ʿArabī al-Qadīm" (The Problem of Method in the Study of Ancient Arabic [Literary] Criticism and its Terminology). *Majallat al-Muslim al-Muʿāṣir*, no. 14, January-April 1990, pp. 55-56.

Elmessiri, Abdelwahab. *Riḥlatī al-Fikriyyah fī al-Budhūr wa al-Judhūr wa al-Thamar: Sīrah Ghayr Dhātiyyah wa Ghayr Mawḍūʿiyyah* (My Journey of Thought into Seeds, Roots, and Fruits: An Account Neither Subjective nor Objective). (Cairo: al-Hay'ah al-ʿĀmmah li Quṣūr al-Thaqāfah, 2000).

Al-Eter, Nur al-Din. *Manhaj al-Naqd fī ʿUlūm al-Ḥadīth* (A Critical Approach to the Hadith Sciences). Reprint. (Damascus: Dār al-Fikr, 1979).

Gadamer, Hans-Georg. *Bidāyat al-Falsafah* (The Beginning of Philosophy). Trans. ʿAli Hakim Salih and Hasan Nazim. (Beirut: al-Kitāb al-Jadīd, 2000).

Al-Ghazālī, Abū Ḥāmid. *Tahāfut al-Falāsifah* (The Incoherence of the Philosophers). Ed. Sulayman Dunya. (Cairo: Dār al-Maʿārif, no date).

__________. *Jawāhir al-Qur'ān wa Duraruhu* (Gems and Pearls of the Qur'an). (Beirut: Dār al-Jīl, 1988).

Al-Ghazyawi, Ali. *Madkhal ilā al-Manhaj al-Islāmī fī al-Naqd al-Adabī* (Introduction to the Islamic Approach to Literary Criticism). Silsilat Kitāb Daʿwat al-Ḥaqq (The Invitation to the Truth Book Series), no. 6. Al-Muhammadiyyah, (Morocco: Ministry of Islamic Endowments, 2000).

Al-Hafni, Abd al-Munim. *Al-Muʿjam al-Shāmil li al-Muṣṭalaḥāt al-Falsafiyyah*. Reprint. (Cairo: Maktabat Madbūlī, 2000).

Al-Hakim, Tawfiq. *ʿAwdat al-Waʿī* (Return of Consciousness). (Cairo: Dār al-Maʿārif, 1972).

Hammam, Abd al-Rahim Said. *Al-Fikr al-Manhajī ʿInd al-Muḥaddithīn* (Methodological Thought Among Hadith Scholars). Doha, *Silsilah Kitāb al-Ummah*, no. 16, Muharram 1408 AH.

Al-Ḥuṣaynī al-Dimashqī, Taqī al-Dīn Abū Bakr Muḥammad al-Ḥusaynī. *Kifāyat al-Akhyār fī Ḥall Ghāyat al-Ikhtiṣār*) (a commentary on Abū Shujāʿ's book on Shāfiʿī jurisprudence entitled *Ghāyat al-Ikhtiṣār*). Part 1. Edited by Ali Abd al-Hamid Baltaji and Muhammad Wahbi Sulayman. (Damascus: Dār al-Khayr, 1994).

Ibn ʿAbd al-Birr, Abū ʿUmar Yusuf. *Jāmiʿ ʿIlm al-Bayān wa Faḍlihi* (A Compendium on Rhetoric and Its Merits). Two volumes. Ed. Abi al-Ashbal al-Zuhayri. (Riyadh: Dār Ibn al-Jawzī, 1994).

Ibn Abī 'Uṣaybiʿah, Muwaffaq al-Dīn Abū al-ʿAbbās Aḥmad ibn al-Qāsim. *ʿUyūn al-Anbā' fī Ṭabaqāt al-Aṭibbā'* (Noteworthy Reports on the Various Classes of Physicians). Annotated by Nizār Riḍā. (Beirut: Dār Maktabat al-Ḥayāh, no date).

Bibliography

Ibn Ashur, Muhammad al-Tahir. *Tafsīr al-Taḥrīr wa al-Tanwīr* (Editing the Right Meaning and Enlightening the New Mind in Interpreting the Holy Book), Part 2. (Tunis: Dār Saḥnūn li al-Nashr wa al-Tawzīʿ, 1997).

__________. *Tafsīr al-Taḥrīr wa al-Tanwīr* (Editing the Right Meaning and Enlightening the New Mind in Interpreting the Holy Book), Part 3. (Tunis: al-Dār al-Tūnisiyyah li al-Nashr, 1984).

__________. *A Laysa al-Ṣubḥ bi Qarīb: al-Taʿlīm al-ʿArabī al-Islāmī* (Does the Morning Not Draw Nigh?: Arab-Islamic Instruction). Second Edition. (Tunis: Dār Saḥnūn and Cairo: Dār al-Salām, 2007).

Ibn Hishām al-Anṣarī, Muḥammad ʿAbd Allāh Jamāl al-Dīn. *Awḍaḥ al-Masālik ilā Alfiyyat Ibn Mālik* (The Clearest Path to [an Understanding of] Ibn Mālik's 'Alfiyyah'). New Revised Edition, vol. 3. (Sidon-Beirut: al-Maktabah al-ʿAṣriyyah, 1966).

Ibn Jazī, Abū al-Qāsim Muḥammad ibn Aḥmad. *Taqrīb al-Wuṣūl ilā ʿIlm al-Uṣūl* (Toward a Proper Understanding of the Principles of Jurisprudence). edited, with commentary, by Abd Allah al-Jaburi. (Amman, Jordan: Dār al-Nafā'is, 2002).

Ibn Kathīr, Abū al-Fidā' Ismāʿīl. *Tafsīr al-Qur'ān al-ʿAẓīm* (An Explanation of the Noble Qur'an), vol. 2. (Cairo: ʿĪsā Al-Bābī al-Ḥalabī, no date).

__________. *Tafsīr al-Qur'ān al-ʿAẓīm* (An Explanation of the Noble Qur'an). Introduced by Abd al-Qadir Arnaut. New Revised Edition, vol. 3. (Damascus-Riyadh: Dār al-Fayḥā', Maktabat Dār al-Salām, no date).

Ibn Khaldūn, ʿAbd al-Raḥmān. *Al-Muqaddimah,* expanded and revised edition. Ed. Abd al-Wahid Wafi. (Cairo: Dār Nahḍat Miṣr, 2004).

Ibn Manẓūr, Abū al-Faḍl Jamāl al-Dīn. Vol. 2. *Lisān al-ʿArab.* (Beirut: Dār Ṣādir and Dār Beirut, no date).

Ibn Rushd, Abū al-Walīd. *Faṣl al-Maqāl fī mā Bayn al-Ḥikmati wa al-Sharīʿah min al-Ittiṣāl* (The Definitive Word on the Link Between Wisdom and the Divinely Revealed Law). Ed. Muhammad Abid al-Jabiri. (Beirut: Markaz Dirāsāt al-Waḥdah al-ʿArabiyyah (Center for Arab Unity Studies), 1997).

__________. *Faṣl al-Maqāl fī mā Bayn al-Ḥikmati wa al-Sharīʿah min al-Ittiṣāl* (The Definitive Word on the Link Between Wisdom and the Divinely Revealed Law). First Edition. Ed. Muhammad ʿAmarah. (Cairo: Dār al-Maʿārif, 1972).

Ibn Taymiyyah, Abū al-ʿAbbās Taqiy al-Dīn. *Dar'u Taʿāruḍ al-ʿAql wa al-Naql* (The Case Against Contradiction Between Reason and Revelation), ed. Muhammad Rashad Salim. (Riyadh: King Muhammad Bin Saud University, 1979).

Ibrahim, Abu Bakr Muhammad Ahmad. *Al-Takāmul al-Maʿrifī wa Taṭbīqātuhu fī al-Manāhij al-Jāmiʿiyyah* (Epistemological Integration and Its Applications in University Curricula), (Herndon, VA: The International Institute of Islamic Thought, 2007).

International Institute of Islamic Thought. *Islāmiyyat al-Maʿrifah: al-Mabādi' wa Khiṭṭat al-ʿAmal wa al-Injāzāt* (The Islamization of Knowledge: General Principles, Plan of Action, and Achievements). (Herndon, VA: The International Institute of Islamic Thought, 1986).

Ishta, Faris. "Madkhal ilā al-Manhajiyyah fī al-ʿUlūm al-Ijtimāʿiyyah" (An Introduction to Methodology in the Social Sciences). *Majallat al-ʿUlūm al-Ijtimāʿiyyah*, Lebanese University, 1991, vol. 1, no. 1, pp. 33-47.

Al-Iṣfahānī, al-Rāghib. *Muʿjam Alfāẓ al-Qur'ān al-Karīm*. Edited by Ibrahim Shams al-Din. (Beirut: Dār al-Kutub al-ʿIlmiyyah, 1997).

Al-Jisr, Nadim. *Qiṣṣat al-Īmān bayn al-Falsafah wa al-ʿIlm wa al-Qur'ān* (The Story of Faith: From Philosophy, to Science, to the Qur'an). Reprint. (Beirut: al-Maktab al-Islāmī, 1969).

Al-Jurjānī, ʿAlī ibn Muḥammad. *Kitāb al-Taʿrīfāt* (Book of Definitions). Edited by Ibrahim al-Abyari. (Beirut: Dār al-Kitāb al-ʿArabī, no date).

Karam, Yusuf. *Tārīkh al-Falsafah al-Yūnāniyyah* (The History of Greek Philosophy). Reprint. (Cairo: Committee on Writing, Translation and Publication, 1966).

Khallāf, ʿAbd al-Wahhāb. *ʿIlm Uṣūl al-Fiqh* (The Science of the Principles of Jurisprudence). Eighth Edition. (Cairo: Maktabat al-Daʿwah al-Islāmiyyah, no date).

Al-Khaṭīb al-Baghdādī, Aḥmad ibn ʿAlī ibn Thābit. *Iqtiḍā' al-ʿIlm al-ʿAmal* (Knowledge Calls for Action). Fifth Edition. Edited by Muhammad Nasiruddin al-Albani. (Damascus: al-Maktab al-Islāmī, 1984).

Madkur, Ibrahim. *Fī al-Falsafah al-Islāmiyyah: Manhaj wa Taṭbīquhu* (On Islamic Philosophy: Method and Application). Reprint. (Cairo: Dār al-Maʿārif, 1983).

Majmaʿ al-Lughah al-ʿArabiyyah. *Al-Muʿjam al-Falsafī* (Dictionary of Philosophy). (Cairo: Majmaʿ al-Lughah al-ʿArabiyyah, 1979).

Malkawi, Fathi, ed. *Naḥwa Binā' Niẓām Maʿrifī Islāmī* (Toward the Construction of an Islamic Epistemological System). (Amman, Jordan: IIIT, 2000).

__________. *ʿĀlam al-Qiyam fī al-Ru'yah al-Manhajiyyah al-Islāmiyyah* (The World of Values in the Islamic Methodological Perspective), forthcoming.

Malkawi, Fathi and Ahmad Odeh. *Asāsiyyāt al-Baḥth al-ʿIlmī fī al-ʿUlūm al-Insāniyyah wa al-Tarbawiyyah* (Foundations of Scientific Research in the Humanities and Educational Sciences). Second Edition. (Irbid: Dār al-Kindī, 1993).

Al-Masʿūdī, Abū al-Ḥasan ʿAlī ibn al-Ḥusayn ibn ʿAlī. *Murūj al-Dhahab wa Maʿādin al-Jawhar* (Meadows of Gold and Its True Essence). Introduced and explained by Mufid Qamihah. (Beirut: Dār al-Kutub al-ʿIlmiyyah, 1985).

Miqdadi, Fuad Kazim. "Maqūlāt fī Fahm al-Khiṭāb al-Thaqāfī al-Taghrībī" (Toward an Understanding of Westernizing Cultural Discourse), *Risālat al-Thaqalayn*, Eleventh Year, no. 41, 2002.

Mirzaq, Abd al-Qadir Muhammad. *Mashrūʿ Adūnīs al-Fikrī wa al-Ibdāʿī: Ru'yah*

Ma^c^rifiyyah (Adunis' Intellectual and Creative Enterprise: An Epistemological Vision). (Herndon, Virginia: The International Institute of Islamic Thought, 2008).

Mustafa, Nadiya Muhammad and Sayf al-Din Abd al-Fattah. *Dawrat al-Minhājiyyah al-Islāmiyyah fī al-ʿUlūm al-Ijtimāʿiyyah: Ḥaql al-ʿUlūm al-Siyāsiyyah Numūdhajan* (A Course on Islamic Methodology in the Social Sciences: The Case of Political Science). (Cairo: IIIT and Markaz al-Ḥaḍārah li al-ʿUlūm al-Siyāsiyyah, 2002).

Al-Najjar, ʿAbd al-Majid. "Al-ʿUmrān wa al-Īmān" (Human Development and Faith). *Majallat Islāmiyat al-Maʿrifah*, Year 2, Issue 8, April 1997, pp. 40-84..

__________. *Mabāḥith fī Manhajiyyat al-Fikr al-Islāmī* (Studies in the Methodology of Islamic Thought). (Beirut: Dar al-Maghrib al-ʿArabī, 1992).

__________. *ʿAwāmil al-Shuhūd al-Ḥaḍārī* (Factors in Cultural Contributions). Part II. (Beirut: Dār al-Gharb al-Islāmī, 1999).

Al-Nashshar, Ali Sami. *Manāhij al-Baḥth ʿInd Mufakkirī al-Islām* (Research Methods Among Muslim Thinkers). (Cairo: Dār al-Salām, 2008).

Al-Nashshar, Mustafa. *Naẓriyat al-ʿIlm al-Arisṭiyyah: Dirāsah fī Manṭiq al-Maʿrifah ʿind Arisṭu* (The Aristotelian Theory of Science: A Study in Aristotle's Logic of Knowledge). Reprint. (Cairo: Dār al-Maʿārif, 1995).

Al-Nīsābūrī, Muslim ibn al-Ḥajjāj. *Ṣaḥīḥ Muslim*. Edited by Abu Suhayb al-Karmi. (Riyadh: Bayt al-Afkār al-Dawliyyah li al-Nashr wa al-Tawzīʿ, 1998).

__________. *Ṣaḥīḥ Muslim* (Beirut: Dār Ibn Ḥazm, 1995).

Pasha, Ahmed Fouad. *Falsafat al-ʿUlūm bi Naẓrah Islāmiyyah* (Philosophy of Science from an Islamic Perspective). First Edition. (Cairo: Self-published, 1984).

__________. *Dirāsāt Islāmiyyah fī al-Fikr al-ʿIlmī* (Islamic Studies in Scientific Thought). (Cairo: Dār al-Hidāyah, 1997).

__________, et. al. *Al-Manhajiyyah al-Islāmiyyah* (Islamic Methodology). (Cairo: The International Institute of Islamic Thought and Dār al-Salam, 2010).

Al-Qahtani, Musfir ibn Ali. *Athar al-Manhaj al-Uṣūlī fī Tarshīd al-ʿAmal al-Islāmī* (The Effect of the Uṣūlī Method on the Systematic Organization of Islamic Action). (Beirut: al-Shabakah al-ʿArabiyyah li al-Abḥāth wa al-Nashr, 2008).

Al-Qaradawi, Yusuf. *Approaching the Sunnah: Comprehension and Controversy*. Translated by Jamil Qureshi (London and Washington: IIIT, 2006).

Al-Qurṭubī, Abū ʿAbd Allāh Muḥammad ibn Aḥmad al-Anṣārī. *Al-Jāmiʿ li Aḥkām al-Qur'ān* (Compendium of the Provisions of the Qur'an). (Beirut: Dār al-Kutub al-ʿIlmiyyah, 1988).

__________. *Al-Jāmiʿ Li Aḥkām al-Qur'ān*. (Beirut: Mu'assasat Manāhil al-ʿIrfān, no date).

Qutb, Sayyid. *Fī ẓilāl al-Qur'ān* (In the Shadows of the Qur'an). Reprint. (Cairo: Dār al-Shurūq, 1978).

__________. *Khaṣā'iṣ al-Taṣawwur al-Islāmī wa Muqawwimātuhu* (Distinguishing

Features and Components of Islamic Conceptualization). Reprint. (Kuwait: International Islamic Federation of Student Organizations (IFSO), 1983).

Al-Raysuni, Ahmad. *Al-Shūrā fī Maᶜrakat al-Binā'*. (Amman, Jordan: IIIT and Dār al-Rāzī, 2007). Published in English as *Al-Shūrā: The Qur'anic Principle of Consultation, A Tool for Reconstruction and Reform*. Translated by Nancy Roberts. (London: IIIT, 2011).

__________. *Al-Fikr al-Maqāṣidī: Qawāᶜiduhu wa Fawā'iduhu* (Aims-Based Thought: Its Guiding Principles and Its Benefits). Pocketbook Series no. 9, published by *Al-Zamān* Newspaper, (Casa Blanca, Morocco: 1999).

__________. *Al-Kulliyāt al-Asāsiyyah li al-Sharīᶜah al-Islāmiyyah* (Basic Universals of Islamic Law). (Rabat: Ḥarakat al-Tawḥīd wa al-Iṣlāḥ, 2007).

__________. *Naẓariyyat al-Taqrīb wa al-Taghlīb wa Taṭbīqātuhā fī al-ᶜUlūm al-Islāmiyyah* (The Theory of Persuasion and Preference and Its Applications to the Islamic Sciences). (Miknas, Morocco: Maṭbaᶜat Muṣᶜab, 1997).

Al-Raysuni, Ahmad and Muhammad Jamal Barut. *Al-Ijtihad: Al-Naṣṣ al-Wāqiᶜ al-Maṣlaḥah* (Innovative Interpretation: Text, Reality, Benefits). *Silsilat Ḥiwārāt al-Qarn* (Dialogues of the Century Series). (Damascus: Dār al-Fikr, 2000).

Al-Rāzī, Abū Bakr Muḥammad ibn Zakariyā. *Kitāb al-Shukūk ᶜalā Kalām Fāḍil al-Aṭibbā', Jalīnūs, fī al-Kutub allatī Nusibat ilayhi* (Reservations Concerning Statements Made by the Illustrious Physician Galen in Those Books Attributed to Him). Edited and introduced by Muhammad Labib Abd al-Ghani. (Cairo: Dār al-Kutub wa al-Wathā'iq al-Qawmiyyah, 2009).

Al-Rāzī, Fakhr al-Dīn. *Al-Tafsīr al-Kabīr*, or *Mafātīḥ al-Ghayb* (The Great Commentary, or Keys to the Unseen), vol. 32. Edited by Imad al-Barudi. (Cairo: al-Maktabah al-Tawfiqiyyah, no date).

Rida, Muhammad Rashid. "Manāfiᶜ al-Awrubbiyyīn wa Maḍārruhum fī al-Sharq – al-Istibdād (3)" (Benefit and Harm from Europeans in the East – Tyranny (3)), *Majallat al-Manār*, vol. 10, no. 4, 1315 AH.

Said, Abd al-Jabbar. "Manhajiyyat al-Taᶜāmul Maᶜa al-Sunnah al-Nabawiyyah (Methodology for Relating to the Prophetic Sunnah). *Islāmiyyat al-Maᶜrifah*, Year 6, Issue no. 18, Fall 1999, pp. 53-88.

Shariati, Ali. *Al-Insān wa al-Islām* (Humanity and Islam). translated by ᶜAbbās al-Tarjumān. (Beirut: Dār al-Rawḍah, 1992).

Shaykh Idris, Jafar. "Qaḍiyat al-Manhaj ᶜInd al-Sayyid Quṭb fī 'Maᶜālim fī al-Ṭarīq'" (The Issue of Method in Sayyid Qutb's 'Maᶜālim fī al-Ṭarīq'), in *The Proceedings of the Seminar on "Directions in Contemporary Islamic Thought"* held in Bahrain. (Riyadh: Maktab al-Tarbiyyah al-ᶜArabi li Duwal al-Khalīj (Arab Education Office for the Gulf States), 1985).

Al-Subkī, ᶜAlī Ibn ᶜAbd al-Kāfī. *Al-Ibhāj fī Sharḥ al-Minhāj: Sharḥ Minhāj al-Wuṣūl ilā ᶜIlm al-Uṣūl* (A Commentary on al-Bayḍāwī's *Minhāj al-Wuṣūl ilā ᶜIlm al-Uṣūl* on the principles of jurisprudence), vol. 1. (Beirut: Dār al-Kutub al-ᶜIlmiyyah, 1995).

Al-Tahānawī, Muḥammad ᶜAlī al-Fārūqī. *Kashshāf Iṣṭilāḥāt al-Funūn*, vol. 1. Edited by Luṭfī Abd al-Badi. (Cairo: al-Hay'ah al-Miṣriyyah li al-Kitāb, 1972).

Al-Tirmidhī, Abū ᶜĪsā Muḥammad Banī ᶜĪsā Ibn Sūrah. *Al-Jāmiᶜ al-Ṣaḥīḥ*, vol. 5. Edited and annotated by Ahmad Muhammad Shakir. (Beirut: Dār al-Kutub al-ᶜIlmiyyah, no date).

Uthman, Sayyid Ahmad. *Al-Dhātiyyah al-Nāḍijah: Maqālāt fī mā Warā' al-Manhaj* (Mature Subjectivity: Essays in Metamethod). (Cairo: Maktabat al-Angelo al-Miṣriyyah, 2000).

Al Yasin, Jasim ibn Muhammad ibn Muhalhal. *Al-Kalimāt al-Manhajiyyah min Kalām Shaykh al-Islām Ibn Taymiyyah* (A Guide to Islamic Methodology Gleaned from the Writings of Ibn Taymiyyah). (Kuwait: Mu'assasat al-Kalimah, no date).

Zayn al-Abidin, Muhammad Surur. *Manhaj al-Anbiyāᶜ fī al-Daᶜwah Ilā Allāh* (The Prophet's Approach to Inviting [Others to Faith in] God). (Birmingham, UK: Dar al-Arqam, 1992).

Zayn al-Abidin, al-Tayyib, ed. *Al-Manhajiyyah al-Islāmiyyah wa al-ᶜUlūm al-Nafsiyyah wa al-Tarbawiyyah* (Islamic Methodology and the Psychological and Educational Sciences), Proceedings of the Fourth International Conference on Islamic Thought at the University of Khartoum. Three volumes. (Herndon, VA: IIIT, 1990).

Al-Zunaydi, Abd al-Rahman ibn Zayd. *Manāhij al-Baḥth fī al-ᶜAqīdah al-Islāmiyyah fī al-ᶜAṣr al-Ḥāḍir: Dirāsah li Manāhjj al-Fikr al-Islāmī al-Muᶜāṣir wa li al-ᶜAnāṣir al-Manhajiyyah fī Dirāsat Uṣūl al-Dīn* (Research Methods of Relevance to Islamic Doctrine in the Modern Age: A Study of Approaches to Contemporary Islamic Thought and the Methodological Components of the Study of the Principles of [the Islamic] Religion). (Riyadh: Markaz al-Dirāsāt wa al-Iᶜlām, Dār Ishbīliyā, 1998).

References in English

Agnos, Michael, ed. *Webster's New World College Dictionary*. Fourth Edition. (Foster City, CA: Webster's New World, 2001).

Bacon, Francis. *The New Organon*. (Cambridge, UK: Cambridge University Press, 2000).

Bakar, Osman. *Classification of Knowledge in Islam: A Study in Islamic Philosophy of Science*. (Kuala Lumpur, Malaysia: Institute for Policy Studies, 1992).

__________. *Tawhid and Science: Essays on the History and Philosophy of Islamic Science*. (Kuala Lumpur, Malaysia: Secretariat for Islamic Philosophy and Science, 1991).

Bibliography

Beeston, A. F. L., et. al. (eds). *Arabic Literature to the End of the Umayyad Period.* (Cambridge: Cambridge University Press, 1983).

Benson, G., R. Glasberg and B. Griffith. *Perspectives on the Unity and Integration of Knowledge.* (New York: Peter Lang, 1998).

Boyer, Ernest. *Scholarship Reconsidered: Priorities of Professoriate.* (Princeton, NJ: Carnegie Foundation for the Advancement of Teaching, 1990).

Broad, William J. "Why They Called It the Manhattan Project." *The New York Times,* (October 30, 2007).

Damasio, Antonio, et. al. (eds.). *Unity of Knowledge: The Convergence of Natural and Human Sciences.* (New York: The New York Academy of Sciences, 2001).

Descartes, René. *Discourse on Method and Meditations on First Philosophy.* Translated by Donald A. Cress. Fourth Edition. (Indianapolis, IN: Hachett Publishing Company, Inc., 1998).

DK Publishing. *Oxford Illustrated American Dictionary.* (New York: Oxford University Press, 1998).

al Fārūqī, Isma^cīl. "Islamization of Knowledge: Problems, Principles and Prospective," in *Islam: Source and Purpose of Knowledge.* (Herndon: IIIT, 1988), pp. 13-63.

__________. *Al-Tawhid: Its Implications for Thought and Life.* Reprint. (Herndon, VA: IIIT, 2000).

Flick, Uwe. *An Introduction to Qualitative Research.* Fourth Edition, (Los Angeles: Sage, 2009).

Godawa, Brian. *Hollywood Worldviews: Watching Films With Wisdom and Discernment.* (Downers Grove, IL: InterVarsity Press, 2002).

Haynes, Stephen. *Professing in the Postmodern Academy.* (Waco, Texas: Baylor University Press, 2002).

Hung, Edwin. *Nature of Science: Problems and Perspectives.* (Belmont, CA: Wadsworth Publishing, 1996).

Iqbal, Muzaffar. *Islam and Science.* (Aldershot, UK: Ashgate Publishing LMT, 2002).

Kuhn, Thomas. *The Structure of Scientific Revolutions.* Second Enlarged Edition. (Chicago: University of Chicago Press, 1970).

Lai, C. H. and Azim Kidwai (eds.). *Ideals and Realities: Selected Essays of Abdus Salam.* Third Edition. (World Scientific Publishing Co., 1989).

McKeon, Richard (ed.). *The Basic Works of Aristotle.* (New York: Random House, 1941).

Moreland, J. P. and William Lane Craig. *Philosophical Foundations for a Christian Worldview.* (Downers Grove, IL: InterVarsity Press, 2003).

Murray, Charles and Catherine Cox. *Apollo: Race to the Moon.* (Clearwater, FL: Touchstone Books, 1990).

Nasr, Seyyed Hossein. *The Need for a Sacred Science.* (New York: State University of New York Press, 1993).

__________. (ed.). *Islamic Spirituality I: Foundations* (*World Spirituality: An Encyclopedic History of the Religious Quest,* Volume 19). (London: Routledge and Kegan Paul, 1987).

__________. *The Need for a Sacred Science.* (New York: State University of New York Press, 1993).

Plowright, David. *Using Mixed Methods: Frameworks for an Integrated Methodology.* (Thousand Oaks, CA: Sage Publications Ltd., 2011).

Rossman, G. B. and S. F. Rallis. *Learning in the Field: An Introduction to Qualitative Research.* Second Edition. (Thousand Oaks, CA: Sage, 2003).

Sardar, Ziauddin. *Explorations in Islamic Science.* (London: Mansell Publications, 1989).

Schwarz, John. *The Complete Guide to the Christian Faith.* (Minneapolis, MN: Bethany House Publishers, 2001).

Teddlie, Charles B. and Abbas Tashakkori. *Foundations of Mixed Methods Research: Integrating Quantitative and Qualitative Approaches in Social and Behavioral Sciences.* (Los Angeles: Sage, 2009).

Wan Daud, Wan Mohd. Nor. *The Concept of Knowledge in Islam and Its Implications for Education in a Developing Country.* (London: Mansell, 1989).

Wilson, Edward O. *Consilience: The Unity of Knowledge.* (New York: Vintage Books, 1999).

World Health Organization. WHO Report on the Global Tobacco Epidemic. (Geneva, Switzerland: WHO, 2009).

INDEX

Abd al-Fattah, Sayf al-Din, 100, 193, 223
Abd al-Rahman, Taha, 61-64, 97
ʿAbd al-Salām, al-ʿIzz ibn, 170
Abdus Salam, Muhammad, 8, 35
Abel, 27
al-Abharī, ʿUmar, 187
Abraham, 94, 139, 188, 195, 247
abrogation of verses, 208
Abu al-Fadl, Mona, 90
Abū Ḥanīfah, 119, 156, 159
AbuSulayman, AbdulHamid,
    Worldview in ideas of, 24-31
    methodology of, 55-57, 223
    on distortions in Muslim thought, 76
    on reform and renewal, 97-99
ʿĀd, people of, 254
Adam, 27, 139-40, 143
adherence (*ittibāʿ*), 279
aesthetics, manifestations of *tawḥīd* in, 237-39
Agathodaemon the Egyptian, 125
agriculture, 258
ahl al-ḥadīth (Traditionists), 171
ahl al-ra'y (people of independent reasoning), 171
Ahmad, Abu Bakr Muhammad, 23-24
ʿĀ'ishah, 40
Alalwani, Taha Jabir, 57-61, 99, 223, 225
ʿAlī ibn Abī Ṭālib, 186
al-ʿAlmawi, 120
analogy (*qiyās*), as source of knowledge, 111
analysis tools, 205-207
analytical models, 79-80
application phase of scientific activity, 6
ʿaql (reason), usage of term, 194-95
Arab mentality, 62
Arabesque, 237
Arif, Nasr, 81
Aristotelian logic, 129-30, 132-34
Aristotle, 120-21, 126, 128, 268
Arkun, Muhammad, 62
art, 237-39
asbāb al-nuzūl (occasions of revelation), 208
ascientific methods, 137
Asclepius, 125
al-Ashʿarī, Abū al-Ḥasan, 158
Ashʿarites, 155-59, 175
Athenians, 128
atom bomb, 35
atom theory, 127
atomistic approach to historical studies, 102
al-Attas, Syed Muhammad Naquib, 11
Augustine, 268
Avicenna, 147
awareness, 88-90
āyah (sign), use of term in Qur'anic text, 28-30

backwardness of Muslim community, 92-93, 170-71
Bacon, Francis, 131-33
Badawi, Abd al-Rahman, 47, 130
al-Baghdādī, ʿAbd al-Qādir, 158
Bakar, Osman
    vision of unity of knowledge, 19-22
al-Bāqillānī, 158, 172
al-Baṣrī, al-Ḥasan, 156

Index

Index

divorce, 243
double-speak, philosophy as, 63
Durkheim, Émile, 135

earth, roundness of, 127, 189-90
economics, manifestation of *tawḥīd* in, 235-37
education, 259-60
educational institutions, importance of, 97-98
effective causes, law of, 173-74
electroweak theory, 8
Elmessiri, Abdelwahab, 79-81
emigration, 233
empirical observation in Aristotelian thought, 129
epistemological integration
  Ahmad's study on, 23-24
  compared with unity of knowledge, 4-6
  conditions for, 274-76
  in conduct, 279-80
  consumptive dimension of, 5
  defined, 1-2
  defining features of, 276-77
  explanatory models, 79-81
  in Islamic worldview, 22-31
  model for, 210-14
  obstacles to, 31-34
  oneness of God as foundation of, 13-22
  paradigm, 76-79
  practical foundation for, 4-6
  priority of particular sciences over others, 28
  relationship between worldview, system and methodology, 82-84
  in research, 277-79
  training program, 281-94
  as used across all schools of thought, 175
  worldview, 71-76
epistemological model, 81
epistemological system, 81-82
established practice (*al-ʿādah al-muḥkamah*), 179-80
European culture, impact of Roman empire on, 130-31. *See also* Western thought
European Organization for Nuclear Research (CERN), 8
evangelism, 46
exegetical tools, 208
existentialism, 137
Experiential-Sufi school, 160-65, 175
experimental scientific method, 149
explanatory models, 79-81
exploitation, as prohibited, 235
extended family, 230
eye, anatomy of, 120

family, 97-98, 213-14, 228-32
al-Fārābī, 12-13, 268
farming, 258
al Fārūqī, Ismaʿīl,
  methodology of, 52-55
  on Islamic art, 238-39
  on religious-secular divide 10
  on unity of knowledge, 13-18
  tawḥīd, 227-28, 235
films, cultural values in, 71
fiqh (understanding), 54, 167. *See also* jurisprudence
fiqh al-ʿumrān, 251
fragmentation of knowledge, 6-7
future, neglect of, 102-103

Gadamer, Hans-Georg, 126
Galen, 120, 125
geographical jurisprudence, 74
al-Ghazālī
  as representing the Sufi school of thought, 13
  on contradictions between reason and revelation, 16-17
  structural unity of knowledge, 30
  on methodology, 47-48
  debate with Ibn Rushd, 99

Index

Index

Index

logic, 99
love, force of, 25
luxury, destructiveness of, 267
ma^crifī, use of term in Elmessiri's work, 80-81

Madkur, Dr. ʿAbd al-Hamid, 161-65
magic eye, 196
magical rites, 143
magnetism, 132
Mahmud, Shaykh Abd al-Halim, 157
Makkah, 253
Mālik ibn Anas, 119, 147, 159
manhaj
  compared with methodology, 45-46
  defined, 40-42
  modern use of term, 110
  Qur'an as reference point for, 85
  Qur'anic terms of relevance to, 42-44
  variant uses of term, 44-45
Manhattan project, 35
maqāmāt (spiritual stations), 162
maqāṣid-based methodology, 65-69
marital relationship, preservation of, 213-14
Marxism, 137
maṣdar (sources) of methodology, 178-79
al-Masʿūdī, 125
material development, 257-58
Mathematics, 127
Maturidites, 155-56, 175
Mazdaists, 125
McKeon, Richard, 130
Messenger of God
  pronounced blessings on those who hear his words, 89
  as interpretation of the Qur'an, 95
  method during the days of, 110-12
  method of Companions of, 85
  method of for issuing verdicts, 116-17
method
  evolution of concept of, 109-10
  during the days of the Messenger of God, 110-12
methodism, 46
Methodists, 46
methodological awareness
  cause and effect, failure to link, 106
  defined, 88-90
  four elements necessary for, 100
  in Muslim community, 100-101
  need for, 90
  unrealistic views of society, 104-105
  in worldview, 101-104
methodological knots, 90
methodological schools
  Experiential-Sufi school, 160-65
  introduced, 146-48
  Juristic-*Uṣūlī* school, 169-74
  rational-scholastic-philosophical, 155-60, 175
  Scientific-Empirical school, 165-69
  unitary methodology, 148-54
methodological tools, 192-94
  reason and sensory perception, 194-97
  function of mind and senses, 200-202
  thought, research and conduct, 202-203
  research tools, 204-210
methodology
  of Abraham, 94
  compared with *manhaj* (method), 45-49
  and evolution of scientific fields, 137-42
  importance of in Islamic thought, 37-39
  in historical studies, 96
  manhaj, defined, 40-42
  Qur'anic method, 112-16, 149-51

Index

pious otherworldliness, 104
Plato, 126, 128, 268
political jurisprudence, 74
political order, manifestations of *tawḥīd* in, 232-35
positivism, 135
positivist-scientific phase of human thought, 148
postmodernism, 137, 152
practical nature of Islam, 233
practice, established (*al-ʿādah al-muḥkamah*), 179-80
pre-Socratic philosophy, 126-28
principle of production, 236
principles
  concept of, 218-22
  introduced, 216-18
  relation with methodological issues, 222-23
  science of, 94-95, 119, 171
production, principle of, 236
progress, societal, 258-61
proof, importance of in Islamic framework, 166
prophets, as sent to all peoples, 124-26
prosperity (*ʿumrān*), 225
Protagoras, 129
psychological world, as source of methodology, 186
purification (*tazkiyah*)
  of community, 246-48
  as complementary and comprehensive, 217
  as a governing value, 239-40
  in the Qur'an, 240-41
  in social relations, 243-44
  of soul, 241-42
  in Sufism, 248-50
  as value-based concept, 225
  of wealth, 244-46
purpose-oriented approach, 276
Pythagoras, 127

qabḍ (dejection) in the Sufi path, 162
al-Qaradawi, Yusuf, 95
al-Qarāfī, Shihāb al-Dīn, 170, 172, 174
qiyās (analogy), as source of knowledge, 111
qualitative data, analysis of, 206-210
Quantum theory, 8
Qur'an
  Abraham, story of, 94
  bada'a (to begin), use of in, 219
  complementarity with sciences, 29-30
  focus of Sufis on, 163
  in Alalwani's methodological determinants, 59
  integrating with created world, 187-92
  interpretation and exegesis, tools required for, 208
  Joseph in, 257
  laws related to family, 229
  method in, 149-51
  minhāj, terms of relevance to, 42-44
  model for dealing with, 90-91
  as methodical authority, 167-68
  purification in, 240-42, 249-50
  as reference point, 85
  relating to, 200-201
  research methodology of, 112-16
  revelation of, 110-11
  and sensory perception, 197-200
  "sign" (*āyah*), use of term, 28-30
  as source of guidance, 212
  as source of Islamic universals, 67-68
  as source of methodology, 182-85
  as springhead of knowledge, 20
  story-telling, as methodological tool in, 112, 210
  ʿumrān in, 252-55, 271
  use of word *ṣadr*, 178
  "wide-awake ear", 88
  worldview of, 26
  z-k-w derivatives, 246-47

Index

Index

scientific experimental method, 149
scientific logic, 132
scientific rationalism, 136
Scientific-Empirical school, 165-69
self-referenced evaluation, 209
sensory perception
  and revelation, 197-200
  as methodological tool, 194-97
  as tool for epistemological integration, 211
  function of in the world, 200-202
sexual relations, 116, 244
al-Shafi'i, Dr. Hasan, 156-59
al-Shāfiʿī, Imam
  works on methodology, 47
  methodological approach introduced by, 66
  as pioneer of principles of jurisprudence, 119, 171
  as a philosopher, 173
shahādah (testimony of faith), 226
al-Shahrastānī, 158
sharīʿah differences among communities, 41
al-Shāṭibī, Imam Abū Isḥāq, 172, 193
al-Shawkānī, Muḥammad ibn ʿAlī, 147, 172-73
al-Shaybānī, Muḥammad ibn al-Ḥasan, 170
Shi'i thought, 156
ship approach, 193
shirʿah, 41
al-Shīrāzī, Quṭb al-Dīn, 13
shirk (association of partners with God), 227
shuhūd (witnesing) in experiential knowledge, 161
sight, sense of, 196
sign (*āyah*), use of term in Qur'anic text, 28-30
ṣirāṭ (way or path), 42
Six Thinking Hats, 203
smoking, 107-108
Snow, Lord S. P., 3
social otherworldliness, 104
social relations, purity in, 243-44
social system, manifestation of *tawḥīd* in, 228-32
social world, as source of methodology, 186
societal change, 269
Socrates, 126
Sophists, 127-29
soul, purification of, 241-42
sources of methodology
  concept of, 178-82
  integrating revelation and created world, 187-92
  introduced, 177-78
  natural world as, 185-87
  revelation as, 182-85
specialization in academic study, danger of, 31
Spengler, Oswald, 137
spiritual guide in Sufism, 162
spiritual knowledge, 20
spiritual stations (*maqāmāt*), 162
story-telling, as methodological tool, 112, 210
strangers, Muslims as, 276
structural unity of the Qur'an, 198
struggle (jihad), 248-50
al-Subkī, Tāj al-Dīn, 44, 171
Sufism, 160-65
  as metaphysical framework for unity of knowledge, 11
  mystical-experiential approach, 147
  purification (*tazkiyah*), 248-50
  as represented by al-Ghazālī, 13
  spiritual vitality of, 54-55
al-Suhrawardī, 147
Sunnah
  defined, 42-43
  faulty approaches to, 95
  as 'hidden revelation', 185
  as methodical authority, 167-68
  Sufism and, 163
Super Proto Synchrotron, 8
superstition, 143

Index

al-Ṭabarī, 2, 147
al-Tahānawī, 48, 120
taḥliyyah (acquisition), 162, 249
tajallī, 249
takāmul, 273. *See also* integration
al-takāmul al-maʿrifī. *See* epistemological integration
takhliyyah (renunciation), 162, 249
ṭarīq (way or path), 42
tasawwuf. *See* Sufism
taṣawwur (conceptualization) in Qutb's thought, 72
al-tawḥīd. *See* oneness of God
tawḥīdī. *See* unitary methodology
al-Tawḥīdī, Abū Ḥayyān, 147
taxation, 237
tazkiyah (purification), 217, 225
teaching, compared with training, 292-94
team thinking, 290-91
terminological studies, 97
testimony of faith, 226
Thales, 126
al-Thawrī, Sufyān, 156
theorization process, 168
Theory of Relativity, 7
thinking tools, 202-203
thinking, training in, 288
thought, mechanisms of, 91-92
Thought-related methodological principles, 223
three-stage theory of human thought, 148
tobacco industry, 107-108
tools. *See* methodological tools
trade, 235-37
traditional methodology, limitations of, 54-55, 57
Traditionists (*ahl al-ḥadīth*), 171
training program
  course requirements, 281-85
  structure, 284
  package, 285-87
  situations, 288-92
  concept of training, 292-94
t-test analysis, 206
Twelver Shi'is, 156

ultra-methodology of Abd al-Rahman, 62
ʿUmar ibn al-Khaṭṭāb, 236
ummah, 231-32
ʿumrah, 253
ʿumrān (prosperity)
  as cultural development, 258-61
  as development, prosperity and life, 261-65
  Ibn Khaldūn's writings on, 265-71
  in Islamic value system, 250-52
  as material development, 257-58
  in the Qur'an, 252-55
  as settling in a place, 256-57
  as state of life, 255-56
  as value-based concept, 225
understanding (fiqh), 54
unitary methodology, 148-54
unity consciousness, 7
unity of knowledge
  as practical foundation for integration, 6-8
  compared with epistemological integration, 4-6
  Islamic discourse on, 9-12
  metaphysical framework for, 11
  and classification of the sciences, 12-13
  al Fārūqī's vision of, 13-18
  Nasr's vision of, 18-19
  Bakar's vision of, 19-22
  complementarity of sciences with divine revelation, 29-30
unity of the community, 232
universal soul, 20-21
university curricula, 23-24, 32-33
usury, 56, 246
Utke, Allen, 6-7

values
  introduced, 216-18, 224-25

Diagrams

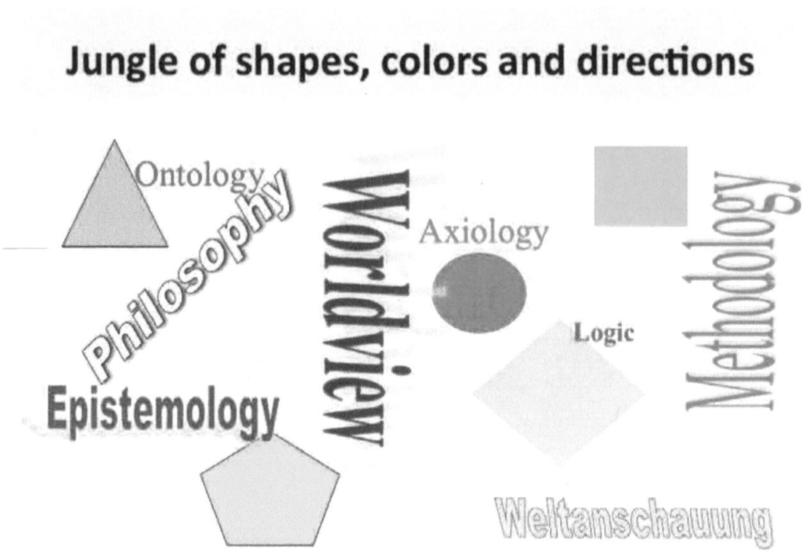

SEE P. 70

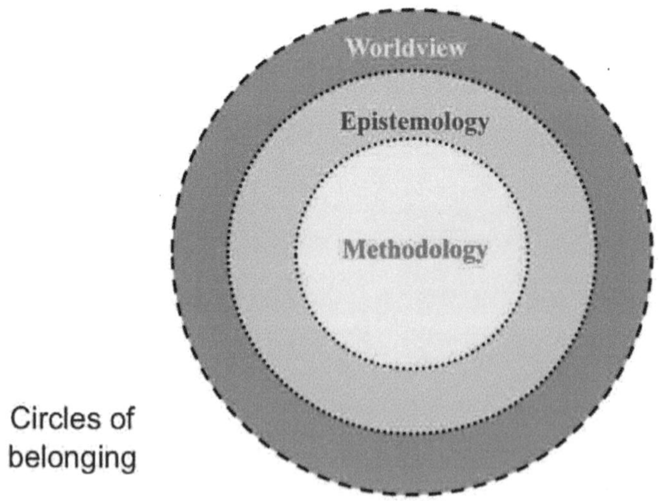

SEE P. 87

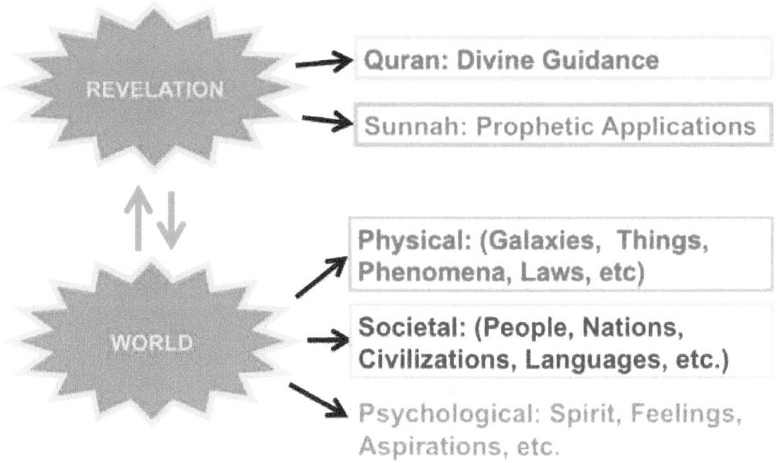

SEE P. 186

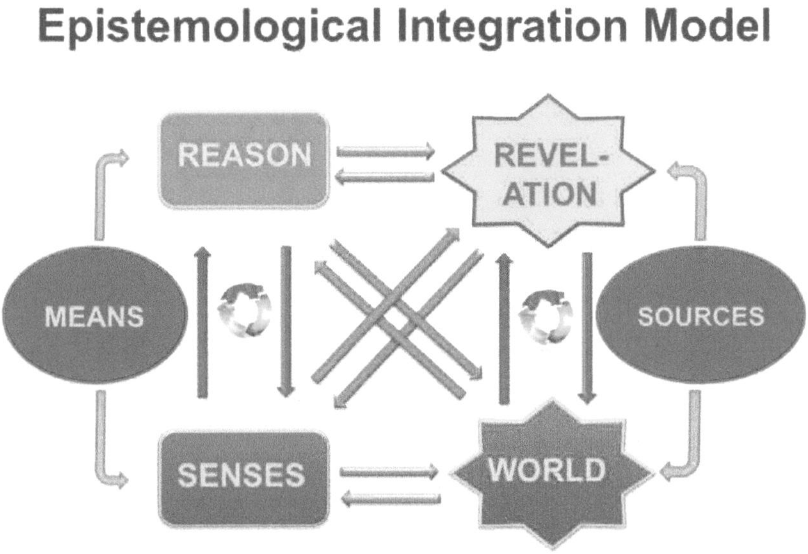

SEE P. 212